Biology 1

FOR OCR

Mary Jones

CAMBRIDGE
UNIVERSITY PRESS

CAMBRIDGE UNIVERSITY PRESS
Cambridge, New York, Melbourne, Madrid, Cape Town, Singapore, Sao Pãulo, Delhi

Cambridge University Press
The Edinburgh Building, Cambridge CB2 8RU, UK

www.cambridge.org
Information on this title: www.cambridge.org/9780521717632

First published 2008

Printed in the United Kingdom at the University Press, Cambridge

A catalogue record for this publication is available from the British Library

ISBN 978-0-521-71763-2 paperback

ACKNOWLEDGEMENTS
Project management: Sue Kearsey
Picture research: Vanessa Miles
Page layout, illustration and preparation of interactive pdfs: Geoff Jones

Contents

1005840358

Introduction

Cambridge OCR Advanced Sciences

The new *Cambridge OCR Advanced Sciences* course provides complete coverage of the revised OCR AS and A Level science specifications (Biology, Chemistry A and Physics A) for teaching from September 2008. There are two books for each subject – one covering AS and one covering A2. Some material has been drawn from the existing *Cambridge Advanced Sciences* books; however the majority is new.

The course has been developed in an innovative format, featuring Cambridge's new interactive PDFs on CD-ROM in the back of the books, and free access to a dedicated website. The CD-ROM provides additional material, including detailed objectives, hints on answering questions, and extension material. It also provides access to web-based e-learning activities (A Level and background revision from GCSE) to help students visualise abstract concepts, understand calculations and simulate scientific processes.

The books contain all the material required for teaching the specifications, and can be used either on their own or in conjunction with the interactive PDFs and the website.

In addition, *Teacher Resource CD-ROMs*, with book PDFs plus extra material such as worksheets, practical activities and tests, are available for each book. These CD-ROMs also provide access to the new *Cambridge OCR Advanced Sciences* Planner website with a week-by-week adaptable teaching schedule.

Biology 1 for OCR – the AS biology text
This book covers the entire OCR AS Biology specification for first examination in 2009. Chapters 1 to 6 correspond to Unit F211, Cells, Exchange and Transport. Chapters 7 to 15 correspond to Unit F212, Molecules, Biodiversity, Food and Health. Each chapter covers one of the numbered sections within the two Modules in Unit F211, and within the three Modules in Unit F212.

The content of the chapters is arranged in the same sequence as in the specification.

The book is designed to be accessible to students who have studied Double Award Science at GCSE, or who have a separate qualification in biology. The language is kept simple, to improve accessibility for all students, while still maintaining scientific rigour throughout. Care is taken to introduce and use all of the specialist terms that students need to acquire during their AS biology studies. In the text, key terms are highlighted in bold.

The depth and breadth of treatment of each topic is pitched at the appropriate level for OCR AS students. The accompanying CD-ROM also contains some material that goes a little beyond the requirements of the specification, which should interest and stretch more able students.

Some of the text and illustrations are based on material in the endorsed text *Biology 1*, which covered the earlier OCR specification, while some is completely new. All of it has been reviewed and revised, ensuring that relevant new findings relating to particular topics are included. In addition to the main content in each chapter, there are How Science Works boxes, describing issues or events related to the biological material, which begin to explore the relevance of these aspects of biology to individuals and to society.

Self assessment questions (SAQs) in each chapter provide opportunities to check understanding and to make links back to earlier work. They often address misunderstandings that commonly appear in examination answers, and will help students to avoid such errors. Past examination questions at the end of each chapter allow students to practise answering exam-style questions. The answers to these, along with exam-style mark schemes and hints on answering questions, are found on the accompanying CD-ROM.

Acknowledgements

We would like to thank the following for permission to reproduce images:

Cover Daniel Cox; p. 3 Richard Kirby (Timeframe Productions Ltd); pp. 4, 8, 9, 13*l*, 17*r*, 18, 79*t*, 79*b*, 96*c*, 157*l*, 172*l*, 191, 225 Phototake Inc; pp. 5, 89 Dr Jeremy Burgess/Science Photo Library; pp. 7*l*, 140 Pascal Goetgheluck/Science Photo Library; p. 7*r* Steve Allen/Science Photo Library; pp. 10, 11*t*, 20 Dennis Taylor; pp. 11*bl*, 13*r* Dr Gopal Murti/Science Photo Library; p. 12 Anton Page, Biomedical Imaging Unit, University of Southampton; p. 14 Biology Media/ Science Photo Library; p. 15*l* Dr Kari Lounatmaa/ Science Photo Library; pp. 15*r*, 167 CNRI/Science Photo Library; p. 16 ISM//Science Photo Library; p. 17*l* Don W. Fawcett/Science Photo Library; pp. 19*l*, 55*t*, 73, 99, 190*r* Biophoto Associates/Science Photo Library; p. 19*r* Marilyn Schaller/Science Photo Library; p. 39*l* David M Dennis; pp. 39*r*, 55*bl*, 55*br*, 175 John Adds; p. 40 Microfield Scientific LTD/Science Photo Library; p. 43*l* Duncan Shaw/Science Photo Library; p. 43*r* © Travelshots.com/Alamy; p. 44 Sidney Moulds/ Science Photo Library; p. 45 M.P. O'Neill/Science Photo Library; p. 47 L. Willatt, East Anglian Regional Genetics Service/Science Photo Library; p. 49 OCR; p. 51 Claude Nuridsany & Marie Perennou/Science Photo Library; p. 56*b* Brian Bell/Science Photo Library; p. 58*t* Photo Insolite Realite/Science Photo Library; p. 65 Science Photo Library; pp. 66, 74, 92*r* Biophoto Associates; pp. 68, 97*br*, 150, 152, 159, 204, 210*l*, 235*r*, 242, 242 extension Geoff Jones; p. 70 Zephyr/ Science Photo Library; p. 84 © Olivier Labalette/ TempSport/Corbis; pp. 92*l*, 97*bl* Andrew Syred; p. 95 NASA; p. 96*t* Ian West; pp. 96*b*, 97*tr* Andrew Syred/ Science Photo Library; p. 97*tl* Dirk Wiersma/Science Photo Library; p. 106 Richard Wehr/Custom Medical Stock Photo/Science Photo Library; p. 108 Hermann Eisenbeiss/Science Photo Library; pp. 113, 217, 231 Eye of Science/Science Photo Library; p. 114 J. Gross, Biozentrum/Science Photo Library; p. 115 Prof. P. Motta/Dept. of Anatomy/University 'La Sapienze', Rome/Science Photo Library; p. 128 Kevin Curtis/ Science Photo Library; p. 137 Simon Fraser/Science Photo Library; p. 138 James King-Holmes/Science Photo Library; p. 144*t* Oak Ridge National Laboratory/ US Department of Energy/Science Photo Library; pp. 144*b*, 160 Gustoimages/Science Photo Library; p. 147 Adam Hart-Davis/Science Photo Library; p. 148 © Peter Cavanagh/Alamy; pp. 153, 161*r*, 226 © Holt Studios International Ltd/Alamy; p. 154*t* Nigel Cattlin/ Holt Studios International/Science Photo Library; p. 154*b* Herve Conge, ISM/Science Photo Library; p. 156 © Peter Llewellyn/Alamy; pp. 157*r*, 221 © David R. Frazier Photolibrary, Inc./Alamy; p. 161*l* Owen Franken/Corbis; p. 162*l* Cordelia Molloy/Science Photo Library; p. 162*r* © Jeremy Hogan/Alamy; pp. 168, 171, 173 World Health Organization; p. 169 Dr Klaus Boller/ Science Photo Library; pp. 172*r*, 174 Andy Crump, TDR, WHO/Science Photo Library; p. 186 © Sally and Richard Greenhill/Alamy; p. 188 Roger De La Harpe/ Africa Imagery; p. 189 © Photofusion Picture Library/ Alamy; p. 190*l* Richard Fosbery; p. 192 Colin Cuthbert/ Science Photo Library; p. 195 Nick Sinclair/Science Photo Library; p. 203*tl* © FLPA/Alamy; p. 203*tr* © Alistair Scott/Alamy; p. 203*bl* © Martin Shields/Alamy; p. 203*br* © Chris Howes/Wild Places Photography/ Alamy; pp. 205, 241*b* © NHPA/Nick Garbutt; p. 210*r* Konrad Wothe; p. 211*tl* Liz Bomford; p. 211*cl* Berndt Fischer; p. 211*bl* Survival Anglia; p. 211 *greenfinch, chaffinch* Mark Hamblin; p. 211 *goldfinch* David Tipling; p. 212*tl* © JUPITERIMAGES/Brand X/Alamy; p. 212*tr* Juniors Bildarchiv; p. 222 © John Carnemolla/Corbis; p. 223*t* © NHPA/Stephen Dalton; p. 223*b* © John Howard/Cordaiy Photo Library Ltd/CORBIS; p. 224 John Durham/Science Photo Library; p. 233 PLI/ Science Photo Library; p. 234*l* Mike Powles; p. 234*r* © Paul Glendell/Alamy; p. 235*l* © Avico Ltd/Alamy; pp. 236*t*, 238 © NHPA/Martin Harvey; p. 236*b* © NHPA/ Robert Thompson; p. 237*t* © ScotImage/Alamy; p. 237*cl* © Organica/Alamy; p. 237*cr* © Mike Read/ Alamy; p. 237*b* © Susan & Allan Parker/Alamy; p. 239*l* © NHPA/Peter & Beverly Pickford; p. 239*r* © NHPA/ Andy Rouse; p. 241*t* © NHPA/Martin Wendler

We would like to thank OCR for permission to reproduce questions from past examination papers, and IUCN and the World Health Organization for permission to reproduce URLs.

Chapter 1

Cell structure

Background

e-Learning

Objectives

All living organisms are made of cells. Cells are the basic units of living things, and most scientists would agree that anything that is *not* made of a cell or cells – for example, a virus – cannot be a living organism.

Some organisms, such as bacteria, have only one cell, and are said to be **unicellular**. Others have millions of cells. Any organism that is made up of more than one cell is said to be **multicellular**.

All cells are very small, but some of them are just large enough to be seen with the naked eye. The unicellular organism *Amoeba*, for example, can just be seen as a tiny white speck floating in liquid if you shake up a culture of them inside a glass vessel. These cells are about 0.1 mm across. However, this is unusually large. Human cells are usually somewhere between 10 μm and 30 μm in diameter (see the box on page 3 for an explanation of 'μm'). Bacterial cells are much smaller, often about 0.5 μm across. To see most cells, a microscope must be used.

Microscopes

The first microscopes were invented in the mid 17th century. They opened up a whole new world for biologists to study. Now biologists would see tiny, unicellular organisms whose existence had previously only been guessed at. They could also see, for the first time, that large organisms such as plants and animals are made up of cells.

Light microscopes

The early microscopes, like the microscopes that you will use in the laboratory, were **light microscopes**. Light microscopes use glass lenses to refract (bend) light rays and produce a magnified image of an object. Figure 1.1 shows how a light microscope works.

Eyepiece lens magnifies and focuses the image from the objective onto the eye.

Objective lens collects light passing through the specimen and produces a magnified image.

Condenser lens focuses the light onto the specimen held between the cover slip and slide.

Condenser iris diaphragm is closed slightly to produce a narrow beam of light.

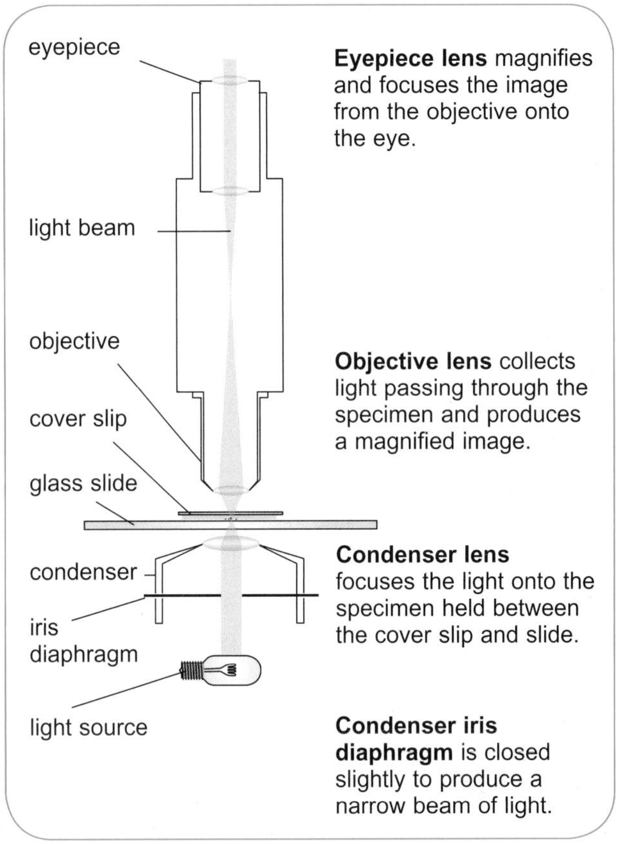

Figure 1.1   How a light microscope works.

The specimen to be observed usually needs to be very thin, and also transparent. To keep it flat, it is usually placed on a glass slide with a very thin glass coverslip on top. For a temporary slide, you can mount the specimen in a drop of water. To make a permanent slide, a liquid that solidifies to produce a clear solid is used to mount the specimen.

The slide is placed on a stage through which light shines from beneath. The light is focused onto the specimen using a **condenser lens**. The light then passes through the specimen and is captured and refracted by an **objective lens**. Most microscopes have three or four different objective lenses, which provide different fields of view and different magnifications. The greater the magnification, the smaller the field of view.

The light rays now travel up to the **eyepiece lens**. This produces the final image, which falls onto the retina of your eye. The image can also be captured using a digital camera or video camera, and viewed or projected onto a screen.

Many biological specimens are colourless when they have been cut into very thin sections, so a **stain** is often added to make structures within the specimen easier to see (Table 1.1). Different parts of a cell, or different kinds of cells, may take up (absorb) a stain more than others. For example, a stain called methylene blue is taken up more by nuclei than by cytoplasm, so it makes a nucleus look dark blue while the cytoplasm is pale blue. Methylene blue is taken up by living cells, but many other stains cannot get through the cell membrane of a living cell and can only be used on dead cells.

Magnification

Using a microscope, or even just a hand lens, we can see biological objects looking much larger than they really are. The object is **magnified**. We can define magnification as the size of the image divided by the real size of the object.

$$\text{magnification} = \frac{\text{size of image}}{\text{real size of object}}$$

For example, we can calculate the magnification of the drawing of a spider in Worked example 1.

Worked example 1

Calculation of the magnification of a drawing.

$$\text{magnification} = \frac{\text{size of image}}{\text{real size of object}}$$

Below is a 'real' spider and a drawing of this spider.

Step 1 Measure the length of the 'real' spider. You should find that it is 10 mm long. The length of the spider in the drawing is 30 mm.

Step 2 Now, substitute these numbers into the equation above:

$$\text{magnification} = \frac{30}{10} = \times 3$$

Notice the '×' sign in front of the number 3. This stands for 'times'. We say that the magnification is 'times 3'.

Stain	Use	Colours produced
methylene blue	staining living cells	dark blue nucleus, light blue cytoplasm (in bacteria, the whole cell takes up the stain)
iodine solution	staining living plant cells	very dark blue starch grains
acidified phloroglucinol	staining lignin (the substance in the cell walls of xylem vessels)	bright red
acetic orcein	staining nuclei and chromosomes	red
eosin	staining cytoplasm and some organelles (it stains dead cells only and so can be used to distinguish between live and dead sperm cells)	pink
light green	staining plant cell walls	green

Table 1.1 Some stains commonly used in light microscopy.

SAQ

1 A person makes a drawing of an incisor tooth. The width of the actual tooth is 5 mm. The width of the tooth in the drawing is 12 mm.
Calculate the magnification of the drawing.

Hint

Answer

Units of measurement

In biology, we often need to measure very small objects. When measuring cells or parts of cells, the most common (and useful) unit is the **micrometre**, written **μm** for short. The symbol μ is the Greek letter mu. One micrometre is one thousandth of a millimetre.

Even smaller structures, such as the organelles within cells, are measured using even smaller units. These are **nanometres**, written **nm** for short. One nanometre is one thousandth of a micrometre.

$$1\,\mu m = \frac{1}{1000}\,mm$$

This can also be written 1×10^{-3} mm, or 1×10^{-6} m.

$$1\,nm = \frac{1}{1000}\,\mu m$$

This can also be written 1×10^{-6} mm, or 1×10^{-9} m.

Often, we are dealing with small units, such as μm. It is important to make sure all your measurements are in the same units. It is often best to convert everything into μm before you begin your calculation, as shown in Worked example 2.

Worked example 2

Calculation of magnification and conversion of units.

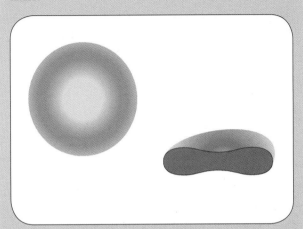

Let us say that we know that the real diameter of a red blood cell is 7 μm and we have been asked to calculate the magnification of the above diagram.

Step 1 Measure the diameter of the cell in the diagram. You should find that it is 30 mm.

Step 2 We have been given its real size in μm, so we need to convert the 30 mm to μm. There are 1000 μm in 1 mm, so 30 mm is 30×1000 μm.

Step 3 Now we can put the numbers into the equation:

$$magnification = \frac{size\ of\ image}{real\ size\ of\ object}$$

$$= \frac{30 \times 1000}{7}$$

$$= \times 4286$$

SAQ

2 This is a **photomicrograph** – a photograph taken using a light microscope. The actual maximum diameter of the cell is 50 μm. Calculate the magnification of the photomicrograph.

Hint

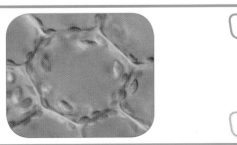

Answer

Worked example 3

Calculating magnification from a scale bar.

This diagram shows a lymphocyte.

6 µm

We can calculate the magnification of the image of the lymphocyte without needing to measure it or to know anything about its original size. We can simply use the **scale bar**. All you need to do is to measure the length of the scale bar and then substitute its measured length and the length that it represents into the equation. (Remember to convert your measurement to µm.)

Step 1 Measure the scale bar. Here, it is 24 mm.

Step 2 Substitute into the equation.

$$\text{magnification} = \frac{\text{size of image}}{\text{real size of object}}$$

$$\text{magnification} = \frac{\text{the length of the scale bar}}{\text{the length the scale bar represents}}$$

$$= \frac{24 \times 1000\,\mu m}{6\,\mu m}$$

$$= \times 4000$$

3 This is a photomicrograph of a transverse section through a leaf. Use the scale bar to calculate the magnification of the photomicrograph.

Hint

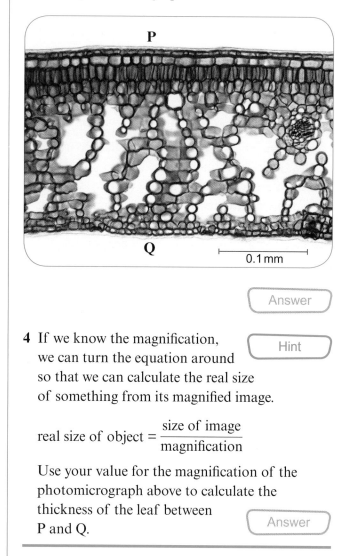

P

Q

0.1 mm

Answer

4 If we know the magnification, we can turn the equation around so that we can calculate the real size of something from its magnified image.

Hint

$$\text{real size of object} = \frac{\text{size of image}}{\text{magnification}}$$

Use your value for the magnification of the photomicrograph above to calculate the thickness of the leaf between P and Q.

Answer

Resolution

Light microscopes have one major disadvantage. They are unable to show objects that are smaller than about 200 nm across ($1\,nm = \dfrac{1}{1000}\,mm$). You might just be able to pick out such a structure, but it would appear only as a shapeless blur.

The degree of detail that can be seen in an image is known as the **resolution**. The tinier the individual points of information on an image – for example, the pixels on a monitor – the better the resolution. To see the very smallest objects, you need a microscope with very high resolution.

The absolute limit of resolution of a microscope is determined by the wavelength of the radiation that it uses. As a rule of thumb, the limit of resolution is about 0.45 times the wavelength. Shorter wavelengths give the best resolution.

The shortest wavelength of visible light is blue light, and it has a wavelength of about 450 nm. So the smallest objects we can expect to be able to distinguish using a light microscope are approximately 0.45 × 450 nm, which is around 200 nm. This is the best resolution we can ever expect to achieve using a light microscope. In practice, it is never quite as good as this.

It's important to understand that resolution is not the same as magnification (Figure 1.2). You could project an image from a light microscope onto an enormous screen, so that it is hugely magnified. There is no limit to how much you could magnify it. But your huge image will just look like a huge blur. There won't be any more 'pixels' in your image – just the same ones that were always there, blown up larger.

Magnification with no change in resolution

This is a photograph of a chloroplast in a plant cell taken with an electron microscope.

The photograph is magnified × 9. But there is no extra detail in the photograph. There has been no increase in resolution.

Increase in resolution with no change in magnification

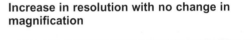

The resolution of the image is increased × 10, by having 10 dots of visual information in each one of the dots (squares) shown on the left. Much more detail of the internal structure of the chloroplast is now shown.

Figure 1.2 Explaining the difference between magnification and resolution.

Electron microscopes

Light is part of the electromagnetic spectrum (Figure 1.3). To get around the limit of resolution imposed by the use of light rays, we can use a different type of wave with a shorter wavelength.

Electron microscopes use beams of electrons instead of light rays (Figure 1.4 and Figure 1.6). Electron beams have much shorter wavelengths than light rays. They therefore have much higher resolution, typically about 400 times better than a light microscope. Using an electron microscope, we can distinguish objects that are only 0.5 nm apart. This means that we can magnify things much more than with a light microscope and still obtain a clear image. With a light microscope, because of the relatively poor resolution, it is only useful to magnify an image up to about 1400 times. With an electron microscope, images remain clear up to a magnification of about 300 000 times.

Some electron microscopes work in a similar way to a light microscope, passing electrons through a thin specimen. They are called **transmission electron microscopes**, TEM for short, and produce images like the one in Figure 1.13.

As with light microscopes, the specimens to be viewed need to be very thin, and to be stained so that the different parts show up clearly in the image that is produced. In electron microscopy, the 'stains' are usually heavy metals, such as lead or osmium (Figure 1.5). Ions of these metals are taken up by some parts of the cells more than others.

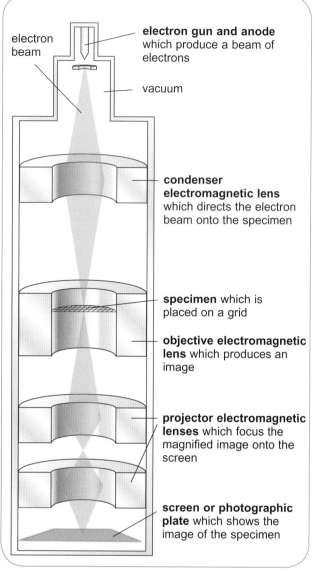

electron gun and anode which produce a beam of electrons

vacuum

condenser electromagnetic lens which directs the electron beam onto the specimen

specimen which is placed on a grid

objective electromagnetic lens which produces an image

projector electromagnetic lenses which focus the magnified image onto the screen

screen or photographic plate which shows the image of the specimen

electron beam

Figure 1.4   How an electron microscope works.

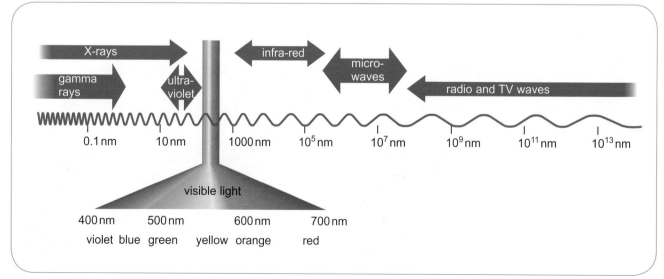

Figure 1.3   The electromagnetic spectrum.

The ions are large and positively charged. The negatively charged electrons do not pass through them, and so do not arrive on the screen. The screen therefore stays dark in these areas, so the structures that have taken up the stains look darker than other areas.

Scanning electron microscopes work by bouncing electron beams off the surface of an object. They give a three-dimensional image, like the one in Figure 1.27. A scanning electron microscope, or SEM, can provide images that can be usefully magnified to almost the same extent as TEM images.

The original images produced by an electron microscope are in black, white and grey only, but false colours are often added using a computer, to make the images look more eye-catching and to help non-specialists to identify the different structures that are visible.

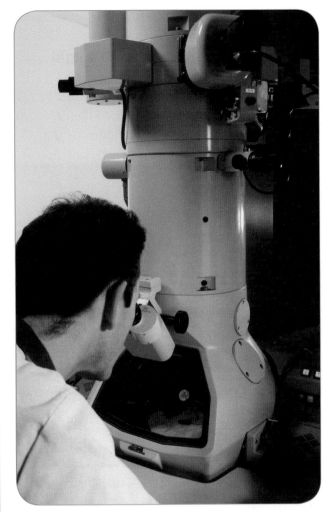

Figure 1.6   Using an electron microscope.

Figure 1.5   These insects are being prepared for viewing in a scanning electron microscope, by having a thin, even layer of gold spattered over them. Gold has large atoms from which electrons will bounce off, giving a clear image of the surface of the insects' bodies.

SAQ

5   Copy and complete the table.

Type of microscope	Best resolution that can be achieved	Best effective magnification that can be achieved
light microscope		
transmission electron microscope		
scanning electron microscope		

Answer

7

Cells

Appearance of cells seen with a light microscope

You are probably already familiar with the structure of animal and plant cells, as they are seen when we use a light microscope. Figure 1.7 is a photomicrograph of an animal cell, and Figure 1.9 is a photomicrograph of a plant cell.

Figure 1.8 is a diagram showing the structures that are visible in an animal cell using a light microscope, and Figure 1.10 is a similar diagram of a plant cell. In practice, you would probably not see all of these things at once in any one cell.

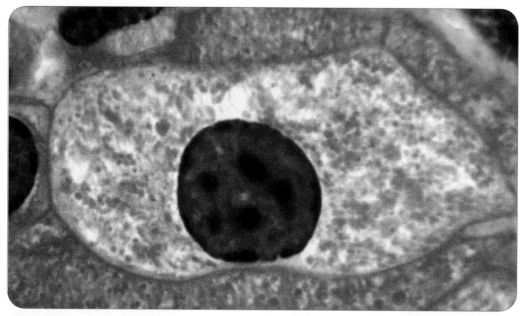

Figure 1.7 Photomicrograph of a stained animal cell (×1800).

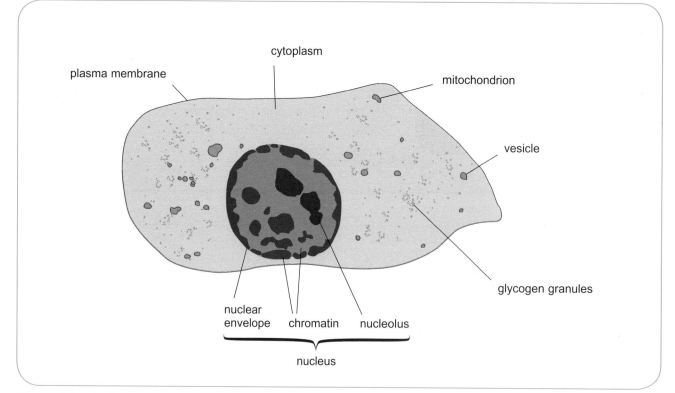

Figure 1.8 A diagram of an animal cell as it appears using a light microscope.

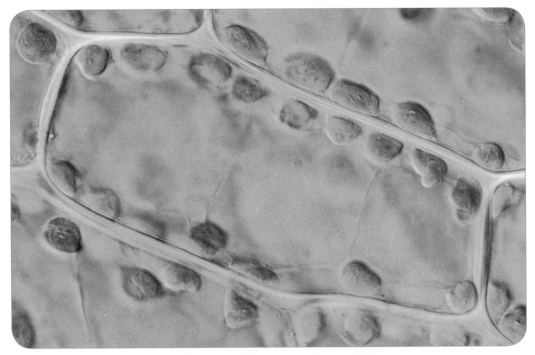

Figure 1.9 Photomicrograph of a cell in a moss leaf (×750).

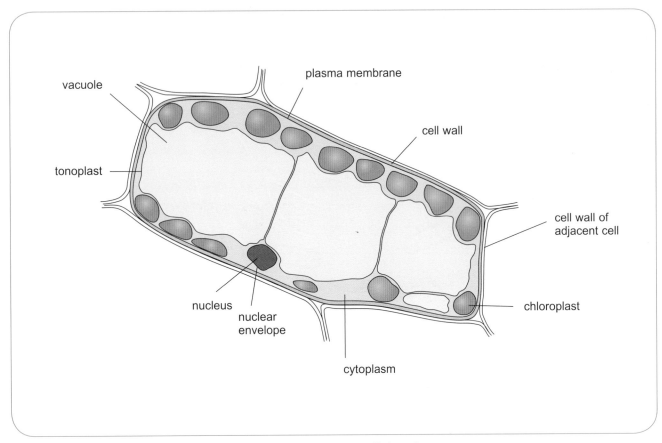

Figure 1.10 A diagram of a plant cell as it appears using a light microscope.

Appearance of cells seen with an electron microscope

As we have seen, electron microscopes are able to resolve much smaller structures than light microscopes. The structure that we can see when we use an electron microscope is called **ultrastructure**.

Figure 1.11 and Figure 1.12 are stylised diagrams summarising the ultrastructure of a typical animal cell and a typical plant cell. Figure 1.13 and Figure 1.15 are electron micrographs of an animal cell and a plant cell. Figure 1.14 and Figure 1.16 are diagrams based on these electron micrographs.

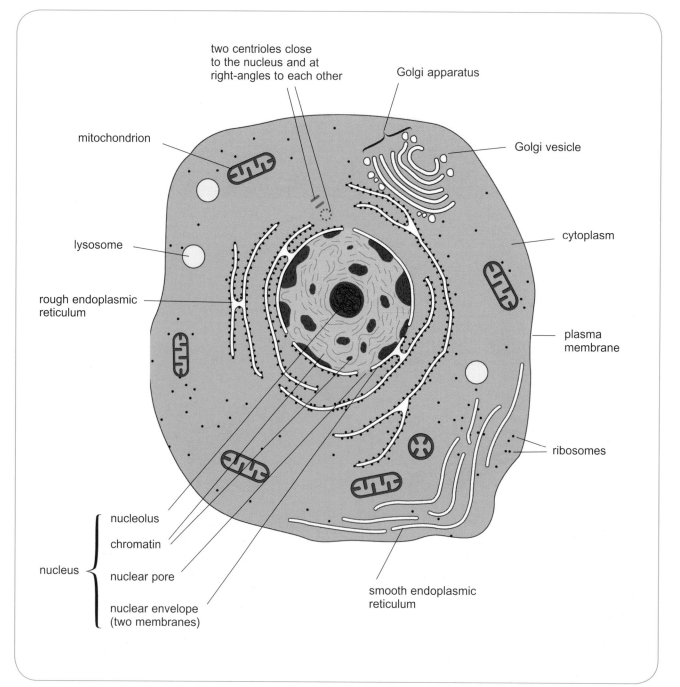

Figure 1.11 Ultrastructure of an animal cell.

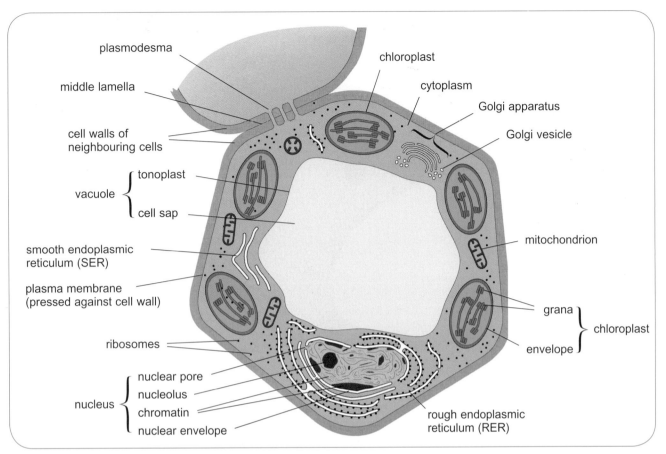

Figure 1.12 Ultrastructure of a plant cell.

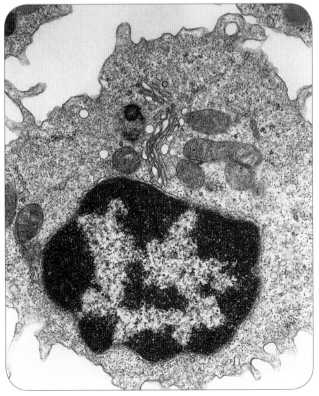

Figure 1.13 Transmission electron micrograph of a white blood cell (× 15 000).

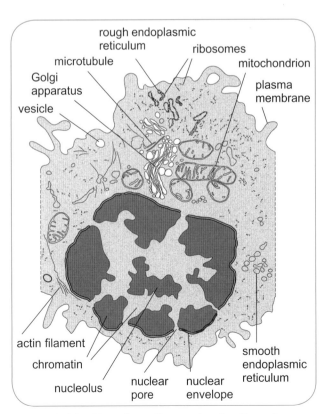

Figure 1.14 Drawing of an animal cell made from the electron micrograph in Figure 1.13.

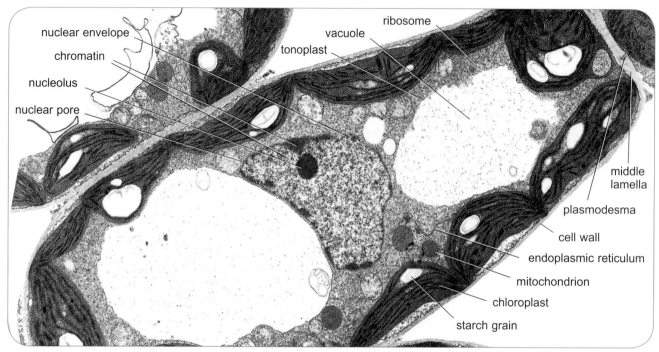

Figure 1.15 Electron micrograph of a plant cell (×5600).

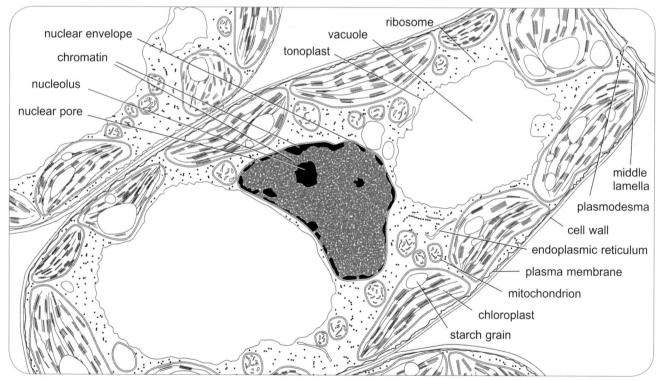

Figure 1.16 Drawing of a plant cell made from the electron micrograph in Figure 1.15.

SAQ

6 State whether the electron micrographs in Figure 1.13 and Figure 1.15 were made using a transmission electron microscope (TEM) or a scanning electron microscope (SEM). How can you tell?

Answer

7 Make a list of all the structures within a cell that are visible with an electron microscope but cannot be clearly seen with a light microscope.

Answer

Structure and function of organelles

The different structures that are found within a cell are known as **organelles**.

Nucleus

Almost all cells have a **nucleus**. Two important exceptions are red blood cells in mammals, and phloem sieve tubes in plants.

The nucleus is normally the largest cell organelle. It has a tendency to take up stains more readily than the cytoplasm, and so usually appears as a dark area (Figure 1.17).

The nucleus is surrounded by two membranes with a small gap between them. The pair of membranes is known as the **nuclear envelope**. There are small gaps all over the envelope, called **nuclear pores**.

The nucleus contains **chromosomes**. Chromosomes are long molecules of DNA. In a non-dividing cell, they are too thin to be visible as individual chromosomes, but form a tangle known as **chromatin,** often darkly stained.

DNA carries a code that instructs the cell about making proteins, and the DNA in the lighter-staining parts of the chromatin can be used for transcription, the first stage of protein synthesis. During transcription, the information on DNA is copied onto molecules of messenger RNA, which travel out of the nucleus, through the nuclear pores, into the cytoplasm.

An especially darkly staining area in the nucleus, the **nucleolus**, contains DNA that is being used to make **ribosomes**, the tiny organelles where protein synthesis takes place.

Endoplasmic reticulum

Within the cytoplasm of every eukaryotic cell, there is a network of membranes, known as the **endoplasmic reticulum**. Some of these membranes have ribosomes attached to them, forming **rough endoplasmic reticulum,** RER for short (Figure 1.18). Some do not, and these form **smooth endoplasmic reticulum,** SER. The RER is usually continuous with the nuclear envelope.

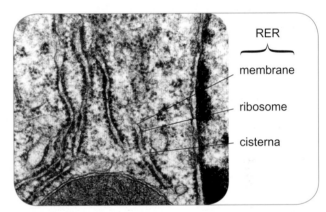

Figure 1.18 Transmission electron micrograph showing endoplasmic reticulum ($\times 40\,000$).

The enclosed spaces formed by the membranes are called **cisternae**. The membranes keep these spaces isolated from the cytoplasm.

RER is where most protein synthesis takes place. Protein synthesis happens on the ribosomes that are attached to the membranes. As the protein molecules are made, they collect inside the cisternae. From here, they can be transported to other areas in the cell – to the Golgi apparatus, for example (page 14).

SER has different roles in different cells. For example, in cells in the ovary and testis it is the site of production of steroid hormones such as oestrogen and testosterone. In liver cells, it is the place where toxins are broken down and made harmless.

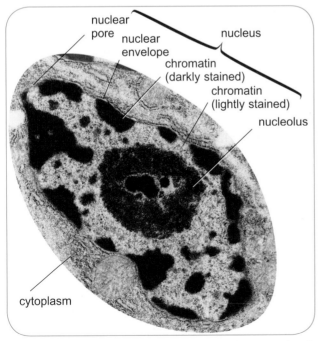

nuclear pore
nuclear envelope
nucleus
chromatin (darkly stained)
chromatin (lightly stained)
nucleolus
cytoplasm

Figure 1.17 Transmission electron micrograph of a nucleus ($\times 10\,000$).

Golgi apparatus

In many cells, a stack of curved membranes is visible, enclosing a series of flattened sacs. This is the **Golgi apparatus** (Figure 1.19). Some cells have several Golgi apparatuses.

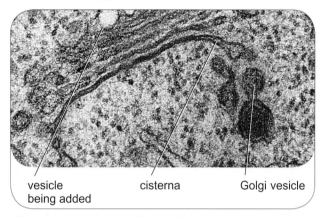

vesicle being added   cisterna   Golgi vesicle

Figure 1.19 Transmission electron micrograph showing a Golgi apparatus (×35 000).

The Golgi apparatus is not a stable structure; it is constantly changing. At one side, tiny membrane-bound **vesicles** move towards the Golgi apparatus and fuse together, forming a new layer to the stack. At the other side, the sacs break down, forming vesicles that move away from the Golgi apparatus (Figure 1.20).

The vesicles that fuse with the Golgi apparatus have come from the endoplasmic reticulum. They contain proteins that were made there. In the Golgi apparatus, these proteins are packaged and processed, changing them into the required product.

Some of the processed proteins are then transported, in the vesicles that bud off from the Golgi apparatus, to the plasma membrane. Here, the vesicles fuse with the membrane and deposit the proteins outside the cell, in a process called **endocytosis**. The production of useful substances in a cell and their subsequent release from it is called **secretion**.

Some vesicles, however, remain in the cell. Some of these contain proteins that function as digestive enzymes, and such vesicles are called **lysosomes**.

Lysosomes

Lysosomes are tiny bags of digestive enzymes. They are surrounded by a single membrane. They are usually about 0.5 μm in diameter. Their main function is to fuse with other vesicles in the cell that contain something that needs to be digested – for example, a bacterium which has been brought into the cell by endocytosis (Chapter 2). They also help to destroy worn-out or unwanted organelles within the cell. The enzymes in the lysosome break down the large molecules in the bacterium or organelle, producing soluble substances that can disperse into the cytoplasm. The head of a sperm cell contains a special type of lysosome called an **acrosome**, whose enzymes digest a pathway into an egg just before fertilisation takes place.

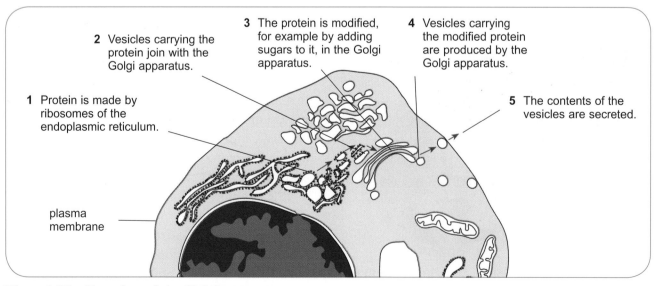

2 Vesicles carrying the protein join with the Golgi apparatus.

3 The protein is modified, for example by adding sugars to it, in the Golgi apparatus.

4 Vesicles carrying the modified protein are produced by the Golgi apparatus.

1 Protein is made by ribosomes of the endoplasmic reticulum.

5 The contents of the vesicles are secreted.

plasma membrane

Figure 1.20 Function of the Golgi apparatus.

Chloroplasts

Chloroplasts are found in some plant cells, but never in animal cells (Figure 1.21). They are the site of photosynthesis.

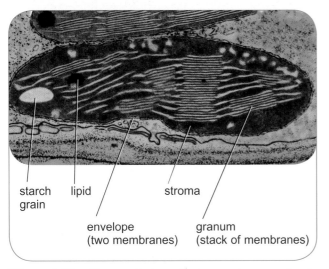

starch grain   lipid   stroma

envelope (two membranes)   granum (stack of membranes)

Figure 1.21 Transmission electron micrograph of a chloroplast (×27000).

A chloroplast has a double membrane, called an **envelope**, surrounding it. These membranes isolate the reactions that take place inside the chloroplast from the rest of the cell.

Inside the chloroplast, there are membranes called **grana** (singular: granum). In places, the grana form stacks called **thylakoids**. The grana contain chlorophyll, and this is where the light-dependent reactions of photosynthesis take place. In these reactions, light energy is captured by chlorophyll and used to split water molecules to provide hydrogen ions, which are then used to make ATP and a substance called reduced NADP. The ATP and reduced NADP are then used to make carbohydrates, using carbon dioxide from the air, in the light-independent reactions. The light-independent reactions take place in the 'background material' of the chloroplast, called the **stroma**.

Chloroplasts often contain **starch grains**. Starch is a carbohydrate that is used as an energy store in plants.

Mitochondria

Mitochondria are found in both plant and animal cells. Like chloroplasts, they are surrounded by a double membrane, also known as an envelope (Figure 1.22).

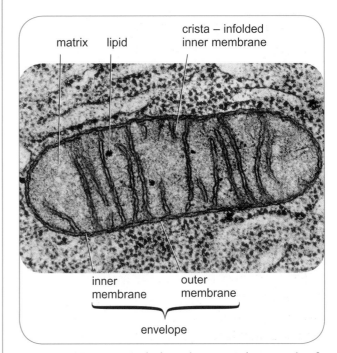

matrix   lipid   crista – infolded inner membrane

inner membrane   outer membrane

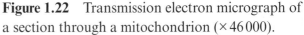

envelope

Figure 1.22 Transmission electron micrograph of a section through a mitochondrion (×46000).

Mitochondria are the site of **aerobic respiration** in a cell. Here, oxygen and energy-containing molecules produced from glucose are used to make **ATP**. ATP is the energy currency of a cell, necessary for every energy-using activity that it carries out. Each cell has to make its own ATP. Cells that use a lot of energy, such as muscle cells, therefore contain a lot of mitochondria.

The inner membrane of the mitochondrion is folded to form **cristae**. Here, ATP is made in a process that has many similarities with the production of ATP on the membranes inside a chloroplast. The 'background material' of the mitochondrion, called the **matrix**, is the site of the stages of aerobic respiration called the Krebs cycle.

Faulty mitochondria

Mitochondria are unusual organelles. Like chloroplasts they have two membranes around them rather than just one, and they contain their own DNA. Mitochondria and chloroplasts have evolved from prokaryotic cells that 'invaded' eukaryotic cells early in their evolutionary history – perhaps 2 billion years ago – and made themselves invaluable by providing enzymes and pathways that help the cell to survive. They have become an integral part of their host cells.

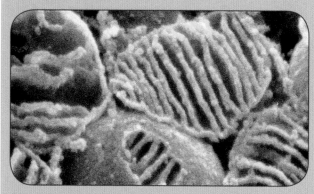

Scanning electron micrograph of a group of mitochondria (×60 000).

All the mitochondria in your cells have been produced from a few mitochondria that were in your mother's egg cell. The genes in mitochondria are passed down the maternal line. When a cell divides (Chapter 3), the mitochondria are shared out between the daughter cells.

The DNA in human mitochondria contains 37 different genes. These genes are not as well protected as those in the nucleus and are particularly prone to mutation. Some of these mutations are harmful, and mitochondria with mutant genes have been linked to a number of human diseases. However, mitochondria are not self-sufficient in DNA, and they rely on proteins that are produced following the code on the DNA in the nucleus. So faults in mitochondria are not necessarily caused by the mitochondria's own genes, but could be a result of a mutation in the nuclear DNA. This is borne out by the fact

that more than 80% of diseases that are linked to faulty mitochondria do not follow a maternal inheritance pattern. This includes some cases of male infertility, caused by a lack of ATP generation in sperm cells, and also a tendency towards the development of type 2 (late onset) diabetes.

But about 1 in every 5000 people are thought to carry mutations in their mitochondrial DNA, and this can sometimes lead to very serious health problems, such as liver, kidney or brain damage. Often, a fetus that has inherited these faulty mitochondria from its mother does not survive and the mother has a miscarriage. Work is in progress to find methods of removing these faulty mitochondria from the mother's egg and replacing them with healthy mitochondria taken from a donor egg. The mother's nucleus would still be present in the egg, so the child would still be genetically hers – except for the genes in her mitochondria.

Licences to carry out such work in the UK are granted by the Human Fertilisation and Embryology Authority. The HFEA has a general ruling that embryos cannot be genetically altered in such a way that the altered genes would be passed on to their own offspring one day – they cannot pass along the 'germ line' from one person to their offspring. Initially, this ruling was thought to exclude the substitution of a mother's mitochondria with someone else's, because mitochondria contain genes. However, in 2006, the HFEA ruled that this would be allowable, and they have granted a licence for research work to be carried out on the technique. Professor John Burn, from the Newcastle Institute of Clinical Genetics, which is the first institution to receive such a licence, says: 'My belief is that what we are doing is changing a battery that doesn't work for one that does. The analogy is with a camera: changing the battery won't affect what's on the film, and changing the mitochondria won't affect the important DNA.'

Vacuole

A vacuole is a membrane-bound organelle that contains liquid. Mature plant cells often have large vacuoles that contain cell sap. The membrane surrounding the vacuole is known as the **tonoplast**. Cell sap contains a variety of substances in solution, especially sugars, pigments and also enzymes.

Plasma (cell surface) membrane

Every cell is surrounded by a **plasma membrane**, sometimes known as the **cell surface membrane**. This is a thin layer made up of lipid (fat) molecules and protein molecules. Its role is to control what enters the cell and what leaves it. You can read about the movement of substances through the plasma membrane in Chapter 2.

Centrioles

Centrioles are found in animal cells but not in plant cells. Centrioles make and organise tiny structures called **microtubules**, which are made of a protein called **tubulin** (Figure 1.23). During cell division, microtubules form the **spindle**, and are responsible for moving the chromosomes around in the cell, and pulling them to opposite ends of the cell. Plant cells also use microtubules during cell division, but they are not organised by centrioles.

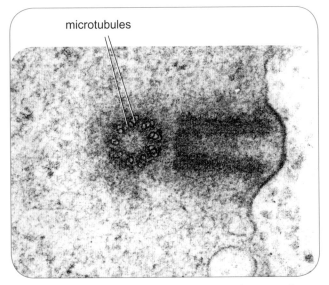

Figure 1.23 Transmission electron micrograph showing the two centrioles of an animal cell (at right angles to each other) (×126000).

Cilia and flagella

Cilia and **flagella** (singular: cilium and flagellum) are long, thin extensions from the surface of a cell, which can produce movement. They are found in some animal cells, and rarely in plant cells – some primitive plants such as liverworts and mosses produce male gametes that swim using flagella.

Cilia and flagella have the same basic structure. The term 'cilia' is used for relatively short structures, usually found in large numbers, whereas 'flagella' are longer and normally found in ones or twos.

Cilia and flagella contain microtubules, always arranged in a 9 + 2 arrangement – that is, with two microtubules in the centre surrounded by a ring made up of nine pairs of microtubules (Figure 1.24 and Figure 1.25). Movement is produced by these microtubules sliding against each other. The movement causes the cilium or flagellum to bend and then straighten. Cilia in a group of ciliated cells usually all move in harmony with each other, looking like a field of wheat as wind sweeps over it.

The movement of cilia can move fluids over the surface of the cell. For example, in the lining of the bronchus, cilia sweep mucus up to the throat, where it is swallowed. Flagella, however, usually cause the cell to swim through a liquid.

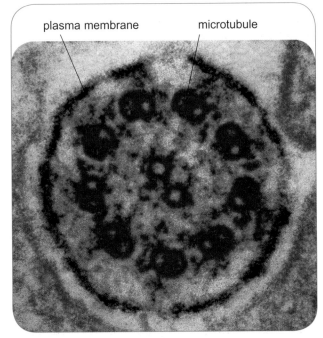

Figure 1.24 Transmission electron micrograph of a transverse section of a cilium or flagellum (×265000).

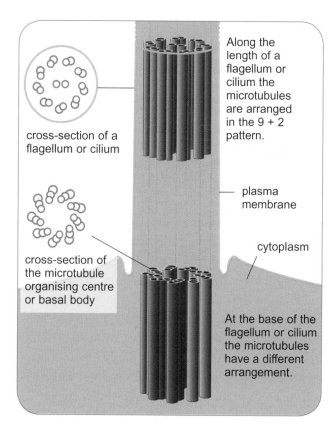

Figure 1.25 Cilia and flagella.

The cytoskeleton

All plant and animal cells contain a network of protein filaments, called **microfilaments**, that act as a 'skeleton' helping to support the cell and to determine its shape. Together with microtubules, these filaments make up the **cytoskeleton** (Figure 1.26).

The cytoskeleton provides mechanical strength for the cell, and also helps to direct movement of organelles within the cell. It provides 'tracks' along which organelles can be moved. The microtubules can act as 'motors', using energy from ATP to pull organelles along the tracks from one place to another. The cytoskeleton can also help the whole cell to move.

Extension

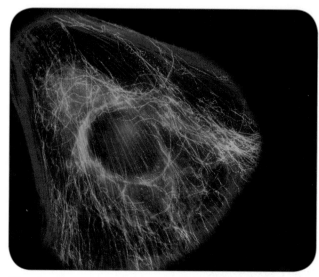

Figure 1.26 Light micrograph showing the cytoskeleton in a kidney cell. Microtubules are stained green, microfilaments red and the nucleus blue (× 5000).

Cell walls

Plant cells are always surrounded by a **cell wall** (Figure 1.27 and Figure 1.28). This is not an organelle, because it is not inside the cell.

Plant cell walls are made of long strands of a carbohydrate called **cellulose**. The cellulose fibres are very strong, and are arranged in a criss-cross manner, held together by a matrix that contains **pectin**. This composite structure has tremendous resistance to stretching forces that might act on it – for example, if the cell has taken up a lot of water and is expanding. The cell wall holds firm, preventing the cell from bursting.

Pectin is also found in the **middle lamella** that cements one cell to another (Figure 1.28).

SAQ

8 Draw a table to compare the structures visible in an animal cell and a plant cell, when they are viewed through an electron microscope.

Hint

Answer

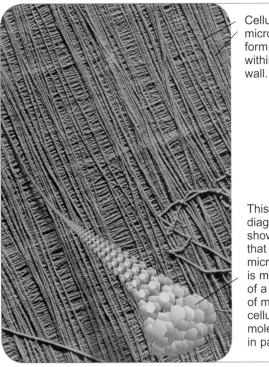

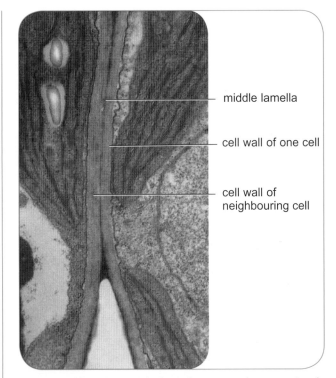

Figure 1.27 Scanning electron micrograph and diagram showing the structure of a plant cell wall (background electron micrograph ×600 000). Notice that the microfibrils lie in different directions in different layers, which greatly increases the mechanical strength of the cell wall.

Figure 1.28 Transmission electron micrograph of plant cell walls. Where two plant cells lie next to each other, a structure called the middle lamella holds the adjacent walls firmly together (×18 000).

Prokaryotic cells

Prokaryotic means 'before nucleus'. Prokaryotes are single-celled organisms that do not have nuclei. Cells that do have nuclei are said to be **eukaryotic**.

The structure of a prokaryotic cell

Figure 1.29 shows the structure of a typical prokaryotic cell. The most obvious difference between this cell and a eukaryotic cell is the lack of a nucleus. The prokaryote's DNA lies free in the cytoplasm.

In eukaryotic cells, the DNA is organised into several chromosomes, in which a long strand of DNA is associated with proteins called **histones**. This is not the case in prokaryotes. The DNA is not usually associated with histones (although histones are present in Archaea), and it is circular rather than linear as in eukaryotes. Another difference is that prokaryotic DNA is always attached to the plasma (cell surface) membrane.

This arrangement of the DNA is so different that some people think we should not use the term 'chromosome' to describe it. However, it has now become common for scientists to talk about bacterial chromosomes, despite the fact that they are not the same as the chromosomes in eukaryotic cells.

Prokaryotes also lack complex membrane-bound organelles, such as mitochondria, chloroplasts and endoplasmic reticulum. They do have ribosomes, but these are smaller than in eukaryotic cells, and they are always free in the cytoplasm rather than attached to membranes.

Prokaryotes are surrounded by a cell wall, but its structure is not at all like that of plant cells. The prokaryote cell wall is made up of fibres of **peptidoglycan**. Like plant cell walls, this cell wall stops the cell bursting if it expands.

Table 1.2 summarises the differences and similarities between eukaryotic cells and prokaryotic cells.

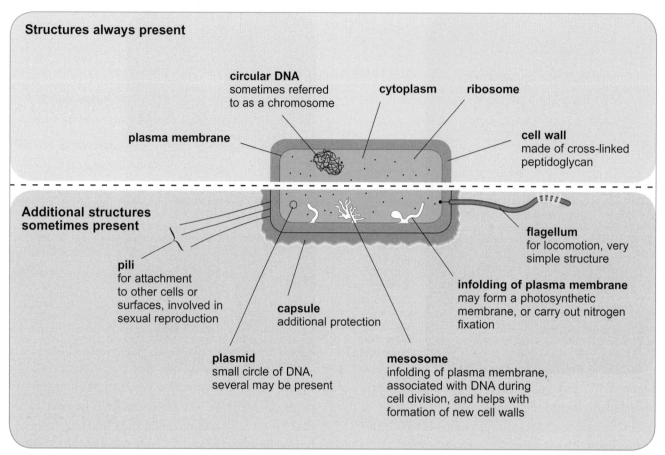

Structures always present

circular DNA
sometimes referred
to as a chromosome

cytoplasm

ribosome

plasma membrane

cell wall
made of cross-linked
peptidoglycan

**Additional structures
sometimes present**

pili
for attachment
to other cells or
surfaces, involved in
sexual reproduction

capsule
additional protection

flagellum
for locomotion, very
simple structure

infolding of plasma membrane
may form a photosynthetic
membrane, or carry out nitrogen
fixation

plasmid
small circle of DNA,
several may be present

mesosome
infolding of plasma membrane,
associated with DNA during
cell division, and helps with
formation of new cell walls

Figure 1.29   The structure of a typical prokaryotic cell.

Structure	Eukaryotic cell	Prokaryotic cell
nucleus	usually present, surrounded by a nuclear envelope and containing a nucleolus	no nucleus, and therefore no nuclear envelope or nucleolus
mitochondria	usually present	never present
chloroplasts	present in some plant cells	never present
endoplasmic reticulum	always present	never present
ribosomes	relatively large, about 30 nm in diameter	relatively small, about 20 nm in diameter
cytoskeleton	always present, made up of microtubules and microfilaments	no cytoskeleton
chromosomes	DNA arranged in several long strands, associated with histones	DNA circular, not associated with histones
cell wall	cellulose cell walls present in plant cells	cell wall always present, made of peptidoglycan
cilia and flagella	sometimes present	some have flagella, but these have a different structure from those in eukaryotic cells

Table 1.2   Comparison of the ultrastructure of eukaryotic and prokaryotic cells.

Summary

Glossary

- All living organisms are made of a cell or cells. Cells and their contents are usually measured in micrometres (μm). One micrometre is one thousandth of a millimetre.

- Light microscopes have much less resolving power than electron microscopes and so the images obtained from light microscopes can only be usefully magnified up to about 1400 times, compared with 300 000 times for an electron microscope.

- The greater resolving power of the electron microscope enables us to see the ultrastructure of a cell – that is, the small organelles that it contains, and their internal structure.

- The following formula can be used to calculate magnifications or the real sizes of objects being viewed:
$$\text{magnification} = \frac{\text{size of image}}{\text{real size of object}}$$

- Specimens to be viewed using a microscope are often stained to make parts of them look darker, or different colours.

- Plant and animal cells are eukaryotic cells, with a nucleus surrounded by an envelope. The nucleus contains the DNA, in the form of chromosomes. All cells are surrounded by a partially permeable plasma membrane.

- Plant and animal cells contain ribosomes for protein synthesis, endoplasmic reticulum for the storage and transport of substances made in the cell, Golgi apparatus for processing and packaging proteins the cell has made, lysosomes containing digestive enzymes and mitochondria to produce ATP by aerobic respiration.

- Plant cells sometimes also contain chloroplasts, where photosynthesis takes place, and they may have a large vacuole containing cell sap. They are surrounded by a fully permeable cellulose cell wall.

- Animal cells contain a pair of centrioles, which organise the microtubules in the cell – for example, when forming the spindle during cell division. Animal cells may also have cilia or flagella, which contain microtubules in a 9 + 2 arrangement and can produce movement.

- Microtubules and microfilaments form the cytoskeleton, holding the cell in shape and helping to move organelles around inside the cell.

- Bacteria are prokaryotic cells, which do not have a nucleus. Their DNA is not associated with histones, and is present as a circular strand. It is attached to the plasma membrane. Prokaryotic cells lack complex membrane-bound organelles such as mitochondria. They have smaller ribosomes than eukaryotic cells. They always have a cell wall, but this is made of peptidoglycan and not cellulose.

Questions

1 a The drawing shows an animal cell <u>nucleus</u> as seen using an electron microscope.

Hint

    i Name the structure labelled W. [1]

    ii The actual diameter of the nucleus, measured along the line XY, is 7 μm.

    Calculate the magnification of the nucleus. Show your working. [2]

b Each part of a cell is specialised to carry out a particular function.

Below is a list of parts of a cell, labelled **A** to **F**. Each of the list of statements, numbered **1** to **6**, refers to one of these parts of the cell.

  A nucleus   **1** where some lipids, including steroids, are made

  B mitochondrion   **2** controls entry of substances into the cell

  C plasma membrane   **3** controls the activities of the cell

  D chloroplast   **4** where polypeptides are made

  E smooth endoplasmic reticulum   **5** where photosynthesis takes place

  F ribosomes   **6** where aerobic respiration takes place

Match a statement to part of the cell. For example, **3** matches with **A**. [5]

OCR Biology AS (2801) January 2003

[Total 8]

Answer

2 a The drawing shows an animal cell as seen under an electron microscope.

Complete the following table by:
- identifying the parts of the cell A to E
- naming the part of the cell responsible for the function stated. The first one has been done for you.

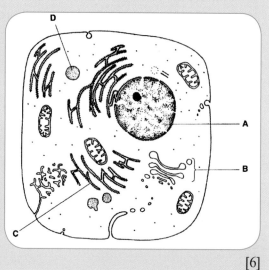

Function	Part of cell	Label
controls activities of the cell	nucleus	A
attaches to mRNA in protein synthesis		
produces secretory vesicles		
contains digestive enzymes		

[6]

b Outline the structure and functions of the cytoskeleton. [4]

OCR Biology AS (2801) January 2005

[Total 10]

Answer

continued

3 With reference to <u>both</u> light and electron microscopy, explain and distinguish between the terms *magnification* and *resolution*.

OCR Biology AS (2801) January 2002

[Total 4]

Hint

Answer

4 The table below compares the features of typical eukaryotic and prokaryotic cells. Copy and complete the table by placing one of the following, as appropriate, in each empty box: a tick (✓), a cross (✗) or the words 'sometimes present'

Feature	Eukaryotic cell	Prokaryotic cell
cell wall	sometimes present	✓
nuclear envelope	✓	
Golgi apparatus		✗
flagellum	sometimes present	
ribosomes		✓
carries out respiration	✓	
chloroplast	sometimes present	

OCR Biology AS (2801) January 2001

[Total 6]

Answer

5 a The diagram shows a drawing of an organelle from a ciliated cell as seen with an electron microscope.

Hint

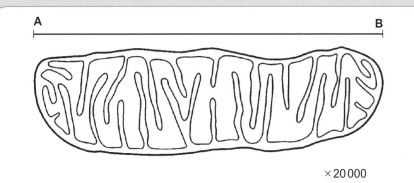

A   B

× 20 000

    i Name the organelle shown in the diagram. [1]

    ii State the function of this organelle. [2]

    iii State why ciliated cells contain relatively large numbers of these organelles. [1]

    iv Calculate the actual length as shown by the line AB in the diagram.
       Express your answer to the <u>nearest micrometre</u> (μm).
       Show your working. [2]

  b An image shown to the same magnification as the diagram above could be produced using a light microscope. Explain why such an image would be of little use when studying cells. [2]

OCR Biology AS (2801) January 2006

[Total 8]

Answer

Chapter 2

Cell membranes

Background

e-Learning

Objectives

Every living cell is surrounded by a membrane. This is called the **plasma membrane**, or the **cell surface membrane**. The plasma membrane defines the limits of the cell. It separates the cell's contents from its external environment, and it controls what can pass from this environment into the cell, and from the cell into the external environment. It is partially permeable.

Membranes are also found inside cells. Some organelles are surrounded by a single membrane – for example, lysosomes. The nucleus, mitochondria and chloroplasts each have two membranes around them, making up an **envelope**. Most eukaryotic cells also have an extensive network of membranes within their cytoplasm, forming the rough endoplasmic reticulum, the smooth endoplasmic reticulum and the Golgi apparatus (Figure 2.1). Like the plasma membrane, these membranes

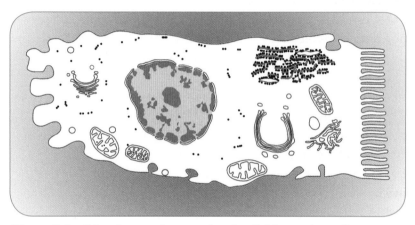

Figure 2.1 Membranes in an animal cell (shown in red).

inside the cell are partially permeable, and therefore able to control what can pass through them. They separate what happens inside the organelle from what is happening in the rest of the cell.

Table 2.1 summarises the functions of membranes around and inside cells. You will find out more about some of these functions in this chapter.

Function	Example
Membranes are partially permeable, controlling what passes through them.	The plasma membrane allows small or uncharged particles to pass through it; protein channels and transporters control the passage of larger or charged particles.
Membranes produce different compartments inside cells.	Mitochondria are surrounded by two membranes, which isolate the reactions taking place inside from the reactions taking place in the cytoplasm.
Membranes are important in cell signalling.	A substance produced by one cell docks into a receptor in the plasma membrane of another, causing something to happen in the second cell.
Membranes can allow electrical signals to pass along them.	The membrane of the axon of a motor neurone transmits action potentials from the central nervous system to a muscle.
Membranes provide attachment sites for enzymes and other molecules involved in metabolism.	The inner membrane of a mitochondrion contains molecules needed for the production of ATP. The inner membrane of a chloroplast contains chlorophyll needed for photosynthesis.

Table 2.1 Functions of membranes.

Structure of cell membranes

All cell membranes have a similar structure. They are normally between 7 nm and 10 nm thick, which makes them invisible with a light microscope but visible using an electron microscope. They are formed from a double layer of molecules called phospholipids, in which many different kinds of **proteins** are situated.

Phospholipid bilayer

Phospholipid molecules have an unusual property. Their heads have a tiny charge, and this attracts them to water molecules. But their tails don't have a charge, and they are repelled from water molecules. We say that the heads of the phospholipids are **hydrophilic** ('water-loving') and the tails are **hydrophobic** ('water-hating') (Figure 2.2).

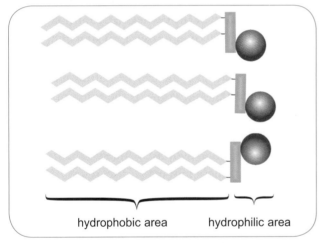

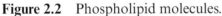

Figure 2.2   Phospholipid molecules.

The cytoplasm inside a cell contains a lot of water, and so does the fluid outside cells. (This is true whether the cell is the single cell of a unicellular organism, or one cell of many in the body of a multicellular organism.) The hydrophilic heads of phospholipid molecules are therefore drawn to these fluids, while the hydrophobic tails are repelled by them. This causes the phospholipids to arrange themselves in a double layer, with heads facing outwards and tails facing inwards. This is called a phospholipid bilayer (Figure 2.3).

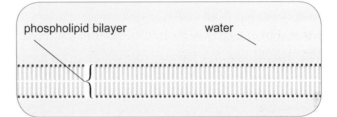

Figure 2.3   A phospholipid bilayer.

Other components of cell membranes

Membranes also contain another type of lipid. This is **cholesterol**. Cholesterol molecules lie alongside the phospholipids, helping to make up the bilayer.

There are also many different protein molecules in cell membranes. They are much larger than phospholipid molecules. Some of the protein molecules lie in the membrane, protruding from both sides. Others float in just the outer layer or the inner layer (Figure 2.4).

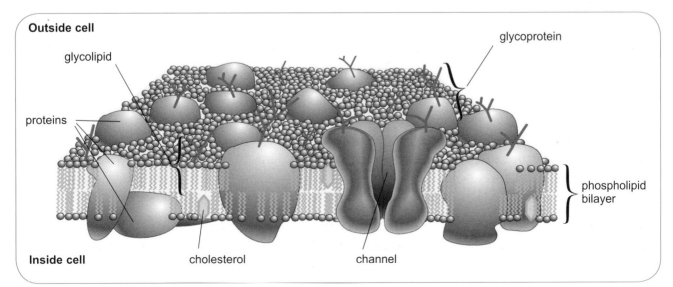

Figure 2.4   Part of a cell surface membrane.

Many of the lipid molecules and protein molecules have short strings of **sugar** molecules attached to them, forming **glycolipids** and **glycoproteins**.

Figure 2.4 shows the structure of a plasma (cell surface) membrane, including all of these components. This is called the **fluid mosaic model** of membrane structure. The term 'fluid' refers to the fact that the molecules in the membrane are in constant motion, moving around within their own layer (they don't normally swap sides). The term 'mosaic' refers to the way the membrane would look if viewed from above, with a mosaic pattern formed by the protein molecules that are scattered throughout.

Table 2.2 summarises the roles of the different components of cell membranes.

SAQ

1 What is the difference between the outer surface and the inner surface of a plasma membrane?

Answer

Cell signalling

A cell must stay in contact with its environment and with other cells in order to survive. Cells must be able to react to changes in their environment. In a multicellular organism, cells in one part of the body must be able to communicate with cells in other parts. A cell therefore needs to be able to pick up 'signals' at its surface to which it may need to respond.

Signals arrive at the plasma membrane from outside the cell as particular substances – for example, a hormone – or changes in electrical potential – as happens in nerve impulses. A receptor in the cell's plasma membrane picks up these signals, and brings about actions within the cell. This process is known as **cell signalling**.

You will meet several different examples of cell signalling as you continue through your Biology course, especially in the context of coordination by hormones and nerve impulses. Cell signalling has potential implications for medicine. For example, why do liver cells in some people not respond to insulin as they should? (This is the cause of type 2 diabetes.) Why do cancer cells not respond to signals that should stop them dividing? Answers to these questions may help to bring about cures or treatments for these and other diseases.

Component	Roles
phospholipid	• forms the bilayer which is the fundamental basis of the membrane in which all other components are embedded • provides a barrier to water-soluble (hydrophilic) substances, such as ions and molecules that carry a charge
cholesterol	• helps to maintain the fluidity of the membrane, preventing it from becoming too stiff when temperatures are low, or too fluid when temperatures are high
protein and glycoprotein	• form channels through which hydrophilic substances can pass; the channels can be opened and closed • act as transporters that can move substances across the membrane up their concentration gradients, with the use of energy from ATP • act as receptor sites, allowing specific molecules from outside the cell, such as hormones, to bind with them and then set up responses within the cell • act as recognition sites, because their precise structure may be specific to a particular type of cell or to a particular individual • act as enzymes

Table 2.2 Roles of the components of cell membranes.

Mechanisms of cell signalling

Figure 2.5 shows three different ways in which cell signalling can occur. In Figure 2.5a, the signal is a chemical that attaches to a protein or glycoprotein acting as an ion channel. When the chemical attaches to the receptor, it makes the channel open and let ions into the cell, bringing about a response.

Figure 2.5b shows a slightly more complex mechanism of cell signalling. Here, the receptor in the plasma membrane interacts with another molecule, a **G-protein**. When the signal molecule attaches to the receptor, the G-protein is activated. The G-protein then activates an enzyme, which brings about a reaction inside the cell.

Figure 2.5c shows a third type of signalling, this time involving a receptor that is also an enzyme. The receptor is made up of two parts. When the signal molecule arrives, it slots into both of these parts, connecting them to one another and forming them into an active enzyme. The enzyme then brings about reactions inside the cell.

Extension

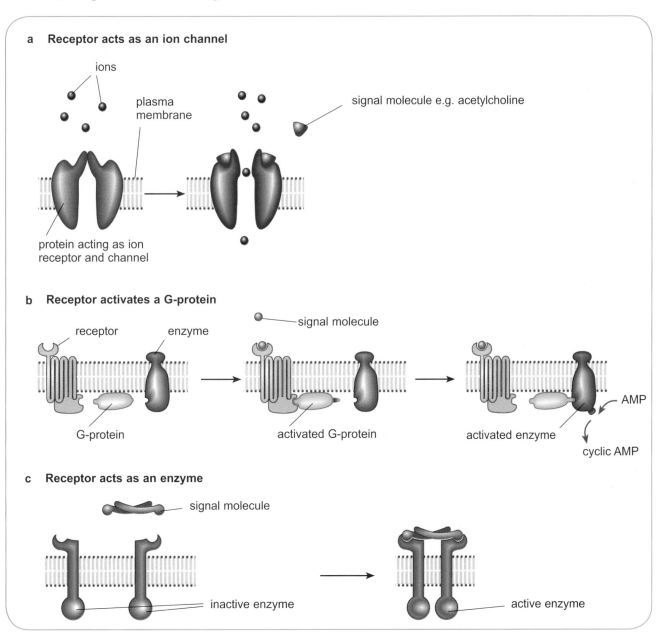

Figure 2.5 Mechanisms of cell signalling: **a** receptor acts as an ion channel; **b** receptor activates a G-protein; **c** receptor acts as an enzyme.

Aspirin and Vioxx

Aspirin seems to have become a wonder drug. Cheap and widely available, not only does it help to relieve pain, but people who are at risk of developing a blood clot in an artery or vein – perhaps because they have atherosclerosis, or are going on a long plane journey – are sometimes recommended to take half an aspirin tablet daily. This is because aspirin reduces the tendency of blood to clot.

Aspirin has these effects because it blocks some important cell-signalling pathways. One of these pathways involves chemicals called prostaglandins. Prostaglandins are made in cells in practically all the tissues in the body, especially after injury. They pass out of the cell and slot into receptors in the membranes of several different kinds of cells, activating G-proteins and bringing about various effects in those cells. For example, some nerve cells respond to prostaglandins by sending pain signals to the brain. Prostaglandins also cause inflammation, where blood capillaries become leaky and allow fluid and white blood cells into the damaged area.

Pain and inflammation in a damaged tissue are useful responses. The pain tells you to take care of that part of your body, and not to do any more damage to it. Inflammation brings white blood cells that can attack and destroy any invading bacteria that have managed to get into the wound. Swelling provides a cushion around the damaged area, helping to protect it while it heals.

But you don't always appreciate these responses of your body to damage! Inflammation has its harmful side, sometimes causing damage to healthy tissue. We would like to be free of pain and to be able to reduce the swelling caused by inflammation. Aspirin does both by stopping the production of prostaglandins. It acts by inhibiting an enzyme inside cells called COX-2, which produces prostaglandins from a lipid called arachidonic acid. With COX-2 out of action, prostaglandin production stops, and inflammation and pain are reduced.

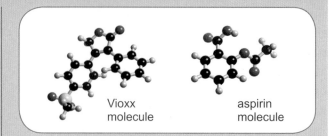

Vioxx molecule   aspirin molecule

Arachidonic acid is also the starting point for making a substance called thromboxane. Thromboxane stimulates platelets to stick together and form blood clots. Aspirin also inhibits the production of thromboxane, which is how it is able to reduce the risk of blood clots forming.

Unfortunately, aspirin also inhibits another enzyme called COX-1, and this enzyme helps to produce the protective layer of mucus that lines the stomach. So taking aspirin makes it more likely that the strong acid in the stomach could damage its walls. People with stomach ulcers are advised not to take aspirin.

As we learn more about the complex metabolic pathways that produce enzymes like COX-1 and COX-2, and about the cell-signalling mechanisms involving prostaglandins and other chemicals, it is becoming possible to produce new drugs that have more narrow-ranging effects than aspirin. One such drug, called Vioxx, was developed to inhibit COX-2 but not COX-1. The idea was that it would reduce pain and inflammation without affecting the stomach lining. The drug went through all the normal testing procedures without difficulty, and was widely prescribed for pain caused by arthritis. However, it was eventually realised that patients taking Vioxx were at an increased risk of developing heart disease. No-one knows quite why this happens. Although the increased risk was very small – 1.5% of people taking Vioxx developed heart problems, compared with 0.78% taking a placebo – it was enough to cause Vioxx to be withdrawn.

Now drug companies are trying to find out more about how COX-1 inhibitors affect cell signalling, hoping that they can find a Vioxx-like substance that will have no harmful side-effects.

Movement across cell membranes

Many substances move into and out of cells through their plasma membranes. Some of these substances move passively – that is, the cell does not have to use energy to make them move. Passive processes include **diffusion**, **facilitated diffusion** and **osmosis**. Other substances are actively moved by the cell, which uses energy to make them move up their concentration gradients. This is called **active transport**.

Diffusion

Particles are constantly moving around randomly. They hit each other and bounce off in different directions. Gradually, this movement results in the particles spreading evenly throughout the space within which they can move. This is **diffusion**.

If there are initially more particles in one place than another, we say there is a **concentration gradient** for them. Diffusion is the net movement of molecules or ions down their concentration gradient – that is, from a place where they are in a high concentration to a place where they are in a lower concentration.

There are usually a large number of different kinds of particles bouncing around inside and outside a cell, on both sides of its plasma membrane. Some of these particles hit the plasma membrane. If they are small – like oxygen and carbon dioxide molecules – and do not have an electrical charge, they can easily slip through the phospholipid bilayer.

Oxygen enters a cell like this. Inside the cell, aerobic respiration constantly uses up oxygen, so the concentration of oxygen inside the cell is low. If there is more oxygen outside the cell, then there is a concentration gradient for oxygen. Oxygen molecules on both sides of the plasma membrane are moving freely around, and some of them hit the plasma membrane and pass through it. This happens in both directions, but because there are more oxygen molecules in a given volume *outside* the cell than *inside*, more of them will pass through the membrane from outside to inside rather than in the opposite direction. The overall effect is for oxygen to move from outside the cell, through the plasma membrane, into the cytoplasm.

Facilitated diffusion

Oxygen and carbon dioxide have small molecules with no electrical charge, and can easily pass through the phospholipid bilayer. However, many other molecules or ions may be too big, or too highly charged, to do this. For example, chloride ions, Cl^-, have an electrical charge and cannot pass through the phospholipid bilayer.

Cells therefore need to provide special pathways through the plasma membrane which will allow such substances to pass through. Such pathways are provided by **channel proteins**. These proteins lie in the membrane, stretching from one side to the other, forming a hydrophilic channel through which ions can pass. The ions pass through by diffusion, down their concentration gradient. This process is called **facilitated diffusion**. It is just like ordinary diffusion, except that the molecules or ions only get through the membrane if they happen to bump into a channel (Figure 2.6).

Each channel formed by a protein will allow only a specific ion or molecule to pass through. The protein can change its shape, making the channel either open or closed. As we have seen, this is used in cell signalling.

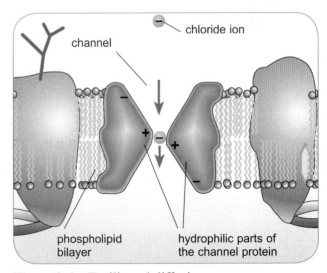

Figure 2.6   Facilitated diffusion.

SAQ

2 Explain under what circumstances carbon dioxide might diffuse into a palisade cell in a leaf, and how the process takes place.

Answer

Osmosis

Water molecules, although they carry a charge (Chapter 7), are very small. They are therefore able to pass through the lipid bilayer by diffusion. This movement of water molecules, down their diffusion gradient, through a partially permeable membrane, is called **osmosis**.

It is not correct to use the term 'concentration' to describe how much water there is in something. Concentration refers to the amount of solute present. Instead, the term **water potential** is used. The symbol ψ (psi) can be used to mean water potential.

The water potential of a solution is a measure of how much water the solution contains in relation to other substances, and how much pressure is being applied to it. A solution containing a lot of water, and under pressure, is said to have a **high water potential**. A solution containing a lot of dissolved substances (solutes) and little water, and not under pressure, has a **low water potential**. You can think of water potential as being the tendency for water to leave a solution.

By definition, pure water at normal atmospheric pressure is given a water potential of 0. The more

solute you dissolve in the water, the lower its water potential gets. Therefore, a solution of sugar has a water potential which is less than 0 – that is, it has a negative water potential.

Just as we don't normally talk about the 'concentration' of water, we don't normally use the term 'concentration gradient' either. Instead, we use the term **water potential gradient**. Water tends to move *down* a water potential gradient, from where there is a lot of water to where there is less of it (Figure 2.7). It diffuses out of a dilute solution (a lot of water – high water potential) and into a concentrated solution (a lot of solute – low water potential).

Why is this important? The cells in your body are surrounded by watery fluids. Blood cells, for example, float in blood plasma. Water can move freely through the plasma membrane of the blood cells, but most of the substances dissolved in the water cannot. If there is a water potential gradient between the contents of a cell and the blood plasma, then water will move either into or out of the cell. If a lot of water moves like this, the cell can be damaged.

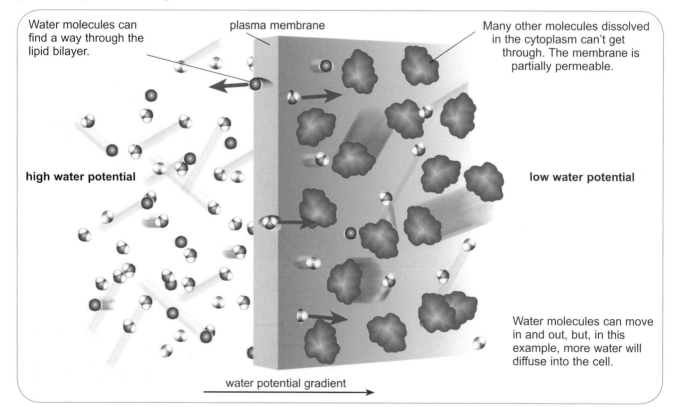

Figure 2.7 How osmosis occurs.

Osmosis and animal cells

Figure 2.8 shows what happens when animal cells are placed in solutions with water potentials higher or lower than the water potential of the cytoplasm inside the cells. If the solution outside the cell has a higher water potential than the cytoplasm, then water enters the cell by osmosis. If the water potential gradient is very high, so much water may enter that the cell bursts.

If the water potential gradient is in the other direction, then water leaves the cell by osmosis. The cell may shrink, sometimes becoming 'star-shaped', described as being '**crenated**'. The concentration of the solutes in the cytoplasm increases, and this may adversely affect metabolic reactions taking place inside the cell.

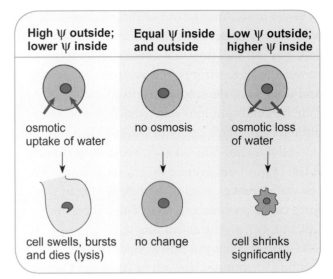

Figure 2.8 Osmosis and animal cells.

Osmosis and plant cells

Figure 2.9 shows what happens when plant cells are placed in solutions with water potentials higher or lower than the water potential of the cytoplasm in the cells.

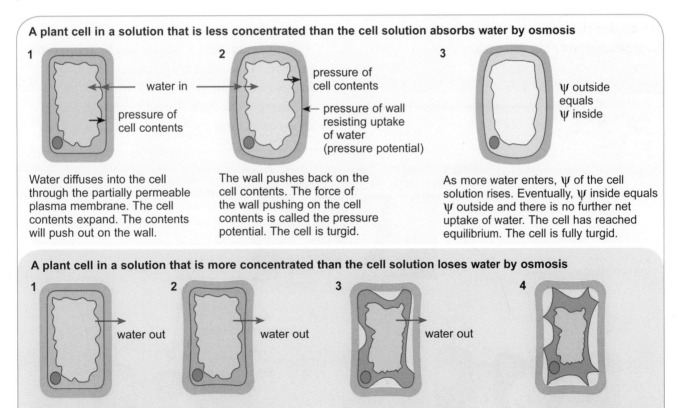

Figure 2.9 Osmosis and plant cells.

Water moves into or out of the cell, down its water potential gradient, just as in an animal cell. The cell wall does not directly affect this movement, because it is fully permeable to water and to most of the solutes dissolved in it.

If the cell is put into water, then – just as in an animal cell – water enters by osmosis. But this time the cell does not burst. This is because, as it swells, it has to push out against the strong cell wall. The cell wall resists expansion of the cell, exerting a force called **pressure potential**. The cell becomes full and stiff, a state called turgor.

If a plant cell is put into a concentrated solution, then water leaves it by osmosis. The cell therefore shrinks. If a lot of water is lost, the contents no longer press outwards on the cell wall, and the cell loses its turgor. It is said to be **flaccid**.

The strong cell wall cannot cave in very much, so as the volume of the cell gets smaller and smaller, the plasma membrane may eventually pull away from the cell wall. The plasma membrane is often damaged in this process. A cell in this state is said to be **plasmolysed**. The cell usually dies.

Extension

Active transport

So far, we have looked at three ways in which substances can move down a concentration gradient (or a water potential gradient) from one side of the plasma membrane to the other. The cell does not have to do anything to make this happen, except perhaps to open a channel to allow facilitated diffusion to take place. These methods are all passive.

However, there are many instances where a cell needs to take up, or get rid of, substances whose concentration gradient is in the 'wrong' direction. This is usually the case with **sodium ions** and **potassium ions**. Most cells need to contain a higher concentration of potassium ions, and a lower concentration of sodium ions, than the concentration outside the cell. To achieve this, cells constantly pump sodium ions out and potassium ions in, up their concentration gradients. This requires energy input from the cell, so it is called **active transport** (Figure 2.10).

Active transport is carried out by **transporter proteins** in the plasma membrane, working in close association with ATP which supplies the energy. The ATP is used to change the shape of the transporter proteins. The shape

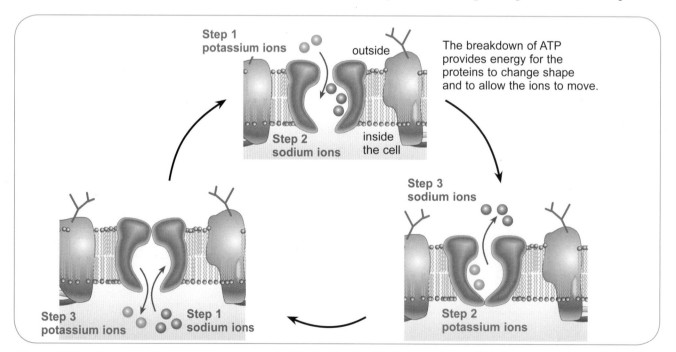

Figure 2.10 An example of active transport – the sodium–potassium pump. Start at step 1 for each ion in turn, and work your way round clockwise. Potassium ions are green and sodium ions are blue.

change moves three sodium ions out of the cell and two potassium ions in. This is going on all the time in most of your cells, and is called the **sodium–potassium pump**. It is estimated that more than a third of the ATP produced in your cells by respiration is used as fuel for the sodium–potassium pump.

Exocytosis and endocytosis

All the mechanisms of movement across membranes that we have looked at so far involve individual ions or molecules moving. Cells can also move substances in bulk across the membrane.

Moving substances *out of* a cell in this way is called **exocytosis** (Figure 2.11). The substance to be released from the cell is contained in a tiny membrane-bound sac called a **vesicle**. The vesicle is moved to the plasma membrane along microtubules. The membrane around the vesicle fuses with the plasma membrane, emptying the vesicle's contents outside the cell.

Moving substances *into* a cell in this way is called **endocytosis**. A good example is the way that

SAQ

3 Suggest what might be moved out of a cell in the pancreas by exocytosis.

Hint

Answer

a phagocyte (a type of white blood cell) engulfs a bacterium. The cell puts out fingers of cytoplasm around the bacterium, which fuse with one another to form a complete ring around it. The bacterium is therefore enclosed in a vacuole, surrounded by a membrane. Enzymes can then be secreted into the vacuole to digest it.

Cells can also move bulk liquids into the cell by endocytosis. The process is the same – fingers of cytoplasm surround a small volume of liquid and form a vacuole around it.

Endocytosis and exocytosis are both active processes, requiring the cell to use energy to make them happen.

How temperature affects membrane permeability

If you cut some pieces of beetroot, wash them and place them in water, the water will remain colourless. If, however, you heat the beetroot pieces, then some of their red colour comes out and the water goes red. Why does this happen?

The red colour in beetroot cells is caused by molecules of a red pigment. The pigment is held in by their cell membranes, which are not permeable to it. However, if you heat the cells, then their membranes become much more permeable. This happens because of the effects of a rise in temperature on the phospholipids and proteins in

Exocytosis

1 Vesicle moves towards plasma membrane.

2 Vesicle joins with plasma membrane.

3 Vesicle contents released – the vesicle membrane is now part of the plasma membrane.

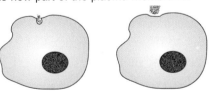

Endocytosis

1 The cell spreads around an object or area of the solution outside the cell.

2 The area enclosed becomes a vesicle.

3 The contents of the vesicle are absorbed into the cytoplasm and the vesicle membrane is recycled.

Figure 2.11 Exocytosis and endocytosis.

the cell membranes.

As the phospholipid molecules get hotter, they vibrate more and more. They move much more than previously, leaving temporary gaps in the membrane through which the pigment molecules can pass.

The protein molecules, too, vibrate more and more as the temperature increases. They may vibrate so much that they begin to come apart and lose their shapes. This, too, leaves gaps in the cell membrane. Very low temperatures, on the other hand, *decrease* membrane permeability. The phospholipids vibrate much less, packing together

tightly and only rarely providing pathways between themselves through which molecules might pass. Protein channels remain in place, but transporter proteins may not work very well, because the low temperatures make it difficult for the cell to provide ATP needed for active transport. Moreover, at low temperatures all molecules and ions will be moving around less, so few of them will hit the membrane and pass through it.

Extension

Summary

Glossary

- Every cell is surrounded by a selectively permeable plasma membrane, which controls what passes through it. The plasma membrane also has important roles in cell signalling.

- Many organelles are also surrounded by membranes; these membranes help to isolate the metabolic reactions inside the organelle from those outside it, and provide extra surface area for the attachment of enzymes and other molecules.

- Membranes are made of a phospholipid bilayer in which proteins are embedded. This is known as the fluid mosaic model. The membranes also contain cholesterol, glycolipids and glycoproteins, each of which has its own functions.

- Cells are able to send and receive signals – for example, in the form of molecules such as hormones. Such signals are received by the plasma membrane; the arrival of a signal may bring about a response in the cell.

- Substances that have small, uncharged molecules can diffuse passively through the phospholipid bilayer. Larger molecules and charged ions pass through channels formed by proteins. If they are diffusing passively down their concentration gradient, this is known as facilitated diffusion.

- Water molecules can move freely across most membranes, by diffusion, down their water potential gradient. This is known as osmosis.

- Cells placed in a solution that has a lower water potential than the cell contents lose water by osmosis, so their volume decreases. Animal cells may become crenated, whilst the cell membrane in plant cells may pull away from the cell wall as the cytoplasm shrinks.

- Cells placed in a solution that has a higher water potential than the cell contents gain water by osmosis, so their volume increases. Animal cells may burst, but plant cells do not because of the strong cell wall that surrounds them.

- Substances can also be moved across membranes against their concentration gradient, using energy in the form of ATP produced by the cell. This is called active transport, and takes place through carrier proteins in the membrane.

- Substances can be moved in bulk across a membrane by exocytosis or endocytosis.

- An increase in temperature increases the movement of the molecules in a membrane, increasing the membrane's permeability.

Questions

1 a Red blood cells of mammals respond to changes in the concentration of salts in the fluid that surrounds them. If they are placed in a solution that has a lower concentration of salts than blood plasma, they swell and may burst. This bursting is known as haemolysis.

Explain why red blood cells may burst when they are placed in a solution that has a lower concentration of salts than blood plasma. [3]

Hint

b An experiment was carried out in which red blood cells were placed in salt solutions of different concentrations. The percentage of cells which were destroyed by haemolysis was recorded. The results are shown in the graph.

The graph shows that the red blood cells do not all haemolyse at the same salt concentration.

i Using the graph, state the salt concentration at which the percentage of haemolysed red blood cells is equal to those that are not haemolysed.

ii Suggest why different red blood cells haemolyse at different salt concentrations.

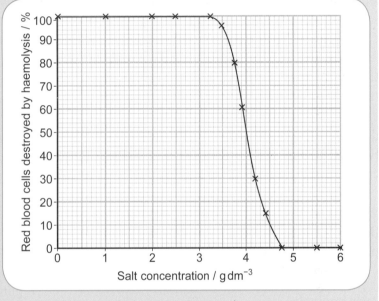

c An experiment was carried out to investigate the uptake of potassium ions by carrot tissue. The experiment was carried out as follows:

● A carrot was cut into discs of uniform size.

● The discs were divided into four groups.

● Equal volumes of a solution containing potassium ions were added.

The temperature remained constant at 21 °C and the experiment was carried out for the same length of time in each case. The experiment was carried out in different oxygen concentrations.

The results are shown in the table.

oxygen concentration / arbitrary units	0	4	11	20
rate of uptake of potassium ions / arbitrary units	7	27	92	100

i Using the information given in the table, state the <u>main</u> process by which potassium ions enter the carrot cells. [1]

ii Give a reason for your answer to i. [1]

iii Suggest an explanation for the uptake of potassium ions in the absence of oxygen. [1]

OCR Biology AS (2801) June 2004 [Total 8]

Answer

Chapter 3

Background

e-Learning

Cell division and cellular organisation

Objectives

The cell cycle

Like most animals, you began your life as a single cell. This cell was a **zygote** – a cell that forms when two gametes fuse. The zygote contained a set of chromosomes from your father and a set of chromosomes from your mother.

All the cells in your body have developed from this single original cell. Soon after it was formed, the zygote divided to form two cells, which then each divided to form a total of four cells. This division went on and on, eventually forming your body containing many millions of cells. Some cells continue to divide even in an adult.

The repetitive process of growing and dividing, growing and dividing is called the **cell cycle** (Figure 3.1). The cell cycle is made up of two main phases, **interphase** and **mitosis**.

Extension

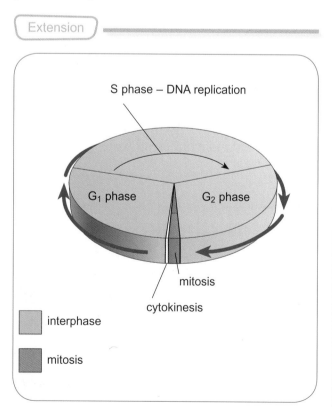

Figure 3.1   The cell cycle.

Interphase

In a cell in a human embryo, one complete cell cycle lasts about 24 hours. About 95% of this time is spent in **interphase**. During interphase, the cell is carrying out all the normal cell activities, such as respiration and protein synthesis. The DNA that makes up its chromosomes is duplicated – a perfect copy is made, so that the DNA can be divided up equally into the two new cells that will be made when the cell divides.

In a human cell, there are 46 **chromosomes**, each of which is made up of one enormously long molecule of DNA. Some time before the cell divides, each DNA molecule is copied. The pair of identical DNA molecules that are now contained in each chromosome remain attached to each other, at a point called the **centromere**. The two identical strands of DNA are called **chromatids** (Figure 3.2 and Figure 3.3).

It is very important that the new DNA molecules that are made are the same as the old ones. Even a small error – a **mutation** – could have harmful effects on the cell. Cells therefore run a 'checking' process on the new DNA. Special proteins work along the DNA molecules, checking for any errors and, where possible, correcting them.

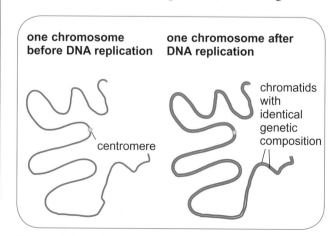

Figure 3.2   Chromosomes in interphase.

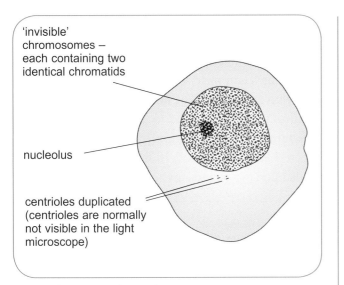

Figure 3.3 Late interphase.

Mitosis

The cell then moves into the next stage of the cell cycle, called **mitosis**. This is the stage during which the nucleus of the cell divides into two nuclei. During mitosis, the two chromatids which make up each chromosome break apart. One of them goes into one new nucleus and one into the other. In this way, the new cells will be genetically identical to each other and to the original parent cell.

Mitosis is made up of four stages: **prophase**, **metaphase**, **anaphase** and **telophase**. The four stages run into one another, without breaks between them.

Prophase

During prophase (Figure 3.4), the chromosomes become visible. Up to now, they have been lying in the nucleus as extremely long and thin threads, so thin that they cannot be seen at all with a light microscope. As prophase begins to get under way, the DNA molecules coil and supercoil, shortening and getting thicker until they eventually form threads that are thick enough to be visible if they are stained.

When the chromosomes appear, they can sometimes be seen to be made of two threads – the chromatids. The chromatids are held together at the centromere. The two chromatids of each chromosome contain identical molecules of DNA, formed in DNA replication during interphase.

As prophase proceeds, the nucleolus disappears. It is also at this stage that the **spindle** begins to form. The **centrioles** move away from each other to opposite ends of the cell. The centrioles organise the formation of the microtubules – long, thin tubes of protein (Figure 3.4).

Metaphase

Now the nuclear membrane breaks down. Its loss means that the whole of the space in the cell is available for manoeuvring the chromosomes. By the time the nuclear membrane breaks down, many of the microtubules have attached themselves to the centromeres of the chromosomes. Each centromere is grabbed by one microtubule on either side. The microtubules pull in opposite directions on the centromeres, bringing the chromosomes to lie at the **equator** of the cell (Figure 3.5).

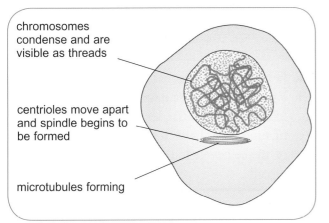

Figure 3.4 Prophase.

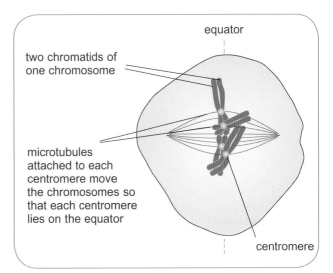

Figure 3.5 Metaphase.

Anaphase

Now the centromeres split. The microtubules are still pulling on them, so the centromeres and the chromatids are pulled apart and moved to either end, or **pole**, of the cell (Figure 3.6).

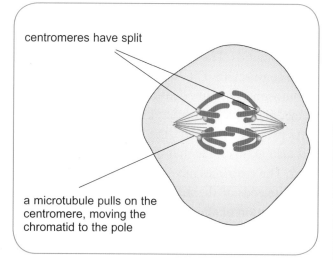

centromeres have split

a microtubule pulls on the centromere, moving the chromatid to the pole

Figure 3.6   Anaphase.

Telophase

The two groups of chromatids have now arrived at the poles. Each group contains a complete set of chromatids, which we can now call chromosomes again. The microtubules making up the spindle fibres break down, so the spindle disappears. New nuclear envelopes form around each group of chromosomes. The chromosomes slowly uncoil and become thinner again, so they effectively disappear (Figure 3.7).

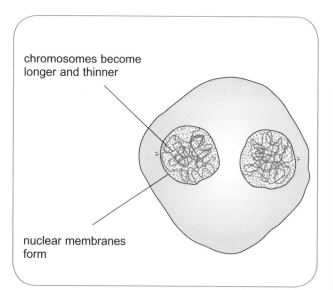

chromosomes become longer and thinner

nuclear membranes form

Figure 3.7   Telophase.

Cytokinesis

Usually, the cytoplasm now divides (Figure 3.8). This forms two new cells, each with a nucleus containing a complete set of chromosomes, and each with a centriole. The new cells are genetically identical to each other and to the original, parent cell.

A summary of mitosis and cytokinesis is shown in Figure 3.9, while Figure 3.10 shows micrographs of mitosis and cytokinesis taking place in plant cells.

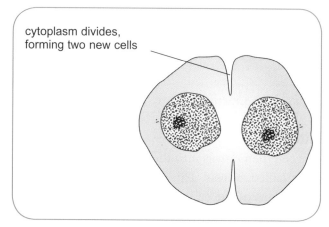

cytoplasm divides, forming two new cells

Figure 3.8   Cytokinesis.

1 A student looked at a prepared slide of a group of cells in various stages of cell division. He identified the stage in 200 cells and counted up how many cells he could see in each stage. The table shows his results.

Stage	Number of cells
interphase	188
prophase	6
metaphase	3
anaphase	1
telophase	2

a How many cells were in a stage of mitosis?

b Explain what these data tell us about the relative lengths of time spent in each stage of the cell cycle in this group of cells.

Hint

Answer

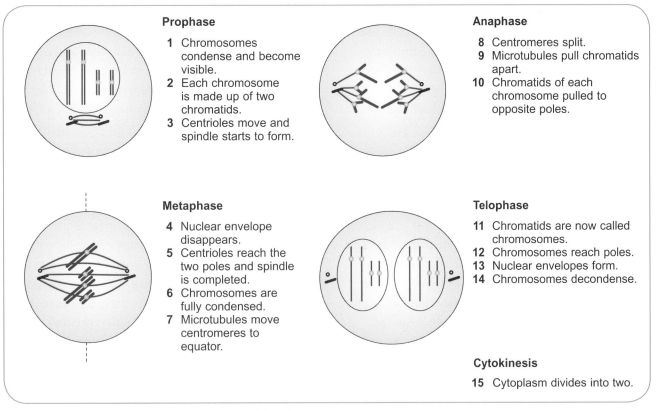

Prophase

1 Chromosomes condense and become visible.
2 Each chromosome is made up of two chromatids.
3 Centrioles move and spindle starts to form.

Anaphase

8 Centromeres split.
9 Microtubules pull chromatids apart.
10 Chromatids of each chromosome pulled to opposite poles.

Metaphase

4 Nuclear envelope disappears.
5 Centrioles reach the two poles and spindle is completed.
6 Chromosomes are fully condensed.
7 Microtubules move centromeres to equator.

Telophase

11 Chromatids are now called chromosomes.
12 Chromosomes reach poles.
13 Nuclear envelopes form.
14 Chromosomes decondense.

Cytokinesis

15 Cytoplasm divides into two.

Figure 3.9 Summary of mitosis and cytokinesis.

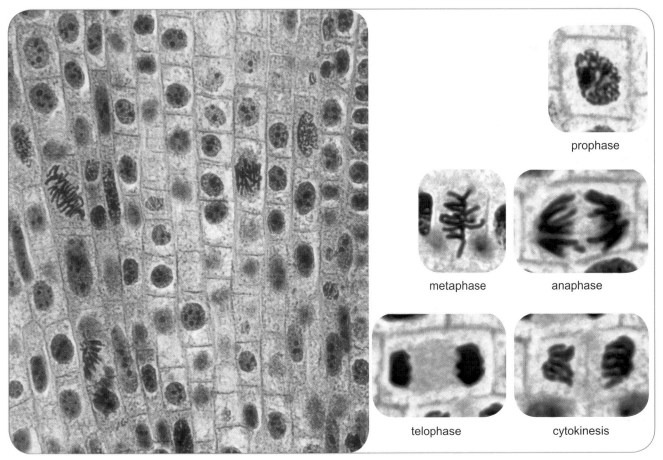

prophase

metaphase   anaphase

telophase   cytokinesis

Figure 3.10 Stages of mitosis in an onion root tip (×100 and ×230).

The significance of mitosis

We have seen that mitosis produces new cells that are genetically identical to the parent cell. Each of these cells has the same number of chromosomes and identical DNA.

This is how cells divide when the body needs more of the same. Mitosis is the type of cell division that occurs in a developing embryo and throughout the growth of a human being.

Mitosis continues to occur in many parts of the body even when we are fully grown. For example, cells in the lining of the alimentary canal divide to provide new cells to replace those which get rubbed off as food moves past them. Mitosis also comes into play when part of the body is damaged and needs repair. For example, if you cut yourself, cells in the skin will produce new cells which spread across the wound to produce a new, protective layer of skin.

In some organisms, mitosis is used for reproduction. For example, strawberry plants grow runners which put down roots and produce new, genetically identical plants. This is **asexual** reproduction, which does not involve gametes or fertilisation. Some animals, for example *Hydra*, can also reproduce in this way.

Single-celled organisms can also reproduce by mitosis. The single-celled fungus, *Saccharomyces cerevisiae*, yeast, reproduces by budding. A new cell is formed from the old one by mitosis, and then breaks away (Figure 3.11).

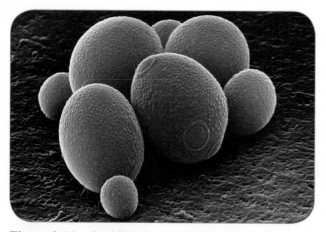

Figure 3.11   Budding in yeast. The cell at the centre shows traces of two buds starting to form. A later stage of budding is seen with the large parent cell and smaller daughter cell at the left.

Differentiation

Your body contains about 10^{13} cells. They have all developed from the single cell with which you began your life – the zygote that was formed by the fusion of an egg cell and a sperm cell. The zygote divided to form a tiny ball of cells called a **blastocyst**, which continued to divide to form an embryo.

In multicellular organisms, there are usually many different kinds of cells. These cells have become specialised to carry out different functions. There is 'division of labour' amongst them.

The body is made up of 'teams' of cells, usually grouped together into **tissues**, which work together closely while each performing their own specialist functions. The specialisation of a cell to carry out a particular function is called **differentiation**.

Once a human cell has differentiated, it usually cannot change into another kind of cell. A heart muscle cell cannot change into a bone cell. A bone cell cannot change into a skin cell.

This is very different from the abilities of the cells in the blastocyst. These cells have the potential to become any of the many different kinds of cells within a human. They are **stem cells**. Stem cells differ from most human cells because:

- they are unspecialised
- they can divide repeatedly to make new cells
- they can differentiate into several kinds of specialised cells.

All the cells in a blastocyst are stem cells, and they can differentiate into any kind of specialised cell. They are therefore said to be '**totipotent**'. Even in an adult person, there are still some stem cells. So far, all the ones that have been found are only able to differentiate into a limited range of cells – for example, there are stem cells in bone marrow that can form white and red blood cells. But they cannot differentiate into neurones, or any other kind of cell.

There is much interest in stem cells, as they could cure many diseases. For example, Parkinson's disease is caused by the death of a particular group of cells in the brain. One day, it may be possible to use stem cells to replace these brain cells.

Extension

Some specialised animal cells

Erythrocytes, otherwise known as red blood cells, transport oxygen in the blood. They have a very short life span. Every second, around 10 million old erythrocytes are destroyed in your spleen, and 10 million new ones are made. They are made from stem cells in the **bone marrow**, especially in the ribs, vertebrae, pelvic bones and skull. These stem cells also make **leucocytes**, the white blood cells. There are several types of these, including **neutrophils** – cells that attack and destroy invading microorganisms by phagocytosis.

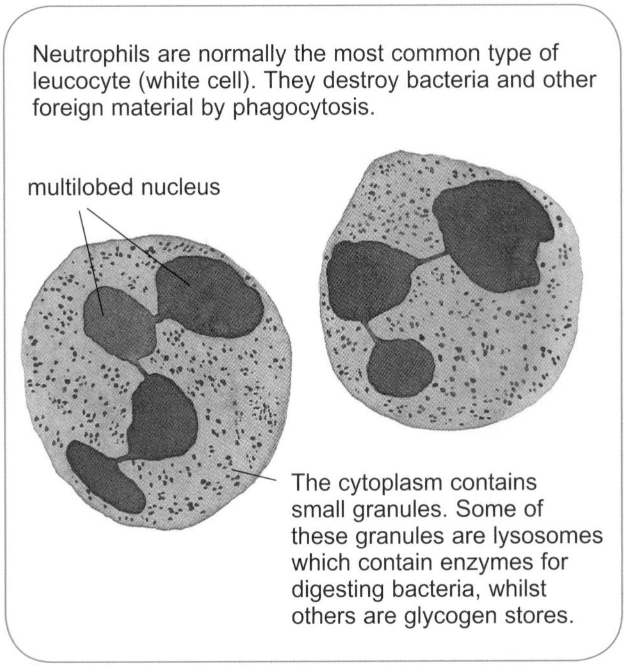

Figure 3.12 and Figure 3.13 show the structures of neutrophils and erythrocytes, and explain how their structures are adapted for their functions. **Spermatozoa**, sperm for short, are the male gametes (Figure 3.14). They are made in the testes throughout a man's life. They are adapted to find and fertilise a female gamete.

Neutrophils are normally the most common type of leucocyte (white cell). They destroy bacteria and other foreign material by phagocytosis.

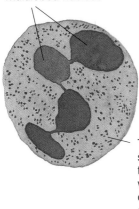

multilobed nucleus

The cytoplasm contains small granules. Some of these granules are lysosomes which contain enzymes for digesting bacteria, whilst others are glycogen stores.

Figure 3.12   Neutrophils.

Erythrocytes transport oxygen and carbon dioxide.

The cell is very small, to allow it to travel through tiny capillaries and so get very close to cells in body tissues.

The cytoplasm is packed with a protein called haemoglobin, which temporarily combines with oxygen or carbon dioxide.

There is no nucleus, to make more room for haemoglobin.

The biconcave shape provides a relatively large surface area : volume ratio, which increases the amount of oxygen and carbon dioxide that can pass into and out of the cell in a certain period of time.

Figure 3.13   Erythrocytes.

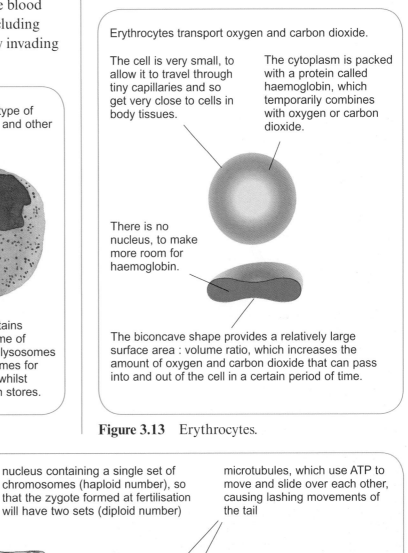

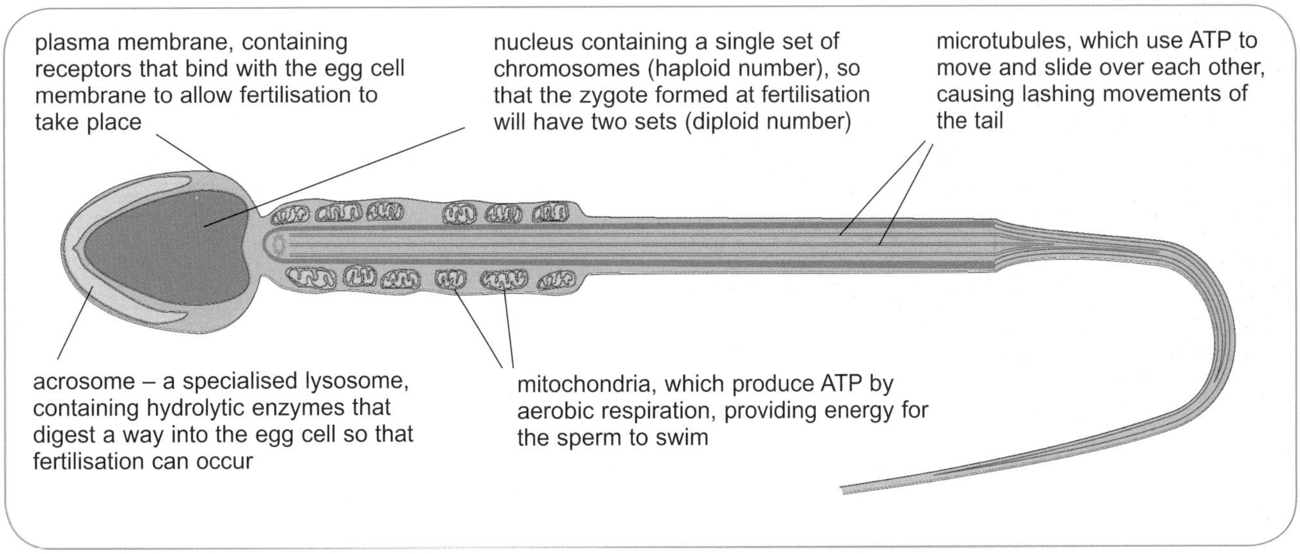

plasma membrane, containing receptors that bind with the egg cell membrane to allow fertilisation to take place

nucleus containing a single set of chromosomes (haploid number), so that the zygote formed at fertilisation will have two sets (diploid number)

microtubules, which use ATP to move and slide over each other, causing lashing movements of the tail

acrosome – a specialised lysosome, containing hydrolytic enzymes that digest a way into the egg cell so that fertilisation can occur

mitochondria, which produce ATP by aerobic respiration, providing energy for the sperm to swim

Figure 3.14   A spermatozoan.

Some specialised plant cells

Plants do not have stem cells – most of their cells retain the ability to differentiate into other kinds of cells throughout their lives. However, there are several parts of a plant where cells are able to divide, and places where this occurs at a high rate are called **meristems**. The meristem just behind the root tip is a good place to find cells in various stages of mitosis, which you can prepare and stain as a 'root tip squash'.

There is another meristem that forms a ring of tissue in the stem, called **cambium**. These cells can divide to form **xylem vessels** on the inside of the ring and phloem sieve tubes on its outside, which help to form these two transport tissues. Figure 3.15 and Figure 3.16 show the structures and functions of these tissues and where they are found in a stem.

The cells that are often considered to be 'typical' plant cells are the **palisade cells** – the main type of photosynthetic cell found in plant leaves. They are, in fact, highly specialised, containing many chloroplasts in which photosynthesis takes place.

Root hair cells are found near the tips of roots. They are specialised epidermal cells – that is, cells that cover the outside of a plant organ. They have long, thin extensions that grow between the soil particles, providing a large surface area that is in contact with the layer of water that is usually present on and between these particles. The water contains various mineral ions in solution, which root hairs absorb. They have a short life, being easily broken as the root grows through the soil. Recently divided cells near the root tip differentiate to form new root hair cells (Chapter 6).

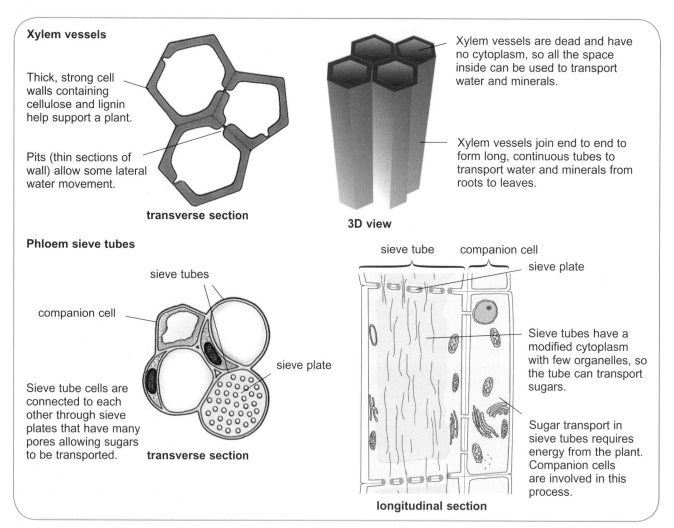

Xylem vessels

Thick, strong cell walls containing cellulose and lignin help support a plant.

Pits (thin sections of wall) allow some lateral water movement.

transverse section

Xylem vessels are dead and have no cytoplasm, so all the space inside can be used to transport water and minerals.

Xylem vessels join end to end to form long, continuous tubes to transport water and minerals from roots to leaves.

3D view

Phloem sieve tubes

sieve tubes

companion cell

sieve plate

Sieve tube cells are connected to each other through sieve plates that have many pores allowing sugars to be transported. **transverse section**

sieve tube   companion cell

sieve plate

Sieve tubes have a modified cytoplasm with few organelles, so the tube can transport sugars.

Sugar transport in sieve tubes requires energy from the plant. Companion cells are involved in this process.

longitudinal section

Figure 3.15 Xylem and phloem tissues. You can see micrographs of xylem tissue and phloem tissue in Chapter 6.

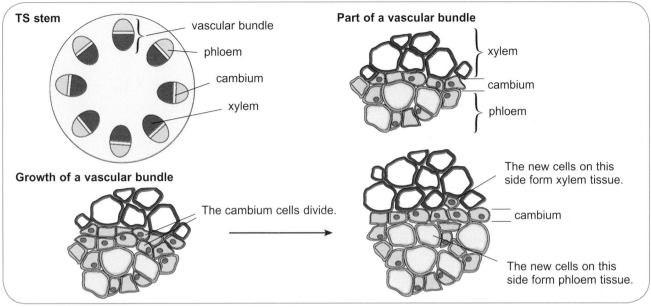

Figure 3.16 Cambium, xylem and phloem in a plant stem.

Dendrochronology

Each spring, as the weather warms up and there is more daylight, trees begin to grow after resting through the winter. Cells in the ring of cambium in the trunk divide, producing new phloem tissue on the outside of the ring, and new xylem tissue on the inside. This process continues throughout the summer, but the new cells produced later in the year are smaller than the ones produced during the period of maximum growth in spring.

The xylem tissue makes up the wood of the trunk. A slice across a tree trunk reveals rings in the wood, corresponding to the yearly growth cycle. The xylem tissue made in spring usually looks light in colour, because the vessels are larger. The summer xylem tissue forms a narrower, darker stripe.

The width of the stripes is determined by how well the tree grew that year, which depends on the weather conditions. In a dry year, the tree will grow less than in a wet year, so the ring for that year will be narrower. This will be true for all the trees growing in that place at that time.

Once the ring patterns of some samples of wood of known age have been analysed, then other samples of wood can be matched against them, looking for matching patterns of narrow and wide rings. This can be used to date the wood – a procedure known as 'dendrochronology'. Dendrochronologists have now built up enough data to establish patterns of growth going back to around 9000 years ago. These can be used to determine when a tree was felled to provide the wood that has been used to build an ancient ship or an old house, for example, as well as showing where the tree grew.

The *Mary Rose* contained wood from trees felled in southern England in 1510.

Tissues, organs and organ systems

The millions of cells inside a multicellular organism such as yourself are not scattered randomly about. Cells that carry out the same function are usually grouped together, forming a tissue. Tissues may be further grouped into organs, and organs into systems. We can define these terms as follows:

- A **tissue** is a collection of cells, together with any intercellular ('between cells') secretion produced by them, that is specialised to perform one or more particular functions. The cells are often of the same type, such as palisade tissue in a plant leaf or squamous epithelium (page 46) in animals.
- An **organ** is a part of the body which forms a structural and functional unit and is composed of more than one tissue. A leaf is an example of a plant organ, and the brain is an example of an animal organ.
- A **system** is a collection of organs with particular functions, such as the excretory, reproductive, cardiovascular and digestive systems in humans.

Figure 3.17 shows the tissues in a leaf.

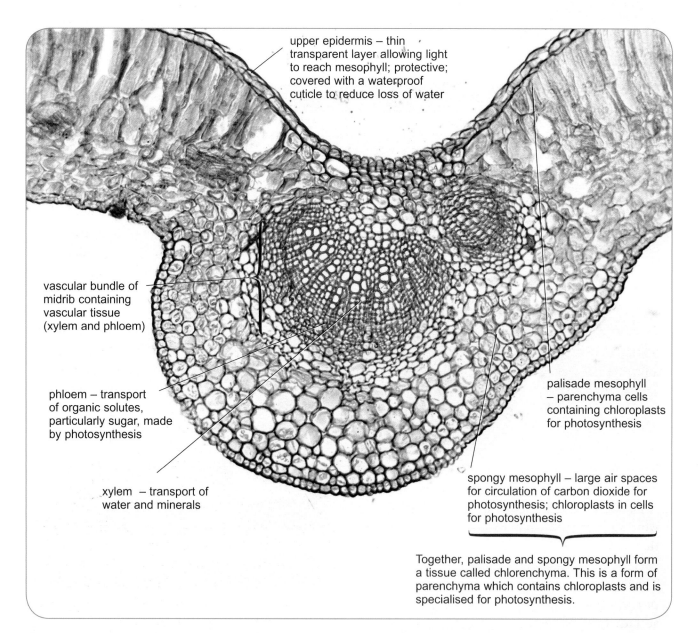

upper epidermis – thin transparent layer allowing light to reach mesophyll; protective; covered with a waterproof cuticle to reduce loss of water

vascular bundle of midrib containing vascular tissue (xylem and phloem)

phloem – transport of organic solutes, particularly sugar, made by photosynthesis

xylem – transport of water and minerals

palisade mesophyll – parenchyma cells containing chloroplasts for photosynthesis

spongy mesophyll – large air spaces for circulation of carbon dioxide for photosynthesis; chloroplasts in cells for photosynthesis

Together, palisade and spongy mesophyll form a tissue called chlorenchyma. This is a form of parenchyma which contains chloroplasts and is specialised for photosynthesis.

Figure 3.17   Transverse section through the midrib of a dicotyledonous leaf, *Ligustrum* (privet) (× 50).

Sponges

Sponges are believed to be amongst the very earliest multicellular animals to have appeared on Earth. The oldest fossil sponges that have so far been discovered are 600 million years old, and it is likely that sponges were around for some time before then.

Sponges are found in seas all over the world, and a few species live in fresh water. At first sight, sponges don't look like animals at all. They remain apparently motionless, generally fixed permanently to the sea bed or a coral reef. Under the microscope, however, they can be seen to have cells with no cell walls – a feature typical of animal cells.

Some of a sponge's cells have long flagella, which beat rhythmically, creating a water current that flows through the sponge's body, and from which the sponge's cells extract food material. The flagellated cells also have microvilli (tiny projections on the cell surface) to increase their surface area and therefore make food absorption more efficient. Other cells are tubular, providing pores through which the water current can circulate. Others secrete the protein collagen, and yet another type secrete little spicules of calcium carbonate or silica, which provide a skeleton for the sponge.

So, like most multicellular organisms, sponges have a range of different types of cells that are specialised for different functions. However, unlike all other groups of animals, sponges do not possess true tissues, organs or systems. The different cells are scattered throughout the sponge's body. This suggests that perhaps they were some of the earliest animals to evolve from the single-celled organisms that lived on Earth long ago.

Sponges have not been of great interest to humans in the past, except as a source of soft, rubbery absorbent material for washing – and even this function has now been almost entirely taken over by plastic sponges. But recently, sponges have become of great interest to pharmaceutical companies.

Unable to move, sponges cannot flee from other animals that eat them. Many of them have evolved a defence mechanism – they secrete toxic chemicals that deter predators, and also prevent other sponges from growing too close to them. Indeed, some other kinds of marine organisms, such as some species of crabs, carry sponges around on their bodies as a defence against predators.

Some of these chemicals show promise as drugs to fight human diseases. For example, a compound called halichondrin, derived from the sponge *Lissodendoryx*, is being developed as a possible anti-cancer drug. The sponge *Dysidea avara* produces a chemical called avarol, which could be used to treat psoriasis – a chronic condition in which red and scaly areas form on the skin. So far, we have only touched the tip of the iceberg, and there may be thousands of chemicals with pharmaceutical potential to be found in sponges.

Some examples of animal tissues

Tissues that cover a surface in an animal are called **epithelial tissues**. The two examples shown in Figure 3.18 are only one cell thick, and so they are *simple* epithelia. The cells rest on a **basement membrane**, which, despite its name, is not a cell membrane at all. It is a network of collagen and glycoproteins that is secreted by the underlying cells, and that holds the epithelial cells in position.

Squamous epithelium covers many surfaces in the human body, including the inner lining of the cheeks, the inner surfaces of blood vessels, and the inner surfaces of the atria and ventricles in the heart. It also forms the walls of the alveoli in the lungs. The individual cells are smooth, flat and very thin. They fit closely together, providing a smooth, low-friction surface over which fluids can move easily. In the alveoli, the thinness of the cells allows rapid diffusion of gases between the alveoli and the blood (Chapter 4).

Ciliated epithelium is made up of cells that possess cilia. Sometimes these cells are shaped like cubes, making up *cuboidal* ciliated epithelium. This tissue lines the ends of the bronchioles in the lungs. Sometimes the cells are tall and narrow, making up *columnar* ciliated epithelium, found in the oviducts.

SAQ

2 Suggest the functions of the ciliated epithelium in:

  a the bronchioles

  b the oviducts.

Answer

Some examples of plant tissues

We have seen how xylem vessels and phloem sieve tubes are specialised for their functions of transporting substances within plants (Figure 3.15). These specialised cells form tissues within plant stems, roots and leaves. Their distribution and structures are also shown in Chapter 6.

Coordination

Division of labour within a multicellular organism means that every cell has its own set of functions in which it specialises. However, it is clearly essential that there is communication and cooperation between cells within a tissue, and between tissues, organs and systems in different parts of the body. Pulling the activities of all the different parts of the body together, so that they work with each other and do appropriate things at appropriate times, is essential if a multicellular organism is to survive.

As we have seen, this communication involves cell signalling. Much of it is done by means of molecules that are produced by one cell and that affect the behaviour of another. These include hormones. In animals, electrical signals, carried by neurones, are another method of communication. Even plants use electrical signals for communication in some circumstances – for example, in the closing of the leaf of a Venus fly trap around a fly that it has captured.

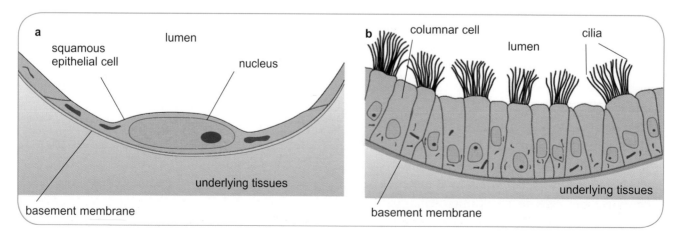

Figure 3.18 Some examples of epithelial tissues, as seen with a light microscope: **a** diagram of a section through squamous epithelium; **b** diagram of a section through ciliated columnar epithelium.

Another type of cell division

All of the specialised cells that are produced as an organism grows are formed by mitosis. As we have seen, this is the type of cell division that is used when the new cells are required to be genetically identical to the parent cell.

However, there is another type of cell division that is needed if an organism has a stage of sexual reproduction in its life cycle. This is called **meiosis**.

In the nucleus of each of your body cells, there are 46 chromosomes. These are actually two *sets* of chromosomes. One set of 23 came from your father, and the other set of 23 came from your mother.

We can see this if images of the chromosomes are 'cut and pasted' to arrange them in order. An arrangement like this is called a **karyotype** (Figure 3.19).

The chromosomes have been arranged and numbered by size, largest first. There are two of each kind, because there are two complete sets. Cells that have two complete sets of chromosomes are called **diploid cells**. The two chromosomes of a kind are said to be **homologous**. This means 'same position', and it refers to the fact that the chromosomes have genes for the same features in the same positions. However, these genes are unlikely to be identical on each chromosome. Most genes have several different varieties, called **alleles**, and some of the alleles on one of a pair of homologous chromosomes are very likely to differ from some of the alleles on the other.

When gametes are formed, a body cell divides by meiosis and produces new cells that have only *one* set of chromosomes. They are **haploid cells**. The new cells get just one chromosome of each homologous pair. They could get either one – the one that originally came from the father, or the one that came from the mother. So there are a very large number of different combinations of chromosomes that could end up in a gamete.

Gametes are therefore **genetically different** from each other. Moreover, any male gamete can fuse with any female gamete at fertilisation, so this offers even more possibilities for different mixtures of genes (Figure 3.20).

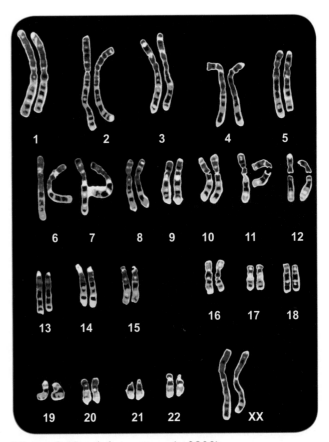

Figure 3.19   A karyotype (× 2800).

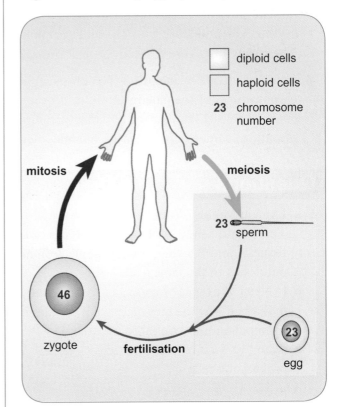

Figure 3.20   The human life cycle. Mitosis produces diploid body cells, and meiosis produces haploid gametes.

Summary

Glossary

- The cell cycle consists of interphase, mitosis and cytokinesis. Mitosis occupies only about 5% of the time, while the rest is used for the duplication and checking of DNA.

- In interphase, DNA replicates, so that each chromosome is made up of two identical chromatids joined at the centromere.

- During mitosis, the nuclear membrane breaks down, spindle fibres form, attach themselves to the condensed chromosomes and manoeuvre them to the equator of the cell. The centromeres then break, and the spindle fibres pull the separated chromatids to opposite ends of the cell. New nuclear membranes form around each group of chromatids. The phases of mitosis are prophase, metaphase, anaphase and telophase.

- During cytokinesis, the cytoplasm splits and two new cells are formed.

- Mitosis produces two daughter cells that are genetically identical to each other and to the parent cell. Mitosis is used for growth, repair and asexual reproduction.

- Multicellular organisms usually contain many types of cells, which have become differentiated to perform different functions. They are often grouped into tissues, containing cells that have the same function – for example, squamous and ciliated epithelium in animals, xylem and phloem in plants. Tissues are grouped into organs, and organs into organ systems.

- When an animal cell has become differentiated, it is normally unable to become any other type of cell. Some cells, however, called stem cells, retain the ability to divide and differentiate. Stem cells in a young embryo are able to differentiate into any kind of cell; in an adult, stem cells appear to have a limited range of specialised cells that they can form. For example, stem cells in bone marrow produce erythrocytes and leucocytes. In plants, cambium cells produce xylem vessels and phloem sieve tubes. These cells are highly adapted for their functions.

- Cells may divide by meiosis, which produces genetically different cells with half the number of chromosomes of the parent cell. Body cells are diploid, meaning that they have two complete sets of chromosomes. Matching, or homologous, chromosomes pair up in meiosis and are then shared out into the daughter cells. These are haploid, meaning that they have only one set of chromosomes.

Questions

1 a Explain what is meant by the term *tissue*. [2]
   The diagram shows cells from two types of epithelial tissue, A and B, as seen under the electron microscope. The cells are not drawn to the same scale.
   b i Name the types of epithelial tissue A and B. [2]
   ii Explain why the cells of tissue B contain many more mitochondria than those in tissue A. [2]
   c State <u>two</u> ways in which the cells of tissues A and B differ from prokaryotic cells. [2]

OCR Biology AS (2801) June 2002

[Total 8]

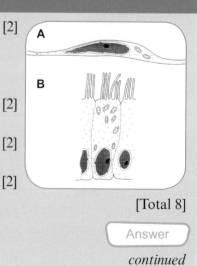

Answer

continued

2 a Describe the role of mitosis. [3]

The diagram shows the stages of the mitotic cell cycle.

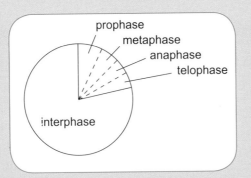

b i Which processes must occur in a cell during interphase before mitosis can take place? [3]

ii In which direction, clockwise or anticlockwise, does the sequence shown in the diagram occur during the mitotic cell cycle? [1]

c Name the stage of mitosis shown in the diagram in which each of the following events occurs.

i Chromosomes split at centromeres. [1]

ii Chromosomes become visible. [1]

iii Nuclear envelope re-forms. [1]

iv Chromatids move to opposite poles of the cell. [1]

v Chromosomes line up along the equator of the spindle. [1]

OCR Biology AS (2801) June 2004 [Total 12]

Answer

3 During the development of the embryo, cells divide by mitosis, grow and differentiate. The cells gradually become organised into tissues and organs.

a i State what is meant by the term *cell differentiation*. [2]

ii Describe the relationship between tissues and organs. [2]

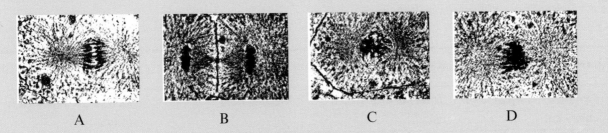

A   B   C   D

b The photographs show an animal cell at different stages of mitosis.

i Arrange the stages shown in the photographs in the correct order by writing their letters in sequence. [1]

ii Compare the genetic makeup of the daughter cells produced by mitosis with that of the original parent cell. [2]

OCR Human Biology AS (2857) January 2005 [Total 7]

Answer

Chapter 4

Exchange

Background

e-Learning

Objectives

Exchange surfaces

All of the cells in your body need constant supplies of oxygen and nutrients, and need to get rid of waste materials, such as carbon dioxide, that are produced in their metabolic reactions. These substances are obtained from, or released to, the external environment, through your body's surface.

Cells and organisms have problems of scale to solve as they get bigger. As an organism gets bigger, both its surface area and its volume increase. However, its surface area does not increase as much as its volume (Figure 4.1). So a large organism such as yourself must find ways of increasing surface area, to provide enough surface to ensure that exchanges with your environment can take place rapidly enough to supply all of your cells with their needs.

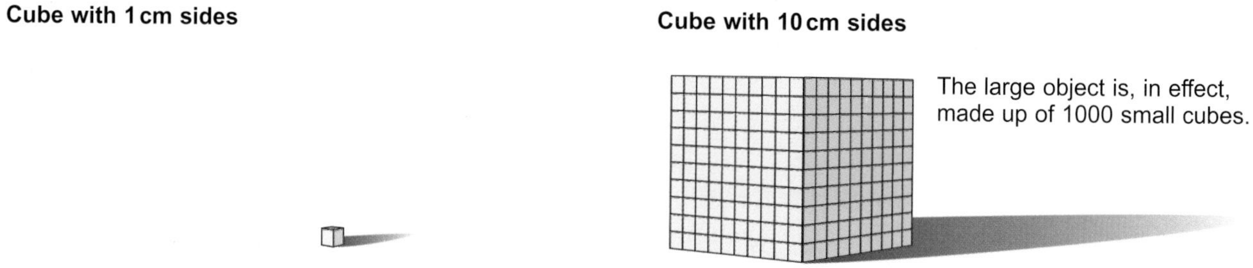

Cube with 1 cm sides

Cube with 10 cm sides

The large object is, in effect, made up of 1000 small cubes.

surface area of one small cube = 6 cm^2
volume of one small cube = 1 cm^3

surface area : volume ratio = $\dfrac{\text{surface area}}{\text{volume}}$

= 6

surface area of large object = 600 cm^2
volume of large object = 1000 cm^3

surface area : volume ratio = $\dfrac{\text{surface area}}{\text{volume}}$

= 0.6

The large object has much less surface area for each 'unit' of volume; it has a much lower surface area to volume ratio.

Figure 4.1 Size and surface area : volume ratio.

SAQ

1 Draw a table like this, with seven more empty rows in it.

Length of one side of a cube / cm	Total surface area / cm^2	Volume / cm^3	Surface area divided by volume
1	6	1	6
2	24	8	3

a Complete your table for cubes with sides up to 10 cm.
b Describe what happens to the surface area : volume ratio as the side length of the cube increases.
c Explain the relevance of this to living organisms.

Hint

Answer

Properties of exchange surfaces

In this chapter, we will look at how oxygen and carbon dioxide are exchanged with your environment, by diffusing across the gas exchange surface in your lungs. All exchange surfaces have features that help substances to move across them as quickly as possible, and in as large a quantity as possible (Figure 4.2).

For terrestrial (land-living) organisms, this can cause problems, because they run the risk of losing water vapour from their bodies across these exchange surfaces. There often has to be some kind of compromise between maximising the area and exposure of the exchange surface, and keeping water loss to an acceptable level.

The list below summarises the features of all exchange surfaces. Table 4.1 shows the ways in which these are achieved in the mammalian lung and in plant leaves.

- The exchange surface should have a *large surface area*. The larger the area across which a substance can diffuse, the more substance can cross the surface in a given time.
- The exchange surface should be *thin*. The shorter the distance across which a substance has to diffuse, the less time it takes.
- There must be a **diffusion gradient** across the exchange surface – in other words, the concentration of the substance on one side of the surface must be different from the concentration on the other, so that the substance diffuses down the gradient.
- In a terrestrial animal, the cells on the surface must be *protected from drying out*. If 'wet' cells are exposed to dry air, water vapour will diffuse out of them and into the air. If too much water is lost, the plasma membrane will lose its structure and the cells will die.

Figure 4.2 Aquatic animals, such as this axolotl, can have their gas exchange surfaces on the outside of their bodies.

SAQ

2 a The volume of an earthworm is about 0.005 dm³. The surface area of its skin is about 0.40 dm². Calculate the surface area : volume ratio of an earthworm.

                                       Hint

   b The volume of a person's body is about 70 dm³. The surface area of the skin is about 180 dm². Calculate the surface area : volume ratio of a person.

   c The surface area of the gas exchange surface inside a person's lungs is about 7000 dm². What is the ratio of the area of gas exchange surface to the volume of the person's body?

   d Use your answers to **a**, **b** and **c** to suggest why earthworms can use their skin for gas exchange, whereas humans need lungs.

                                       Answer

Feature of exchange surface	Mammalian lungs	Plant leaves
Large surface area	Lungs contain millions of tiny alveoli.	Plants have highly branched shapes with many leaves, providing a relatively large surface area : volume ratio. Air spaces inside plant leaves ensure that many cell surfaces are exposed to air.
Thin	Alveolar walls and capillary walls are each only one cell thick.	Plant leaves are usually only a few cells thick; gases can reach most cells directly from the air. Stomata allow direct contact of the air spaces inside the leaf with the air outside it. Gases diffuse directly from air spaces into the cells that need them.
Diffusion gradient	Breathing movements replace oxygen-poor and carbon dioxide-rich air inside the lungs with atmospheric air. Blood flow through capillaries takes away oxygen-rich and carbon dioxide-poor blood and brings in blood low in oxygen and high in carbon dioxide.	In daylight, photosynthesis in palisade and spongy mesophyll cells uses carbon dioxide, lowering its concentration inside the leaf to below that in air. At night, respiration produces a diffusion gradient in the opposite direction. Oxygen diffuses in at night, and out during daylight.
Protection from drying out	The alveoli are tucked away deep inside the body, away from direct exposure to dry air. Cells secrete a watery fluid that covers the cells lining the alveoli, keeping them moist despite the loss of some water by evaporation into the air.	Stomata can close to prevent movement of gases, including water vapour, out of the leaf. A waxy cuticle covers the rest of the leaf, to reduce water loss from cells on the leaf surface.

Table 4.1 Gas exchange surfaces in mammals and plants.

SAQ

3 Emphysema is a disease that is frequently caused by smoking. In emphysema, the walls of the alveoli break down, creating larger and fewer spaces in the lungs.

In an investigation of the effects of smoking on lung surface area : volume ratios, samples of lung tissue of equal volume were taken from 10 normal lungs and 10 lungs from people with emphysema. The mean surface area of the samples from the normal lungs was 0.275 µm, and the mean surface area of the samples from lungs with emphysema was 0.170 µm.

a Explain how the breakdown of alveolar walls leads to a decrease in surface area : volume ratio of the gas exchange surface. [Hint]

b Use the results of the study to explain why a person with emphysema has difficulty in getting enough oxygen into the blood. [Answer]

The mammalian gas exchange system

Figure 4.3 shows the gross structure of the mammalian gas exchange system. The lungs are inside the **thorax** (chest), surrounded by a pair of **pleural membranes** that secrete **pleural fluid**. This provides an airtight, slippery covering that allows the lungs to inflate and deflate easily.

Air passes down into the lungs through the **trachea**, which branches into the left **bronchus** and right bronchus. Each bronchus branches repeatedly to form smaller tubes called **bronchioles**, which end in bunches of tiny sacs called **alveoli**. Each alveolus has a **blood capillary** very closely associated with it, and it is here that oxygen and carbon dioxide diffuse between the air inside the lungs and the blood inside the capillaries.

Lungs have no muscles, so movement is produced by muscles in the **diaphragm** – a sheet of tissue containing muscle, that separates the thorax from the abdomen – and the muscles between the **ribs**, which are called intercostal muscles. The rib cage also protects the lungs from damage, as well as protecting the heart, which is partly beneath the left lung.

Epithelial tissue in the airways

The tubes leading down to the lungs are lined by cells that are adapted to remove particles from the air before it reaches the lungs.

The cells making up the epithelial tissue that lines the trachea and bronchi are of two main types – **ciliated cells** and **goblet cells** (Figure 4.4). All of these cells sit on a **basement membrane** which contains fibres made from proteins that the cells beneath them have secreted.

Each cilium is about 3–4 µm long, and there are many of them on each ciliated cell. Each cilium contains microtubules which can slide past each other, causing the cilium to bend.

The numerous goblet cells in between the ciliated cells secrete **mucus**. Mucus contains substances called glycoproteins, whose molecules include very long chains of sugar molecules – it is these that make mucus so slimy and sticky. Mucus forms a complete protective covering over the epithelium. This not only stops the cells from drying out, but also traps particles from the air, preventing them from reaching the alveoli where they could cause damage.

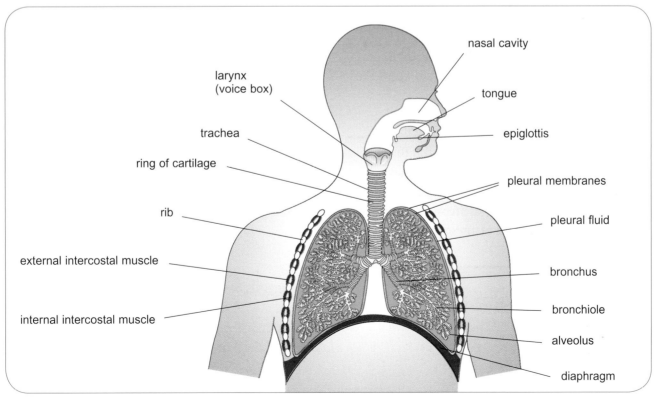

Figure 4.3 The mammalian gas exchange system.

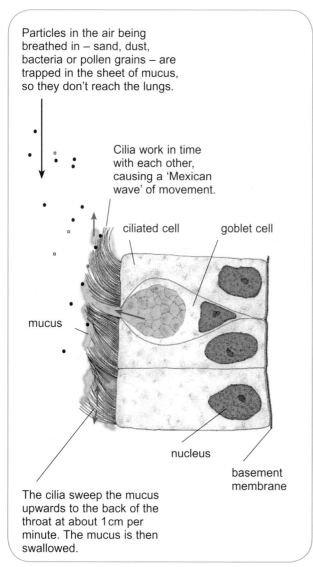

Particles in the air being breathed in – sand, dust, bacteria or pollen grains – are trapped in the sheet of mucus, so they don't reach the lungs.

Cilia work in time with each other, causing a 'Mexican wave' of movement.

ciliated cell   goblet cell

mucus

nucleus

basement membrane

The cilia sweep the mucus upwards to the back of the throat at about 1 cm per minute. The mucus is then swallowed.

Figure 4.4   How the ciliated epithelium keeps the lungs clean.

SAQ

4 Ciliated cells have more mitochondria than many other types of cells. Goblet cells have a lot of rough endoplasmic reticulum and Golgi apparatus. Explain how these features relate to the functions of each of these types of cells.

Answer

Other tissues in the airways

The walls of the airways contain several other types of tissues, besides the ciliated epithelium that lines the trachea and bronchi. These tissues include cartilage, smooth muscle and elastic tissue (Figure 4.5 and Figure 4.6).

Cartilage is a tough tissue that helps to support the walls of the trachea and bronchi. The bronchioles do not contain cartilage. Like bone, cartilage is very strong, but it is more flexible than bone. Rings of cartilage in the walls of the trachea and bronchi help to hold these tubes open as the air pressure inside them changes during breathing. In the trachea, the cartilage is arranged in C-shaped rings. In the bronchi, it occurs in a more irregular pattern.

Smooth muscle is found in the walls of the trachea, bronchi and bronchioles. It is a type of muscle that contracts slowly and steadily and can remain contracted for long periods of time. It is **involuntary** muscle, meaning that you have no conscious control over its contraction. When the smooth muscle contracts, it narrows the airways. This is useful in changing the diameter of the small bronchioles – they can be made wider when

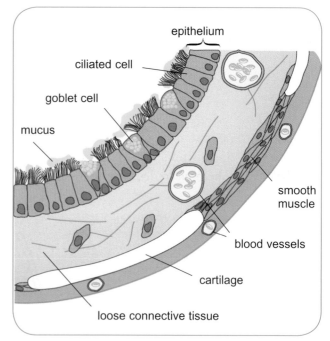

epithelium

ciliated cell

goblet cell

mucus

smooth muscle

blood vessels

cartilage

loose connective tissue

Figure 4.5   The histology of a bronchus wall.

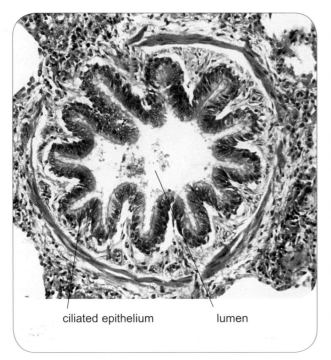

ciliated epithelium   lumen

Figure 4.6 Photomicrograph of a bronchiole (×80).

a person is exercising and needs to get air into and out of the lungs more rapidly than normal. In people who suffer from asthma, the smooth muscle can contract in response to otherwise harmless substances in the air, or for other reasons, and this causes considerable breathing difficulties. Drugs called beta agonists can be inhaled to help make the muscles relax.

Elastic fibres are found in the walls of all of the airways, even the very smallest ones. They are especially important where they occur around the alveoli. During breathing in, the alveoli expand, stretching the elastic fibres. During breathing out, the fibres recoil, helping to decrease the volume inside the lungs and forcing air out.

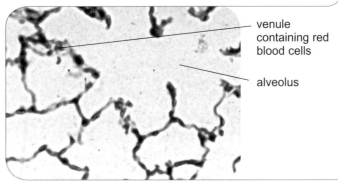

venule containing red blood cells

alveolus

Figure 4.7 The structure of alveolar tissue.

Structure of alveoli

The alveoli, tucked deep inside the lungs, are the gas exchange surface. Here, atmospheric air is brought as close as possible to the blood, so that gases can diffuse quickly and easily between the two.

Figure 4.7 shows the structure of alveolar tissue. You can see that it is essentially made up of air spaces, divided by thin walls. The wall of each alveolus is a single layer of flattened cells, each cell being only about 5 μm thick. Blood capillaries, also with walls made up of single cells, are in close contact with them. The distance across which oxygen diffuses to pass from the alveolar air space into the blood inside a capillary is therefore very small.

In between the alveolar walls, elastic fibres provide strength and flexibility, so that the alveolar volume can easily increase during breathing in and decrease when you breathe out.

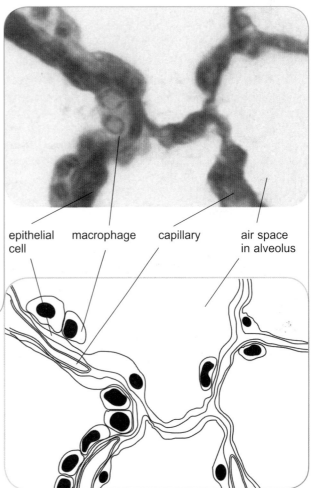

epithelial   macrophage   capillary   air space
cell   in alveolus

Macrophages constantly patrol the alveolar surfaces. They scavenge for any harmful material that may have escaped the ciliated epithelium on the way into the lungs, such as bacteria, particulates from smoke, or dust particles. Macrophages are phagocytes, and will engulf and digest whatever they find. Some types of particles, however, cannot be digested, and they can cause serious harm. Asbestos fibres, for example, can accumulate in the lungs despite the best efforts of macrophages, and lead to serious disease (Figure 4.8).

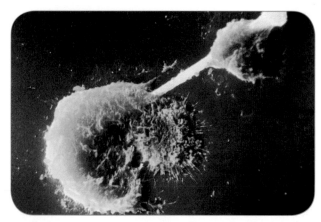

Figure 4.8 Two macrophages attempting to engulf an asbestos fibre. The fibres cannot be broken down and eventually puncture the macrophages. The contents of the macrophages leak out and they die.

Surfactant and respiratory distress syndrome

The inner surfaces of the alveoli are kept moist by the secretion of a watery fluid from the cells of the alveolar wall. Surface tension could easily cause the wet walls to stick together, making it difficult for the alveoli to expand when breathing in. To prevent this, the fluid contains a detergent-like substance called a **surfactant**, which reduces surface tension.

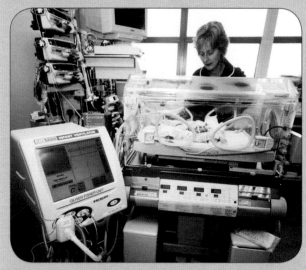

While a baby is still in the uterus, it does not use its lungs for gas exchange. Oxygen is supplied to its body through the umbilical cord, which contains two veins bringing blood from the placenta, where oxygen from the mother's blood diffuses into the baby's blood.

As the baby's lungs are not yet being used, there is no need for surfactant to be secreted, so this does not happen until fairly late in pregnancy. If a baby is born very prematurely, then its lungs may not be producing enough surfactant to stop the alveoli from sticking together. In this situation, the newborn baby may be unable to inflate its lungs when it tries to breathe. This condition is called respiratory distress syndrome of the newborn, often shortened to RDS. The more premature a baby, the greater the chance of RDS.

In a special baby unit at a hospital, a baby with RDS will be given extra oxygen, perhaps supplied under pressure to force the alveoli open. The baby may be placed inside a machine that rhythmically changes the air pressure around the baby's thorax, creating pressure gradients between the external air and the air in the lungs, which cause air to move in and out of the lungs. The baby may even be given surfactant through a tube leading to the lungs.

RDS usually gets worse before it gets better, and it may be several weeks before the baby can be taken off oxygen and out of the breathing machine. However, unless there are complications, there is a good chance that the baby will recover fully.

The mechanism of breathing

As our gas exchange surface is tucked away deep inside the lungs, it is necessary to bring fresh supplies of air into contact with this surface. We do this by **breathing**. Breathing can be defined as making movements that move air into and out of the lungs.

The lungs have no muscles, so they cannot move by themselves. Breathing movements are caused by two sets of muscles – the **intercostal muscles** between the ribs and the **diaphragm muscles**. These are shown in Figure 4.9.

Contraction of the external intercostal muscles and of the muscles in the diaphragm increases the volume of the thoracic cavity. This lowers the pressure within the thoracic cavity to below the pressure of the air outside the body. Air therefore flows down the pressure gradient and into the thorax. The only way in is through the trachea and into the lungs, so air is drawn into the lungs. The lungs inflate.

To breathe out, these muscles all relax. The elastic fibres between the alveoli, which were stretched when the lungs expanded, go back to their normal length. As the volume of the thoracic cavity decreases, the pressure inside it increases. This forces air out of the lungs.

Figure 4.9 shows how these events take place.

Extension

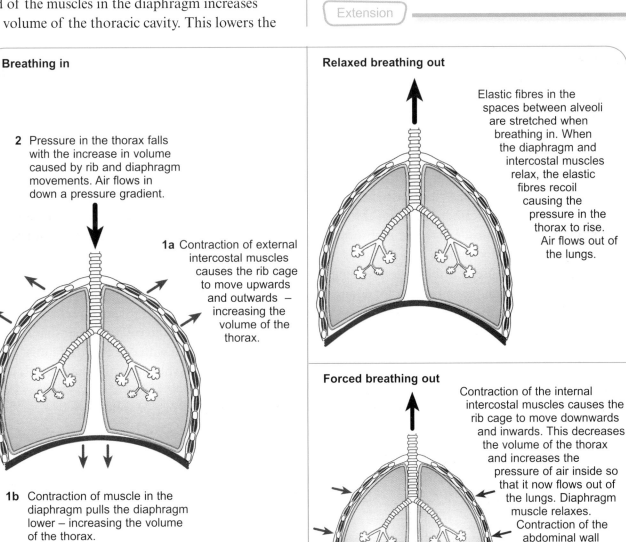

Breathing in

2 Pressure in the thorax falls with the increase in volume caused by rib and diaphragm movements. Air flows in down a pressure gradient.

1a Contraction of external intercostal muscles causes the rib cage to move upwards and outwards – increasing the volume of the thorax.

1b Contraction of muscle in the diaphragm pulls the diaphragm lower – increasing the volume of the thorax.

Relaxed breathing out

Elastic fibres in the spaces between alveoli are stretched when breathing in. When the diaphragm and intercostal muscles relax, the elastic fibres recoil causing the pressure in the thorax to rise. Air flows out of the lungs.

Forced breathing out

Contraction of the internal intercostal muscles causes the rib cage to move downwards and inwards. This decreases the volume of the thorax and increases the pressure of air inside so that it now flows out of the lungs. Diaphragm muscle relaxes. Contraction of the abdominal wall raises pressure in the abdomen and raises the diaphragm.

Figure 4.9 The mechanism of breathing.

Measuring lung volumes

The volumes of air that are moved into and out of the lungs during breathing can provide useful information about the health of a person's lungs. These volumes can be measured using an instrument called a **spirometer** (Figure 4.10)

How a spirometer works

In the type of spirometer shown in Figure 4.10, a person breathes in and out into an enclosed air chamber. The air is trapped between the spirometer float and the water. As the person breathes in, the volume of air inside the chamber decreases, and the float drops down. As the person breathes out, the volume of air inside the chamber increases, and the float is pushed up.

The float is attached to a pen, which writes on paper attached to a revolving drum. The movement of the spirometer float is therefore recorded as a series of 'up and down' lines on the paper.

The air chamber can be filled with atmospheric air, or it can be filled with medical grade oxygen. The spirometer can be used with or without soda lime (see Figure 4.10). When soda lime is present, the air that the person breathes out passes through it, and all the carbon dioxide in the air is absorbed by the soda lime and does not go into the air chamber. This can be useful if the person is going to be breathing through the spirometer for a long period, to avoid them re-breathing air that has become quite rich in carbon dioxide. It can also be useful if you want to measure the volume of oxygen that has been consumed over a period of time (page 59).

Tidal volume and ventilation rate

Figure 4.11 shows a spirometer trace that was produced while a person breathed normally using a spirometer. Each time he breathed out, the pen went up, and each time he breathed in it went down. The chart shows four breaths in and five breaths out.

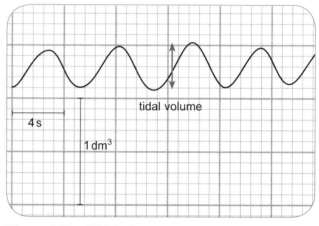

Figure 4.11 Tidal air movements.

The chart can be calibrated so that we know what volume of air is represented by a particular distance moved up or down by the pen. In this example, ten small squares on the vertical represent $1\,dm^3$ of air, and 5 small squares on the horizontal represent $4\,s$. You can think of the spirometer trace as a graph, with time on the x-axis and volume on the y-axis.

The chart can be used to measure the person's **tidal volume**. This is the volume of air that is breathed in and out with one breath. In this example, the tidal volume of the third breath is $0.4\,dm^3$.

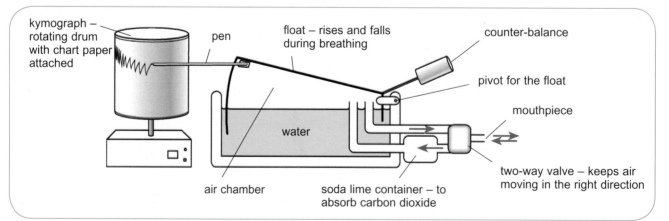

Figure 4.10 A spirometer.

5 Calculate the mean tidal volume shown in the spirometer trace in Figure 4.11.

Hint

Answer

We can also use the chart to work out the person's **breathing rate** – the number of breaths taken per minute. This can then be used to calculate the **ventilation rate**. This is the total volume of air breathed in or out in one minute. If you take 12 breaths per minute, and your mean tidal volume is $0.5\,dm^3$, then your ventilation rate is 12 breaths per minute $\times\,0.5\,dm^3 = 6\,dm^3$ per minute.

6 Calculate the mean breathing rate, in breaths per minute, shown by the spirometer trace in Figure 4.11. Then use this value, and your answer to SAQ 5, to determine the ventilation rate.

Hint

Answer

Vital capacity

Your **vital capacity** is the very greatest volume of air you can move into and out of your lungs with one breath. It can be measured by breathing out every bit of air that you can from your lungs, and then taking your very largest breath in. The spirometer trace that is produced would look something like Figure 4.12.

When you breathe out deeply, you obviously move more air out of your lungs than during normal, relaxed breathing. This extra air breathed out is your **expiratory reserve volume**. The extra air you breathe *in* when you take a very deep breath is your **inspiratory reserve volume**. Your vital capacity is your tidal volume plus your expiratory reserve volume plus your inspiratory reserve volume.

7 Use the spirometer trace in Figure 4.12 to find the person's vital capacity.

Answer

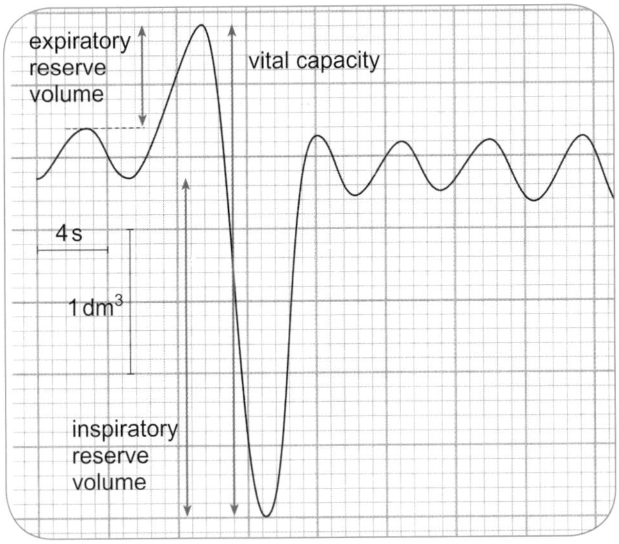

Figure 4.12 Vital capacity.

Measuring oxygen consumption

If the chamber of the spirometer is filled with oxygen, you can use it to measure how much oxygen you use over a period of time.

For this investigation, there must be soda lime in the container. Each time you breathe in, you take oxygen from the chamber and the float drops. When you breathe out, the unused oxygen in your expired air goes back into the air chamber, but the carbon dioxide in your expired air is absorbed by the soda lime. So the total volume of gas going back into the chamber is less than you took from it. With each breath, the volume of oxygen in the spirometer gets less and less, so the traces drawn by the pen go down and down. If we measure *how much* they go down over a period of time, this tells us the volume of oxygen that you have used.

Figure 4.13 shows the kind of spirometer trace you might get. The difference in the volume of air inside the spirometer chamber at the start of the session and at the end is $0.4\,dm^3$. This is the volume of oxygen that the subject used. The time taken for this volume of oxygen to be used was 24 seconds. So the rate of consumption of oxygen was $1\,dm^3\,min^{-1}$.

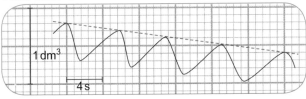

Figure 4.13 Measuring oxygen consumption.

SAQ

8 A spirometer's air chamber was filled with oxygen, and soda lime was used to absorb all the carbon dioxide in expired air. A subject breathed in and out of the spirometer while at rest. She then exercised vigorously for 5 minutes, and then breathed in and out of the spirometer again. The graph shows the spirometer trace.

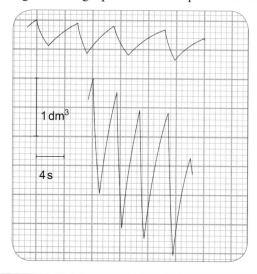

a Calculate the breathing rate before exercise, and the breathing rate after exercise Show your working.

b Calculate the mean tidal volume before exercise, and the mean tidal volume after exercise. Show your working.

c Calculate the rate of oxygen consumption before exercise and the rate of oxygen consumption after exercise.

d You probably have some knowledge of aerobic respiration, anaerobic respiration and oxygen debt from your GCSE studies. Use this knowledge to try to explain the difference between the figures you have calculated for before and after exercise.

Summary

Glossary

- Multicellular organisms may need specialised exchange surfaces to increase the surface area : volume ratio. A good exchange surface should have a large surface area, be thin and be able to maintain a diffusion gradient. The cells on the surface must be protected from drying out.

- Alveoli in the human lung are very small, and there are large numbers of them, so providing a very large surface area. The distance between the air in the alveolus and the blood in the capillaries is very small. Breathing movements supply freshly inspired air to the alveoli, and blood flow brings deoxygenated blood to the alveolus and removes oxygenated blood, so maintaining diffusion gradients for oxygen and carbon dioxide.

- The airways leading to the lungs are lined with ciliated epithelium containing goblet cells that produce mucus. The mucus traps particles in the air and the cilia sweep the mucus upwards, away from the lungs.

- The walls of the trachea and bronchi contain cartilage, which supports them and prevents them from collapsing when air pressure inside them is low. Smooth muscle in the walls of the trachea, bronchi and bronchioles can contract to narrow the airway. Elastic fibres in the walls of all the airways, and in alveolar tissue, allow the lungs to inflate and deflate. This is especially important in ensuring that the alveoli deflate when breathing out.

- Air is moved into and out of the lungs by breathing movements. During breathing in, the external intercostal muscles and the muscles in the diaphragm contract. This increases the volume of the thoracic cavity, decreases the pressure within it and therefore causes air to flow in from outside, down a pressure gradient. During breathing out, these muscles relax, which decreases the volume of the thoracic cavity. Recoil of the elastic fibres in the lungs causes them to deflate, forcing air out of the body.

continued

● Tidal volume is the volume of air moved in or out of the lungs in one breath. Vital capacity is the maximum volume of air that can be moved in or out of the lungs in one breath. These values can be measured using a spirometer.

● Oxygen uptake can be measured by recording the fall in volume of the air in a spirometer over several breaths.

Questions

1 The diagram shows a transverse section of a bronchus from the lung of a mammal.

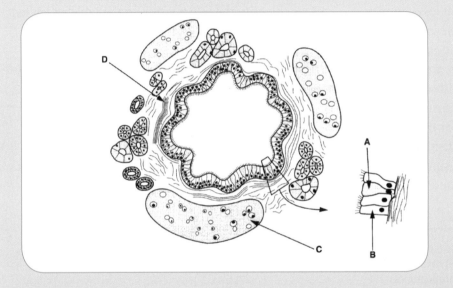

  a Name A to D. [4]

  b Describe how the cells lining the bronchus protect the alveoli from damage. [4]

  c There are elastic fibres between the cells lining the gaseous exchange surface in the alveoli. Describe the function of these fibres. [3]

  d The table shows some measurements of a person's breathing. Ventilation rate is the volume of air breathed in during one minute.

tidal volume at rest	$500\,cm^3$
vital capacity	$4600\,cm^3$
breathing rate at rest	12 breaths per minute
ventilation rate during exercise	$20\,000\,cm^3\,min^{-1}$

With reference to the table,

  i calculate the ventilation rate at rest [1]

  ii explain the meaning of the term *vital capacity* [2]

  iii state how the person increased their ventilation rate even though their breathing rate remained constant. [1]

OCR Biology AS (2802) June 2001 [Total 15]

Answer

Chapter 5

Transport in animals

e-Learning

Objectives

Types of transport system

Why do humans have a blood system? The answer is fairly obvious even to a non-scientist: our blood system transports substances such as nutrients and oxygen around the body. However, there are many organisms that either have much less complex transport systems or do not have any kind of transport system at all. Before looking in detail at the human transport system, we will consider why some organisms can manage without one.

A quick survey of some organisms that have very simple transport systems, or none at all, will provide an important clue. Table 5.1 lists six kinds of organisms, and gives a brief summary of the type of transport system that each has.

SAQ

1 Using the information in Table 5.1, suggest how important each of the following factors appears to be in determining whether or not an organism needs an efficient transport system. In each case, identify the information in the table which led you to your answer.

a size
b surface area : volume ratio
c level of activity

Answer

All living cells require a supply of nutrients, such as glucose. Most living cells also need a constant supply of oxygen. There will also be waste products, such as carbon dioxide, to be disposed of.

Type of organism	Single-celled	Cnidarians (jellyfish and sea anemones)	Insects	Green plants	Fish	Mammals
Size range	all microscopic	some microscopic, some up to 60 cm	less than 1 mm to 13 cm	1 mm to 150 m	12 mm to 10 m	35 mm to 34 m
Example	*Paramecium* 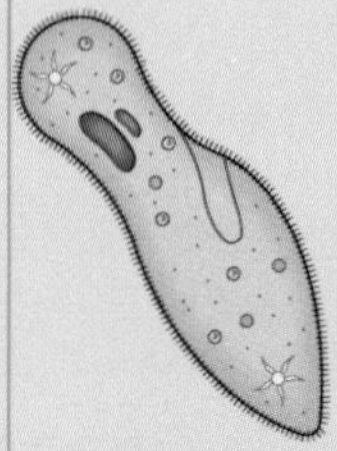	sea anemone 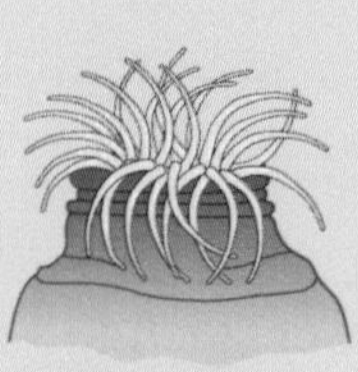	locust 	*Pelargonium* 	goldfish 	human 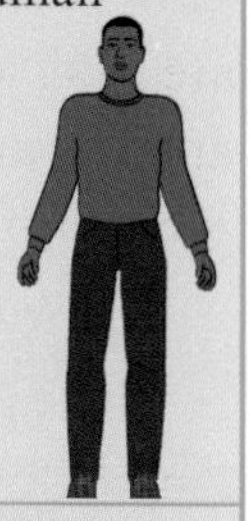
Level of activity	move in search of food	jellyfish swim slowly; anemones are sedentary and move very slowly	move actively; many fly	no movement of whole plant; parts such as leaves may move slowly	move actively	move actively
Type of transport system	no specialised transport system	no specialised transport system	blood system with pumps	xylem and phloem make up transport system; no pump	blood system with pump	blood system with pump

Table 5.1   Different transport systems.

Very small organisms, such as the single-celled protozoan *Paramecium*, can meet their requirements for the supply of nutrients and oxygen, and the removal of waste, by means of diffusion. The very small distances across which substances have to diffuse mean that the speed of supply or removal is sufficient for their needs. These tiny organisms have a large surface area:volume ratio, so there is a relatively large area of membrane across which gases can diffuse.

Even larger organisms, such as cnidarians, can manage by diffusion alone. A cnidarian's body is made up just two layers of cells, so every cell is within a very small distance of the water in which these organisms live, and with which they exchange materials. They, too, have relatively large surface area:volume ratios. Moreover, cnidarians are not very active animals, so their cells do not have large requirements for glucose or oxygen, nor do they produce large amounts of waste products. Diffusion, slow though it is, is quite adequate to supply their needs.

Larger, more active organisms, such as insects, fish and mammals, cannot rely on diffusion alone. Cells, often deep within their bodies, are metabolically very active, with requirements for rapid supplies of nutrients and oxygen, and with relatively large amounts of waste products to be removed. These organisms have well-organised transport systems, with pumps to keep fluids moving through them. Plants, although large, are less metabolically active than these groups of animals and, as you will see in Chapter 6, have evolved a very different type of transport system, with no obvious pump to keep fluids moving.

Open and closed circulatory systems

The human blood system, like that of all vertebrates, is a **closed circulatory system**. This means that the blood is always enclosed in vessels.

Insects, however, have an **open circulatory system** (Figure 5.1). Here, although the blood is pumped around the body by a heart and flows out of the heart in arteries, it is not then contained within vessels but fills the body cavity, which is called a **haemocoel** ('blood space').

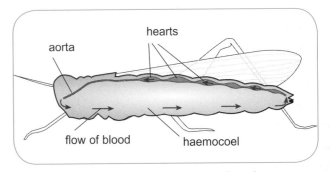

Figure 5.1 The transport system of an insect.

In insects, the blood does *not* transport oxygen around the body. Insects have a gas exchange system which is not at all like that of humans. Insects have an arrangement of tubes called **tracheae**, which penetrate deep into the body and carry air from the atmosphere directly to the tissues (Figure 5.2). The insect gas exchange surfaces are therefore very close to the cells that are using oxygen and making carbon dioxide, so diffusion is sufficient to satisfy their demands.

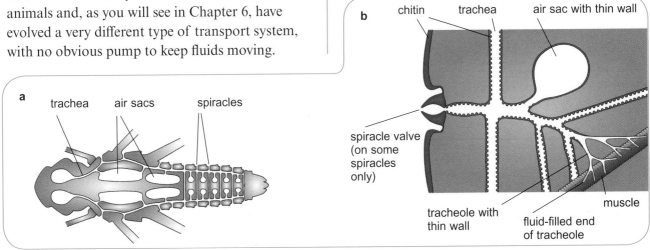

Figure 5.2 The gas exchange system of an insect: **a** dorsal view; **b** detail of parts of the gas exchange system.

2 To answer these questions, look at Figure 5.2.

  a Explain how the insect gas exchange system provides a large surface area for gas exchange.

  b Suggest why there are spirals of chitin (a tough, supporting material) around the tracheae.

> Hint

  c Suggest why having valves on the spiracles is important for terrestrial insects.

> Hint

> Answer

Single and double circulatory systems

The human circulation system is a **double circulatory system** (Figure 5.3). One part serves the lungs, and is called the **pulmonary circulation**. The other part serves the rest of the body, and is called the **systemic circulation**.

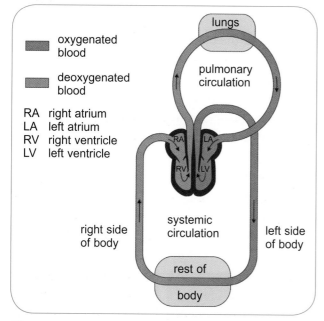

Figure 5.3 A double circulatory system. This is a general plan of the mammalian transport system.

3 a Is the transport system shown in Figure 5.3 a closed system or an open system? Explain your answer.

  b How many times does the blood pass through the heart on one journey round the body in a double circulatory system?

> Answer

Fish, however, have a **single circulatory system** (Figure 5.4). Here, the blood is pumped out of the heart to the gills (the equivalent of our lungs) where it picks up oxygen. But, instead of going back to the heart, the blood continues on around the rest of the body.

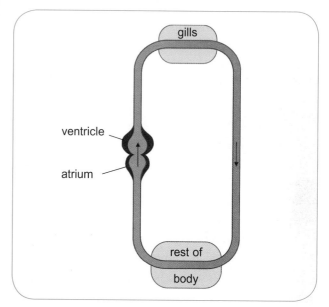

Figure 5.4 A single circulatory system in a fish.

This system is not as efficient as the mammalian system at getting oxygenated blood to the tissues. As blood from the heart reaches the gas exchange organs, it travels through many tiny capillaries, where it loses much of its pressure. In humans, the oxygenated blood returns to the heart, where the left ventricle pumps it out into the aorta. The oxygenated blood moves quickly out of the heart, and moves fast along the arteries, rapidly delivering oxygen to respiring tissues. In a fish, however, the blood from the gill capillaries is simply collected back up into vessels and carried on its way to the rest of the body, without being repressurised by the heart.

4 State two differences between the circulatory systems of an insect and a fish.

> Answer

The mammalian heart

Structure of a human heart

The heart of an adult human has a mass of around 300 g and is about the size of your fist (Figure 5.5). It is a bag of muscle, filled with blood. Figure 5.6 shows the appearance of a human heart, looking at it from the front of the body.

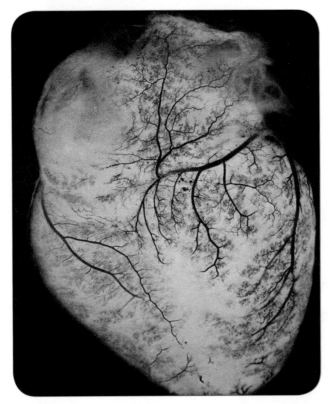

Figure 5.5   A human heart.

The muscle of which the heart is made is called cardiac muscle. This muscle is able to contract and relax rhythmically, 24 hours a day, throughout your life.

In Figure 5.6, you can see the blood vessels that carry blood into and out of the heart. The large, arching blood vessel is the largest artery, the **aorta**, with branches leading upwards towards the head and the main flow turning back downwards to the rest of the body. The other blood vessel leaving the heart is the **pulmonary artery**. This, too, branches very quickly after leaving the heart, into two arteries, one taking blood to the left lung and one to the right. Running vertically on the right-hand side of the heart are the two large veins, the **venae**

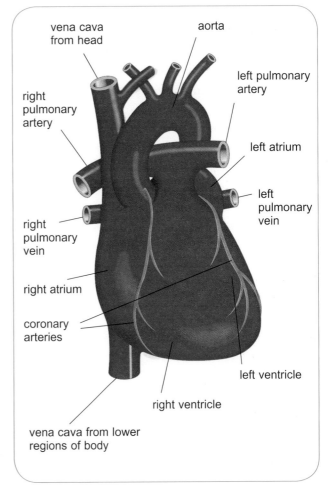

Figure 5.6   Diagram of the external structure of a human heart, seen from the front.

cavae (singular: vena cava), one bringing blood downwards from the head and the other bringing it upwards from the rest of the body. The **pulmonary veins** bring blood back to the heart from the left and right lungs.

On the surface of the heart, the **coronary arteries** can be seen (Figures 5.5 and 5.6). These branch from the aorta and deliver oxygenated blood to the muscle of the walls of the heart.

If the heart is cut open vertically (Figure 5.7), it can be seen to contain four chambers. The two chambers on the left of the heart are completely separated from those on the right by a wall of muscle called the **septum**. Blood cannot pass through this septum; the only way for blood to get from one side of the heart to the other is to leave the heart, circulate around either the lungs or the rest of the body, and then return to the heart.

The upper chamber on each side is called an **atrium**. The two atria receive blood from the veins. You can see from Figure 5.7 that blood from the venae cavae flows into the right atrium, while blood from the pulmonary veins flows into the left atrium.

The lower chambers are **ventricles**. Blood flows into the ventricles from the atria, and is then squeezed out into the arteries. Blood from the left ventricle flows into the aorta, while blood from the right ventricle flows into the pulmonary arteries.

The atria and ventricles have valves between them, which are known as the **atrio-ventricular valves**. The one on the left is the **mitral** or **bicuspid valve**, and the one on the right is the **tricuspid valve**.

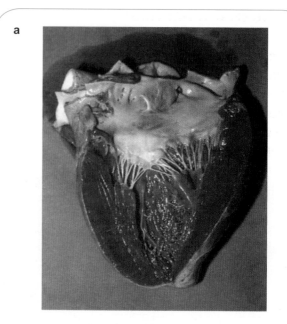

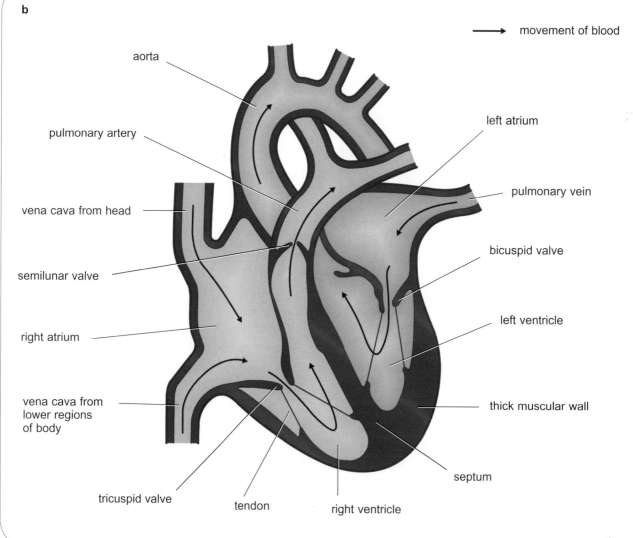

Figure 5.7 Vertical sections through a human heart: **a** the heart has been cut through the left atrium and ventricle only; **b** both sides of the heart are shown.

The cardiac cycle

Your heart beats around 70 times a minute at rest. The **cardiac cycle** is the sequence of events that makes up one heart beat.

As the cycle is continuous, a description of it could begin anywhere. We will begin with the time when the heart is filled with blood, and the muscle in the atrial walls contracts. This stage is called **atrial systole** (Figure 5.8). The pressure developed by this contraction is not very great, because the muscular walls of the atria are only thin, but it is enough to force the blood in the atria down through the atrio-ventricular valves into the ventricles. The blood from the atria does not go back into the pulmonary veins or the venae cavae, because these have semilunar valves to prevent backflow.

About 0.1 s after the atria contract, the ventricles contract. This is called **ventricular systole**. The thick, muscular walls of the ventricles squeeze inwards on the blood, increasing its pressure and pushing it out of the heart. As soon as the pressure in the ventricles becomes greater than that in the atria, this pressure difference forces the atrio-ventricular valves shut, preventing blood from going back into the atria. Instead, the blood rushes upwards into the aorta and pulmonary artery, pushing open the semilunar valves in these vessels as it does so.

Ventricular systole lasts for about 0.3 s. The muscle then relaxes, and the stage called **ventricular diastole** begins. The pressure in the ventricles drops. The high-pressure blood which has just been pushed into the arteries would flow back into the ventricles, but for the presence of the semilunar valves, which snap shut as the blood fills their cusps.

During diastole, as the whole of the heart muscle relaxes, blood from the veins flows into the two atria. The blood is at a very low pressure, but the thin walls of the atria are easily distended, providing very little resistance to the blood flow. Some of the blood flows down into the ventricles. The atrial muscle then begins to contract, pushing blood forcefully down into the ventricles, and the whole cycle begins again.

Figure 5.9 shows how the atrio-ventricular and semilunar valves work.

The walls of the ventricles are much thicker than the walls of the atria, because the ventricles need to develop much more force when they contract, to push the blood out of the heart and around the body. For the right ventricle, the force required is relatively small, as the blood goes only to the lungs, which are very close to the heart. The left ventricle has to develop sufficient force to push blood all around the rest of the body. So the muscular wall of the left ventricle needs to be thicker than that of the right ventricle.

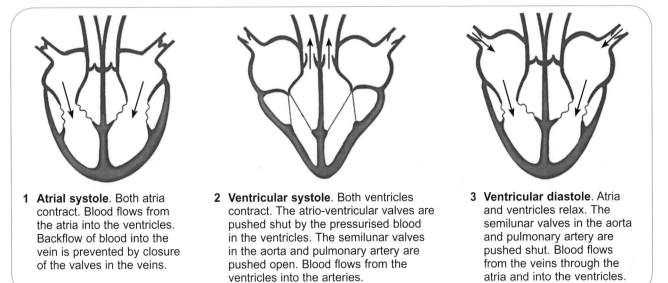

1 **Atrial systole**. Both atria contract. Blood flows from the atria into the ventricles. Backflow of blood into the vein is prevented by closure of the valves in the veins.

2 **Ventricular systole**. Both ventricles contract. The atrio-ventricular valves are pushed shut by the pressurised blood in the ventricles. The semilunar valves in the aorta and pulmonary artery are pushed open. Blood flows from the ventricles into the arteries.

3 **Ventricular diastole**. Atria and ventricles relax. The semilunar valves in the aorta and pulmonary artery are pushed shut. Blood flows from the veins through the atria and into the ventricles.

Figure 5.8   The cardiac cycle. Only three stages in this continuous process are shown.

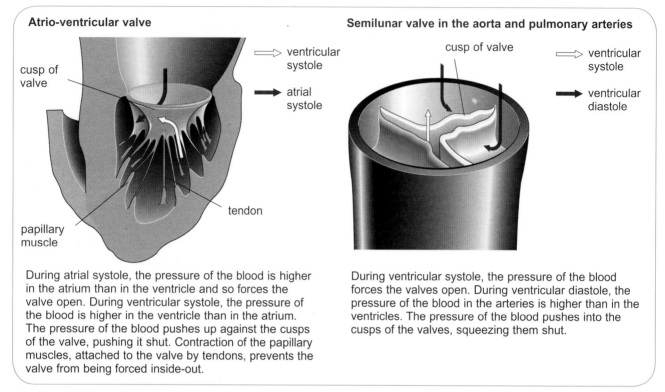

Atrio-ventricular valve

cusp of valve

papillary muscle

tendon

⟹ ventricular systole

➡ atrial systole

Semilunar valve in the aorta and pulmonary arteries

cusp of valve

⟹ ventricular systole

➡ ventricular diastole

During atrial systole, the pressure of the blood is higher in the atrium than in the ventricle and so forces the valve open. During ventricular systole, the pressure of the blood is higher in the ventricle than in the atrium. The pressure of the blood pushes up against the cusps of the valve, pushing it shut. Contraction of the papillary muscles, attached to the valve by tendons, prevents the valve from being forced inside-out.

During ventricular systole, the pressure of the blood forces the valves open. During ventricular diastole, the pressure of the blood in the arteries is higher than in the ventricles. The pressure of the blood pushes into the cusps of the valves, squeezing them shut.

Fig 5.9 How the heart valves function.

Drugs to help the heart

The heart rate is controlled by a patch of muscle in the heart called the **pacemaker**, or **sino-atrial node (SAN)**.

Two nerves carry impulses from the brain to the SAN. One of these is the vagus nerve. It releases a transmitter substance called acetycholine next to the cells in the SAN. Acetylcholine slots into receptors in the plasma membranes of these cells, and makes the cells beat more *slowly*.

The other nerve, called the sympathetic nerve, releases a different chemical called noradrenalin. This has the opposite effect to acetylcholine, and makes the cells in the SAN beat more *rapidly*. The hormone adrenaline, released from the adrenal glands just above the kidneys when a person is frightened or excited, has the same effect.

There are several drugs that can be used to help a person who has problems with their rate of heartbeat. Two of these are digoxin and propranolol.

Digoxin inhibits a Na–K pump in the plasma membrane of the heart muscle cells. This pump

Digoxin was discovered in foxgloves.

usually keeps sodium concentration inside the cells at a low level. When the pump is slowed, sodium ions accumulate inside the cells. This also increases the concentration of calcium ions in them, which increases the force of muscle contraction.

Propranolol has the opposite effect. It belongs to a class of drugs called beta blockers. They work by decreasing the effect of noradrenalin on the SAN, reducing the heart rate. Beta blockers are often given to people with angina, a pain in the chest that is a sign that the coronary arteries are not supplying enough oxygen to the heart muscle.

SAQ

5 Figure 5.10 shows the pressure changes in the left atrium, left ventricle and aorta throughout two cardiac cycles. Make a copy of this diagram.

a i How long does one heart beat (one cardiac cycle) last?

ii What is the heart rate represented on this graph, in beats per minute?

b The contraction of the muscles in the ventricle wall causes the pressure inside the ventricle to rise. When the muscles relax, the pressure drops again. On your copy of the diagram, mark the following periods:

i the time when the ventricle is contracting (ventricular systole)

ii the time when the ventricle is relaxing (ventricular diastole).

c The contraction of muscles in the wall of the atrium raises the pressure inside the atrium. This pressure is also raised when blood flows into the atrium from the veins, while the atrial walls are relaxed. On your copy of the diagram, mark the following periods:

i the time when the atrium is contracting (atrial systole)

ii the time when the atrium is relaxing (atrial diastole).

d The atrio-ventricular valves open when the pressure of the blood in the atria is greater than that in the ventricles. They snap shut when the pressure of the blood in the ventricles is greater than that in the atria. On your diagram, mark the points at which these valves open and close.

e The opening and closing of the semilunar valves in the aorta depends, in a similar way, on the relative pressures in the aorta and ventricles. On your diagram, mark the points at which these valves open and close.

f The right ventricle has much less muscle in its walls than the left ventricle, and only develops about one-quarter of the pressure developed on the left side of the heart. On your diagram, draw a line to represent the probable pressure inside the right ventricle during the 1.3 s shown.

Answer

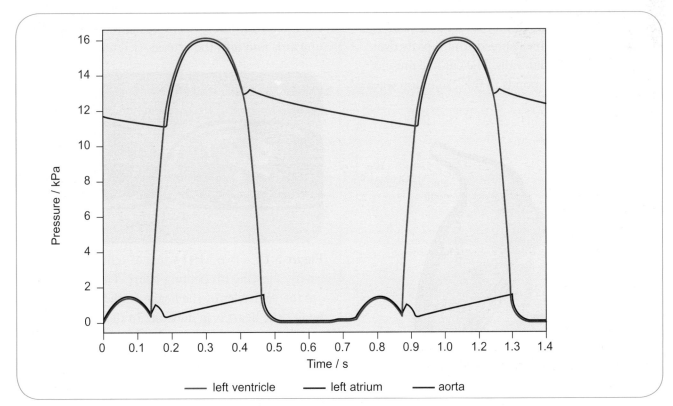

Figure 5.10 Pressure changes in the heart during the cardiac cycle.

Control of the heart beat

Cardiac muscle differs from the muscle in all other areas of the body in that it is **myogenic**. This means that it automatically contracts and relaxes; it does not need to receive impulses from a nerve to make it contract. If cardiac muscle cells are cultured in a warm, oxygenated solution containing nutrients, they contract and relax rhythmically, all by themselves. Cardiac muscle cells joined together contract together, in unison.

However, the individual muscle cells in a heart cannot be allowed to contract at their own natural rhythms. If they did, parts of the heart would contract out of sequence with other parts; the cardiac cycle would become disordered and the heart would stop working as a pump. The heart has its own built-in controlling and coordinating system which prevents this happening.

The cardiac cycle is initiated in a small patch of muscle in the wall of the right atrium, called the **sino-atrial node** or **SAN** (Figure 5.11). It is often called the **pacemaker**. The muscle cells in the SAN set the pace and rhythm for all the other cardiac muscle cells. Their natural rhythm of contraction is slightly faster than the rest of the heart muscle. Each time they contract, they set up a wave of electrical activity, which spreads out rapidly over the whole of the atrial walls. The cardiac muscle in the atrial walls responds to this excitation wave by contracting, in the same rhythm as the SAN. Thus, all the muscle in both atria contracts almost simultaneously.

As we have seen, the muscles of the ventricles do not contract until *after* the muscles of the atria. (You can imagine what would happen if they all contracted at once.) This delay is caused by a feature of the heart that briefly delays the excitation wave in its passage from the atria to the ventricles.

There is a band of fibres between the atria and the ventricles which does not conduct the excitation wave. As the wave spreads out from the SAN, it cannot pass through these fibres. The only route is through a small patch of conducting fibres, known as the **atrio-ventricular node** or **AVN**. The AVN picks up the excitation wave as it spreads across the atria and, after a delay of about 0.1 s, passes it on to a bunch of conducting fibres, called the **Purkyne tissue**, which runs down the septum between the ventricles. This transmits the excitation wave very rapidly down to the base of the septum, from where it spreads outwards and upwards through the ventricle walls. As it does so, it causes the cardiac muscle in these walls to contract, from the bottom up, squeezing blood upwards and into the arteries (Figure 5.12).

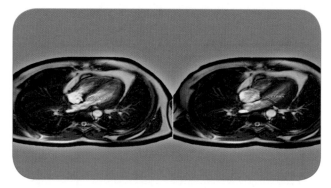

Figure 5.12   Two MRI scans of a man's chest cavity, showing his beating heart. The orange areas are the ventricles of the heart. In the left-hand image, the heart is in diastole. In the right-hand image, the ventricles are contracting – you can see that the volume inside them is less.

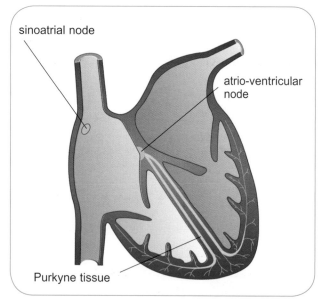

sinoatrial node

atrio-ventricular node

Purkyne tissue

Figure 5.11   The sino-atrial node and atrio-ventricular node.

Electrocardiograms

It is quite easy to detect and record the waves of electrical excitation as they travel through the heart muscle. Electrodes can be placed on the skin over opposite sides of the heart, and a recording is made of the electrical potentials. The result is essentially a graph of voltage against time. It is called an **electrocardiogram** or **ECG**. Figure 5.13 shows an ECG for a healthy heart.

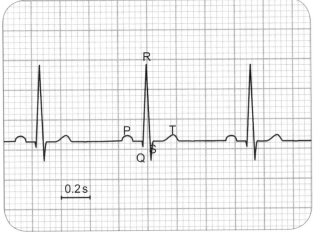

Figure 5.13   A normal ECG.

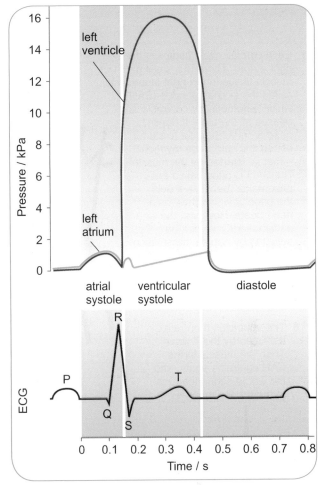

Figure 5.14   An ECG, and how it relates to the cardiac cycle.

Figure 5.14 explains how the peaks and troughs of the ECG relate to the pressure changes we have already looked at. If you look very carefully, you can see that the ups and downs in the ECG happen just *before* the ups and downs in the pressure graph. For example, the P wave on the ECG comes before the pressure rise in the left atrium. This is because the ECG records the electrical impulses that are spreading over the heart, and these electrical impulses *cause* the contraction

of the muscle in the heart walls. So the P wave in the ECG represents the wave of electrical activity spreading through the walls of the atria (Figure 5.15), which is quickly followed by the contraction of the atrial muscle and therefore the rise in pressure in the atria.

SAQ

6 This diagram shows a normal ECG. The paper on which the ECG was recorded was running at a speed of $25\,\mathrm{mm\,s^{-1}}$.

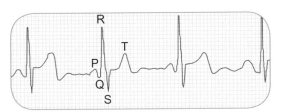

   a Calculate the heart rate in beats per minute.

   b The time interval between Q and T is called the **contraction time**.

      i Suggest why it is given this name.

      ii Calculate the contraction time from this ECG.

   c The time interval between T and Q is called the **filling time**.

      i Suggest why it is given this name.

      ii Calculate the filling time from this ECG.

   Answer

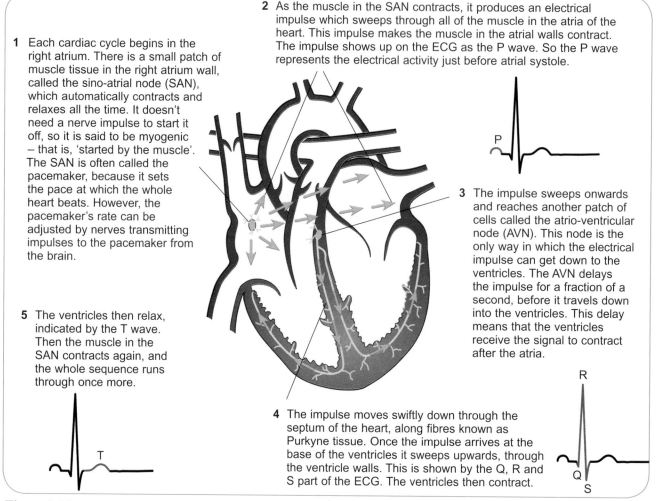

1 Each cardiac cycle begins in the right atrium. There is a small patch of muscle tissue in the right atrium wall, called the sino-atrial node (SAN), which automatically contracts and relaxes all the time. It doesn't need a nerve impulse to start it off, so it is said to be myogenic – that is, 'started by the muscle'. The SAN is often called the pacemaker, because it sets the pace at which the whole heart beats. However, the pacemaker's rate can be adjusted by nerves transmitting impulses to the pacemaker from the brain.

2 As the muscle in the SAN contracts, it produces an electrical impulse which sweeps through all of the muscle in the atria of the heart. This impulse makes the muscle in the atrial walls contract. The impulse shows up on the ECG as the P wave. So the P wave represents the electrical activity just before atrial systole.

3 The impulse sweeps onwards and reaches another patch of cells called the atrio-ventricular node (AVN). This node is the only way in which the electrical impulse can get down to the ventricles. The AVN delays the impulse for a fraction of a second, before it travels down into the ventricles. This delay means that the ventricles receive the signal to contract after the atria.

4 The impulse moves swiftly down through the septum of the heart, along fibres known as Purkyne tissue. Once the impulse arrives at the base of the ventricles it sweeps upwards, through the ventricle walls. This is shown by the Q, R and S part of the ECG. The ventricles then contract.

5 The ventricles then relax, indicated by the T wave. Then the muscle in the SAN contracts again, and the whole sequence runs through once more.

Figure 5.15 How electrical impulses move through the heart.

Figure 5.16 shows two examples of abnormal ECGs. The first shows ventricular fibrillation, in which the muscle in the ventricle walls just flutters. This could be because of serious damage to the heart muscle, which has caused it to stop beating – in other words, a heart attack or cardiac arrest. For any chance of survival, the person needs treatment with a defibrillator, which administers electric shocks, to try to get the heart muscle beating normally again.

The second ECG in Figure 5.16 shows a condition called heart block. There are many different kinds of heart block, a term which refers to problems with the movement of the electrical signals from one part of the heart to another. In this person, the signals are taking much longer than usual to pass from the atria to the ventricles, and you can see that the time interval between the P and R sections is longer than in Figure 5.13. This could be caused by damage to the Purkyne fibres.

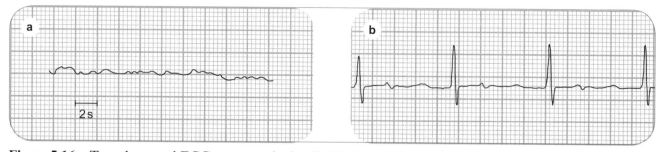

Figure 5.16 Two abnormal ECGs: **a** ventricular fibrillation; **b** heart block.

Blood vessels

When blood first leaves the heart, it is travelling in vessels called **arteries**. Arteries always carry blood away from the heart. The largest arteries divide into smaller ones, and these continue to divide to form much smaller vessels called **arterioles**. These in turn divide into even smaller vessels called **capillaries**. Capillaries then join up with each other to form **venules** and these finally merge to form **veins**, which carry blood back to the heart. The structures of the walls of arteries, veins and capillaries are shown in Figure 5.17 and Figure 5.18.

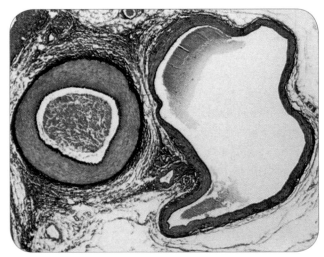

Figure 5.18   Micrograph of an artery and vein (×15).

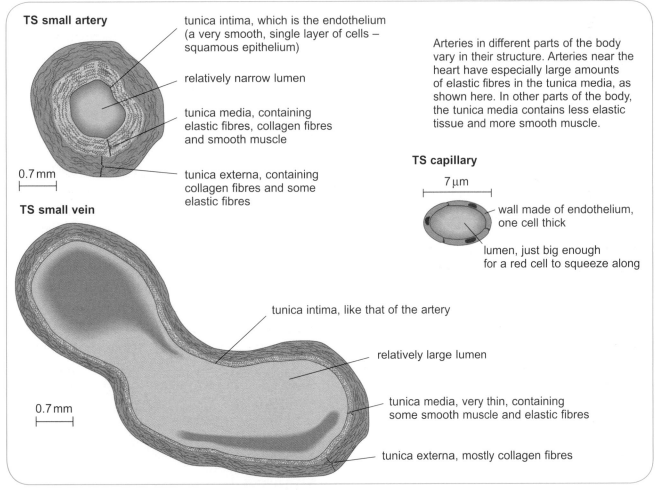

TS small artery

tunica intima, which is the endothelium (a very smooth, single layer of cells – squamous epithelium)

relatively narrow lumen

tunica media, containing elastic fibres, collagen fibres and smooth muscle

tunica externa, containing collagen fibres and some elastic fibres

0.7 mm

Arteries in different parts of the body vary in their structure. Arteries near the heart have especially large amounts of elastic fibres in the tunica media, as shown here. In other parts of the body, the tunica media contains less elastic tissue and more smooth muscle.

TS capillary

7 μm

wall made of endothelium, one cell thick

lumen, just big enough for a red cell to squeeze along

TS small vein

tunica intima, like that of the artery

relatively large lumen

tunica media, very thin, containing some smooth muscle and elastic fibres

tunica externa, mostly collagen fibres

0.7 mm

Figure 5.17   The tissues making up the walls of arteries, capillaries and veins.

Arteries

The function of arteries is to transport blood swiftly and at high pressure to the tissues.

Both arteries and veins have walls made up of three layers:

- an inner **endothelium** (lining tissue), made up of a layer of flat cells fitting together like jigsaw pieces; called squamous epithelium, this is very smooth, and so reduces friction as blood flows over its surface
- a middle layer called the **tunica media** ('middle coat') containing smooth muscle, collagen and elastic fibres
- an outer layer called the **tunica externa** ('outer coat') containing elastic fibres and collagen fibres.

The distinctive feature of an artery wall is its strength and elasticity. Blood leaving the heart is at a very high pressure. Blood pressure in the human aorta may be around 120 mm Hg, or 16 kPa. (Blood pressure is still measured in the old units of mm Hg even though kPa is the SI unit – mm Hg stands for 'millimetres of mercury' and refers to the distances which mercury is pushed up the arm of a U-tube when a sphygmomanometer is used; 1 mm Hg is equivalent to about 0.13 kPa.) To withstand the pressure surges, artery walls must be extremely strong and able to expand and recoil.

Arteries have the thickest walls of any blood vessel. The human aorta, the largest artery and the one where pressure is highest, has an overall diameter of 2.5 cm close to the heart, and a wall thickness of about 2 mm. Although 2 mm may not seem very great, the composition of the wall provides great strength and resilience. The tunica media, which is by far the thickest part of the wall, contains large numbers of elastic fibres. These allow the wall to stretch as pulses of blood surge through at high pressure as a result of the contraction of the ventricles. As the ventricles relax, the blood pressure drops, and the elastic artery walls recoil inwards.

Therefore, as blood at high pressure enters an artery, the artery becomes wider, which reduces the pressure slightly, so it is a little below what it would be if the wall could not expand. As blood at lower pressure enters an artery, the artery wall recoils inwards, giving the blood a small 'push' and raising the pressure a little. The overall effect is to 'even out' the flow of blood. However, the arteries are not entirely effective in achieving this: if you feel your pulse in your wrist, you can feel the artery, even at this distance from your heart, being stretched outwards with each surge of blood from the heart.

As arteries reach the tissue to which they are delivering blood, they branch into smaller vessels called **arterioles**. The walls of arterioles are similar to those of arteries, but they have a greater proportion of smooth muscle. This muscle can contract, narrowing the diameter of the arteriole and reducing blood flow through it. This helps to control the volume of blood flowing into a tissue at different times. For example, during exercise, arterioles that supply blood to muscles in your legs will be wide (dilated) as their walls relax, while those carrying blood to the gut wall will be narrow (constricted).

Extension

Capillaries

Arterioles branch to form the tiniest of all blood vessels, the capillaries (Figure 5.19). Their function is to take blood as close as possible to all cells, allowing rapid transfer of substances between the blood and the cells. Capillaries form a network throughout every tissue in the body except the cornea and cartilage. These networks are sometimes known as **capillary beds**. Although individual capillaries are very small, there are so many of them that their total cross-sectional area is considerably greater than that of the arteries.

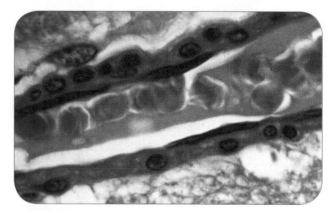

Figure 5.19 Micrograph of a blood capillary containing red blood cells (× 900).

Capillaries are often no more than 7 or 8 μm in diameter. This is about the same size as a red blood cell, so these can only pass through the capillaries in single file. This makes sure that every red blood cell, carrying its load of oxygen, is brought as close as possible to the cells in the surrounding tissues. This speeds up the transfer of oxygen to the cells and the removal of carbon dioxide. The gases move by diffusion, down their concentration gradients.

Capillaries have very thin walls, only one cell thick, which also speeds up transfer of materials between the blood and the tissues. Many substances pass across the endothelial cells in vesicles, by endocytosis and exocytosis (Chapter 2). The vesicles can even fuse to form tiny holes right through a cell. In most capillaries, there are also tiny gaps between the individual cells that form the endothelium, allowing easy transfer of substances dissolved in the plasma out of the capillary to the surrounding cells.

SAQ

7 Suggest why there are no blood capillaries in the cornea of the eye.

<Answer>

<Extension>

Veins

As blood leaves a capillary bed, the capillaries join together to form **venules** and then **veins**. The function of veins is to return blood to the heart.

The blood which enters veins is at a much lower pressure than in arteries. In humans, a typical value for venous blood pressure is about 5 mm Hg or even less. Veins therefore have no need for thick, elastic walls. The walls are so thin that veins collapse when a section of tissue is cut to make a microscope slide. The walls have the same three layers as arteries, but the tunica media is much thinner with far fewer elastic fibres and muscle fibres.

The low blood pressure in veins creates a problem: how can this blood be returned to the heart? The problem is most obvious if you consider how blood can return upwards from your legs. Unaided, the blood in your leg veins

would sink and accumulate in your feet. Many of the veins run within, or very close to, several leg muscles. Whenever you tense these muscles, they squeeze inwards on the veins, temporarily raising the pressure within them. This in itself would not help to push the blood back towards the heart – blood would just squidge up and down as you walked. To keep the blood flowing in the right direction, veins contain semilunar valves, formed from their endothelium (Figure 5.20). The valves allow blood to move towards the heart, but not away from it. When you contract your leg muscles, the blood in the veins is squeezed through the valves, but cannot drop back past them.

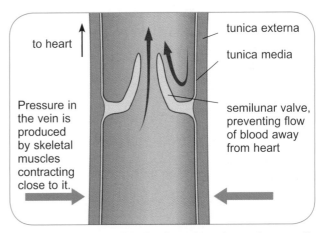

Figure 5.20 Longitudinal section through a small vein and a valve.

Table 5.2 summarises the differences between arteries, veins and capillaries, and Figure 5.21 shows how blood pressure changes as it travels on a complete journey from the heart, through the systemic circulatory system, back to the heart and finally through the pulmonary circulatiory system.

SAQ

8 Explain what causes each of the following:

<Hint>

a Blood pressure oscillates (goes up and down) in the arteries.

b Blood pressure drops in the arterioles and in the capillaries.

c Blood pressure rises in the pulmonary artery, but not so high as in the aorta.

<Answer>

	Artery	**Vein**	**Capillary**
Elastic tissue in wall	Large amount, especially in arteries close to the heart. This allows the wall to stretch and recoil as high-pressure blood pulses through.	Small amount. Blood in veins is at low pressure, so there is no need for the walls to be elastic.	None.
Smooth muscle in wall	Relatively large amount in small arteries and arterioles. Contraction of this muscle reduces the size of the lumen, which can divert blood from one area to another.	Small amount. All blood in veins is travelling back to the heart, so there is no advantage in being able to divert it to different tissues.	None.
Thickness of wall	Relatively thick. Artery walls must be strong enough to withstand the high pressure of the blood flowing inside them.	Relatively thin. The blood in veins is at low pressure, so there is no need for a thick wall.	The wall is only one cell thick. Moreover, these cells are thin and flattened, so the wall is as thin as possible. This allows rapid transfer of substances by diffusion between the blood and tissue fluid.
Endothelium (inner lining)	Very smooth. This allows blood to flow freely and quickly. A rough wall would present more resistance to blood flow. Intact endothelium decreases the likelihood of a thrombus (blood clot) forming.	As arteries.	The wall of a capillary is made of endothelium only, with no other layers of tissue. The thin endothelium and pores speed up exchange of substances with the tissues.
Presence of valves	There are no valves in arteries, except those in the aorta and pulmonary artery as they leave the heart.	Veins have valves, which allow blood to flow towards the heart but not away from it. They are necessary because of the low pressure of blood in the veins.	There are no valves in capillaries.
Diameter of lumen	Relatively small compared with veins.	Relatively large. The wide lumen of a vein provides less resistance to blood flow than the narrow lumen of an artery, allowing blood at low pressure to move through easily.	Tiny. Many capillaries are only 8 µm wide. This brings the blood as close as possible to the cells in the tissues with which it is exchanging materials such as oxygen and carbon dioxide.

Table 5.2   Summary of blood vessel structure and function.

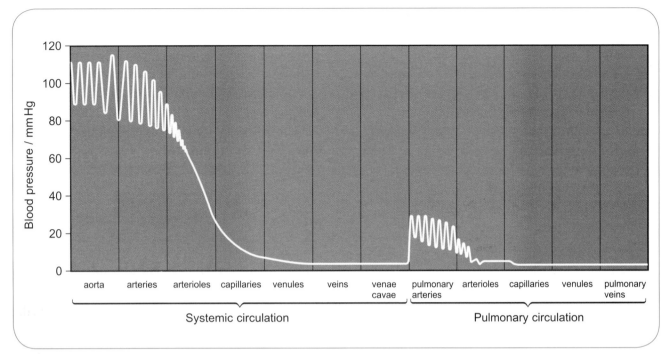

Figure 5.21 Blood pressure in different regions of the human circulatory system.

Blood plasma, tissue fluid and lymph

Blood is composed of cells floating in a pale yellow liquid called **plasma**. Blood plasma is mostly water, with a variety of substances dissolved in it. These solutes include nutrients, such as glucose, and waste products, such as urea, that are being transported from one place to another in the body. They also include protein molecules, called **plasma proteins**, that remain in the blood all the time.

How tissue fluid is formed

As blood flows through capillaries within tissues, some of the plasma leaks out through capillary walls and seeps into the spaces between the cells of the tissues. Almost one-sixth of your body consists of spaces between your cells. These spaces are filled with leaked plasma, which is known as **tissue fluid**.

Tissue fluid is very similar in composition to blood plasma. However, it contains far fewer protein molecules than plasma, as these are too large to escape easily through the tiny holes in the capillary endothelium.

Red blood cells are much too large to pass through, but some white blood cells can squeeze through and move freely around in the tissue fluid. Table 5.3 shows the sizes of the molecules of some of the substances in blood plasma, and the relative ease with which they pass from capillaries into tissue fluid.

Substance	Relative molecular mass	Permeability of capillary wall to this substance
water	18	1.00
sodium ions	23	0.96
urea	60	0.8
glucose	180	0.6
haemoglobin	68 000	0.1
albumin	69 000	0.000 01

Table 5.3 Relative permeability to different substances of capillaries in a muscle. The permeability to water is given a value of 1; the other values are given relative to this.

SAQ

9 Use the information in Table 5.3 to answer these questions.

   a How does the permeability to a substance of the capillary walls appear to depend on the relative molecular mass of that substance?

   b In a respiring muscle, would you expect the net diffusion of glucose to be from the blood plasma to the muscle cells, or vice versa? Explain your answer.

   c Albumin is the most abundant plasma protein. Suggest why it is important that capillary walls should be almost impermeable to albumin.

   Answer

The amount of fluid which leaves the capillaries and forms tissue fluid is the result of two opposing pressures. Particularly at the arterial end of a capillary bed, the blood pressure inside a capillary is enough to push fluid out into the tissue. However, we have seen that water moves by osmosis from regions of low solute concentration (high water potential) to regions of high solute concentration (low water potential). Since tissue fluid lacks the high concentrations of proteins that are present in blood plasma, the imbalance leads to a water potential gradient, encouraging the movement of water back into the capillaries from the tissue fluid. The net result of these competing processes is that fluid tends to flow *out* of the capillaries into the tissue fluid at the arterial end of a capillary bed, and *into* the capillaries at the venous end. Overall, however, more fluid flows out than flows back in, so there is a net loss of fluid as blood passes through a capillary bed.

Tissue fluid is the immediate environment of each individual body cell. It is through tissue fluid that exchanges of materials between cells and the blood occur. Within our bodies, many processes take place to maintain the composition of tissue fluid at a constant level, to provide an optimum environment in which cells can work.

Lymph

About 90% of the fluid that leaks from capillaries eventually seeps back into them. The remaining 10% is collected up and returned to the blood system through a series of tubes called **lymph vessels** or **lymphatics**. These are tiny, blind-ending vessels, which are found in almost all tissues of the body. The end of one of these vessels is shown in Figure 5.22.

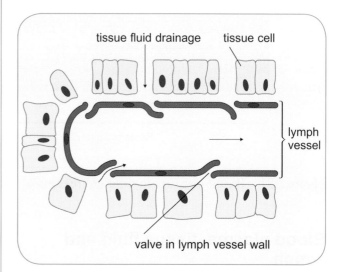

Figure 5.22 Drainage of tissue fluid into a lymph vessel.

Tissue fluid can flow into the lymphatics through tiny valves, which allow it to flow in but not out. These valves are wide enough to allow large protein molecules to pass through. This is very important, as such molecules are too big to get into blood capillaries, and so cannot be taken away by the blood. If your lymphatics did not take away the protein in the tissue fluid between your cells, you could die within 24 hours. If the rate of loss of fluid from blood plasma into the tissue fluid is not the same as the rate of removal of tissue fluid as lymph, then there can be a build-up of tissue fluid, called **oedema**.

SAQ

10 We have seen that capillary walls are not very permeable to plasma proteins. Suggest where the protein in tissue fluid has come from.

   Answer

The fluid inside lymphatics is called **lymph**. It is virtually identical to tissue fluid.

In some tissues, the lymph is rather different than in other tissues. For example, the tissue fluid and lymph in the liver have particularly high concentrations of protein. High concentrations of lipid are found in the lymph in the walls of the small intestine, where lipids are absorbed from digested food.

Lymphatics join up to form larger lymph vessels, which gradually transport lymph back up to the large veins which run just beneath the collarbone, the **subclavian veins** (Figure 5.23). Lymph is moved through lymphatics in the same way as blood in veins – there are valves to prevent backflow, and the contraction of surrounding muscles provides pressure. Lymph flow is very slow, and only about 100 cm^3 per hour flows through the largest lymph vessel, the thoracic duct, in a resting human. This is a big contrast with blood flow, which moves at about 80 cm^3 per second.

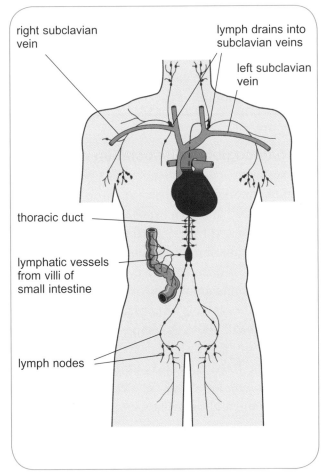

right subclavian vein

lymph drains into subclavian veins

left subclavian vein

thoracic duct

lymphatic vessels from villi of small intestine

lymph nodes

Figure 5.23   The human lymphatic system.

Blood

You have about 5 dm^3 of blood in your body, with a mass of about 5 kg. Suspended in the blood plasma, you have around 2.5×10^{13} red blood cells, 5×10^{11} white blood cells and 6×10^{12} platelets (Figure 5.24). In this chapter, we will look at the structure and functions of red blood cells, also known as **erythrocytes**.

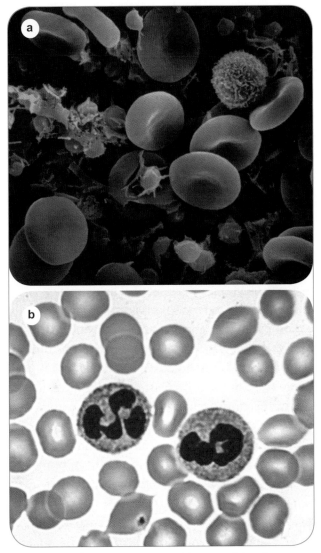

Figure 5.24   Micrographs of human blood. **a** This is a false-colour scanning electron micrograph. Red blood cells are coloured red. The purple sphere is a white blood cell. Platelets are coloured yellow ($\times 900$). **b** This photograph is taken with a normal light microscope. This blood has been stained so that the nuclei of the white cells are dark purple ($\times 850$).

The structure of erythrocytes

Erythrocytes are small cells, with no nucleus (Figure 5.25). Their red colour is caused by the red pigment **haemoglobin**, Hb, a globular protein (Chapter 7). The main function of erythrocytes is to transport oxygen, and also carbon dioxide, between the lungs and respiring tissues.

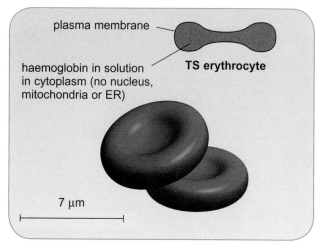

plasma membrane

TS erythrocyte

haemoglobin in solution in cytoplasm (no nucleus, mitochondria or ER)

7 μm

Figure 5.25 Erythrocytes.

Erythrocyte structure is unusual in three ways.

- Erythrocytes are very small. The diameter of a human red blood cell is about 7 μm, compared with the diameter of an 'average' liver cell of 40 μm. This small size means that all haemoglobin molecules within the cell are close to the cell's plasma membrane, and can therefore exchange oxygen easily with the fluid outside the cell. It also means that capillaries can be only 8 μm wide and still allow erythrocytes to squeeze through them, bringing oxygen as close as possible to the cells that require it.
- Erythrocytes are shaped like a biconcave disc. The 'dent' in each side of the cell, like its small size, increases its surface area : volume ratio. This means that oxygen can diffuse rapidly into and out of the cell.
- Erythrocytes have no nucleus, no mitochondria and no endoplasmic reticulum. This leaves more room for haemoglobin.

The role of haemoglobin

Oxygen is transported around the body in combination with haemoglobin. Each haemoglobin molecule can combine with eight oxygen atoms, forming **oxyhaemoglobin**. Haemoglobin combines with oxygen when oxygen is at a high concentration, and releases it in areas where it is at a low concentration. This means that it picks up oxygen at the lungs, and releases it in tissues.

SAQ

11 Which of these functions could be carried out in a red blood cell? Explain each answer.
   a protein synthesis
   b cell division
   c lipid synthesis

   Answer

12 In a healthy adult human, there are about 150 g of haemoglobin in each dm^3 of blood.
   a 1 g of haemoglobin can combine with 1.3 cm^3 of oxygen at body temperature. How much oxygen can be carried in 1 dm^3 of blood?
   b At body temperature, 0.025 cm^3 of oxygen can dissolve in 1 cm^3 of water. Assuming that blood plasma is mostly water, how much oxygen could be carried in 1 dm^3 of blood if we had no haemoglobin?

   Answer

The haemoglobin dissociation curve

To investigate how haemoglobin behaves in different conditions, samples are extracted from the blood and then exposed to different concentrations, known as **partial pressures**, of oxygen. The amount of oxygen that combines with each sample of haemoglobin is then measured.

The maximum amount of oxygen with which a haemoglobin sample can possibly combine is given a value of 100%. A sample of haemoglobin that has combined with this maximum amount is said to be 100% saturated. At lower oxygen concentrations, less oxygen combines with the haemoglobin, and so it is less saturated. We can plot the percentage saturation of haemoglobin against the different partial pressures of oxygen. This gives us a curve known as a **dissociation curve** (Figure 5.26).

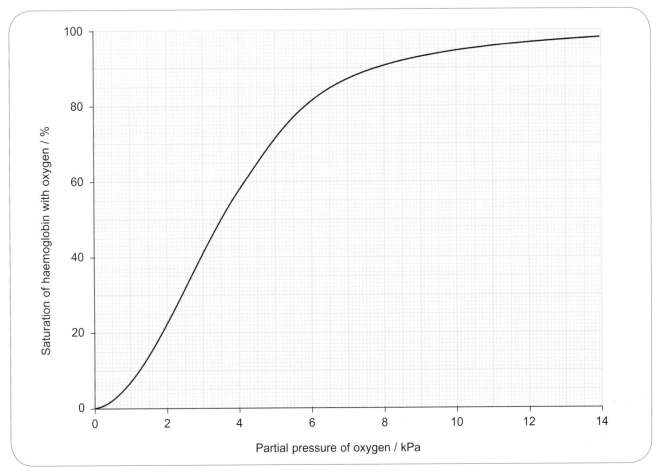

Figure 5.26 The haemoglobin dissociation curve.

You can see that, in general, the greater the partial pressure of oxygen, the greater the percentage saturation of the haemoglobin. This is what we would expect. The more oxygen there is, the more is taken up by the haemoglobin.

Think about the haemoglobin inside an erythrocyte in a capillary in the lungs. Here, where the partial pressure of oxygen is high, the haemoglobin will be 95–97% saturated with oxygen. In an actively respiring muscle, however, where the partial pressure of oxygen is much lower, the haemoglobin will be only about 20–25% saturated with oxygen. This means that the haemoglobin coming from the lungs loses a lot of its oxygen when it arrives at a muscle. The released oxygen diffuses out of the red blood cell and into the muscle, where it can be used in respiration.

Extension

SAQ

13 Use the dissociation curve in Figure 5.26 to answer these questions.
   a i The partial pressure of oxygen in the alveoli of the lungs is about 12 kPa. What is the percentage saturation of haemoglobin in the lungs?
   ii If 1 g of fully saturated haemoglobin is combined with 1.3 cm^3 of oxygen, how much oxygen will 1 g of haemoglobin in the capillaries in the lungs be combined with?
   b i The partial pressure of oxygen in an actively respiring muscle is about 2 kPa. What is the percentage saturation of haemoglobin in the capillaries in this muscle?
   ii How much oxygen will 1 g of haemoglobin in the capillaries of this muscle be combined with?

Answer

Carbon dioxide transport

Carbon dioxide is constantly produced in respiring tissues, and is transported in the blood to the lungs, where it is excreted.

The carbon dioxide from the tissues diffuses into the blood plasma. Then, one of three things can happen to it (Figure 5.27).

● Some of it remains as carbon dioxide molecules, dissolved in the plasma. About 5% of the total carbon dioxide carried in the blood is in this form.

● Some of the carbon dioxide diffuses into the erythrocytes. In the cytoplasm of the erythrocytes, there is an enzyme called **carbonic anhydrase**. This enzyme catalyses the following reaction:

$$CO_2 + H_2O \xrightarrow{\text{carbonic anhydrase}} H_2CO_3$$

carbon   water   carbonic
dioxide   acid

The carbonic acid then **dissociates** (splits):

$$H_2CO_3 \longrightarrow H^+ + HCO_3^-$$

carbonic   hydrogen   hydrogencarbonate
acid   ion   ion

The hydrogen ions quickly combine with the haemoglobin molecules inside the erythrocyte. This forms **haemoglobinic acid**, which makes the haemoglobin release the oxygen that it is carrying. The hydrogencarbonate ions diffuse out of the erythrocyte and into the blood plasma. They remain here in solution, and are carried to the lungs. About 85% of carbon dioxide is transported like this.

● Some of the carbon dioxide that diffuses into the erythrocytes escapes the attentions of carbonic anhydrase. Instead, it combines directly with haemoglobin, forming a compound called **carbaminohaemoglobin**. About 10% of the carbon dioxide is transported in this form.

When blood reaches the lungs, all of these reactions go into reverse. Carbon dioxide diffuses out of the blood and into the air in the alveoli. This leaves the haemoglobin molecules free to combine with oxygen, ready to begin another circuit of the body.

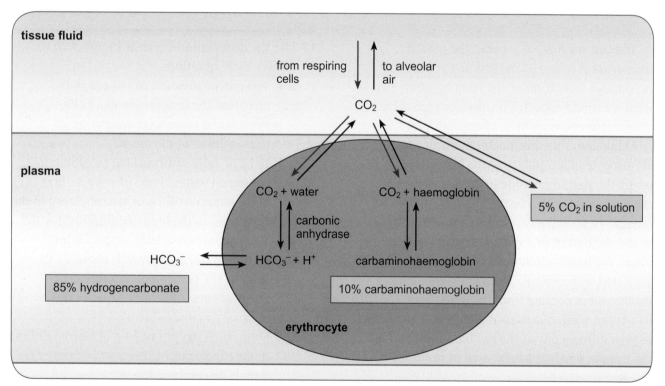

Figure 5.27 Carbon dioxide transport in the blood. The blood carries carbon dioxide partly as undissociated carbon dioxide in solution in the plasma, partly as hydrogencarbonate ions in solution in the plasma and partly combined with haemoglobin in the erythrocytes.

The Bohr shift

We have seen that, when there is a lot of carbon dioxide around, the high concentration of carbon dioxide causes events in the erythrocyte that make the haemoglobin release some of its oxygen. This is called the **Bohr effect**, after Christian Bohr who discovered it in 1904. It is exactly what the body needs. High concentrations of carbon dioxide are found in respiring tissues, which need oxygen. These high carbon dioxide concentrations cause haemoglobin to release its oxygen even more readily than it would otherwise do.

If a dissociation curve is drawn for haemoglobin at high concentrations of carbon dioxide, the curve lies to the right of and below the 'standard' curve (Figure 5.28). We can say that a high carbon dioxide concentration lowers the affinity of haemoglobin for oxygen.

Fetal haemoglobin

A developing fetus obtains its oxygen not from its own lungs, but from its mother's blood. In the placenta, the mother's blood is brought very close to that of the fetus, allowing diffusion of various substances from the mother to the fetus and vice versa.

Oxygen arrives at the placenta in combination with haemoglobin, inside the mother's erythrocytes. The partial pressure of oxygen in the blood vessels in the placenta is relatively low, because the fetus is respiring. The mother's haemoglobin therefore releases some of its oxygen, which diffuses from her blood into the fetus's blood.

The partial pressure of oxygen in the fetus's blood is only a little lower than that in its mother's blood, which should mean that the diffusion of oxygen from mother to fetus is very slow. However, the haemoglobin of the fetus is not the same as its mother's. Fetal haemoglobin combines more readily with oxygen than adult haemoglobin does. Fetal haemoglobin is said to have a higher affinity for oxygen than adult haemoglobin.

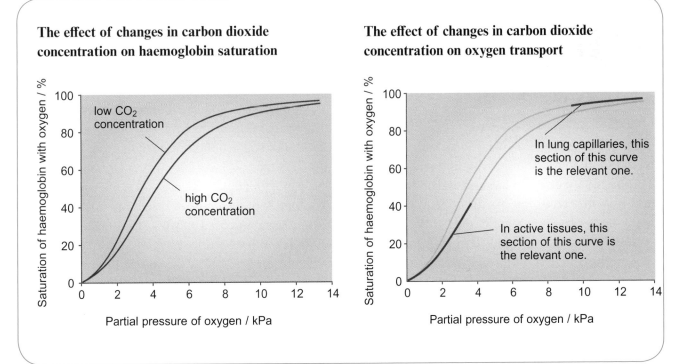

Figure 5.28 Dissociation curves for haemoglobin at two different partial pressures of carbon dioxide; the shift of the curve to the right when the haemoglobin is exposed to higher carbon dioxide concentration is called the Bohr effect.

A dissociation curve for fetal haemoglobin (Figure 5.29) shows that, at any partial pressure of oxygen, fetal haemoglobin is more saturated than adult haemoglobin. The curve lies *above* and to the left of the curve for adult haemoglobin. So, at any particular partial pressure of oxygen, fetal haemoglobin will take oxygen from adult haemoglobin.

Extension

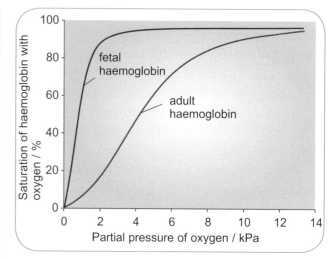

Figure 5.29 Dissociation curves for adult and fetal haemoglobin.

Blood doping

At the 1984 Olympic Games, held in Los Angeles, American cyclists won medals for the first time in 72 years. More surprisingly, no fewer than four of them won medals. It emerged that they had used a technique called 'blood doping' to enhance their performance.

Over the next few years many athletes used blood doping. Several months before competition, 1 dm³ of blood was taken from the athlete and then frozen. As the athlete continued in his or her training, their blood volume would gradually return to normal. Then, a few hours before the competition, the red cells were thawed and transfused back into their body.

Blood doping was done because it raised the quantity of haemoglobin in the athlete's blood. This meant that the blood could carry more oxygen, so the muscles were able to carry out aerobic respiration more quickly. This especially helped athletes taking part in endurance sports, such as cycling and cross-country skiing.

By 1998, more sophisticated ways of achieving the same effect were being used. These involved a hormone called erythropoetin, or EPO for short. This hormone is produced by the kidneys and increases the rate of production of red blood cells. Some cyclists who took part in the Tour de France in 1998 had injected this hormone.

The use of blood doping is now officially banned. This is because it is seen as being unfair, and also because it can be very dangerous. Blood doping increases the risk of clots developing in blood vessels, and it is thought that several European cyclists died from this between 1987 and 1990. But still people continued to do it. In March 2002, at the Salt Lake City winter Olympics, a cleaner found discarded blood transfusion equipment at the house in which the Austrian skiing team had been staying. Investigations found that three of the skiers had received blood transfusions just before the competition.

Blood doping is very difficult to detect. However, tests are now available that can distinguish between the EPO that is naturally produced in the body and the EPO which can be bought and injected. Another test which is very useful is to measure the haemoglobin concentration in the blood. If this is well above normal, then blood doping is suspected.

Summary

Glossary

- Large, multicellular, active organisms need transport systems to deliver oxygen, glucose and other substances to cells, and to remove their waste products, because their surface area : volume ratio is too low for direct diffusion.

- Mammals have a double circulatory system, in which blood is returned to the heart after passing the gas exchange surface. In the heart, its pressure is increased before moving through the systemic system. Fish have a single circulatory system, in which blood travels directly around the body after passing the gills.

- Vertebrates have a closed circulatory system, where blood is always within vessels. Insects have an open system, where blood fills the body cavity.

- The human heart has two atria and two ventricles. Blood enters the heart by the atria and leaves from the ventricles. A septum separates the right side (containing deoxygenated blood) from the left side (containing oxygenated blood). The ventricles have thicker walls than the atria, and the left ventricle has a thicker wall than the right. This is related to the pressure the muscles in the walls need to produce when they contract.

- Semilunar valves in the veins and in the entrances to the aorta and pulmonary artery, and atrio-ventricular valves, prevent backflow of blood.

- The heart is made of cardiac muscle, which is myogenic. The sino-atrial node (SAN) sets the pace for the contraction of muscle in the heart. Excitation waves spread from the SAN across the atria, causing their walls to contract. The AVN slows down the spread to the ventricles. The Purkyne fibres conduct the wave to the base of the ventricles, so these contract after the atria and from the bottom up. One complete cycle of contraction and relaxation is called the cardiac cycle.

- An electrocardiogram (ECG) shows the electrical activity of the heart.

- Arteries have thicker, more elastic walls than veins, to allow them to withstand the high pressure of pulsing blood. Veins have thinner walls and valves, to aid the flow of blood at low pressure back to the heart. Capillaries have leaky walls, only one cell thick, which allow rapid transfer of substances between tissues and the blood.

- Plasma leaks from capillaries to form tissue fluid. This is collected into lymphatics and returned to the blood at the subclavian veins.

- Erythrocytes carry oxygen in the form of oxyhaemoglobin. Haemoglobin combines with oxygen at high partial pressures of oxygen, and releases it when the partial pressure is low. When carbon dioxide is present, the affinity of haemoglobin for oxygen is lowered, and the dissociation curve lies to the right of and below the normal curve. This is called the Bohr shift.

- Carbon dioxide is carried in the blood as carbon dioxide molecules in solution in the plasma, as HCO_3^- ions in solution in the plasma, and as carbaminohaemoglobin in the erythrocytes. Carbonic anhydrase in the erythrocytes is responsible for the formation of the HCO_3^- ions.

- Fetal haemoglobin has a higher affinity for oxygen than adult haemoglobin, and its dissociation curve lies to the left of and above the curve for adult haemoglobin. This allows effective transfer of oxygen from mother to fetus across the placenta.

Questions

1 Figure 1 and Figure 2 are diagrams to show how the internal structure of the heart and its associated circulatory system in a simplified form. Figure 1 represents the system for a mammal and Figure 2 that for a frog (an amphibian).

Both systems are described as closed systems. The mammalian system is also described as a complete double circulation but the frog as a partial double circulation.

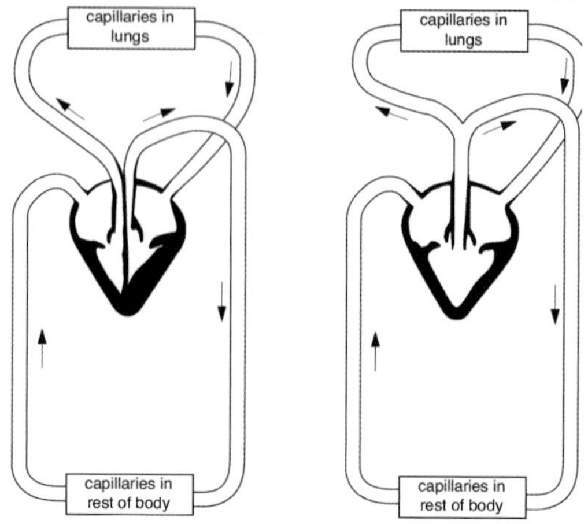

Figure 1   **Figure 2**

   a State what is meant by a closed system. [1]

   b Use the information in the two figures above to suggest why the mammalian system is called a <u>complete</u> double circulation whilst that of the frog is called a <u>partial</u> double circulation. [3]

   c Suggest why the system shown for the frog may be less effective at supplying the body tissues with oxygen. [2]

OCR Biology AS (2803) June 2006 [Total 6]

Hint

Answer

2 The table contains information about various components of the mammalian circulatory system.

	Blood in aorta	**Tissue fluid**	**Lymph**	**Blood in vena cava**
red blood cells	many		none	many
white blood cells		some	some	many
glucose concentration	high	high		high
pressure	high	low	low	

   a i Copy the table, and complete each of the empty boxes with the most appropriate word. [4]

      ii Explain the differences recorded in the table for glucose and pressure. [4]

   b The blood also contains hydrogencarbonate ions (HCO_3^-). Describe how these ions are formed in the blood. [3]

OCR Biology AS (2803) June 2006 [Total 11]

Hint

Answer

Chapter 6

Transport in plants

Background

e-Learning

Objectives

Plant transport systems

Plant cells, like animal cells, need a regular supply of oxygen and nutrients. All plants are multicellular, and some of them are very large, so the problem of surface area:volume ratio applies to them just as it does to animals (Chapter 5). Most plants, however, have a much more branching shape than animals, and this provides a much larger surface area:volume ratio for exchange with their environment than in an animal of the same body mass.

The requirements of plants differ from those of animals in several ways, both in the nature of the nutrients and gases required and the rate at which these need to be supplied.

- **Carbon dioxide**: Photosynthesising plant cells need a supply of carbon dioxide during daylight. They obtain this from the air. Aquatic plants get carbon dioxide from the water that surrounds them.
- **Oxygen**: All living plant cells need oxygen for respiration. Cells that are actively photosynthesising produce more than enough oxygen for their needs. Cells that are not photosynthesising have to take in oxygen from their environment, but they do not respire at such a high rate as mammals and so they do not need such a rapid oxygen supply.
- **Organic nutrients**: Some plant cells make many of their own organic food materials, such as glucose, by photosynthesis. However, many plant cells do not photosynthesise and need to be supplied with organic nutrients from photosynthetic or storage cells.
- **Inorganic ions and water**: All plant cells require a range of inorganic ions and also water. These are taken up from the soil, by roots, and are transported to all areas of the plant.

The energy requirements of plant cells are, on average, far lower than those of cells in a mammal. This means that their rate of respiration and, therefore, their requirement for oxygen and glucose are considerably less than those of mammals. Plants can therefore manage with a much slower transport system.

One of the main requirements of the photosynthetic regions of a plant is sunlight. Plants have evolved thin, flat leaves which present a large surface area to the Sun. This also makes it easy for oxygen and carbon dioxide to diffuse into and out of the leaves, reaching and leaving every cell quickly enough so that there is no need for a transport system to carry gases.

As a result of these differences between the structures and requirements of a plant and a mammal, it is not surprising that they have evolved different transport systems. In fact, plants have *two* transport systems, one for carrying mainly water and inorganic ions from the roots to the parts above ground, and one for carrying substances made by photosynthesis from the leaves to other areas. In neither of these systems do fluids move as rapidly as blood does in a mammal, nor is there an obvious pump. Neither plant transport system carries oxygen or carbon dioxide, which travel to and from cells and the environment by diffusion alone.

SAQ

1 Explain why plants do not need a transport system to distribute oxygen or carbon dioxide.

Hint

Answer

Water transport in plants

Figure 6.1 outlines the pathway taken by water as it is transported through a plant. Water from the soil enters a plant through its root hairs and then moves across the root into the xylem tissue in the centre. It then moves upwards in the xylem vessels through the root into the stem and finally into the leaves.

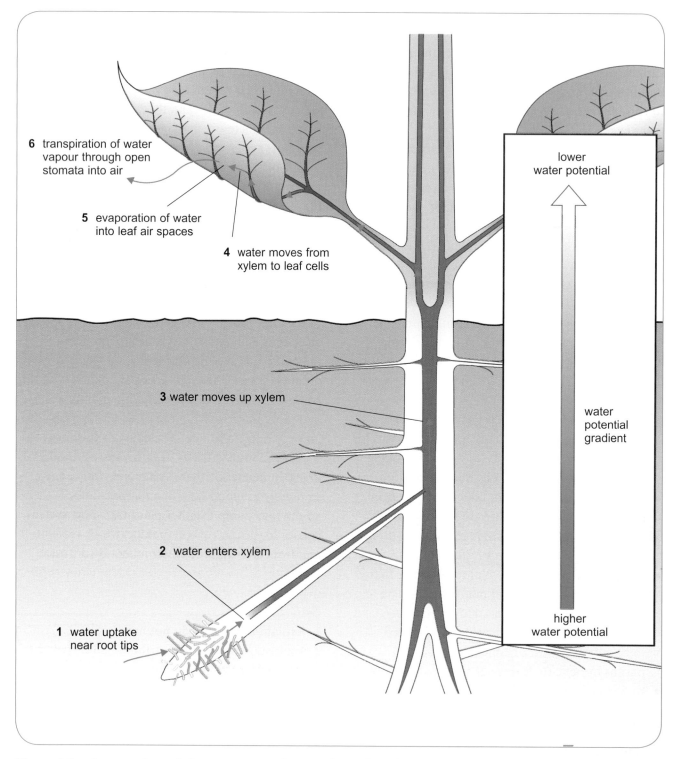

6 transpiration of water vapour through open stomata into air

5 evaporation of water into leaf air spaces

4 water moves from xylem to leaf cells

3 water moves up xylem

2 water enters xylem

1 water uptake near root tips

lower water potential

water potential gradient

higher water potential

Figure 6.1 An overview of the movement of water through a plant; water moves down a water potential gradient from the soil to the air.

James Cameron Gifford Library - Issue Receipt

JCG01(right)

Customer name: Tosheva, Bogomila

Title: Biology 1 for OCR / Mary Jones.
ID: 1005840358
Due: 17/01/2018 23:59

Total items: 1
15/11/2017 16:58

All items must be returned before the due date and time.
The Loan period may be shortened if the item is requested.

www.nottingham.ac.uk/library

From soil into root hair

The roots of plants have very thin, single-celled extensions of some of the cells that make up the outer layer (epidermis) of the root. They are called **root hairs**, and they are a specialised exchange surface for the uptake of water and mineral ions.

Each root hair is only about 200–250 μm across, but this is large enough for them to be visible with the naked eye (Figure 6.2). There may be thousands of them on each tiny branch of a root, so together they provide an enormous surface area that is in contact with the soil surrounding the root.

Soil is made up of particles of minerals and humus. Between the soil particles there are air spaces. Unless the soil is very dry, there is a thin layer of water covering each soil particle. The root hairs make contact with this water, and absorb it by osmosis. The water moves into the root hair because there is a lower concentration of solutes in the soil than there is inside the root hair cell. The water potential outside the root hair is therefore higher than the water potential inside, so water moves passively down the water potential gradient into the cells (Figure 6.3).

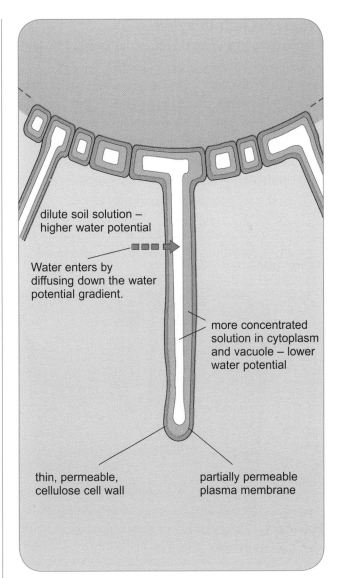

Figure 6.3 Water uptake by a root hair cell.

Water can also enter the root without going into a cell at all. It can seep into the cell walls of the root hair cells, and then move through these and other cell walls all the way into the centre of the root.

SAQ

2 The root hairs of a plant and the alveoli of the lungs are exchange surfaces.
Describe the features that they have in common.

(Answer)

(Extension)

Figure 6.2 A root of a young radish showing the root hairs.

From root hair to xylem

Figure 6.4 and Figure 6.5 show the internal structure of a young root. Water that has been taken up by the root hairs travels across the **cortex** and into the centre of the root. It does this because the water potential inside the xylem vessels is lower than the water potential in the root hairs and the cells in between. Water moves passively down this water potential gradient, from the root hairs at the edge of the root to the xylem in the centre.

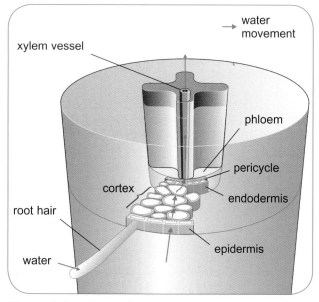

Figure 6.4 The pathway of water movement from root hair to xylem.

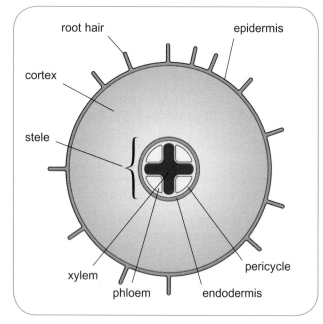

Figure 6.5 Transverse section of a young root to show the distribution of tissues.

The water takes two different routes through the cortex. The cells of the cortex, like all plant cells, are surrounded by cell walls made of many layers of cellulose fibres criss-crossing each other. Water soaks into these walls rather as it would soak into filter paper, and then seeps across the root from cell wall to cell wall, and through the spaces between the cells, without ever entering a cell. This route is called the **apoplast pathway** (Figure 6.6a).

Some water, however, enters the cells and moves from cell to cell by osmosis, or through strands of cytoplasm that make direct connections between adjacent cells, called **plasmodesmata** (Figure 6.6b). This is called the **symplast pathway**.

The relative importance of these two pathways depends on the species of plant and the environmental conditions.

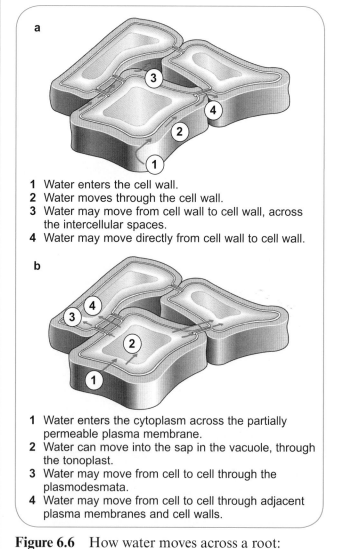

a

1 Water enters the cell wall.
2 Water moves through the cell wall.
3 Water may move from cell wall to cell wall, across the intercellular spaces.
4 Water may move directly from cell wall to cell wall.

b

1 Water enters the cytoplasm across the partially permeable plasma membrane.
2 Water can move into the sap in the vacuole, through the tonoplast.
3 Water may move from cell to cell through the plasmodesmata.
4 Water may move from cell to cell through adjacent plasma membranes and cell walls.

Figure 6.6 How water moves across a root: **a** the apoplast pathway; **b** the symplast pathway.

When the water reaches the **stele** (Figure 6.5), the apoplast pathway is barred. The cells in the outer layer of the stele, called the **endodermis**, have a thick, waterproof, waxy substance called **suberin** in their walls (Figure 6.7). This band of suberin, called the **Casparian strip**, forms an impenetrable barrier to water in the walls of the endodermis cells. The only way for the water to cross the endodermis is through the cytoplasm of these cells. This arrangement gives the plant control over what ions pass into its xylem vessels, as everything has to cross a plasma membrane on the way in.

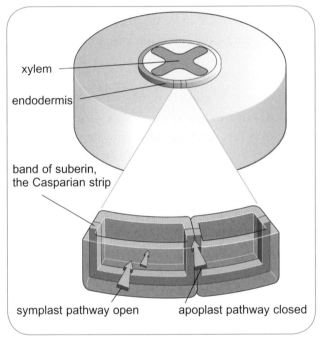

Figure 6.7   The Casparian strip.

Up through the xylem vessels

Water is carried from the roots all the way up to the top of the plant inside **xylem vessels**. In a large tree, the distance from the roots to the topmost leaf could be tens of metres. Yet there is no pump making the water move. What force causes water to travel up a plant?

To answer this question, we need to understand what is happening to the water in the leaves, because this is what drives the process. It is also important to know something about the structure of the xylem vessels, as this too helps to keep the water moving.

We have already looked briefly at the structure of xylem vessels, in Chapter 3. Xylem vessels are made up of many long, narrow cells called **xylem elements** stacked end to end. Xylem elements began as living cells, with cytoplasm, nucleus and cellulose cell walls. However, they then differentiated into extremely specialised structures – and died. Xylem elements contain no living material, and are just the empty shells of the cells from which they developed.

Figure 6.8 and Figure 6.9 show the structure of xylem vessels. Each xylem element has a wall made of cellulose and a substance called **lignin**. Lignin is a very strong, waterproof material. It is important not only in keeping water inside the xylem vessels, but also in helping to support the plant. The wood of tree trunks and branches is made of xylem vessels.

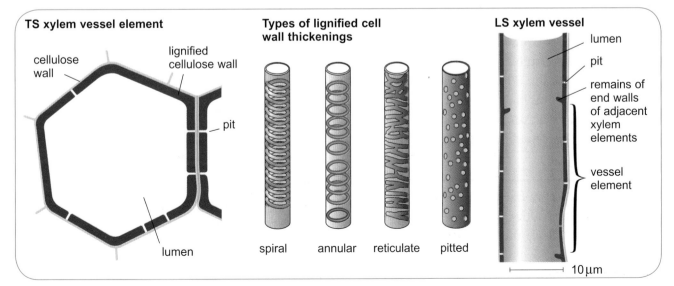

Figure 6.8   The structure of xylem vessels.

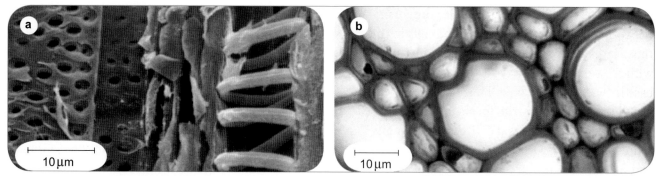

Figure 6.9 **a** Scanning electron micrograph of a longitudinal section through part of a buttercup stem, showing xylem vessels. The young vessel on the right has a spiral band of lignin around it, while those on the left are older and have more extensive coverings of lignin with many pits.

b Light micrograph of a transverse section of xylem vessels. They have been stained so that the lignin appears red. The xylem vessels are the large empty cells. You can also see smaller parenchyma cells between them; these do not have lignified walls, and each contains a nucleus and cytoplasm.

The end walls of the xylem elements usually disappear completely, so that the stack of elements makes up a continuous tube, like a drainpipe, reaching all the way from the roots, through the stem (Figure 6.10) and up to the very top of the plant. There are usually several xylem vessels side by side. Water can move sideways between them, and out of the xylem vessel into the surrounding cells, though **pits** in their walls. These are small gaps where no lignin has been deposited, leaving just the cellulose cell wall, through which water can easily move.

You can think of xylem vessels as being like a group of drinking straws. To pull water up a straw, you put your mouth over the top and suck. 'Sucking' means reducing the pressure. Because you have reduced the pressure at the top of the straw, there is a pressure gradient from the bottom of the straw to the top. The liquid moves down this pressure gradient, from the relatively high pressure at the bottom to the relatively low pressure at the top.

The liquid moves up the straw, and up through

xylem vessels, by **mass flow**. Mass flow is the way that water moves in a river, or up a drinking straw, or out of a tap. A whole body of water flows along together. This is very different from diffusion or osmosis, which rely on the random movements of individual molecules.

The column of water in the xylem vessels holds together because individual water molecules are attracted to each other. This attraction is called **cohesion**, and you will find out why it exists in Chapter 7. The water molecules are also attracted to the sides of the xylem vessels, and this is known as **adhesion**. This gives them a tendency to 'crawl' up the inner surface of the vessel. Cohesion and adhesion help the whole column of water to flow up the xylem vessel without breaking. Xylem

SAQ

3 Use the scale bar in Figure 6.9b to calculate the width of the lumen (space) inside the xylem vessels that are shown in transverse section.

Hint

Answer

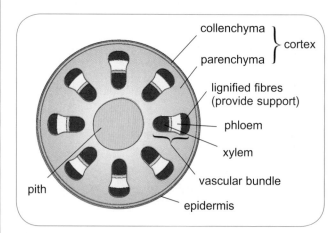

Figure 6.10 Transverse section through a young stem to show the distribution of tissues.

vessels are very narrow – usually somewhere between 0.01 mm and 0.2 mm in diameter – and this means that more of the water is in contact with the sides of the vessel than would be the case if the vessels were wider. Adhesive forces are therefore relatively high. So, to move water up xylem vessels, there needs to be a pressure gradient. Something must lower the pressure at the top. The process that does this is **transpiration**.

From leaf to atmosphere – transpiration

Figure 6.11 shows the structure of a leaf. The cells in the **spongy mesophyll** layers are not tightly packed, and there are many spaces around them filled with air. The water in the cells seeps into the walls, so these cell walls are always wet. Some of this water evaporates into the air spaces, so that the air inside a leaf is usually saturated with water vapour.

These air spaces are in direct contact with the air outside the leaf, through small pores called **stomata**. If the air outside the leaf contains less water vapour than inside it, then there is a water potential gradient from the air spaces inside the leaf to the outside. Water vapour therefore diffuses out through the stomata. This is called transpiration (Figure 6.12).

As water evaporates from the cell walls of the mesophyll cells, water moves into them to replace

it. This water comes from the xylem vessels in the leaf. This removal of water from the top of the xylem vessels reduces its pressure. The water pressure at the top of the xylem vessel is therefore less than the water pressure at the bottom, so water flows up the vessel – just like water up a drinking straw. Cohesion between the water molecules keeps them moving together without the column breaking, all the way up to the top of even the tallest trees.

The continuous movement of water from the roots, up through the xylem, into the leaves and then out into the atmosphere is known as the **transpiration stream**. The plant does not have to provide any energy at all to make it happen. The driving force is supplied by the difference in water potential between the air and the soil. The water moves down a water potential gradient.

SAQ

4 Explain how each of these features adapts xylem vessels for their function of transporting water from roots to leaves.
 a total lack of cell contents
 b no end walls in individual xylem elements
 c a diameter of between 0.01 mm and 0.2 mm
 d lignified walls
 e pits

> Answer

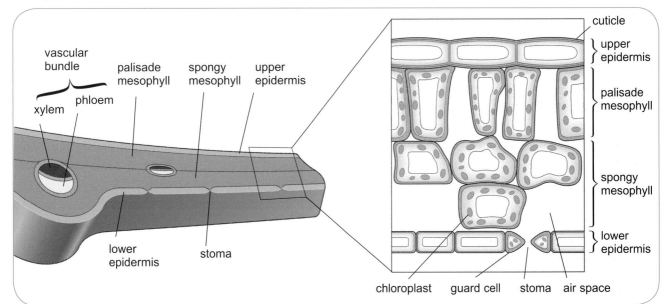

Figure 6.11 The structure of a leaf; water enters the leaf as liquid water in the xylem vessels, and diffuses out as water vapour through the stomata.

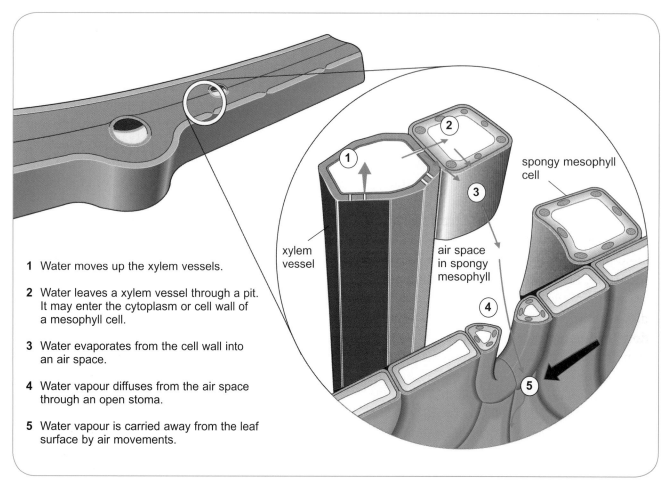

1 Water moves up the xylem vessels.

2 Water leaves a xylem vessel through a pit. It may enter the cytoplasm or cell wall of a mesophyll cell.

3 Water evaporates from the cell wall into an air space.

4 Water vapour diffuses from the air space through an open stoma.

5 Water vapour is carried away from the leaf surface by air movements.

Figure 6.12 Water movement through a leaf.

Factors affecting transpiration

Anything that increases the water potential gradient between the air spaces in the leaf and the air outside, or that speeds up the movement of the water molecules, will increase the rate of transpiration.

- **Humidity**: Humidity is a measure of how much water vapour is held in the air. In conditions of low humidity – that is, when the air is dry – there is a steep water potential gradient between the leaf and the air. Transpiration rates are therefore greater in low humidity than in high humidity.

- **Temperature**: An increase in temperature causes an increase in the kinetic energy of water molecules. This increases the rate of evaporation of water from the cell walls into the air spaces, and also the rate of diffusion of the water vapour out of the leaf. An increase in temperature therefore increases the rate of transpiration.

- **Light intensity**: Light does not normally have any direct effect on the rate of transpiration during the daytime. However, many plants close their stomata at night, when it is dark and they are unable to photosynthesise and so do not need to use carbon dioxide from the air. In especially dry conditions, the plant may close its stomata even when light levels are ideal for photosynthesis, to avoid losing too much water from its leaves. There is often a compromise to be reached between allowing in enough carbon dioxide for photosynthesis, and not letting out too much water vapour.

In hot conditions, the evaporation of water from the plant's leaves can have a very useful cooling effect, in a similar manner to the evaporation of sweat from your skin.

Extension

Transpiration and climate

Most of us are aware that cutting down rainforests reduces photosynthesis, increasing the amount of carbon dioxide in the air and contributing to global warming. But fewer people realise how transpiration can affect climate.

Aerial photographs, historical records and data and computer models from NASA have been used to look at the effects of changes in land cover on climate in the USA. In the mid-west, the natural vegetation was grassland, but as this has been replaced by agricultural land, the average temperature in those regions has dropped by almost 1 °C. This is because grass does not transpire as much as crops. The extra transpiration from the crop plants increases the humidity of the air and has a cooling effect.

In contrast, when forest is removed to grow crops, as has happened on the east coast of the USA, the reverse effect is seen. Forest trees transpire much more than most crop plants, and so the air above the farmland often contains less water vapour than the air above a forest. As forest has been replaced by farmland, the climate in these regions has become warmer.

There have also been effects on local rainfall – slightly more rainfall where there are forests, compared to areas where forest has been replaced by crops. But these are much less marked than the temperature changes.

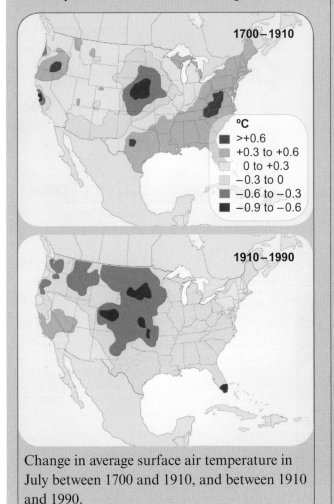

Change in average surface air temperature in July between 1700 and 1910, and between 1910 and 1990.

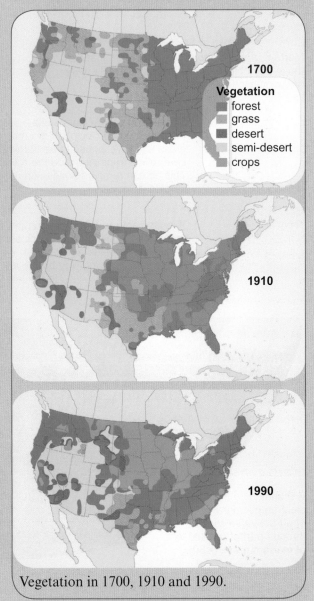

Vegetation in 1700, 1910 and 1990.

Xerophytes

A **xerophyte** is a plant that is adapted to live in dry conditions. Plants that live in hot deserts are xerophytes, but some very cold places can also be dry. Moreover, plants cannot absorb water from the soil when the water is frozen.

Xerophytes generally have adaptations that help them to obtain more water, and other adaptations that help them to reduce the rate at which they lose water vapour from their leaves.

Figure 6.13 and Figure 6.14 shows some examples of xerophytes and their adaptations.

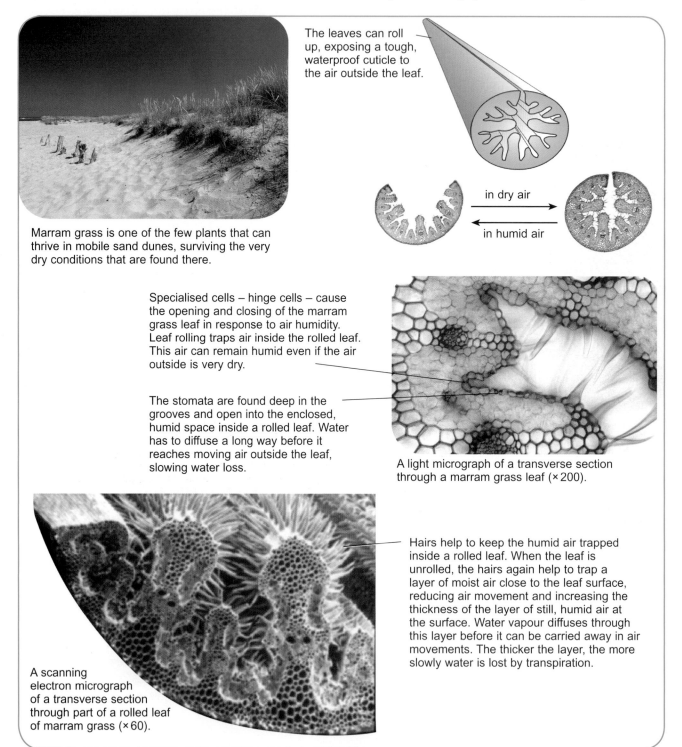

The leaves can roll up, exposing a tough, waterproof cuticle to the air outside the leaf.

in dry air

in humid air

Marram grass is one of the few plants that can thrive in mobile sand dunes, surviving the very dry conditions that are found there.

Specialised cells – hinge cells – cause the opening and closing of the marram grass leaf in response to air humidity. Leaf rolling traps air inside the rolled leaf. This air can remain humid even if the air outside is very dry.

The stomata are found deep in the grooves and open into the enclosed, humid space inside a rolled leaf. Water has to diffuse a long way before it reaches moving air outside the leaf, slowing water loss.

A light micrograph of a transverse section through a marram grass leaf (×200).

Hairs help to keep the humid air trapped inside a rolled leaf. When the leaf is unrolled, the hairs again help to trap a layer of moist air close to the leaf surface, reducing air movement and increasing the thickness of the layer of still, humid air at the surface. Water vapour diffuses through this layer before it can be carried away in air movements. The thicker the layer, the more slowly water is lost by transpiration.

A scanning electron micrograph of a transverse section through part of a rolled leaf of marram grass (×60).

Figure 6.13 The adaptations of marram grass, *Ammophila arenaria*, for dry conditions.

Opuntia is a cactus with flattened, photosynthetic stems that store water. The leaves are reduced to spines, which reduces the surface area from which transpiration can take place and protects the plant from being eaten by animals.

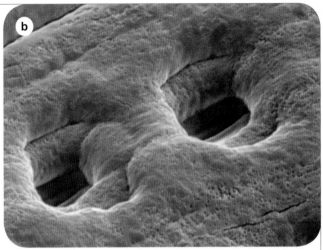

False-colour SEM of a needle from a Sitka spruce (×1500), a large tree from Canada and Alaska. Its leaves are in the form of needles, greatly reducing the surface area available for water loss. Its leaves are covered in a layer of waterproof wax and have sunken stomata, as shown here.

TS SEM of *Phlomis italica* leaf showing its 'trichomes' (×20). These are tiny hair-like structures that act as a physical barrier to the loss of water, like the marram grass hairs. Phlomis is a small shrub that lives in dry habitats in the Mediterranean regions of Europe and North Africa.

The cardon, *Euphorbia canariensis*, grows in dry areas of Tenerife. It has swollen, succulent stems that store water and photosynthesise. The stems are coated with wax, which cuts down water loss. The leaves are extremely small.

Figure 6.14 Some adaptations shown by xerophytes.

Hint

SAQ

5 Use the information in Figure 6.13 and Figure 6.14, and any other information you can find, to construct a table describing and explaining features of xerophytes. You could use a table like the one below. Try to find at least six different features.

Feature	How it helps the plant to conserve water

Answer

Comparing rates of transpiration

It is not easy to measure the rate at which water vapour is leaving a plant's leaves. This makes it very difficult to investigate directly how different factors, such as temperature or wind speed, affect the rate of transpiration. However, it *is* relatively easy to measure the rate at which a plant stem takes up water. A very high proportion of the water taken up by a stem is lost in transpiration. As the rate at which transpiration is happening directly affects the rate of water uptake, this measurement can give a very good approximation of the rate of transpiration.

The apparatus used for this is called a **potometer** (Figure 6.15). It is essential that everything in the potometer is completely watertight and airtight, so that no leakage of water occurs and so that no air bubbles break the continuous water column. To achieve this, it helps if you can insert the plant stem into the apparatus with everything submerged in water, so that air bubbles cannot enter the xylem when you cut the stem. It also helps to cut the end of the stem with a slanting cut, as air bubbles are less likely to get trapped against it.

Potometers can be simpler than the one in Figure 6.15. You can manage without the reservoir (though this does mean it takes more time and effort to refill the potometer) and the tubing can be straight rather than bent. In other words, you can manage with just a straight piece of glass tubing.

As water evaporates from the leaves, more water is drawn into the xylem vessels that are exposed at the cut end of the stem. Water is drawn along the capillary tubing. If you record the position of the meniscus at set time intervals, you can plot a graph of distance moved against time. If you expose the plant to different conditions, you can compare the rate of water uptake.

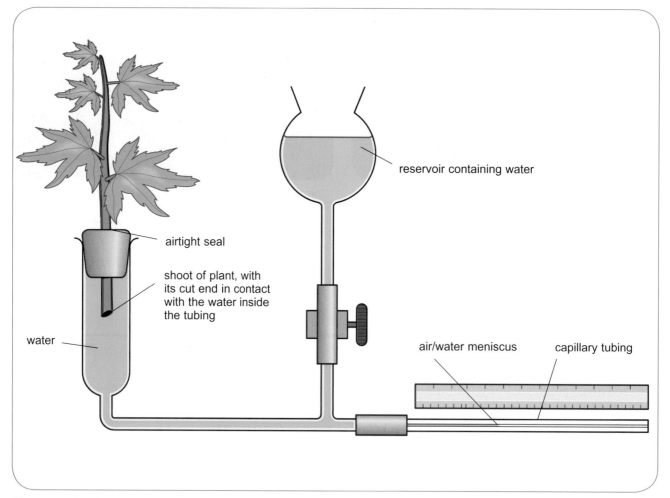

reservoir containing water

airtight seal

shoot of plant, with its cut end in contact with the water inside the tubing

water

air/water meniscus

capillary tubing

Figure 6.15   A potometer.

Translocation

Translocation is the term used to describe the transport of soluble organic substances within a plant. These are substances that the plant itself has made – such as sugars, which are made by photosynthesis in the leaves. These substances are sometimes called **assimilates**. The main substance transported in phloem is sucrose.

Assimilates are transported in **sieve elements**. Sieve elements are found in **phloem tissue**, together with several other types of cells including **companion cells**. Sieve elements and companion cells work closely together to achieve translocation.

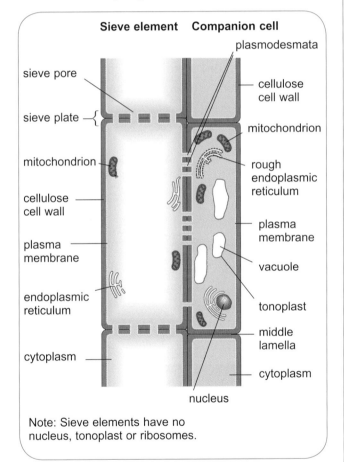

Figure 6.16 A phloem sieve element and its companion cell.

Extension

Sieve elements

Figure 6.16 shows the structure of a sieve tube and its accompanying companion cell. A sieve tube is made up of many elongated sieve elements, joined end to end vertically to form a continuous column. Each sieve element is a living cell. They are very narrow, often between 10 and 15 µm in diameter. Like a 'normal' plant cell, a sieve element has a cellulose cell wall, a plasma membrane and cytoplasm containing endoplasmic reticulum and mitochondria. However, the amount of cytoplasm is very small and only forms a thin layer lining the inside of the wall of the cell. There is no nucleus, nor are there any ribosomes.

Perhaps the most striking feature of sieve elements is their end walls. Where the end walls of two sieve elements meet, a **sieve plate** is formed. This is made up of the walls of both elements, perforated by large pores. These pores are easily visible with a good light microscope. When sieve plates are viewed using an electron microscope, strands of fibrous protein can sometimes be seen passing through these pores from one sieve element to another (Figure 6.17). However, these strands are produced by the sieve element in response to the damage caused when the tissue is cut during preparation of the specimen for viewing. In living phloem, the protein strands are not present, and so the pores are open and present little barrier to the free flow of liquid through them.

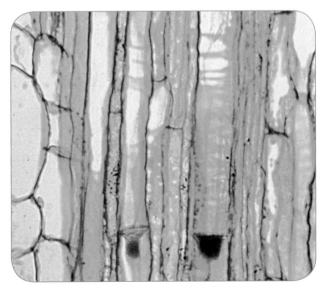

Figure 6.17 Photomicrograph showing phloem sieve elements (×600).

Companion cells

Each sieve element has at least one companion cell lying close beside it. Companion cells have the structure of a 'normal' plant cell, with a cellulose cell wall, a plasma membrane, cytoplasm, a vacuole and a nucleus. However, the number of mitochondria and ribosomes is rather larger than usual, and the cells are metabolically very active. Also, the vacuole remains small and does not form a large central vacuole.

Companion cells are very closely associated with the neighbouring sieve elements. Many plasmodesmata (strands of cytoplasm) pass through their cell walls, providing a direct pathway between the cytoplasm of the companion cell and the cytoplasm of the sieve element.

The contents of sieve tubes

The liquid inside phloem sieve tubes is called **phloem sap**, or just sap. Table 6.1 shows the composition of the sap of the castor oil plant, *Ricinus communis*.

Solute	Concentration in $mol\,dm^{-3}$
sucrose	250
potassium ions, K^+	80
amino acids	40
chloride ions, Cl^-	15
phosphate ions, PO_4^{3-}	10
magnesium ions, Mg^{2+}	5
sodium ions, Na^+	2
nitrate ions, NO_3^-	0
plant growth substances (e.g. auxin)	small traces

Table 6.1 Composition of sap in *Ricinus communis*.

SAQ

6 Which of the substances in Table 6.1 are synthesised by the plant?

Answer

It is not easy to collect enough phloem sap to analyse its contents. When phloem tissue is cut, the sieve elements respond by rapidly blocking the sieve pores. The pores are blocked first by plugs of phloem protein, and then, within hours, by a carbohydrate called **callose**. However, castor oil plants are unusual in that their phloem sap does continue to flow for a while, making it relatively easy to collect.

Aphids are a good way of collecting sap. Aphids, such as greenfly, feed by inserting their tubular mouthparts, called stylets, into the phloem of plant stems and leaves (Figure 6.18). Phloem sap flows through the stylet into the aphid. If the stylet is cut near the aphid's head, the sap continues to flow. It seems that the small diameter of the stylet does not allow sap to flow out rapidly enough to switch on the plant's phloem 'clotting' mechanism.

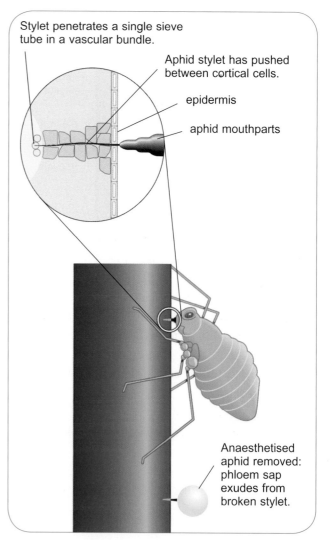

Stylet penetrates a single sieve tube in a vascular bundle.

Aphid stylet has pushed between cortical cells.

epidermis

aphid mouthparts

Anaesthetised aphid removed: phloem sap exudes from broken stylet.

Figure 6.18 Using an aphid to collect phloem sap.

How translocation occurs

Phloem sap, like the contents of xylem vessels, moves by mass flow. However, whereas in xylem vessels differences in pressure are produced by a water potential gradient between soil and air, requiring no energy input from the plant, this is not so in phloem transport. To create the pressure differences needed for mass flow in phloem, the plant has to use its own energy. Phloem transport is therefore an *active* process, in contrast to the *passive* transport in xylem.

The pressure difference is produced by **active loading** of sucrose into the sieve elements at the place from which sucrose is to be transported. This is typically in a photosynthesising leaf. As sucrose is loaded into the sieve element, this decreases the water potential in the sap inside it. Therefore, water follows the sucrose into the sieve element, moving down a water potential gradient by osmosis.

At another point along the sieve tube, sucrose may be removed by other cells. Root cells, for example, may use sucrose delivered by phloem. Sucrose will often be at a relatively low concentration in these cells, because they are using it up. So sucrose simply diffuses out of the phloem and into the root cell, and water follows by osmosis.

So, in the leaf, water moves into the sieve tube. In the root, it moves out of it. This creates a pressure difference, with the pressure at the 'leaf' end of the phloem sieve tube being greater than that at the 'root' end. The pressure difference causes the liquid inside the tube to flow from the high pressure area to the lower one, by mass flow.

Any area of a plant from which sucrose is loaded into the phloem is called a **source**. An area that takes sucrose out of the phloem is called a **sink** (Figure 6.19).

Sinks can be anywhere in the plant, both above and below the photosynthesising leaves. So sap flows both upwards and downwards. This contrasts with the situation in xylem, where flow is always upwards. Within any one phloem sieve tube, however, the flow is all in one direction.

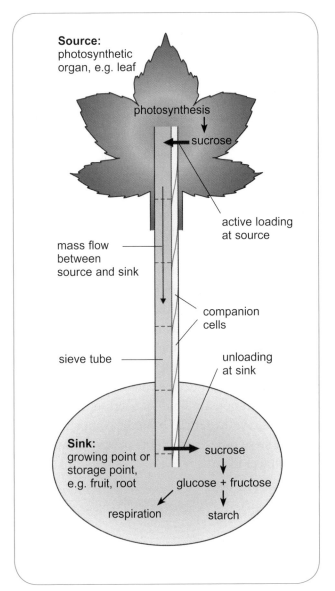

Figure 6.19   Sources, sinks and mass flow in phloem.

SAQ

7 Which of the following are sources, and which are sinks?

  a a nectary in a flower

  b a developing fruit

  c the storage tissue of a potato tuber when the potato is just starting to sprout

  d a growing potato tuber

Loading sucrose into phloem

In leaf mesophyll cells, photosynthesis produces sugars. Some of these are converted into sucrose, which can be transported in the phloem to other parts of the plant.

Sucrose is soluble, so it dissolves in the water in the cell. It can move out of a mesophyll cell and across the leaf, by either the apoplast or symplast pathway.

Sucrose is loaded into companion cells by active transport (Figure 6.20). This is done in a rather roundabout way. First, hydrogen ions are pumped out of the cell by active transport, using ATP as the energy source. This creates a large excess of hydrogen ions outside the cell. They can move back into the cell down their concentration gradient, through a protein that acts as a carrier for both hydrogen ions and sucrose at the same time. The sucrose molecules are carried through this co-transporter into the companion cell, against the concentration gradient for sucrose. The sucrose molecules can then move from the companion cell into the sieve tube, through the plasmodesmata that connect them.

Unloading sucrose from phloem

Unloading occurs in any tissue that requires sucrose. It is likely that the sucrose moves out of the phloem and into the tissue by facilitated diffusion. Once in the tissue, the sucrose is converted into something else by enzymes. This decreases its concentration and therefore maintains a concentration gradient from the phloem into the tissue. One such enzyme is invertase, which converts sucrose to glucose and fructose.

SAQ

8 Draw a table and use it to compare the structure of xylem vessels and phloem sieve tubes. You could include cell structure (walls, diameter, cell contents and so on), substances transported and methods of transport.

Answer

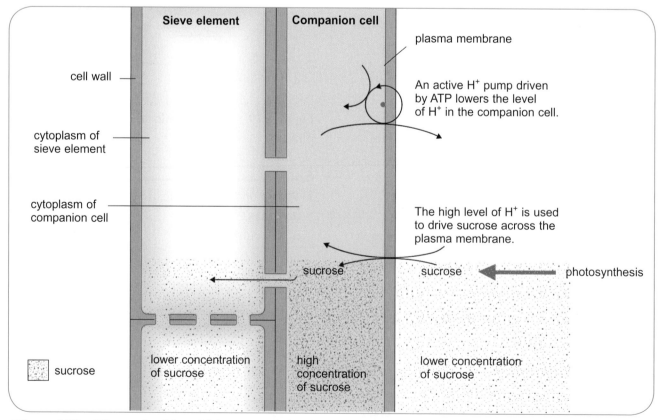

Figure 6.20 The method by which sucrose is loaded into phloem.

Evidence for the mechanism of phloem transport

Until the late 1970s and 1980s, there was considerable argument about whether or not phloem sap did or did not move by mass flow, in the way we have described. The stumbling block was the presence of the sieve pores and phloem protein, as it was felt that these must have some important role. Several hypotheses were put forward, which tried to provide a role for the phloem protein. It is now known that the phloem protein is not present in living, active phloem tissue, and so there is no need to provide it with a role when explaining the mechanism of phloem transport.

There is now a lot of evidence that phloem transport does occur by mass flow. The rate of transport in phloem is about 10000 times faster than it would be if substances were moving by diffusion rather than by mass flow. The actual rates of transport measured match closely with those calculated from measured pressure differences at source and sink, assuming that the pores in the sieve plates are open and unobstructed.

Experimental work has investigated the sucrose–hydrogen co-transporter in plant cells, and it is understood how this works. There is also plenty of circumstantial evidence that this takes place, for example:

- phloem sap always has a relatively high pH, often around 8; this is what you would expect if hydrogen ions are being actively transported *out* of the neighbouring companion cell
- there is a difference in electrical potential across the plasma membrane of companion cells, which is more negative inside than outside; this could be caused by the greater concentration of positively charged hydrogen ions outside the cell than inside.

Summary

Glossary

- Plants are large, but have branching shapes, which increase the surface area:volume ratio. They have a relatively low metabolic rate compared to animals, and so can use diffusion to supply oxygen and carbon dioxide to their cells.

- Water is transported through a plant in xylem vessels. The water moves passively, down a water potential gradient from the soil to the air.

- Water moves into the root hairs by osmosis, and crosses the root cortex by the apoplast pathway (between the cells) or the symplast pathway (through the cells).

- The Casparian strip bars the apoplast pathway when the water arrives at the endodermis, so water has to pass through the cytoplasm of the endodermal cells and then into the xylem vessels.

- Xylem vessels are stacks of dead, empty xylem elements. These have no end walls, and their side walls are impregnated with lignin. Adhesion of water molecules to their walls and cohesion of water molecules to each other help the water column inside xylem vessels to move upwards by mass flow without breaking.

- Transpiration in the leaves provides the driving force for water movement through the plant. Water evaporates from the wet cell walls of cells inside the leaf, and then diffuses out through stomata into the air. Water moves from xylem vessels in the leaf into the leaf cells, by osmosis. This lowers the pressure at the top of the xylem so that water moves up the xylem by mass flow, down a pressure gradient.

- Transpiration is increased by high temperatures and high wind speeds, and is decreased by high humidity. A potometer can be used to compare rates of transpiration.

continued

- Xerophytes are plants that are adapted to live in dry conditions. They have structures and mechanisms that help them to obtain as much water as possible, to store water and to limit the loss of water from their leaves.

- Substances that the plant has made, such as sucrose, are transported in phloem tubes. These are made up of sieve elements, which are living cells with perforated end walls. Sieve elements have no nucleus.

- Companion cells are closely associated with phloem sieve elements. Some of them actively load sucrose into a phloem sieve element, which reduces its water potential. Water therefore moves into the sieve element by osmosis. At the other end of the phloem tube, sucrose is removed by cells that are using it. This makes the pressure at the one end of the tube less than that at the other, so the liquid inside the tube flows from the high pressure area to the low pressure area by mass flow.

- A place where sucrose is loaded into the phloem is called a source. A place where sucrose is removed from it is called a sink.

Questions

1 The diagram shows the results of an investigation to compare rates of transpiration and water absorption by a plant during a hot day in summer. There was no shortage of soil water available to the plant throughout the investigation, which was carried out over 24 hours starting at midnight.

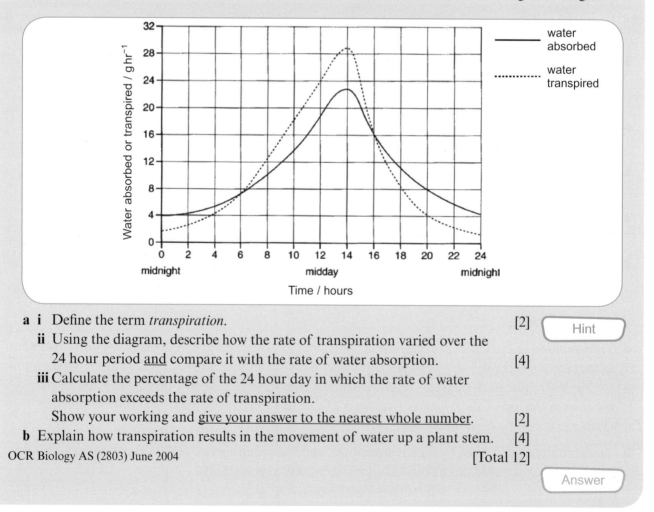

    a i Define the term *transpiration*. [2]

      ii Using the diagram, describe how the rate of transpiration varied over the 24 hour period **and** compare it with the rate of water absorption. [4]

     iii Calculate the percentage of the 24 hour day in which the rate of water absorption exceeds the rate of transpiration.
        Show your working and give your answer to the nearest whole number. [2]

    b Explain how transpiration results in the movement of water up a plant stem. [4]

OCR Biology AS (2803) June 2004   [Total 12]

Hint

Answer

Chapter 7

Biological molecules

Objectives

The human body is made of many different types of molecules. Most of your body is water, which has small molecules made of two atoms of hydrogen combined with one atom of water, formula H_2O. The other main types of molecules in organisms are proteins, carbohydrates, fats and nucleic acids. These molecules make up your structure, and they also undergo chemical reactions – known as **metabolic reactions** – that make things happen in and around your cells.

Up until the mid 1950s, we did not know very much about the structures of these molecules or how their structures might relate to the ways in which they behave. Since then, there has been an explosion of knowledge and understanding, and today a major industry has been built on the many applications to which we can put this knowledge. Biotechnology makes use of molecules and reactions in living organisms, and research continues to find new information about how molecules behave, and new uses for this technology in fields including medicine, agriculture, mining and food production.

In this chapter, we will look at the structures of the main types of molecules found in our bodies – and in those of every other living organism (Table 7.1). We will also see how these structures relate to the functions of the molecules.

water	60
protein	19
fat	15
carbohydrate	4
other	2

Table 7.1   Body composition (percentage of total mass).

Water

Water is by far the most abundant molecule in our bodies. It is also one of the smallest and one of the simplest. Yet water is an amazing substance, with a collection of properties that are shared by no other. It is difficult to imagine how life of any kind could exist without water. The search for other life in the universe begins by searching for other planets that may have liquid water on them.

The structure of a water molecule

Figure 7.1 shows the structure of a water molecule. It is made up of two hydrogen atoms covalently bonded to one oxygen atom. The bonds are very strong, and it is very difficult to split the hydrogen and oxygen atoms apart.

A covalent bond is an electron-sharing bond, and in this case the sharing is not equal. The oxygen atom gets slightly more than its fair share, and this gives it a very small negative charge. This is written δ^- (delta minus). The hydrogen atoms have a very small positive charge, δ^+ (delta plus).

These tiny charges mean that water molecules are attracted to each other – the positively charged hydrogen atoms on one molecule are attracted to the negatively charged oxygen atoms on other molecules. The attraction is called a **hydrogen bond**.

In solid water – ice – the hydrogen bonds hold the water molecules in a rigid lattice formation. As in all solids, the molecules vibrate, but they do not move around. In liquid water, the molecules have more kinetic energy, moving around past each other, forming fleeting hydrogen bonds with each other. In water vapour, the molecules are far apart, scarcely interacting with each other at all.

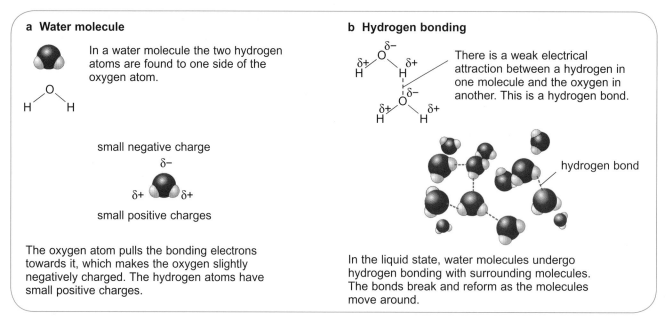

a Water molecule

In a water molecule the two hydrogen atoms are found to one side of the oxygen atom.

small negative charge
δ−

δ+   δ+

small positive charges

The oxygen atom pulls the bonding electrons towards it, which makes the oxygen slightly negatively charged. The hydrogen atoms have small positive charges.

b Hydrogen bonding

There is a weak electrical attraction between a hydrogen in one molecule and the oxygen in another. This is a hydrogen bond.

hydrogen bond

In the liquid state, water molecules undergo hydrogen bonding with surrounding molecules. The bonds break and reform as the molecules move around.

Figure 7.1   **a** The structure of a water molecule; **b** hydrogen bonding.

Water, heat and temperature

If you heat water, the temperature of the water rises. Temperature relates to the amount of kinetic energy that the water molecules have. As heat energy is added to the water, a lot of the energy is used to break the hydrogen bonds between the water molecules. Because so much heat energy is used for this, there is less heat energy available to raise the temperature. Water therefore requires a lot of heating in order to increase its temperature by very much. We say that it has a high **specific heat capacity**.

You make good use of this property. Being largely water, your body does not change its temperature quickly. Large changes in the temperature of your external environment have relatively small effects on the temperature of your body. This is true for all living organisms.

For organisms that live in water, it means that the temperature of their external environment is relatively stable. It takes a lot of heat in order to change the temperature in, say, a lake or the sea.

The energy needed to break the hydrogen bonds between water molecules also affects water's boiling point. Other substances with molecules of a similar size and construction – such as hydrogen sulfide, H_2S – form gases at room temperature. There are no hydrogen bonds holding the hydrogen sulfide molecules together, so they are free to fly off into the air. However, because of the hydrogen bonds, water at room temperature is liquid. It has to be heated to 100°C before the molecules have enough energy to break apart from one another so that the water turns from a liquid to a gas. If water was not a liquid at the temperatures found on Earth, then life as we know it would not exist here.

Once again, our bodies make good use of this property of water. A great deal of heat energy is needed to make water change into a gas. When liquid sweat lies on the surface of the skin, the water in the sweat absorbs heat energy from the body as it evaporates (Figure 7.2). The heat needed to do this is called **latent heat** of evaporation. It is our major cooling mechanism. It also helps to cool plant leaves in hot climates, as water evaporates from the surfaces of the mesophyll cells inside them.

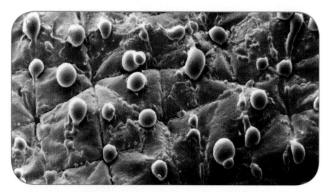

Figure 7.2   This SEM shows sweat droplets emerging from pores on human skin (×25).

Solvent properties

Water is an excellent solvent. The tiny charges on its molecules attract other molecules or ions that have charges on them (Figure 7.3). The molecules and ions spread around in between the water molecules. This is called **dissolving**.

When an ionic compound such as sodium chloride dissolves in water, the sodium ions and the chloride ions become separated from each other. This makes it easy for them to react with other ions or molecules. Many reactions, including most metabolic reactions, will only take place in solution.

Water can flow, and therefore it can carry dissolved substances from one place to another. This happens in our blood, and in the xylem vessels and phloem sieve tubes of a plant. Urea, the main nitrogenous excretory product of mammals, is removed from the body dissolved in water in the form of urine.

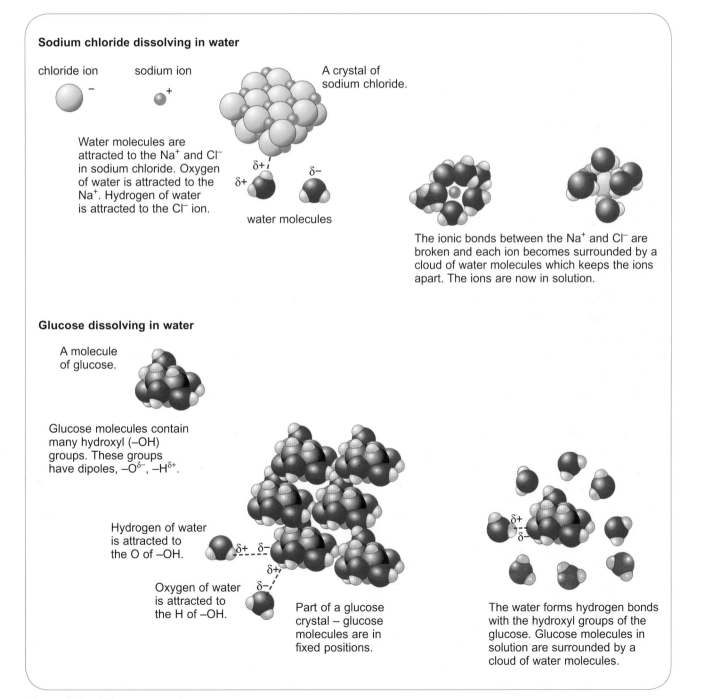

Sodium chloride dissolving in water

chloride ion

sodium ion

A crystal of sodium chloride.

Water molecules are attracted to the Na⁺ and Cl⁻ in sodium chloride. Oxygen of water is attracted to the Na⁺. Hydrogen of water is attracted to the Cl⁻ ion.

water molecules

The ionic bonds between the Na⁺ and Cl⁻ are broken and each ion becomes surrounded by a cloud of water molecules which keeps the ions apart. The ions are now in solution.

Glucose dissolving in water

A molecule of glucose.

Glucose molecules contain many hydroxyl (–OH) groups. These groups have dipoles, $–O^{\delta-}$, $–H^{\delta+}$.

Hydrogen of water is attracted to the O of –OH.

Oxygen of water is attracted to the H of –OH.

Part of a glucose crystal – glucose molecules are in fixed positions.

The water forms hydrogen bonds with the hydroxyl groups of the glucose. Glucose molecules in solution are surrounded by a cloud of water molecules.

Figure 7.3   Water as a solvent.

Density and viscosity

Water molecules are pulled closely together by the hydrogen bonds between them, and this makes water a relatively dense liquid. The density of pure water is $1.0\,\mathrm{g\,cm^{-3}}$. Compare this, for example, with ethanol, which has a density of only $0.79\,\mathrm{g\,cm^{-3}}$.

Most living organisms, containing a lot of water, have a density which is quite close to that of water. This makes it easy for them to swim. Aquatic organisms often have methods of slightly changing their average density – for example, by filling or emptying parts of their body with air – to help them to float or to sink.

It takes quite a lot of effort to swim through water. You have to push aside the molecules, which are attracted to one another and therefore reluctant to move apart. We say that water is a fairly viscous fluid. This is why aquatic organisms are often streamlined; their shape helps them to cut through water more easily.

Cohesion and surface tension

Water molecules tend to stick together. This is called **cohesion**. Even in a tall column of water, the forces holding the molecules to each other help to prevent the column from breaking.

Within a body of water each water molecule is attracted to others all around it. However, on the surface, the uppermost molecules only have other molecules *below* them, not above. So they are pulled downwards. These pulling forces draw them closer together than in other parts of the pond. This phenomenon is called **surface tension**. It forms a strong layer on the surface of the water – so strong that small animals are able to walk on it without difficulty (Figure 7.4).

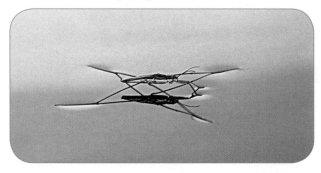

Figure 7.4 The water strider hunts by running over the surface of the water.

Proteins

Proteins are substances whose molecules are made of many **amino acids** linked together in long chains. Figure 7.5 shows the structure of an amino acid.

All amino acids have a central carbon atom. Carbon atoms have four bonds which can hold them firmly to other atoms. In an amino acid, the central carbon forms one bond with a **carboxyl group**, –COOH. There is another bond with a hydrogen atom, and a third bond with an **amino group**, $-NH_2$. The fourth bond, however, can be with any one of a whole range of different groups. The letter R is used to show this group. In animals such as humans, there are about 20 different amino acids, each with a different **R group**.

The amino acids that make up a protein are linked together during protein synthesis, which happens on the ribosomes in a cell. Here, separate amino acids are brought close to each other, and react together to form a linkage between them called a **peptide bond**. Figure 7.6 shows how this is done. Peptide bonds are very strong; they involve **covalent bonds**, in which the atoms share electrons with each other. As the peptide bond is formed, two hydrogen atoms from one amino acid and one oxygen atom from another amino acid join together to form a water molecule. Reactions where water is formed and released are called **condensation reactions**.

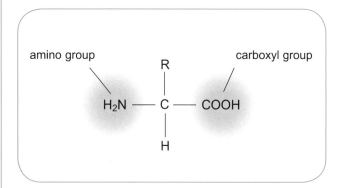

Figure 7.5 The basic structure of all amino acids.

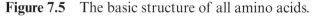

SAQ

1 Explain how cohesion helps with water transport in a plant.

Answer

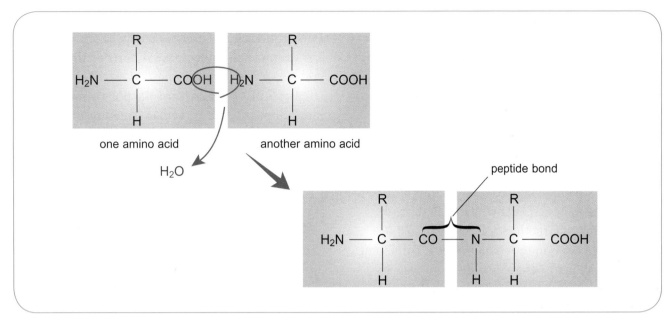

Figure 7.6 The formation of a peptide bond by a condensation reaction.

On the ribosome, a long chain of amino acids is formed, all linked together by peptide bonds. This chain is called a **polypeptide**. Protein molecules, as we shall see, contain one or more chains of polypeptides. Haemoglobin, for example, contains four polypeptides all coiled up with each other.

Polypeptides can be broken down by breaking their peptide bonds. This happens, for example, when protein molecules are digested in the stomach by protease enzymes. The reaction is called a **hydrolysis** reaction. 'Hydro' means 'water' and 'lysis' means 'breaking apart'. In this reaction, combination with a water molecule breaks the peptide bond between two amino acids and separates them (Figure 7.7).

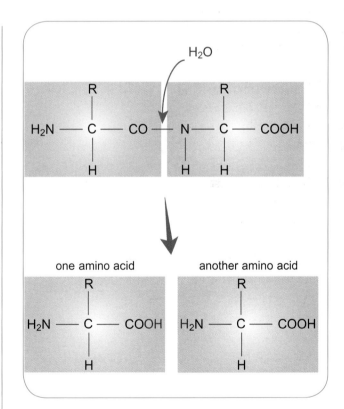

Figure 7.7 The breakage of a peptide bond by a hydrolysis reaction.

SAQ ____

2 a The simplest amino acid is glycine. Its R group is a single hydrogen atom. How many atoms are there altogether in a molecule of glycine?

b Write the molecular formula of glycine.

Answer

Primary structure

If we look at the different amino acids in polypeptide chains, and the sequence in which they are linked together, we find that, for a particular polypeptide, they are always the same. This sequence is called the **primary structure** of the molecule.

As there are approximately 20 different amino acids, which can be linked together in any order, and as a polypeptide may contain hundreds of amino acids, there is a nearly infinite number of possible primary structures. A change in just one of the amino acids in the chain makes it a different protein, which may behave in a different way. In a haemoglobin molecule, there are two different types of polypeptide chain, which have slightly different primary structures – Figure 7.8 shows the amino acid sequence of part of each chain, called α (alpha) and β (beta) chains.

Each of the 20 different amino acids has its own name – for example, valine, leucine and cysteine. Often, their names are abbreviated to three letters, such as val, leu and cys.

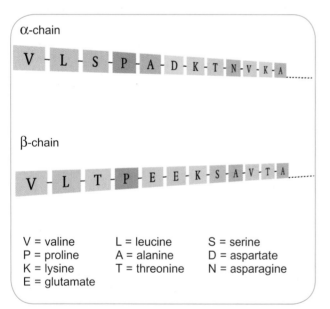

α-chain

V - L - S - P - A - D - K - T - N - V - K - A

β-chain

V - L - T - P - E - E - K - S - A - V - T - A

V = valine   L = leucine   S = serine
P = proline   A = alanine   D = aspartate
K = lysine   T = threonine   N = asparagine
E = glutamate

Figure 7.8   The first 12 amino acids of the α and β polypeptide chains in haemoglobin. The total length of the α-chain is 141 amino acids while the β-chain is 146 amino acids long.

Extension

Secondary structure

Polypeptide chains do not usually lie straight. For example, in some proteins parts of the chain coil into a regular pattern called an α-helix (Figure 7.9). Other parts of the polypeptide chain may adopt a different regular structure, called a β-fold. These regular arrangements make up the **secondary structure** of the protein.

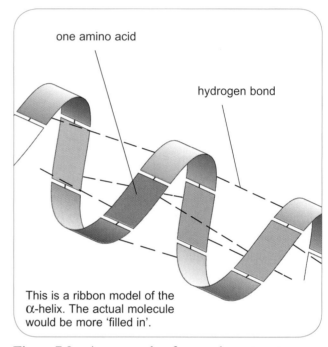

one amino acid

hydrogen bond

This is a ribbon model of the α-helix. The actual molecule would be more 'filled in'.

Figure 7.9   An example of secondary structure – an α-helix.

The shape of the α-helix or the β-fold is maintained by **hydrogen bonds** that form between different amino acids in the chain. A hydrogen bond is an attraction between an atom with a very small negative charge and another atom with a very small positive charge. In an α-helix in a polypeptide, the hydrogen bonds form between the oxygen of the –CO group of one amino acid (very small negative charge) and the hydrogen of the –NH$_2$ group (very small positive charge) of the amino acid four places ahead of it in the chain.

Hydrogen bonds are nowhere near as strong as the covalent bonds in peptide bonds, as they do not involve sharing electrons, and the charges that attract one another are relatively small. However, if there are a lot of them, as there are in a protein, then between them they can be a major force in holding together the shape of a molecule.

Tertiary structure

The chain can now fold round itself even more. The overall shape formed by this is called the **tertiary structure**. Imagine a curly cable attached to a kettle, for example. The regular coils are equivalent to the secondary structure – like an α-helix. If you then twist the coil into a particular shape, this is the equivalent of the tertiary structure of a protein. The tertiary structure is held by hydrogen bonds, and also by three other types of bonds – **disulfide bonds**, **ionic bonds** and **hydrophobic interactions**.

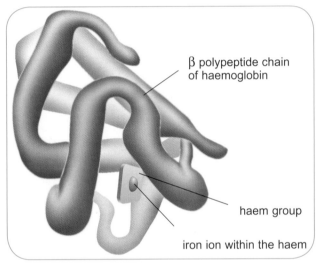

β polypeptide chain of haemoglobin

haem group

iron ion within the haem

Figure 7.10 Tertiary structure of one β polypeptide chain of haemoglobin.

Figure 7.10 shows the tertiary structure of one of the β polypeptide chains in a haemoglobin molecule. Each of the polypeptide chains winds itself around a little group of atoms with an iron ion (Fe^{2+}) at the centre. This group of atoms is called a **haem** group, and it is essential to the functioning of the haemoglobin molecule in its role as an oxygen transporter. The iron ion in each of the four haem groups in a haemoglobin molecule is able to bond with two oxygen atoms, so that one haemoglobin molecule is able to carry eight oxygen atoms in all.

In haemoglobin, the chain is curled up into a ball, forming a **globular protein** (Figure 7.10). Enzymes (Figure 7.11) are also globular proteins. In some other proteins, such as **collagen**, the shape is long and thin. Collagen is a **fibrous protein**. Figure 7.12 shows the different kinds of bonds that help to hold a polypeptide in its secondary and tertiary structures. These bonds hold each protein molecule in a very precise shape. This shape determines the function of the molecule.

The places in which the different kinds of bonds can form are determined by the amino acid sequence in the protein – its primary structure. Even a change of a single amino acid can have a big effect on the protein's tertiary structure, and therefore its ability to carry out its function.

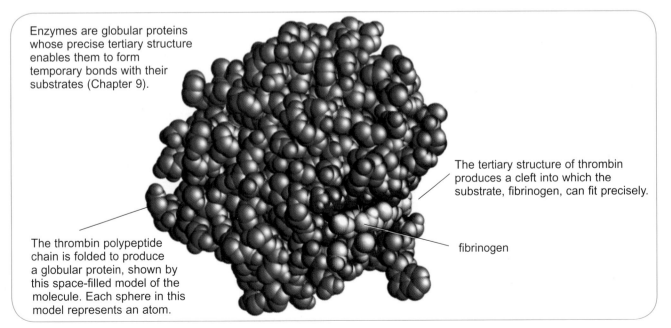

Enzymes are globular proteins whose precise tertiary structure enables them to form temporary bonds with their substrates (Chapter 9).

The tertiary structure of thrombin produces a cleft into which the substrate, fibrinogen, can fit precisely.

fibrinogen

The thrombin polypeptide chain is folded to produce a globular protein, shown by this space-filled model of the molecule. Each sphere in this model represents an atom.

Figure 7.11 The enzyme thrombin (blue) and its substrate fibrinogen (brown) attached to each other.

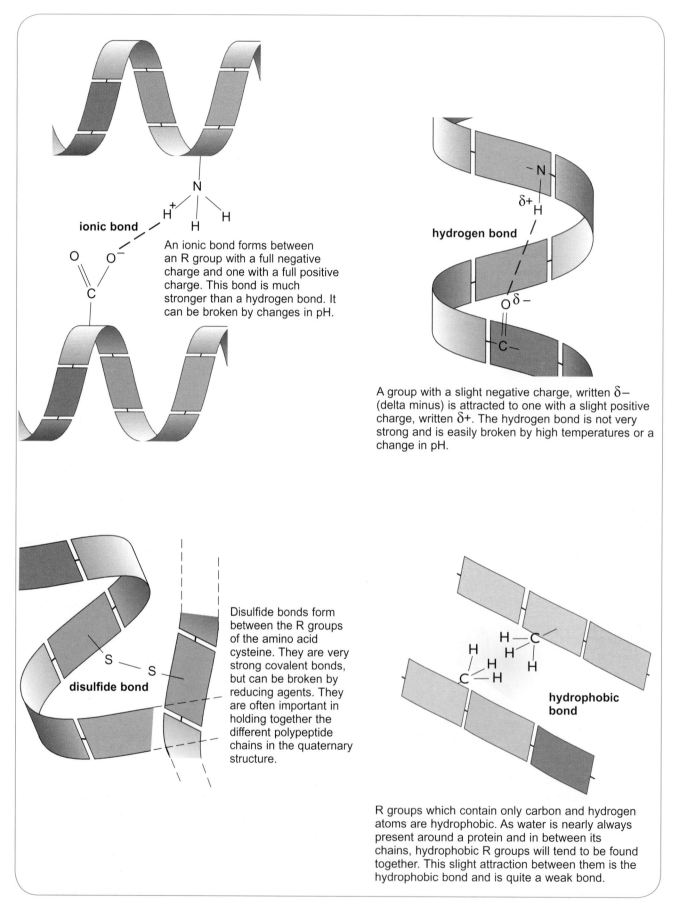

ionic bond

An ionic bond forms between an R group with a full negative charge and one with a full positive charge. This bond is much stronger than a hydrogen bond. It can be broken by changes in pH.

hydrogen bond

A group with a slight negative charge, written $\delta-$ (delta minus) is attracted to one with a slight positive charge, written $\delta+$. The hydrogen bond is not very strong and is easily broken by high temperatures or a change in pH.

disulfide bond

Disulfide bonds form between the R groups of the amino acid cysteine. They are very strong covalent bonds, but can be broken by reducing agents. They are often important in holding together the different polypeptide chains in the quaternary structure.

hydrophobic bond

R groups which contain only carbon and hydrogen atoms are hydrophobic. As water is nearly always present around a protein and in between its chains, hydrophobic R groups will tend to be found together. This slight attraction between them is the hydrophobic bond and is quite a weak bond.

Figure 7.12   Bonds that hold protein molecules in shape.

Quaternary structure

There is still one more level of complexity to come. We mentioned earlier that a haemoglobin molecule is made of four polypeptide chains. These four chains fit together to make the complete haemoglobin molecule. The shape that they produce is called the **quaternary structure** of the protein (Figure 7.13). This shape is held by the same kinds of bonds as the tertiary structure. (The name 'quaternary' doesn't refer to the four chains – it refers to the fourth level of structure. A protein made of just two cross-linked polypeptide chains still has a quaternary structure.)

Extension

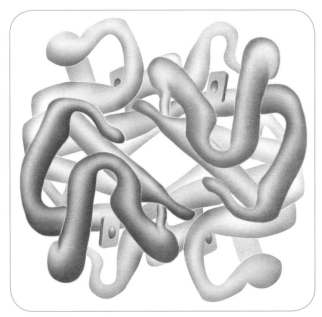

Figure 7.13 Quaternary structure of a haemoglobin molecule. The two α-chains are shown in blue, and the two β-chains in brown.

Haemoglobin, sickle cell anaemia and malaria

In many parts of sub-Saharan Africa, children are quite frequently born with an illness called sickle cell anaemia. This condition is also seen in other parts of the world, but by far the greatest number of cases is seen in parts of Africa and Asia. The disease is also seen in people whose ancestors came from those parts of the world but who now live elsewhere. It is an inherited disease.

A person with sickle cell anaemia has red blood cells that have a strong tendency to go seriously out of shape when oxygen levels in the blood are low. The cells form a sickle shape instead of their usual biconcave disc shape. They are no longer able to carry oxygen, and they get stuck in capillaries, leading to great pain and serious damage to tissues. A 'sickle cell crisis' like this can be fatal.

Sickle cell anaemia is caused by a tiny difference in the primary structure of the β polypeptide in haemoglobin. The difference is so small that it is difficult to imagine it can cause such serious harm. Just one amino acid is different. Where there should be the amino acid glutamate, there is a valine instead.

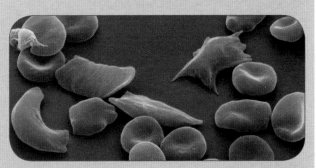

SEM showing sickled and normal red blood cells.

The position of this amino acid is on the outside of the haemoglobin molecule. Glutamate has a small charge on it, which makes it associate with water molecules and helps to make haemoglobin soluble in water. But valine has no charge. The presence of valine decreases the solubility of the haemoglobin, because valine does not interact with water. Instead, especially when oxygen concentrations are low, the valine molecules interact with each other. They stick together, and this makes the haemoglobin molecules stick together. They form fibres, pulling the red blood cell out of shape and causing a potentially fatal sickling crisis.

Collagen – a fibrous protein

We have seen that haemoglobin is a globular protein. It is soluble in water, and is found dissolved in the cytoplasm of red blood cells.

Collagen, however, is a fibrous protein. It is found in skin, tendons, cartilage, bones, teeth and the walls of blood vessels. It is an important **structural protein**, not only in humans but in almost all animals, and is found in structures ranging from the body wall of sea anemones to the egg cases of dogfish.

Figure 7.14 shows the molecular structure of collagen. It consists of three polypeptide chains, each in the shape of a helix. These three helical polypeptides wind around each other to form a 'rope'.

Almost every third amino acid in each polypeptide is glycine, the smallest amino acid. Its small size allows the three strands to lie close together and form a tight coil. Any other amino acid would be too large. The three strands are held together by hydrogen bonds.

Each complete, three-stranded molecule of collagen interacts with other collagen molecules running parallel to it. Bonds form between the R groups of lysines in molecules lying next to each other. These cross-links hold many collagen molecules side by side, forming **fibrils**. The ends of the parallel molecules are staggered – if they were not, there would be a weak spot running right across the collagen fibril. Fibrils associate to form bundles called **fibres**. Collagen has tremendous tensile strength – that is, it can resist strong pulling forces. The human Achilles tendon, which is almost all collagen fibres, can withstand a pulling force of $300\,N$ per mm^2 of cross-sectional area (Figure 7.15).

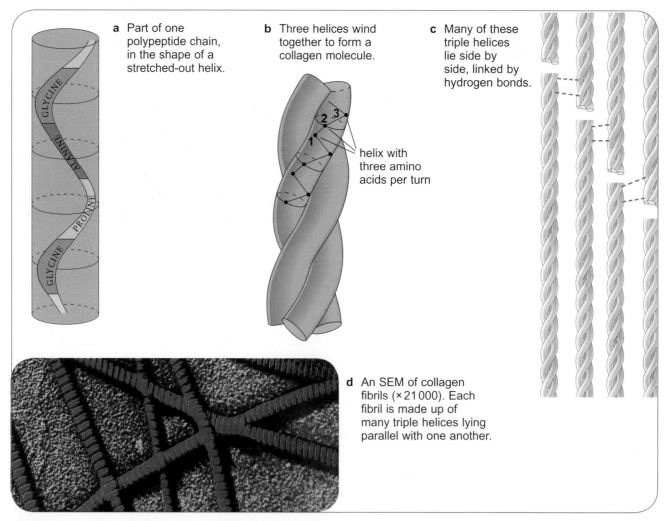

a Part of one polypeptide chain, in the shape of a stretched-out helix.

b Three helices wind together to form a collagen molecule.

helix with three amino acids per turn

c Many of these triple helices lie side by side, linked by hydrogen bonds.

d An SEM of collagen fibrils (× 21 000). Each fibril is made up of many triple helices lying parallel with one another.

Figure 7.14   The structure of collagen; the diagrams and photographs begin with the very small and work up to the not-so-small.

A comparison of globular and fibrous proteins

Table 7.2 compares the structure and properties of globular and fibrous proteins.

Many – but by no means all – globular proteins are soluble in water, and they are often metabolically active. Enzymes, for example, are globular proteins, as are antibodies and some hormones, including insulin and glucagon. Globular proteins that are insoluble in water include the transporter molecules found in cell membranes. Globular proteins must have a very precise shape, because this determines their function, and they therefore have a very precise primary structure, always being made of exactly the same sequence of amino acids making up a chain of exactly the same length. In contrast, fibrous proteins may have a rather more variable primary structure, with a limited range of different amino acids that can be joined together to form chains of varying lengths.

Fibrous proteins are not soluble in water, and they are not usually metabolically active (Figure 7.15). Most of them, like collagen, have a structural role. For example, keratin forms hair and nails, and is found in the upper layers of the skin, which it makes waterproof. The soluble globular protein fibrinogen, found in blood plasma, is converted into the insoluble fibrous protein fibrin when a blood vessel is damaged. The fibrin fibres form a network across the wound, in which platelets can be trapped to form a blood clot.

The solubility of these two types of protein depends on their structure. To be soluble in water, a molecule needs to be not too large (Figure 7.15), and also to have groups with an electrical charge on the outside of the molecule. This makes them able to interact with water molecules (page 107). Globular proteins generally have these features; when the polypeptide chains fold, they do so with R groups carrying charges on the outside of the molecule, and R groups without charges on the inside. Fibrous proteins, in contrast, are generally much too large to be soluble in water.

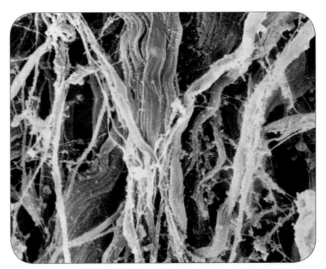

Figure 7.15 An SEM of human collagen fibres ($\times 3000$). Each fibre is made of many fibrils. The fibres are large enough to be seen with a light microscope and much too large to dissolve in wter.

	Globular proteins	Fibrous proteins
Examples	haemoglobin, enzymes, antibodies, transporters in membranes, some hormones (e.g. insulin)	collagen, keratin, elastin
Primary structure	very precise, usually made up of a non-repeating sequence of amino acids forming a chain that is always the same length	often made up of a repeating sequence of amino acids, and the chain can be of varying length
Solubility	often soluble in water	insoluble in water
Functions	usually metabolically active, taking part in chemical reactions in and around cells	usually metabolically unreactive, with a structural role

Table 7.2 A comparison of globular and fibrous proteins.

Carbohydrates

Carbohydrates are substances whose molecules are made of **sugar** units. The general formula for a sugar unit is $C_nH_{2n}O_n$. Carbohydrates include sugars, starches and cellulose. Sugars are always soluble in water and taste sweet. Starches and cellulose, which are both examples of **polysaccharides**, are insoluble in water and do not taste sweet.

Monosaccharides

A carbohydrate whose molecules contain just one sugar unit is called a **monosaccharide**. Glucose, fructose and galactose are examples of monosaccharides. Glucose is the main respiratory substrate in cells, providing energy when it is oxidised. All sugars taste sweet, and fructose is often found in fruits and in nectar – here, it attracts insects and other animals, which might then inadvertently disperse the plant's seeds, or transfer pollen from one flower to another.

Figure 7.16 shows the structure of the monosaccharide **glucose**. Glucose is a sugar containing six carbon atoms, and so it is said to be a **hexose**. Glucose molecules can exist in two forms, known as α-glucose and β-glucose.

There are several other types of hexose sugars. They all have the same molecular formula as glucose, but their atoms are arranged differently.

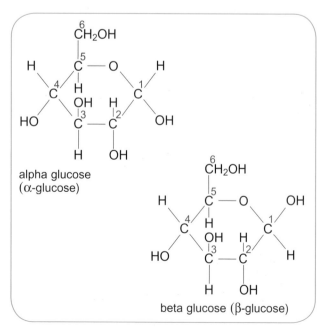

Figure 7.16 The structure of glucose molecules.

Disaccharides

Two monosaccharide molecules can link together to form a sugar called a **disaccharide**. For example, two α-glucose molecules can react to form **maltose** (Figure 7.17). This is a condensation reaction. The linkage formed between the two monosaccharides is called a **glycosidic bond**. It involves covalent bonds, and is very strong. Like monosaccharides, disaccharides are soluble in water and taste sweet.

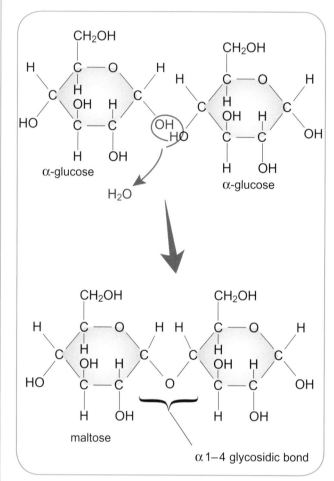

Figure 7.17 The formation of a glycosidic bond by a condensation reaction.

SAQ

3 a Use the information in Figure 7.16 to write the molecular formula for glucose.

b What is the one difference between an α-glucose molecule and a β-glucose molecule?

[Answer]

[Extension]

In maltose, the glycosidic bond is formed between carbon atom 1 of one molecule and carbon atom 4 of the other. Both molecules are in the α form. We can describe this as an α 1–4 glycosidic bond.

When carbohydrates are digested, glycosidic bonds are broken down by carbohydrase enzymes. The enzyme that breaks maltose apart is called **maltase**. This is a hydrolysis reaction (Figure 7.18).

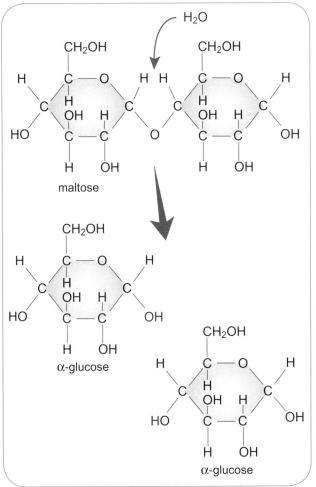

Figure 7.18 The breakage of a glycosidic bond by a hydrolysis reaction.

Polysaccharides

Linking together thousands of α-glucose molecules with 1–4 glycosidic bonds produces the carbohydrate **amylose**, found in **starch**. This is how plants store the carbohydrate that they make in photosynthesis. Starch is insoluble and metabolically inactive, so it does not interfere with chemical reactions inside the cell, nor does it affect the water potential.

Amylose molecules coil around to form a long spiral (Figure 7.19). This makes them very compact, so a lot of starch can be stored in a small space. The coil is held in shape by hydrogen bonds.

Cellulose is also a polysaccharide made of thousands of glucose molecules, but this time they are β-glucose and they are linked with β 1–4 glycosidic bonds (Figure 7.20). Cellulose molecules do not coil, but lie straight. Rather than forming hydrogen bonds within themselves, each molecule forms hydrogen bonds with its neighbour. This produces bundles of molecules lying side by side, all held together by thousands of hydrogen bonds. These bundles are called **fibrils**, and they themselves form larger bundles called **fibres**. You can see these fibres in micrographs of cellulose cell walls. They are structurally very strong. Cellulose is difficult to digest, and very few animals have an enzyme that can break its β 1–4 glycosidic bonds.

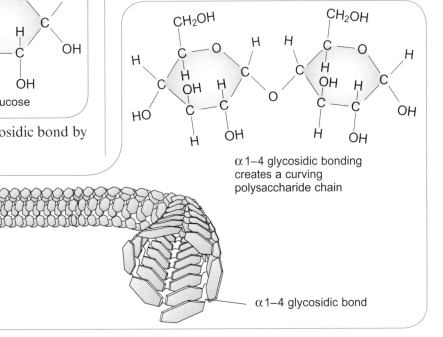

α 1–4 glycosidic bonding creates a curving polysaccharide chain

α 1–4 glycosidic bond

Figure 7.19 The structure of amylose.

Whereas plants contain amylose (starch) and cellulose, animal cells never contain either of these polysaccharides. Instead, they store carbohydrate as **glycogen**. This has a structure similar to amylose – it is made up of α glucose molecules linked by 1–4 glycosidic bonds. However, unlike amylose, it also has branches, where 1–6 glycosidic bonds are formed (Figure 7.21). This makes it more difficult for glycogen molecules to form helices, so they are not as tightly coiled as starch molecules. They also tend to be shorter.

Glycogen stores are found in the liver and in muscles, where little dark granules of glycogen can often be seen in photomicrographs. They can be easily broken down to form glucose by an enzyme called **glycogen phosphorylase**, which is activated by insulin when blood glucose levels are low.

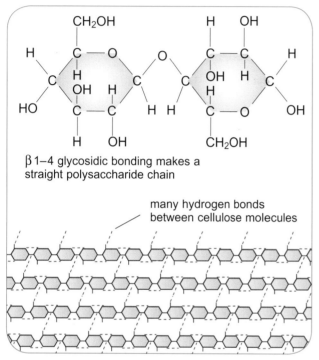

β 1–4 glycosidic bonding makes a straight polysaccharide chain

many hydrogen bonds between cellulose molecules

Figure 7.20   The structure of cellulose.

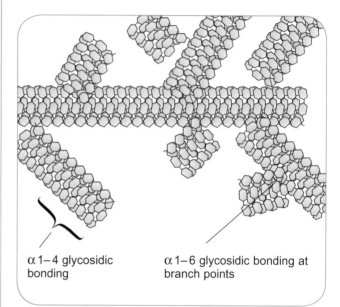

α 1–4 glycosidic bonding

α 1–6 glycosidic bonding at branch points

Figure 7.21   The structure of glycogen.

Extension

SAQ

4 Copy and complete this table to compare the structures and functions of amylose, cellulose and glycogen.

	Amylose	Cellulose	Glycogen
Monosaccharide from which it is formed	α-glucose	β-glucose	α-glucose
Type(s) of glycosidic bond			
Overall shape of molecule			
Hydrogen bonding within or between molecules			
Solubility in water			
Function			

Answer

Lipids

Lipids are a group of substances that – like carbohydrates – are made up of carbon, hydrogen and oxygen. However, they have a much higher proportion of hydrogen than carbohydrates. They are insoluble in water.

Lipids include fats, which tend to be solid at room temperatures, and oils, which tend to be liquid. In general, animals produce mostly fats and plants mostly oils, although there are many exceptions to this rule.

Triglycerides

Triglycerides get their name because their molecules are made of three **fatty acids** attached to a **glycerol** molecule (Figure 7.22). Fatty acids are acids because they contain a **carboxyl group**, –COOH.

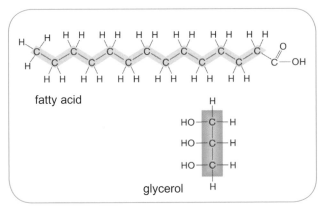

Figure 7.22 The structures of a fatty acid and glycerol.

SAQ

5 Where in the body might ester bonds be broken, and what is the name of the enzyme that catalyses this reaction?
Answer

6 a Use Figure 7.22 and Figure 7.23 to work out the molecular formula of one triglyceride.
  b How do the proportions of carbon, hydrogen and oxygen in a triglyceride differ from their proportions in a carbohydrate such as glucose?
Answer

The carboxyl groups of fatty acids are able to react with the –OH (**hydroxyl**) groups of glycerol, forming **ester bonds** (Figure 7.23). These linkages involve covalent bonds, and so are very strong. As with the formation of peptide bonds and glycosidic bonds, this is a condensation reaction. The breakage of an ester bond is a hydrolysis reaction.

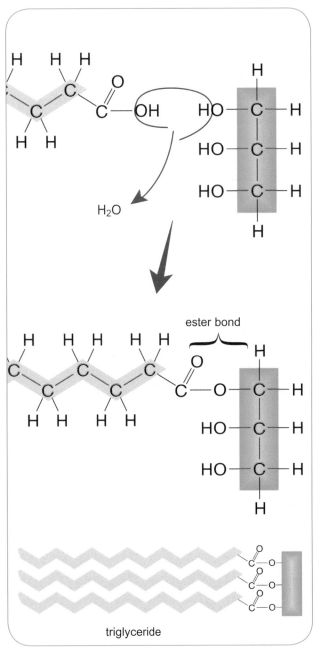

Figure 7.23 How a triglyceride is formed from glycerol and three fatty acids.

Extension

119

Triglycerides are insoluble in water. This is because none of their atoms carries an electrical charge, and so they are not attracted to water molecules. They are said to be **hydrophobic**.

A diet rich in saturated fats may increase the cholesterol level in the blood, increasing the risk of developing heart disease (Chapter 10). Foods are frequently labelled with the proportions of saturated and unsaturated fats that they contain.

A **saturated fat** is one in which the fatty acids all contain as much hydrogen as they can. Each carbon atom in the fatty acid 'tail' is linked to its neighbouring carbon atoms by single bonds, while the other two bonds are linked to hydrogen atoms. An **unsaturated fat**, however, has one or more fatty acids in which at least one carbon atom is using *two* of its bonds to link to a neighbouring carbon atom, so it only has one bond spare to link to hydrogen (Figure 7.24). This double carbon–carbon bond forms a 'kink' in the chain.

Triglycerides are rich in energy, and they are often used as energy stores in living organisms. One gram of triglyceride can release twice as much energy as one gram of carbohydrate when it is respired, so they make compact and efficient stores. In humans, cells in a tissue called **adipose tissue** are almost filled with globules of triglycerides, and they make very good thermal insulators. Animals that live in cold environments, such as whales and polar bears, often have especially thick layers of adipose tissue beneath the skin.

Stored triglycerides also provide a place in which fat-soluble vitamins, especially vitamin D and vitamin A, can be stored.

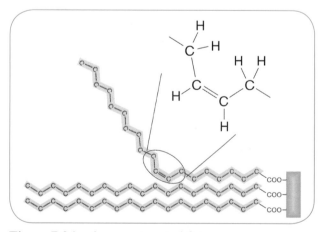

Figure 7.24 An unsaturated fat.

Phospholipids

A phospholipid is like a triglyceride in which one of the fatty acids is replaced by a phosphate group (Figure 7.25).

Whereas the fatty acid tails of a phospholipid are hydrophobic, the phosphate heads are **hydrophilic** – that is, they are attracted to water molecules. This is because the phosphate group has a negative electrical charge on it, which is attracted to the tiny positive electrical charge on the hydrogen atoms in a water molecule. So, when it is in water, the two ends of a phospholipid molecule do different things. The phosphate is drawn towards water molecules and dissolves in them. The fatty acids are repelled by water molecules and avoid them. In water, the phospholipid molecules arrange themselves in a sheet called a **bilayer** (Figure 7.26).

You should recognise this bilayer as the basic structure of a cell membrane. Phospholipids are one of the most important molecules in a cell. Without them, there could be no plasma membrane and the cell would simply cease to exist.

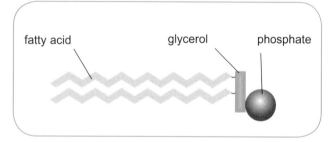

Figure 7.25 A phospholipid molecule.

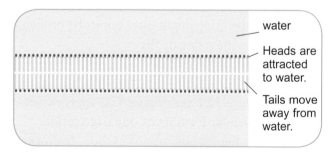

Figure 7.26 A phospholipid bilayer.

SAQ

7 Some fats are described as 'monounsaturated' while others are 'polyunsaturated'. Suggest what these names mean.

Answer

Cholesterol and steroids

Some people classify cholesterol as a lipid, whereas others do not. Here, we will include cholesterol within the group of compounds we call lipids. Figure 7.27 shows the structure of a cholesterol molecule. Cholesterol and other substances with similar structures, which are formed from it, are called **steroids**.

There are a huge number of different kinds of steroids in the body. Many of them are hormones – for example, testosterone and oestrogen. Cholesterol itself is a major constituent of cell membranes (Chapter 1), where it helps to regulate the fluidity of the membrane.

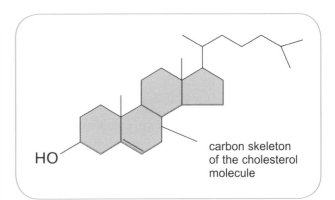

carbon skeleton of the cholesterol molecule

Figure 7.27   The structure of a cholesterol molecule.

Summary

Glossary

- Water molecules have tiny negative charges in one part of the molecule, and tiny positive charges in another part. These charges attract water molecules to each other, and these attractions are called hydrogen bonds.

- Because of its hydrogen bonds, water is a liquid at normal temperatures. It has a high specific heat capacity and a relatively high boiling point. A lot of heat is required to make it turn from liquid to gas, and this helps to cool animals and plants. Cohesion between water molecules is important in maintaining columns of water in xylem vessels.

- Water is an excellent solvent. Substances in solution can undergo metabolic reactions, and be transported around the body of a plant or animal.

- Proteins are large molecules made of many amino acids linked together by peptide bonds. A chain of amino acids is called a polypeptide. Peptide bonds are made during protein synthesis on ribosomes. The reaction is a condensation reaction. Peptide bonds are broken, for example, in digestion. The reaction is a hydrolysis reaction.

- The sequence of amino acids in a protein is its primary structure. The regular coiling of the polypeptide chain is its secondary structure, and its overall three-dimensional shape is its tertiary structure. The association of two or more polypeptides to form the protein molecule is its quaternary structure.

- The secondary structure of a protein is held together by hydrogen bonds. Tertiary and quaternary structures involve hydrogen bonds, ionic bonds, disulfide bonds and hydrophobic interactions.

- Globular proteins – for example, haemoglobin – have ball-shaped molecules. They are often soluble and usually metabolically reactive. Fibrous proteins – for example, collagen – have long, thin molecules. They are insoluble and often have a structural role.

- Carbohydrates include sugars and starches. A monosaccharide is a sugar with one sugar unit, while a disaccharide has two. Polysaccharides have many sugar units linked together into long chains.

continued

- Sugars link together through glycosidic bonds. The formation of a glycosidic bond is a condensation reaction, and its breakage is a hydrolysis reaction. Bonds are named according to the form (α or β) of the sugar molecules involved and the numbers of the carbon atoms. For example, in maltose there is an α1–4 glycosidic bond linking the two glucose molecules.

- Sugars taste sweet and are soluble in water. They are important energy sources when they are oxidised in respiration. Polysaccharides are not sweet and are insoluble. Starch and glycogen are energy stores, while cellulose forms plant cell walls.

- Lipids (fats and oils) are made of glycerol linked by ester bonds to fatty acids. The formation of an ester bond is a condensation reaction, and its breakage is a hydrolysis reaction. Lipids are insoluble in water. Triglycerides are important energy stores. Phospholipids form cell membranes.

- Cholesterol is a lipid that helps to maintain the fluidity of cell membranes. It is used to make steroids such as oestrogen and testosterone.

Questions

1 There are many different polysaccharides found in plants and animals. Gum arabic is classed as a complex polysaccharide and is produced by the tree *Acacia senegal*. It seeps out from the cut surface when the tree is damaged.

   The molecules of gum arabic have a branched structure and are soluble in water. It is classed as a heteropolysaccharide, which means that it is made up of a number of different sugars. Hydrolysis of gum arabic produces four different monosaccharides.

   a Describe what happens during the hydrolysis of a polysaccharide molecule. [2]

   b Gum arabic is similar to other polysaccharides in a number of ways but also differs from them. Copy and complete the table below, comparing gum arabic with other polysaccharides.

	Gum arabic	Amylopectin (a component of starch)	Cellulose	Glycogen
branched structure	yes	yes		
heteropolysaccharide	yes		no	
found in animals / plants	plants		plants	
function in organism	healing			energy store

[8]

OCR Biology AS (2801) June 2003

[Total 10]

Answer

continued

Questions

2 a i State the components needed to synthesise a triglyceride. [2]

   ii Name the chemical reaction by which these components are joined. [1]

  b State <u>one</u> function of triglycerides in living organisms. [1]

Lipase is an enzyme that catalyses the hydrolysis of triglycerides. It is a soluble globular protein.

   The function of an enzyme depends upon the precise nature of its tertiary structure. The diagram represents the structure of an enzyme. the black strips represent the disulfide bonds which help to stabilise its tertiary structure.

  c i Describe the nature of the disulfide bonds that help to stabilise the tertiary structure of a protein such as lipase. [2]

   ii Name <u>two other</u> types of bonding that help to stabilise the tertiary structure. [2]

Region A in the diagram is a secondary structure.

  d Describe the nature of region A. [2]

OCR Biology AS (2801) January 2001   [Total 10]

> Answer

3 a The diagram represents part of a collagen molecule.

  i Collagen is a protein made of three chains of amino acids, twisted together like a rope.

   State the name given to a chain of amino acids. [1]

  ii Name the amino acid that forms a high proportion of the collagen molecule. [1]

  iii Collagen has tremendous strength, having about one quarter of the tensile strength of mild steel. Using information given in the diagram to help you, explain how the structure of collagen contributes to its strength. [2]

  b Complete the following passage by inserting the most appropriate terms in the spaces provided.

Cellulose and collagen are both fibrous molecules. Cellulose, a carbohydrate, is the main component of the _____ _____ in plants.

Cellulose is made of chains of many _____ glucose molecules which are joined by 1–4 _____ bonds. Each glucose molecule is rotated _____ ° relative to its neighbour, resulting in a _____ chain. Adjacent chains are held to one another by _____ bonds. [6]

OCR Biology AS (2801) January 2005   [Total 10]

> Answer

Chapter 8

Background

e-Learning

Objectives

Polynucleotides

It is amazing to realise that until the middle of the 20th century we did not even know that DNA is the genetic material. Our DNA carries the genetic code – a set of instructions telling the cell the sequence in which to link together amino acids when proteins are being synthesised. Slight differences in the structure of these proteins may result in slight differences in our metabolic reactions. Partly for this reason, we are all slightly different from one another.

You probably know that DNA is a 'double helix'. A DNA molecule is made of two long chains of **nucleotide** molecules, linked together to form a twisted ladder. Each chain is called a **polynucleotide**.

The structure of DNA

DNA stands for **deoxyribonucleic acid**. When it was discovered, it was given the name 'nucleic acid' because it was mostly found in the nuclei of cells and is slightly acidic.

Each nucleotide in a DNA molecule contains:
- a phosphate group
- the five-carbon sugar, **deoxyribose**
- an organic base.

Figure 8.1 shows the components of a nucleotide in DNA. The base can be any one of four. These are **adenine**, **guanine**, **thymine** and **cytosine**. They are usually abbreviated to A, G, T and C. Adenine and guanine each contain two rings in their structure. They are known as **purine bases**. Thymine and cytosine have only one ring. They are known as **pyrimidine bases**.

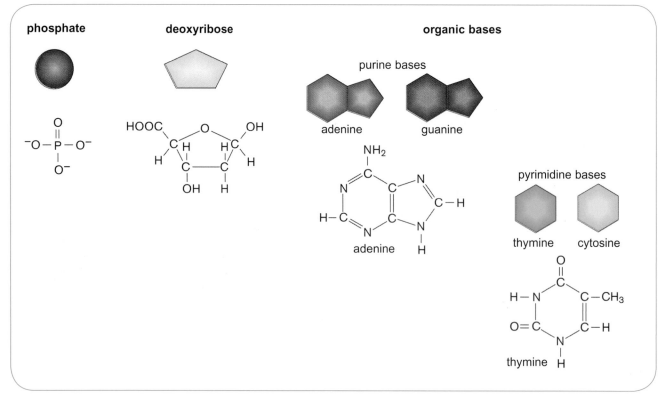

Figure 8.1 The components of a nucleotide in DNA.

Figure 8.2 shows how these components are linked in nucleotides and how the nucleotides link together to form long chains called polynucleotides.

You can see that the base in each nucleotide sticks out sideways from the chain. In DNA, two chains of nucleotides lie side by side, one chain running one way and the other in the opposite direction (Figure 8.3 and Figure 8.4). They are said to be **anti-parallel**. The bases of one chain link up with the bases of the other by means of **hydrogen bonds**. The whole molecule twists to produce the double helix shape.

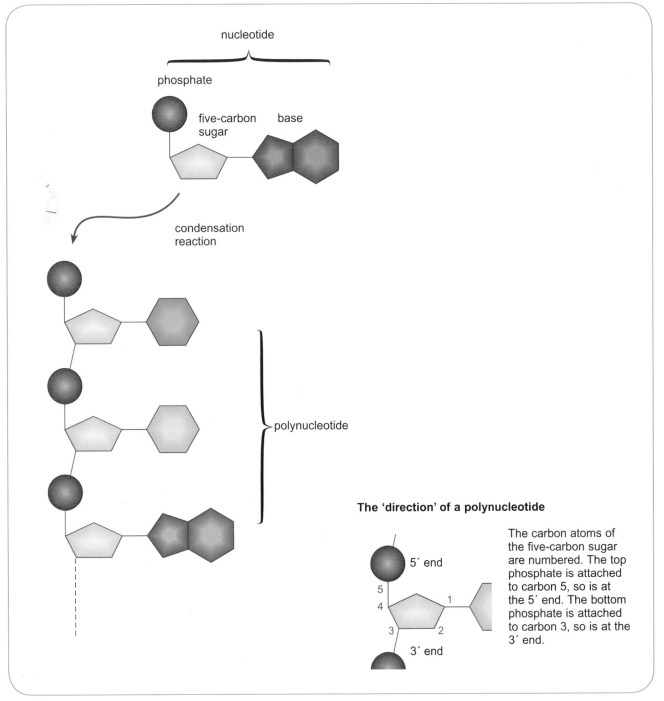

Figure 8.2   How nucleotides join to form a polynucleotide.

The key to the ability of DNA to hold and pass on the code for making proteins in the cell is the way in which these bases link up. There is just the right amount of space for one large base – a purine – to link with one smaller base – a pyrimidine. And the linking is even more particular than that. A can only link with T, and C can only link with G. This is called **complementary base pairing**.

Complementary base pairing ensures that the code carried on a molecule of DNA can be copied perfectly over and over again, so that it can be passed down from cell to cell and from generation to generation. It is also what enables the code on the DNA to be used to instruct the protein-making machinery in a cell to construct exactly the right proteins. You will find out much more about this if you continue studying biology to A2 level.

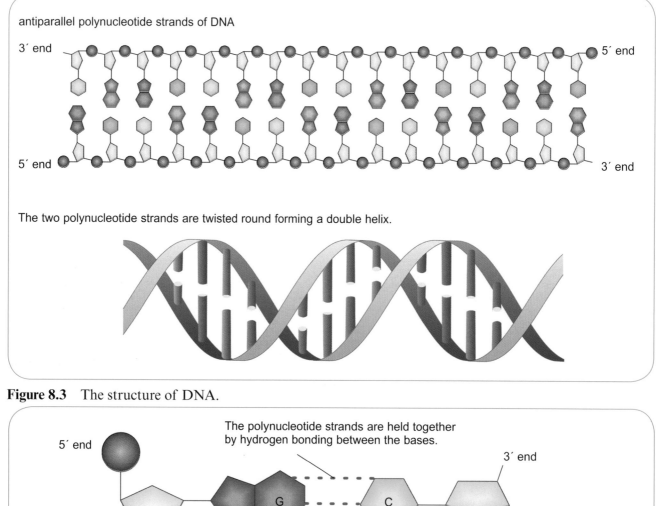

antiparallel polynucleotide strands of DNA

3′ end

5′ end

5′ end

3′ end

The two polynucleotide strands are twisted round forming a double helix.

Figure 8.3 The structure of DNA.

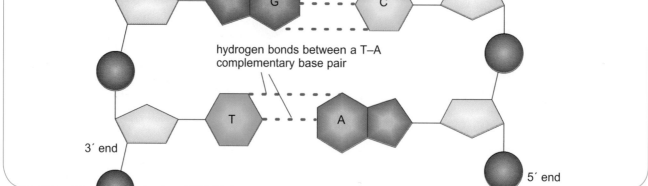

The polynucleotide strands are held together by hydrogen bonding between the bases.

5′ end

3′ end

G

C

hydrogen bonds between a T–A complementary base pair

T

A

3′ end

5′ end

Figure 8.4 Hydrogen bonding joining the bases in DNA.

DNA replication

We have seen that, before a cell divides by mitosis, its DNA replicates to produce two copies. One copy is passed on to each daughter cell. DNA replication takes place during interphase of the cell cycle (Chapter 3).

Figure 8.5 and Figure 8.6 show how DNA replication takes place. This method is called **semi-conservative replication**, because each of the new DNA molecules is made of one old strand and one new strand of DNA.

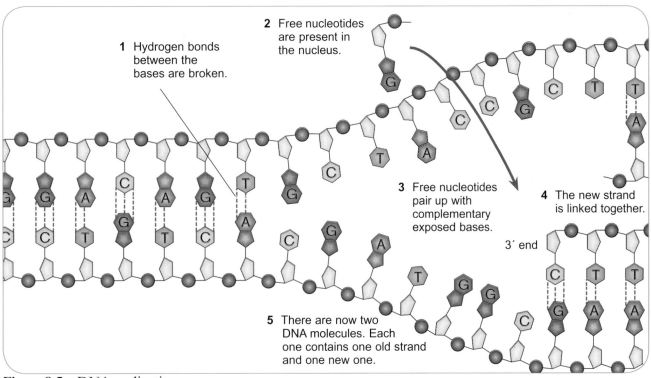

1 Hydrogen bonds between the bases are broken.

2 Free nucleotides are present in the nucleus.

3 Free nucleotides pair up with complementary exposed bases.

4 The new strand is linked together.

3′ end

5 There are now two DNA molecules. Each one contains one old strand and one new one.

Figure 8.5 DNA replication.

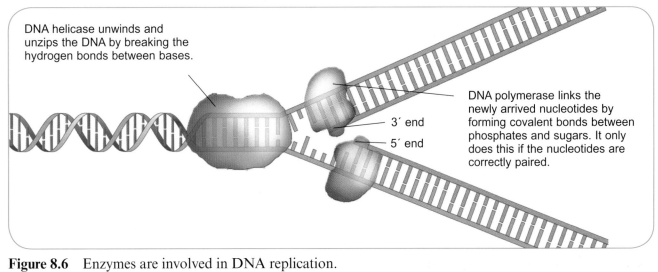

DNA helicase unwinds and unzips the DNA by breaking the hydrogen bonds between bases.

3′ end
5′ end

DNA polymerase links the newly arrived nucleotides by forming covalent bonds between phosphates and sugars. It only does this if the nucleotides are correctly paired.

Figure 8.6 Enzymes are involved in DNA replication.

The role of DNA

DNA carries a code that is used by the cell when making proteins. The sequence of bases in the DNA molecules determines the sequence of amino acids that are strung together when a protein molecule is made on the ribosomes.

A length of DNA that codes for making one polypeptide is called a **gene**. It is thought that there are around 30 000 genes in our cells (Figure 8.7).

The code is read in groups of three 'letters' – that is, triplets of bases. As we have seen, there are four bases in a DNA molecule, A, T, C and G. A sequence of three bases in a DNA molecule codes for one amino acid (Figure 8.8).

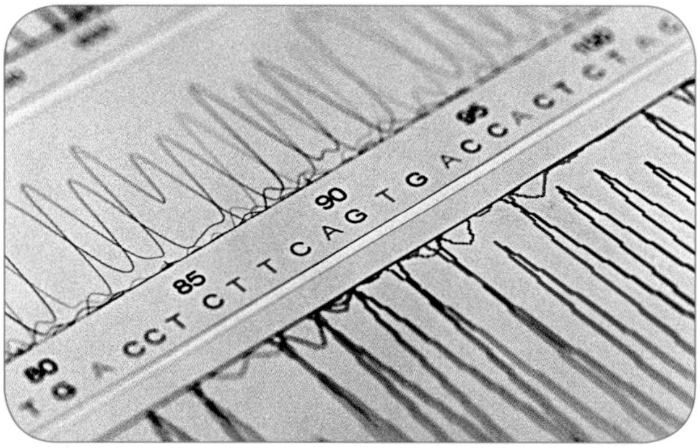

The structure of RNA

DNA is not the only polynucleotide in a cell. There are also polynucleotides which contain the sugar **ribose** rather than deoxyribose. They are therefore called **ribonucleic acids**, or **RNA** for short. Figure 8.9 shows the structure of RNA. RNA is generally single stranded, while DNA is generally double stranded. Another difference between them is that RNA always contains the base **uracil** (U) instead of thymine.

While DNA stores the genetic information in the nucleus of a cell, RNA is involved with using that information to make proteins.

Figure 8.7 The Human Genome Project has worked out the base sequence in each human chromosome.

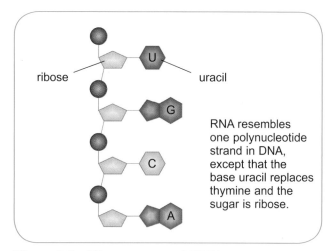

RNA resembles one polynucleotide strand in DNA, except that the base uracil replaces thymine and the sugar is ribose.

Figure 8.9 The structure of RNA.

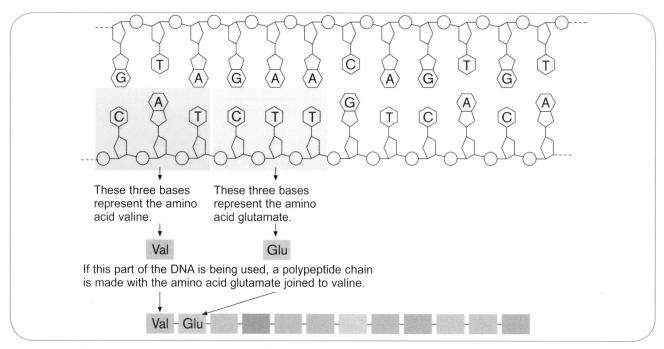

Figure 8.8 How DNA codes for amino acid sequences in proteins.

The sequence of bases on part of a DNA molecule – a gene – is used to build an RNA molecule with the complementary base sequence. This RNA molecule then travels out into the cytoplasm and attaches to a ribosome. Working with other RNA molecules, the base sequence is used to determine the sequence of amino acids that are strung together to make a protein molecule. The base sequence on the DNA therefore determines the primary structure of the protein that is made.

SAQ

2 Use a table, or a list of bullet points, to summarise the differences between DNA and RNA.

Answer

Extension

Summary

Glossary

- DNA is deoxyribonucleic acid. It is a double-stranded molecule made up of two strands of nucleotides.

- A DNA nucleotide is made up of a phosphate group, a five-carbon sugar called deoxyribose, and a base. There are four bases in DNA – adenine, guanine, cytosine and thymine. They are usually abbreviated to A, G, C and T.

- Adenine and guanine are purine bases. Cytosine and thymine are pyrimidine bases.

- The nucleotides in a strand of DNA are linked to each other by strong covalent bonds between the phosphate groups and deoxyribose. The phosphate groups bond to carbon 5 and to carbon 3 of the deoxyribose ring. The end of the molecule where the phosphate is bonded to carbon 5 is called the 5′ end, while the other is the 3′ end.

- The two strands of a DNA molecule are linked to each other by weak hydrogen bonds between the bases. A always bonds with T, and C always bonds with G. A and T are linked by two hydrogen bonds. C and G are linked by three hydrogen bonds.

- The two strands of a DNA molecule run in opposite directions. They are said to be anti-parallel. They twist around each other to form a double helix.

- The DNA molecules in a cell nucleus are replicated before cell division takes place. First, the two strands of the molecule are untwisted and unzipped. Free DNA nucleotides pair up with the exposed bases on both strands. They are then linked together by the formation of bonds between their deoxyribose and phosphate groups. This is catalsyed by the enzyme DNA polymerase. Two new molecules are therefore formed, each identical to the original one. Each new molecule contains one old strand and one new strand, so the process is called semi-conservative replication.

- The sequence of bases in a DNA molecule codes for the sequence of amino acids in a protein to be made on the ribosomes. Three bases code for one amino acid. A sequence of DNA nucleotides that codes for one polypeptide is known as a gene.

- RNA is ribonucleic acid. There are several kinds of RNA. Most are single stranded. They contain the pentose sugar ribose, rather than deoxyribose. They contain the base uracil instead of thymine.

- During protein synthesis, an RNA molecule is built up against one of the DNA strands in a gene. The RNA then travels out of the nucleus to a ribosome, where its sequence of bases is used to determine the sequence of amino acids in the polypeptide that is being constructed on the ribosome.

Questions

1 Figure 1 represents a nucleotide which forms part of a DNA molecule.

  a i Name A to C. [3]

    ii State which part of the nucleotide contains nitrogen. [1]

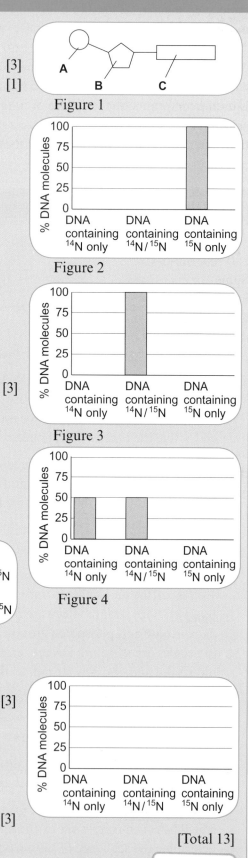

Figure 1

During research into the mechanism of DNA replication, bacteria were grown for many generations in a medium containing only the 'heavy' isotope of nitrogen, ^{15}N. This resulted in all the DNA molecules containing only ^{15}N. This is illustrated in Figure 2.

Figure 2

These bacteria were then grown in a medium containing only 'light' nitrogen, ^{14}N. After the time taken for the DNA to replicate once, the DNA was analysed. The results are shown in Figure 3.

  b Explain how these data support the semi-conservative hypothesis of DNA replication. [3]

Figure 3

The bacteria continued to grow in the 'light' nitrogen, ^{14}N, medium until the DNA had replicated once more. The DNA molecules were analysed. The results are shown in Figure 4.

    Figure 5 shows simple diagrams of DNA molecules, indicating the nitrogen content of each.

Figure 5

Figure 4

  c With reference to Figure 5, select the letter or letters which best represent the bacterial DNA in Figure 2, Figure 3 and Figure 4. [3]

The bacteria continued to grow in the 'light' nitrogen, ^{14}N, medium until the DNA had replicated once more. The DNA molecules were analysed.

  d Copy and complete the bar chart to the right to indicate the expected results of the composition of these DNA molecules. [3]

OCR Biology AS (2801) January 2002

[Total 13]

Answer

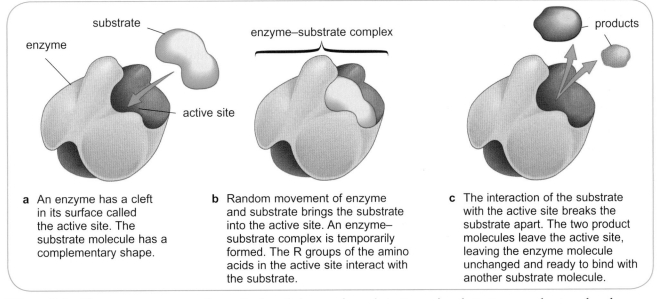

Chapter 9

Enzymes

Objectives

Enzymes are protein molecules that can be defined as **biological catalysts**. A catalyst is a substance that speeds up a chemical reaction, but remains unchanged at the end of the reaction. Virtually every metabolic reaction that takes place within a living organism is catalysed by an enzyme. Many enzyme names end in -ase, such as protease or ATPase.

How enzymes work

Some enzymes act inside cells, and are known as **intracellular** enzymes. Examples include **hydrolases** found inside lysosomes, which hydrolyse (break down) substances that a cell has taken in by phagocytosis. **ATPases** are also intracellular enzymes found, for example, inside mitochondria, where they are involved in the synthesis of ATP during aerobic respiration.

Some enzymes act outside cells, and are known as **extracellular** enzymes. These include the digestive enzymes in the alimentary canal, such as amylase, which hydrolyses starch to maltose.

Enzymes are globular proteins. Like all globular proteins, enzyme molecules are coiled into a precise three-dimensional shape – their tertiary

structure – with hydrophilic R groups (side chains) on the outside of the molecules, making them soluble in water. Enzyme molecules also have a special feature in that they possess an **active site** (Figure 9.1). The active site of an enzyme is a region, usually a cleft or depression, to which another particular molecule can bind. This molecule is the **substrate** of the enzyme. The shape of the active site allows the substrate to fit perfectly, and to be held in place by temporary bonds that form between the substrate and some of the R groups of the enzyme's amino acids. This combined structure is called the **enzyme–substrate complex** (Figure 9.2). Each type of enzyme will usually act on only one type of substrate molecule. This is because the shape of the active site will only allow one shape of molecule to fit, like a key fitting into a lock. In most enzymes, when the substrate fits into the active site, the shape of the whole enzyme changes slightly so that it can accommodate and hold the substrate in exactly the right position for the reaction to occur. This is called **induced fit** – the arrival of the substrate molecule causes a change in the shape of the enzyme.

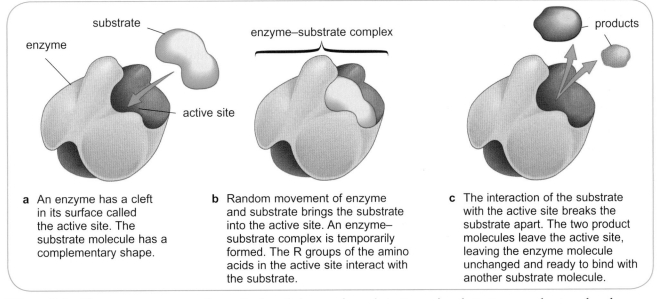

a An enzyme has a cleft in its surface called the active site. The substrate molecule has a complementary shape.

b Random movement of enzyme and substrate brings the substrate into the active site. An enzyme–substrate complex is temporarily formed. The R groups of the amino acids in the active site interact with the substrate.

c The interaction of the substrate with the active site breaks the substrate apart. The two product molecules leave the active site, leaving the enzyme molecule unchanged and ready to bind with another substrate molecule.

Figure 9.1   How an enzyme catalyses the breakdown of a substrate molecule to two product molecules.

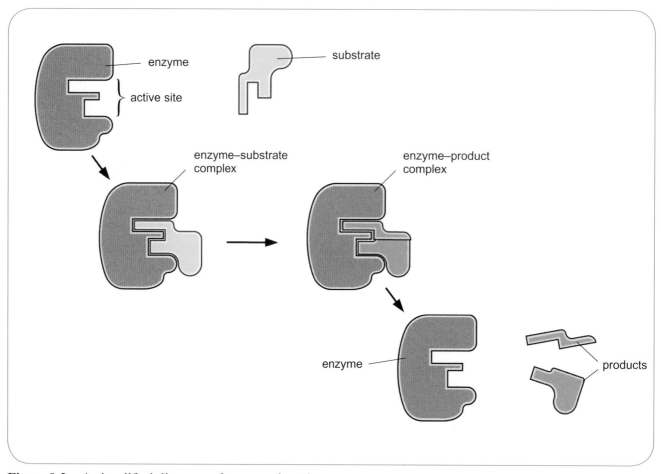

Figure 9.2   A simplified diagram of enzyme function.

Whether it works by a simple lock-and-key mechanism, or by induced fit, the enzyme and its substrate must be a perfect match. The enzyme is said to be **specific** for this substrate.

The enzyme may catalyse a reaction in which the substrate molecule is split into two or more molecules. Alternatively, it may catalyse the joining together of two molecules – for example, when linking amino acids to form polypeptides during protein synthesis on ribosomes. Interaction between the R groups of the enzyme and the atoms of the substrate can break, or encourage formation of, bonds in the substrate molecule. As a result, one, two or more **products** are formed.

When the reaction is complete, the product or products leave the active site. The enzyme is unchanged by the process, so it is now available to receive another substrate molecule. The rate at which substrate molecules can bind to the enzyme's active site, be formed into products and leave can be very rapid. A molecule of the enzyme catalase, for example, can bind with hydrogen peroxide molecules, split them into water and oxygen and release these products at a rate of 10^7 molecules per second. In contrast, one of the enzymes involved in photosynthesis, called rubisco, can only deal with three molecules per second.

Activation energy

We have seen that enzymes increase the rates at which chemical reactions occur. Most of the reactions that occur in living cells would occur so slowly without enzymes that they would effectively not happen at all.

In many reactions, the substrate will not be converted to a product unless it is temporarily given some extra energy. This energy is called **activation energy** (Figure 9.3). One way of increasing the rates of many chemical reactions is to increase the energy of the reactants by heating them. You have probably done this on many occasions by heating substances that you want to react together. In the Benedict's test for reducing sugar, for example, you need to heat the Benedict's reagent and sugar solution together before they will react.

Mammals also use this method of speeding up their metabolic reactions. Our body temperature is maintained at 37 °C, which is usually considerably warmer than the temperature of the air around us. But even raising the temperature of cells to 37 °C is not enough to give most substrates the activation energy that they need to change into products. We cannot raise body temperature much more than this, because temperatures above about 40 °C begin to cause irreversible damage to many of the molecules from which we are made, especially protein molecules. Enzymes are a solution to this problem because they decrease the activation energy of the reaction that they catalyse (Figure 9.3). They do this by holding the substrate or substrates in such a way that their molecules can react more easily. Reactions catalysed by enzymes take place rapidly at a much lower temperature than they would without them.

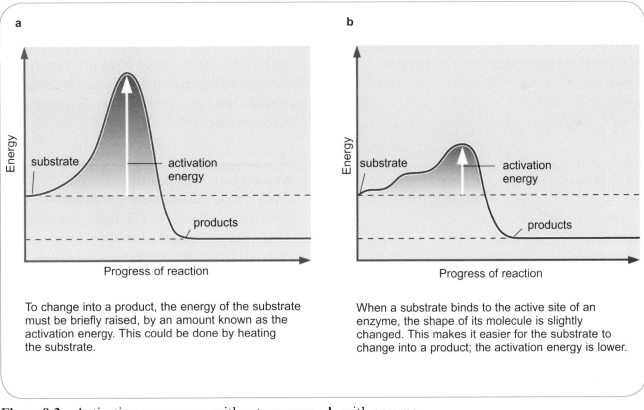

To change into a product, the energy of the substrate must be briefly raised, by an amount known as the activation energy. This could be done by heating the substrate.

When a substrate binds to the active site of an enzyme, the shape of its molecule is slightly changed. This makes it easier for the substrate to change into a product; the activation energy is lower.

Figure 9.3 Activation energy: **a** without enzyme; **b** with enzyme.

The course of a reaction

You may be able to carry out an investigation into the rate at which substrate is converted into product during an enzyme-controlled reaction. Figure 9.4 shows the results of such an investigation, using the enzyme catalase. This enzyme is found in the tissues of most living things and catalyses the breakdown of hydrogen peroxide into water and oxygen. (Hydrogen peroxide is a very toxic product of several different metabolic reactions.) It is an easy reaction to follow because the oxygen that is released can be collected and measured.

The reaction begins very swiftly. As soon as the enzyme and substrate are mixed, bubbles of oxygen are released. A large volume of oxygen can be collected in the first minute of the reaction. As the reaction continues, however, the rate at which oxygen is released gradually slows down. The reaction gets slower and slower, until it eventually stops.

The explanation for this is quite straightforward. When the enzyme and substrate are first mixed, there are many substrate molecules. Enzyme and substrate bind at incredible speed so, at any moment, virtually every enzyme molecule has a substrate molecule in its active site. The rate at which the reaction occurs will depend only on how many enzyme molecules there are, and the speed at which each enzyme molecule can bind with another substrate molecule.

However, as more and more substrate is converted into product, there are fewer and fewer substrate molecules to bind with enzymes. Enzyme molecules may be 'waiting' for a substrate molecule to move in their direction and, by chance, hit their active site. As fewer substrate molecules are left, the reaction gets slower and slower, until it eventually stops.

The curve in Figure 9.4 is therefore steepest at the beginning of the reaction: the rate of an enzyme-controlled reaction is always fastest at the beginning. This rate is called the **initial rate of reaction**. You can measure the initial rate of the reaction by calculating the slope of a tangent to the curve, as close to time 0 as possible. An easier way of doing this is simply to read off the graph the amount of oxygen given off in the first 30 seconds. In this case, the initial rate of oxygen production is $2.7\,cm^3$ of oxygen per 30 seconds, or $5.4\,cm^3$ per minute.

SAQ

1 Why is it better to calculate the initial rate of reaction from a curve such as the one in Figure 9.4, rather than simply measuring how much oxygen is given off in the first 30 seconds?

Hint

Answer

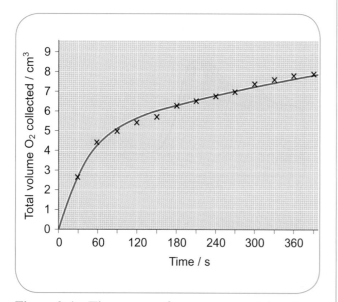

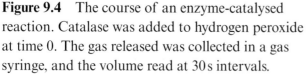

Figure 9.4 The course of an enzyme-catalysed reaction. Catalase was added to hydrogen peroxide at time 0. The gas released was collected in a gas syringe, and the volume read at 30 s intervals.

The effect of enzyme concentration

Figure 9.5 shows the results of an investigation in which different concentrations of catalase were added to the same volume of a hydrogen peroxide solution. You can see that the shapes of all five curves in Figure 9.5a are similar. In each case, the reaction begins very quickly (steep curve) and then gradually slows down (curve levels off). The amounts of hydrogen peroxide are the same in all five reactions, so the total amount of oxygen eventually produced will be the same. Eventually, all the curves will meet.

To compare the rates of these five reactions, in order to look at the effect of enzyme concentration on reaction rate, it is fairest to look at the rate *right at the beginning* of the reaction. This is because, once the reaction is under way, the amount of substrate in each reaction begins to vary, as substrate is converted to product at different rates in each of the five reactions. It is only at the very beginning of the reaction that we can be sure that differences in reaction rate are caused only by differences in enzyme concentration.

To work out this initial rate for each enzyme concentration, we can calculate the slope of the curve 30 seconds after the beginning of the reaction. (Ideally, we should do this for an even earlier stage of the reaction – as close to time 0 as possible, as explained earlier – but in practice this is impossible.) We can then draw a second graph (Figure 9.5b) showing this initial rate of reaction plotted against enzyme concentration.

This graph shows that the initial rate of reaction increases linearly as enzyme concentration increases. In these conditions, reaction rate is directly proportional to the enzyme concentration. This is just what common sense says should happen. If you double the number of enzyme molecules present, then twice as many active sites will be available for the substrate to slot into. As long as there is plenty of substrate available, the initial rate of a reaction increases linearly with enzyme concentration.

SAQ

2 Sketch the shape that Figure 9.5b would have if excess hydrogen peroxide was not available.

Hint

Answer

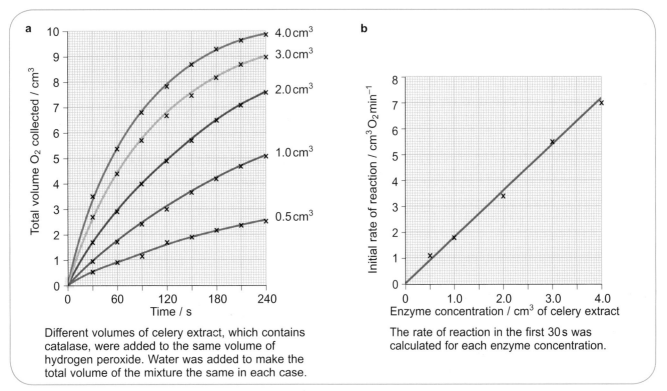

a Different volumes of celery extract, which contains catalase, were added to the same volume of hydrogen peroxide. Water was added to make the total volume of the mixture the same in each case.

b The rate of reaction in the first 30 s was calculated for each enzyme concentration.

Figure 9.5   The effect of enzyme concentration on the rate of an enzyme-catalysed reaction.

Measuring reaction rate

It is easy to measure the rate of the catalase–hydrogen peroxide reaction, because one of the products is a gas, which is released and can be collected. Unfortunately, it is not always so easy to measure the rate of a reaction. If, for example, you wanted to investigate the rate at which amylase breaks down starch to maltose, it would be very difficult to observe the course of the reaction because the substrate (starch) and the product (maltose) remain as colourless substances in the reaction mixture.

The easiest way to measure the rate of this reaction is to measure the rate at which starch disappears from the reaction mixture. This can be done by taking samples from the mixture at known times, and adding each sample to some iodine in potassium iodide solution. Starch forms a blue–black colour with this solution, but maltose does not. Using a colorimeter, you can measure the intensity of the blue–black colour obtained, and use this as a measure of the amount of starch still remaining. If you do this over a period of time, you can plot a curve of amount of starch remaining against time. You can then calculate the initial reaction rate in the same way as for the catalase–hydrogen peroxide reaction.

It is even easier to observe the course of this reaction if you mix starch, iodine in potassium iodide solution, and amylase in a tube, and take regular readings of the colour of the mixture in this one tube in a colorimeter. However, this is not ideal, because the iodine interferes with the reaction and slows it down.

The effect of substrate concentration

Figure 9.6 shows the results of an investigation in which the concentration of catalase was kept constant, and the concentration of hydrogen peroxide was varied. Once again, curves of oxygen released against time were plotted for each reaction, and the initial rate of reaction calculated for the first 30 seconds. These initial rates of reaction were then plotted against substrate concentration.

As substrate concentration increases, the initial rate of reaction also increases. Again, this is just what we would expect – the more substrate molecules there are around, the more often an enzyme's active site can bind with one. However, if we go on increasing substrate concentration, keeping the enzyme concentration constant, there comes a point where every enzyme active site is working continuously. If more substrate is added, the enzyme simply cannot work faster: substrate molecules are effectively 'queuing up' for an active site to become vacant. The enzyme is working at its maximum possible rate, known as V_{max}.

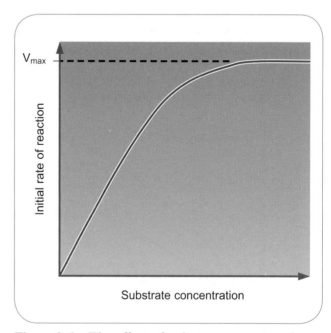

Figure 9.6 The effect of substrate concentration on the rate of an enzyme-catalysed reaction.

SAQ

3 a Sketch the curve you would expect to obtain if the amount of starch remaining was plotted against time.
    Hint

  b How could you use this curve to calculate the initial reaction rate?
    Answer

Temperature and enzyme activity

Figure 9.7 shows how the rate of a typical enzyme-catalysed reaction varies with temperature. At low temperatures, the reaction takes place only very slowly. This is because molecules are moving relatively slowly. Substrate molecules will not often collide with the active site of an enzyme molecule, and so binding between substrate and enzyme is a rare event. As temperature rises, the enzyme and substrate molecules move faster. Collisions happen more frequently, so that substrate molecules enter the active sites more often. Moreover, when they do collide, they do so with more energy, so more of them will have sufficient activation energy to react. It is easier for bonds to be broken so that the reaction can occur.

As temperature continues to increase, the speed of movement of the substrate and enzyme molecules also continues to increase. However, above a certain temperature the structure of the enzyme molecules vibrates so energetically that some of the bonds holding the enzyme molecule in its precise shape begin to break. This is especially true of hydrogen bonds. The enzyme molecule begins to lose its shape and activity and is said to be **denatured**. This is often irreversible.

In the reaction illustrated in Figure 9.7, at temperatures just above 40 °C, the substrate molecule fits less well into the active site of the enzyme, so the rate of the reaction slows down slightly compared with its rate just below 40 °C. At higher temperatures, the substrate no longer fits at all, or can no longer be held in the correct position for the reaction to occur.

The temperature at which an enzyme catalyses a reaction at the maximum rate is called the **optimum temperature**. Most human enzymes have an optimum temperature of around 40 °C. By keeping our body temperatures at about 37 °C, we ensure that enzyme-catalysed reactions occur at close to their maximum rate. It would be dangerous to maintain a body temperature of 40 °C, because even a slight rise above this would begin to denature enzymes.

Enzymes from other organisms may have different optimum temperatures. Some enzymes, such as those found in bacteria that live in hot springs, have much higher optimum temperatures (Figure 9.8). Some plant enzymes have lower optimum temperatures, depending on their habitat.

Figure 9.8   Bacteria living in hot springs such as this one in Yellowstone National Park, USA, are able to tolerate very high temperatures. Enzymes from such organisms are proving useful in various industrial applications.

SAQ

4   How could you carry out an experiment to determine the effect of temperature on the rate of breakdown of hydrogen peroxide by catalase?

Hint

Answer

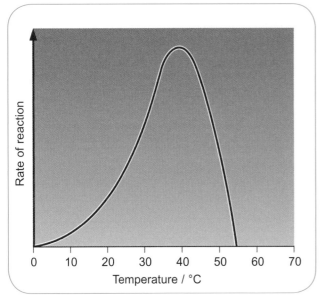

Figure 9.7   The effect of temperature on the rate of an enzyme-controlled reaction.

pH and enzyme activity

Figure 9.9 shows how the activity of an enzyme is affected by pH. Most enzymes work fastest at a pH somewhere around 7 – that is, in fairly neutral conditions. Some, however, such as the protease pepsin which is found in the acidic conditions of the stomach, have a different optimum pH (Figure 9.10).

pH is a measure of the concentration of hydrogen ions in a solution; the lower the pH, the higher the hydrogen ion concentration. Hydrogen ions can interact with the R groups of amino acids – this influences the way in which they bond with each other and therefore affects tertiary structure. A pH that is very different from the optimum pH can cause denaturation of an enzyme.

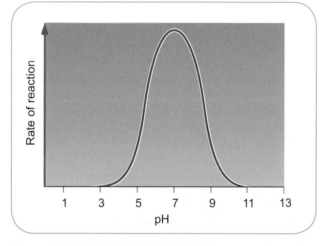
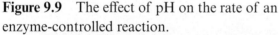

Figure 9.9 The effect of pH on the rate of an enzyme-controlled reaction.

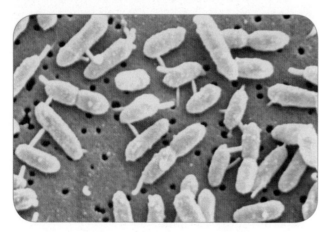

Figure 9.10 The prokaryote *Acidiphillum* is able to live in very acidic conditions; its enzymes have a low optimum pH. It may prove useful in breaking down acidic wastes from mining operations.

Enzyme inhibitors

A substance that slows down or stops an enzyme-controlled reaction is said to be an **inhibitor**.

As we have seen, the active site of an enzyme fits, or adjusts to fit, one particular substrate perfectly. It is possible, however, for some *other* molecule to bind to an enzyme's active site if it is very similar to the enzyme's substrate. This could inhibit the enzyme's function.

If the inhibitor molecule binds only briefly to the site then there is competition between it and the substrate for the site. If there is much more of the substrate than the inhibitor present, substrate molecules can easily bind to the active site in the usual way and so the enzyme's function is hardly affected. However, if the concentration of the inhibitor rises or that of the substrate falls, it becomes more and more likely that the inhibitor will collide with an empty site and bind with the enzyme, rather than the substrate. This is known as **competitive inhibition** (Figure 9.11). It is said to be **reversible** because it can be reversed by increasing the concentration of substrate.

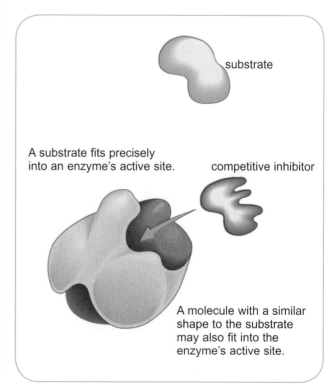

A substrate fits precisely into an enzyme's active site.

substrate

competitive inhibitor

A molecule with a similar shape to the substrate may also fit into the enzyme's active site.

Figure 9.11 Competitive inhibition.

Sometimes, the inhibitor can remain permanently bonded with the active site and causes a permanent block to the substrate. This kind of inhibition is **irreversible**. Even if more substrate is added, it cannot displace the inhibitor from the active site. The antibiotic penicillin works like this. It permanently occupies the active site of an enzyme that is essential for the synthesis of bacterial cell walls.

A different kind of inhibition takes place if a molecule can bind to another part of the enzyme, rather than the active site. This can seriously disrupt the normal arrangement of bonds holding the enzyme in shape. The resulting distortion ripples across the molecule to the active site, making it unsuitable for the substrate. The enzyme's function is blocked no matter how much substrate is present so this is **non-competitive inhibition** (Figure 9.12). It can be **reversible inhibition** or **irreversible inhibition**, depending on whether the inhibitor bonds briefly or permanently with the enzyme. Digitalis – a substance extracted from foxglove plants – is an example of a non-competitive inhibitor. It binds with the enzyme ATPase, resulting in an increase in the contraction of heart muscle.

In an enzyme-catalysed reaction, the graph of initial rate of reaction against substrate concentration is changed if an inhibitor is present. The shape of the graph shows whether competitive or non-competitive inhibition is occuring (Figure 9.13).

Inhibitors that seriously disrupt enzyme-controlled reactions can act as **metabolic poisons**, preventing vital chemical reactions that take place in the body. For example, a toxin found in the death cap mushroom, called alpha-amanitin, inhibits enzymes that catalyse the production of RNA from DNA. When this happens, cells are no longer able to synthesise proteins. This mushroom is one of the deadliest fungi known.

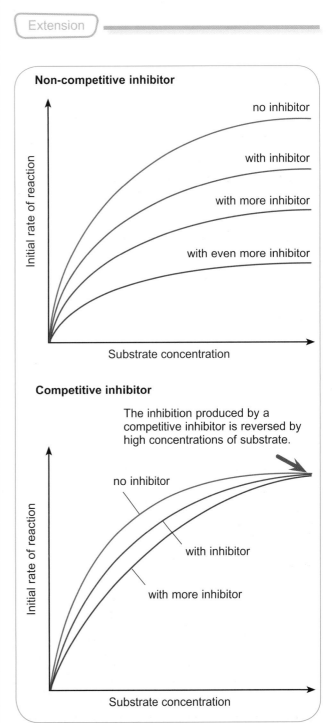

Figure 9.13 The effect of increasing substrate concentration on non-competitive and competitive inhibition.

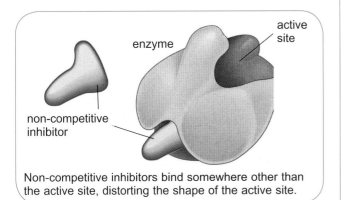

Figure 9.12 Non-competitive inhibition.

Cofactors and coenzymes

Many enzymes require the presence of another substance in order to function. These substances are called **cofactors** or **coenzymes**.

There is no absolutely clear-cut distinction between a cofactor and a coenzyme. However, most biologists use the term 'cofactor' for simple molecules or inorganic ions, and the term 'coenzyme' for larger molecules. Both cofactors and coenzymes usually work by binding briefly with the enzyme. They sometimes alter its shape so that it can bind more effectively with its substrate, and sometimes help the enzyme to transfer a particular group of atoms from one molecule to another.

For example, chloride ions act as cofactors for salivary amylase. They bind with amylase, slightly changing its shape and making it easier for starch molecules to fit into its active site. Another example arises in blood clotting, where calcium ions are essential cofactors for the enzyme thrombin, which catalyses the change of the soluble, globular protein fibrinogen into the insoluble, fibrous protein fibrin.

An example of a coenzyme is **coenzyme A**. This is needed in many metabolic pathways, including aerobic respiration.

Many cofactors are made from vitamins. For example, vitamin B_3 is required for the synthesis of coenzyme A.

Leeches and blood clotting

It is very important that blood should only clot when required, but that when it is required it clots quickly. One of the essential reactions that happens in order to form a blood clot is the changing of the soluble protein fibrinogen into the insoluble protein fibrin, brought about by the enzyme thrombin.

Fibrinogen is always present in the blood plasma. Thrombin is only produced when a blood vessel is damaged. An inhibitor called antithrombin, like fibrinogen, is also present in the plasma, and it binds to thrombin, partly covering its active site and stopping it from binding with its substrate. The quantities of thrombin and antithrombin in the blood are precisely balanced to make sure that blood only clots in the right place and at the right time.

Leeches feed on blood. They do not want it to clot – they need it to flow freely from the small wound they make. In their saliva is an enzyme, hirudin, which, like antithrombin, binds thrombin and inhibits its action, acting as an anticoagulant.

Leeches are still used in medicine. They are especially useful after replacement surgery – for example, if someone has lost an ear in an

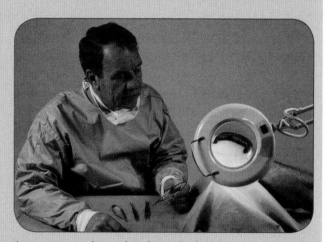

A surgeon using a leech to drain blood from damaged tissue.

accident and has had it sewn back on. Surgeons can generally reconnect arteries successfully because they have relatively thick walls, but the thin-walled veins are often impossible to connect. This means that blood is delivered effectively to the replaced organ, but not removed. Leeches fulfil this role. They act as substitute veins after surgery, helping to remove excess blood, preventing it from clotting and keeping it flowing smoothly as the body repairs itself.

Summary

● Enzymes are globular proteins, which act as catalysts by lowering activation energy. They control virtually all metabolic reactions, both intracellularly and extracellularly.

● Each enzyme acts on only one particular substrate, because there has to be a perfect match between the shape of the substrate and the shape of the active site, in order for an enzyme–substrate complex to form. Usually, binding with the substrate will cause a change in the enzyme's shape, so that it accommodates the substrate perfectly; this is called induced fit.

● Anything that affects the shape of the active site, such as high temperature, a change in pH or the binding of a non-competitive inhibitor with the enzyme molecule, will reduce the activity of the enzyme.

● Competitive inhibitors slow down the rate of reaction, by competing with the substrate for the active site. The degree of inhibition is related to the relative concentrations of the inhibitor and the substrate.

● Enzyme inhibition may be reversible or irreversible, depending on how tightly and for how long the inhibitor binds to the enzyme.

● Some metabolic poisons and medicinal drugs are enzyme inhibitors.

● Many enzymes require the presence of cofactors or coenzymes in order to catalyse their reactions.

Glossary

Questions

1 Two students carried out an investigation into the effect of pH on the activity of a lysosomal enzyme. Student A drew a graph, shown in the diagram.

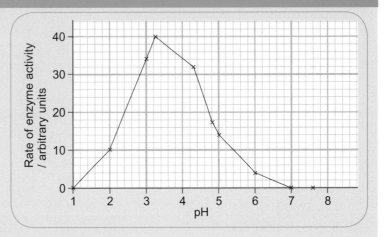

a i A teacher asked two students to state the optimum pH for this enzyme. Student A gave the answer 'pH 3.25' but student B gave the answer 'somewhere between pH 3.0 and pH 4.3'.

The teacher said that student B had given the better answer.
Explain why student B's answer was better. [2]

ii Explain why this enzyme is not active at pH 7. [2]

b Explain the effects of enzyme concentration, substrate concentration and competitive inhibitors on the rate of an enzyme-controlled reaction. [9]

OCR Biology AS (2801) January 2006 [Total 13]

Answer

continued

2 The enzyme urease catalyses the following reaction:

urea + water ⟶ ammonium carbonate

Ammonium carbonate readily gives off ammonia.

The indicator bromo-thymol blue is yellow in neutral solution and blue in alkaline solution. In an investigation, urease was mixed with bromo-thymol blue. The mixture was divided equally between five test-tubes, labelled A to E. One test-tube was placed in each of five water baths at the temperatures shown in the table, until they reached the desired temperature. The same mass of urea was then added to each test-tube. The test-tubes were maintained at their temperatures and the time taken for the contents of each test-tube to turn blue was recorded.

The results of the investigation are shown in the table.

a Suggest why the indicator changed colour after urea was added to the enzyme. [1]

b With reference to the table,
  i state what you can conclude about the optimum temperature of the enzyme [1]
  ii explain the fact that the <u>time taken</u> for the blue colour to appear is greater at 15 °C than at 35 °C and is greater at 55 °C than at 35 °C. [4]

Test-tube	Temperature / °C	Time taken for blue colour to appear / s
A	0	89
B	15	21
C	35	5
D	45	17
E	55	33

The indicator was added to a separate sample of urea and to a separate sample of urease.

In neither test-tube was a blue colour produced.

c Explain why the indicator was added to separate samples of both urea and urease. [2]

d Copy the axes, and sketch the curves you would expect if an enzyme-controlled reaction was carried out under optimum conditions with
  i a fixed quantity of enzyme [2]
  ii excess substrate. [1]

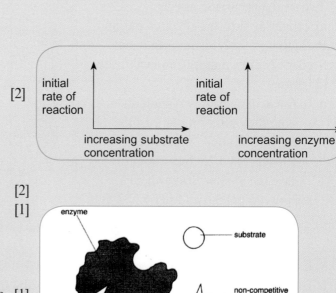

The diagram represents an enzyme, its substrate and a <u>non-competitive</u> inhibitor.

e With reference to the diagram,
  i copy the diagram and label the active site [1]
  ii explain how the inhibitor has its effect. [3]

OCR Biology AS (2801) June 2001   [Total 15]

Answer

Chapter 10

Diet and food production

Objectives

Nutrition

The food we eat provides us with the energy that our cells use, and also with the materials that are needed to construct tissues. We are **heterotrophs** – like all animals, we rely on organic substances in our diet that have been made by plants (Table 10.1). Plants are **autotrophs**, using inorganic substances to build organic substances such as carbohydrates, proteins and lipids. These substances contain energy that originated as energy in sunlight.

Nutrient	Function	Good food sources	Notes
carbohydrates	provide energy, which is released by respiration inside body cells	bread, rice, potatoes, pulses (beans, lentils and peas), breakfast cereals	includes sugars and starches; starches are better than sugars because they take longer to digest and the energy in them is released more steadily
proteins	formation of new cells and tissues, and of many important substances, including haemoglobin, collagen and enzymes; can be respired to provide energy	meat, eggs, fish, dairy products, pulses	proteins contain 20 different amino acids, of which 8 are essential in the diet as the body cannot make them from other amino acids
lipids	making cell membranes, and steroid hormones; provide energy when broken down in respiration – fats provide twice as much energy per gram as carbohydrates or proteins	dairy products, red meat, oily fish, plant oils	lipids contain several different fatty acids, of which two are essential in the diet; foods containing lipids are also important sources of fat-soluble vitamins
vitamin A (fat soluble)	making the pigment rhodopsin, found in the rod cells in the eye and essential for vision	meat, egg yolks, carrots	daily doses at around 100 times the recommended daily intake are toxic
vitamin C (water soluble)	making collagen	citrus fruits, blackcurrants, potatoes	
vitamin D (fat soluble)	formation of bones and teeth	dairy foods, oily fish, egg yolks	this vitamin is also made in the skin when exposed to sunlight
iron	formation of haemoglobin	meat, beans, chocolate, shellfish, eggs	shortage of iron in the diet is a common cause of anaemia
calcium	bone formation and blood clotting	dairy products, fish	lack of calcium in the diet can increase the risk of osteoporosis

Table 10.1 Nutrients and their roles in the body.

A balanced diet

A good diet contains a full range of all the different nutrients. A **balanced diet** contains all of these nutrients, in approximately the correct proportions. The amount of energy in the diet should be approximately equal to the amount of energy used by the body each day.

SAQ

1 a Which of the nutrients listed in Table 10.1 are organic chemicals?

  b Which of the nutrients listed in Table 10.1 provide us with energy?

Answer

Malnutrition

The term **malnutrition** is often misunderstood. We tend to associate it with pictures of starving children in drought-stricken regions of Africa, or in refugee camps. But malnutrition does not necessarily mean starvation – it literally means 'bad eating' and refers to the result of any diet that is seriously unbalanced.

In Britain, one of the most serious effects of malnutrition in the early 21st century is **obesity** (Figure 10.1). An obese person is seriously overweight. One definition of obesity is having a body mass index (BMI) of more than 30. (To calculate your body mass index, divide your mass, in kilograms, by your height, in metres, squared.) Obesity results from consistently eating nutrients that contain more energy than the body uses. The 'spare' energy is stored in the form of fat, which builds up as **adipose tissue** underneath the skin and around the body organs. Obesity seriously increases the risk of developing heart disease, type II diabetes and arthritis (Figure 10.2).

The incidence of obesity has been steadily increasing. Almost all of us have easy access to as much food as we want, and much of this food is very 'energy-dense' – it contains a lot of kilojoules per gram. This is often true of fast food, such as burgers and fries. On the other side of the coin, many of us do not use up a great deal of energy each day; we have become much more sedentary, spending more time sitting and relaxing rather than walking or playing sport. The combination of eating more and exercising less is building up what many nutritionists are calling the 'obesity time bomb'. The increasing number of people who are obese now will result in an increasing number of people with obesity-related diseases in the future.

Figure 10.1 A normal mouse and an obese mouse.

Figure 10.2 Obesity is most damaging when fat accumulates around the abdomen. It greatly increases the risk of developing type II diabetes.

What causes obesity?

There's no doubt that some people have a much greater tendency to put on weight than others. While quite a bit of this can be put down to environment and lifestyle – including the diet eaten, amount of exercise taken and straightforward willpower – scientists have long believed that there is also a strong genetic influence on our likelihood of becoming obese. For example, studies of identical twins show that they have a very high resemblance in their tendency to become obese, even if they are brought up in completely different environments.

It seems likely that genetic influences on obesity are polygenic – that is, there are many different genes that each have a small effect. There are just a few examples of a single gene that can have a large effect, but they are very rare. For example, a two-year-old boy who weighed almost 30 kg was found to have a mutation in a gene that normally codes for a protein called leptin, which has been linked to the control of appetite.

The discovery of leptin was first made in mice, in 1994. Various strains of mice are kept and bred in laboratories, and one of these strains is extremely obese (Figure 10.1). The obese mice were found to have a single gene mutation that prevented them from making leptin. Leptin is made in fat storage cells, in adipose tissue. The more fat there is, the more leptin is made. Leptin travels in the blood to all parts of the body, where it has several different target organs. Among these is the brain – leptin provides an 'I am full' signal to the brain, suppressing appetite. As fat stores dwindle, less leptin is produced and the mouse feels hungrier. The obese mice have no leptin, so their brains never get a 'full' signal, and they always feel hungry.

There were high hopes that this discovery might help to explain obesity in humans. We also produce leptin, and it was thought that perhaps giving people leptin might suppress their appetites and help them to lose weight. But results of trials have not been encouraging. Leptin may play a role in our desire to eat, but it isn't a magic bullet that can reduce obesity. Indeed, many obese people already have high levels of leptin in their blood, and it seems that the problem is more in the way the brain responds to it than the actual production of leptin by the fat cells.

Various other studies have found potential candidate genes that might affect the tendency to put on weight. One of the best studies was reported in 2007. A group of researchers in Britain had been looking for a genetic link to the tendency to develop type II diabetes. They had screened 2000 people with type II diabetes, and found a strong correlation with the presence of a particular allele (variety of a gene) called FTO. The link was so strong that the team decided to expand their study, and to look not only at diabetes but also obesity. They used a huge sample of 38 759 people, from Britain, Italy and Finland. They found that people who were heterozygous for this allele were, on average, 1.2 kg heavier than people who did not have it. People who were homozygous for the allele were, on average, 3 kg heavier. Around 50% of people were heterozygous and 16% homozygous.

It looks as though this research has identified one of the many genes that are probably involved in determining the likelihood of becoming obese. There must be many more yet to be discovered. But we cannot put all the blame on genes. There is no suggestion that our genes have changed in the last 50 years, but there is no doubt that the proportion of obese people has increased greatly. This can only be down to lifestyle. Some of us may find it more difficult than others to keep our weight down, but we can still take care over diet and exercise and try to maintain weight at a healthy level.

Extension

Diet and the cardiovascular system

If you live to be 80 years old, your heart will beat at least 2.5 billion times. Your lungs will inflate and deflate at least 600 million times. Inevitably the body systems become less efficient as we get older, but there is a great deal that we can do to help to keep both the cardiovascular system and the gaseous exchange system working strongly, even as we age.

Coronary heart disease

Coronary heart disease, often abbreviated to **CHD**, is a common disorder of the blood vessels that supply the heart muscle with oxygenated blood. It is a major cause of death in developed countries. In the United Kingdom, around 3–4% of men between the ages of 35 and 74 die each year as a direct result of CHD. For women, the risk is around half of this figure. It is the single most common cause of death – 30% of all deaths among men, and 22% of deaths among women, are caused by CHD. Every year, 156 000 people in England and Wales die from CHD.

The ability of the cardiac muscle to contract depends on it receiving a continuous supply of oxygen. The muscle uses the oxygen for aerobic respiration, which provides the energy that it uses for contraction. If the oxygen supply fails, then the muscle cannot contract. Heart muscle lacking oxygen quickly dies.

CHD is caused by **atherosclerosis** in the coronary arteries (the section about the structure of the heart in Chapter 5 and Figure 10.3). Atherosclerosis is sometimes known as 'hardening of the arteries'.

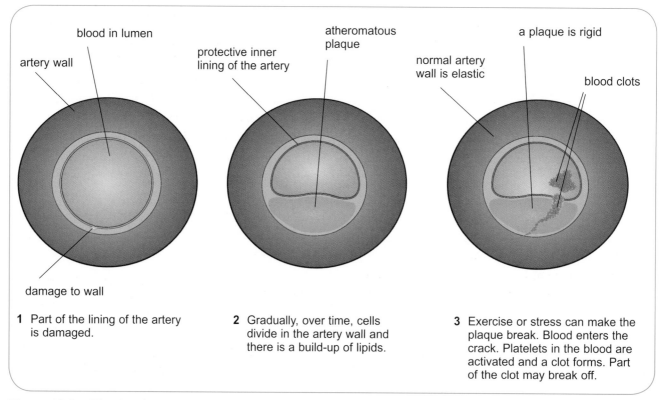

Figure 10.3   The development of an atheromatous plaque.

Atherosclerosis can lead to the coronary arteries becoming blocked. Usually, the blockage is due to the build-up of material inside the artery walls, which makes the space through which blood can flow – the lumen – much narrower. Atherosclerosis can also occur in other arteries, including those supplying the brain.

Atherosclerosis develops slowly, and people do not normally show any symptoms until they are at least 40 years old. It occurs naturally as part of the ageing process. However, in some people it progresses more rapidly and this can be due to a variety of factors that tend to damage the lining of arteries. These include high blood pressure, the presence of harmful chemicals such as those in tobacco smoke, or low-density lipoproteins (LDLs, described on pages 148 – 150). The damage, and the attempts by the body to repair itself, build up tissue and chemicals in the artery wall. These deposits are known as an **atheromatous plaque**.

Once the plaque has reduced the lumen of a coronary artery by 50% or more, the flow of blood through the artery cannot keep up with the oxygen requirements of the heart muscle during exercise. The person experiences pain when exercising, known as **angina**. The pain is often in the left shoulder, chest and arm, but for some people also in the neck or the left side of the face.

Blood clots can form on and around the plaque. Such a blood clot is called a **coronary thrombosis**. This happens because platelets in the blood come into contact with collagen (a fibrous protein, described on in Chapter 7) in the artery wall. The platelets then secrete chemicals that stimulate the blood to form a clot.

The blood clot narrows the artery even more. It may break off and get stuck in a smaller vessel. The part of the heart that is supplied by this blood vessel stops beating, and some of the muscle cells may die. This is known as a **myocardial infarction** and is an extremely dangerous condition.

Myocardial infarction

'Myo' means 'muscle', and the myocardium is the muscular wall of the heart. 'Infarction' is a term describing the loss of sufficient blood flow to a tissue to allow it carry out its normal activity. Around 90% of instances of myocardial infarction are caused by a coronary thrombosis.

If the infarction involves a large amount of muscle, the person may die almost immediately. Severe myocardial infarction may cause the heart to stop beating. This is called **cardiac arrest** (heart attack) (Figure 10.4). No pulse can be felt, and the victim rapidly loses consciousness.

Others may not lose consciousness, but experience such severe pain that they call for help straight away. If less muscle is affected, the pain may be less severe, and the patient may wait several hours before calling a doctor. Sometimes, they may not even realise that they have had a minor infarction, and do nothing. The pain is usually felt near the centre of the thorax, behind the sternum, and is described as 'crushing' or 'bursting'.

The commonest time of day for acute myocardial infarction is first thing in the morning, when the patient has just got up. There is another peak around 5 p.m. Friday is the commonest day of the week for a myocardial infarction, and there are fewer at weekends. No-one really understands the reasons for these patterns, but it is thought that stress or excitement may be involved, causing a rise in blood pressure, which may rupture a plaque in a coronary artery.

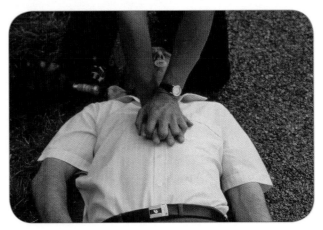

Figure 10.4 A paramedic applying chest compressions to get the heart to beat again after cardiac arrest.

Diet and coronary heart disease

It seems that every week there is some new advice about what we should and should not do to maintain a healthy heart. In the 1950s, people were told to drink milk and eat eggs to stay healthy (Figure 10.5). Then the health experts decided that these, and many other 'fatty' foods, were bad for us. In 2003, the Atkins diet, which entails cutting out practically all carbohydrate-rich foods and eating as much protein- and fat-containing food as you like, became extraordinarily popular. Why so much confusion?

The difficulty is that we cannot quickly and easily do properly controlled experiments into the effect on human health of a particular factor in the diet. There are too many variables involved that we cannot control. In particular, it seems that small differences in our genes make us respond to a particular type of diet in different ways.

Figure 10.5 In the 1950s, a classic advertising slogan 'Go to work on an egg' was used by the British Egg Marketing Board. TV commercials were to be reshown on their 50th anniversary in 2007, but were banned on the grounds that they did not promote a balanced diet.

However, there *is* a great deal of evidence that shows that having a high level of **cholesterol** in the blood does increase the risk of suffering from CHD. What is less clear is the extent to which diet affects blood cholesterol levels. There is some evidence that eating a diet high in **saturated fats** can increase your blood cholesterol level and therefore your risk. However, other investigations do not support this view. Overall, there is as yet no hard evidence that makes a direct link between the amount of cholesterol that you eat and your risk of heart disease.

HDLs and LDLs

The structures, properties and functions of fats (lipids) and cholesterol are described in Chapter 7. We have already seen (Chapter 1) that cholesterol is an important constituent of cell membranes. If we do not take in enough in our diet, then the liver makes cholesterol that can be transported around the body and used by cells.

Cholesterol is not soluble in water, and so it cannot be transported in solution in the blood plasma. It is carried in the blood plasma in the form of **lipoproteins** – tiny balls made up of various lipids, cholesterol and proteins (Figure 10.6).

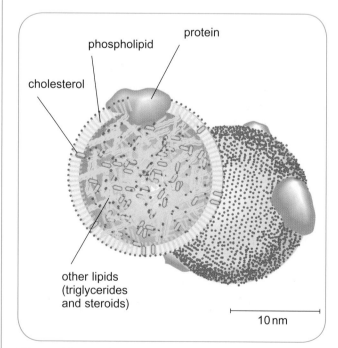

Figure 10.6 Lipoproteins.

Lipoproteins come in several varieties, with different proportions of protein molecules and lipid molecules, including cholesterol. Proteins tend to be denser than lipids, so the more protein there is, the greater the density of the lipoprotein. The lipoproteins are named according to their densities (Table 10.2).

High-density lipoproteins – HDLs	a lot of protein and relatively small amounts of lipids
Low-density lipoproteins – LDLs	more lipid and less protein than HDLs
Chylomicrons	contain a lot of lipid and very little protein

Table 10.2   Types of lipoproteins.

HDLs usually pick up cholesterol from body cells that are dying, or whose membranes are being restructured, and transport it to the liver. **LDLs** usually carry lipids and cholesterol from the liver to other parts of the body. Chylomicrons are formed in the wall of the ileum from fats which have been digested and absorbed. They transport lipids from the small intestine to the liver.

Cholesterol and CHD

LDLs have a tendency to deposit the cholesterol that they carry in the damaged walls of arteries. This cholesterol makes up a large proportion of an atheromatous plaque (Figure 10.3). There is a positive link between the level of LDLs in the blood and the risk of suffering from CHD and possibly a heart attack.

HDLs, on the other hand, seem actually to protect against CHD. They remove cholesterol from tissues, including the tissues in the walls of blood vessels.

In the past, health professionals were simply concerned about the quantity of cholesterol in the blood. Now attention has shifted to the relative proportions of 'good' HDLs and 'bad' LDLs. The higher the proportion of HDLs, the lower the risk of heart disease.

So how can someone increase their proportion of HDLs? Diet does have an effect in some people. A diet that is very rich in saturated fats (fats from animal-derived foods) may result in a high LDL concentration. A person who eats that sort of diet may benefit from switching to one that is low in saturated fats. This would probably involve reducing the amounts of meat and dairy products in the diet, and increasing the amounts of plant-derived foods and fish. Almost all studies show a link between eating fish and protection against CHD.

SAQ

2 A study followed 639 people with a family history of CHD over a period of 14 years. Some had an LDL:HDL of more than 8, while some had an LDL:HDL of less than 8. The graph shows the probability of survival of a person in each of these groups over the 14 years of the study.
   a Explain why the survival probability is 100% at 0 years.
   b Suggest why the graph is drawn so that it goes down in steps rather than in a smooth line. [Hint]
   c Describe the conclusions that can be drawn from these data. [Hint] [Answer]

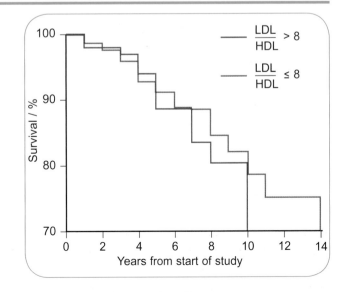

149

We have seen that the amount of cholesterol in the diet is not directly linked to the development of atherosclerosis. This is because the cholesterol in our blood does not all come from cholesterol that we eat. The liver makes cholesterol, and if there is insufficient in the blood it will make more. If we eat more cholesterol, the liver reduces its production of it. Various studies suggest that the greatest effect a low-fat, low-cholesterol diet can have on LDL concentration is to reduce it on average by around 10%.

A much more effective way of reducing LDLs is to use drugs called **statins**. These inhibit an enzyme in the liver cells which catalyses one of the reactions involved in the synthesis of cholesterol.

Salt and CHD

Blood pressure is the pressure that the blood exerts on the walls of the vessels through which it is travelling. The pressure in an artery in the arm, for a healthy young person, should be between 120 mm Hg and 139 mm Hg during systole (when the heart muscle is contracting) and between 80 mm Hg and 89 mm Hg during diastole. If a person's resting blood pressure is excessively and persistently high, they are said to have **hypertension**.

Hypertension increases the risk of CHD. It causes the walls of arteries to thicken and stiffen. This increases the risk of damage to the epithelium lining the vessel, which is often followed by the development of atheromatous plaques. It also means that the heart has to pump blood at higher pressures, increasing the workload on the heart.

In many cases, the cause of high blood pressure is not clear. A diet high in salt may sometimes be part of the problem. A high salt concentration in the blood draws water into the blood by osmosis, thus increasing the blood volume and therefore the blood pressure. The kidneys should react to this situation by excreting more liquid with more salt in it, but they do not always do this.

People with chronic (long-term) hypertension may be advised to eat a low-salt diet. They may also be given diuretics ('water pills'), which make the kidneys excrete large amounts of fluid. This reduces the volume of fluid in the body, and so reduces blood pressure.

Proving the link

For many years, doctors have urged people with high blood pressure to eat less salt, to decrease their risk of developing coronary heart disease or having a stroke.

But there was no hard evidence to support this recommendation. Despite doctors' and scientists' suspicions, no-one had actually shown that reducing the salt in your diet is good for your health. Because the evidence was so shaky (and some people suggested that the little evidence there was even showed that a low-salt diet was bad for you) many people did not follow their doctor's advice.

It was not until April 2007 that a careful piece of research actually showed that this link genuinely exists – yes, eating less salt really is good for your health.

The research followed 2400 people with high blood pressure – all volunteers – over a period of 15 years. Half were shown how to look for low-salt foods when they were shopping, and eat a low-salt diet, while half ate a 'normal' diet, with as much salt as they wanted.

The results showed incontrovertibly that those eating a low-salt diet had a 20% lower risk of death from all causes. In all, 200 people had developed cardiovascular disease. Of these, 112 came from the group that had not been recommended to eat a low-salt diet. Only 88 were in the low-salt group.

Some processed foods high in salt.

Sources of food

Almost all of our food comes originally from plants. Many people are vegan or vegetarian and eat only plant-derived foods. Others eat animal-derived foods such as meat, eggs and milk, but even these depend ultimately on plants. Plants are the producers in food chains, making carbohydrates by photosynthesis and then using these to manufacture proteins, lipids and vitamins.

In almost every country in the world, plant-derived foods form the staple diet. Figure 10.7 shows the staple foods in southern Asia. These are all plant foods that contain a large amount of carbohydrate, generally in the form of starch. They tend to supply the bulk of a person's diet, providing a large proportion of their energy needs and many vitamins and minerals. Other foods eaten in smaller quantities, such as leafy vegetables, eggs, meat and fish, provide proteins and other vitamins. Many people in Britain also eat a diet based around a staple food. Diets vary according to cultures – so some people may eat a diet containing a lot of potatoes, while others eat a lot of bread (made from wheat) or rice. But things have changed greatly in the last 50 years, and many people now eat a diet much richer in fats and proteins than in the past. The traditional plant-based staple foods are not usually energy-rich – they do not contain much lipid, and they do contain plenty of fibre. The modern, high-energy diet tends to be low in fibre, and much richer in lipid and quick-release carbohydrates (sugars, rather than starches). It is probable this that is largely responsible for the increases in obesity and the incidence of type II diabetes.

SAQ

3 Write food chains to show the origin of each of these foods, ending each chain with a human: bread (made from wheat flour), yogurt, beef steak, eggs

Hint

Answer

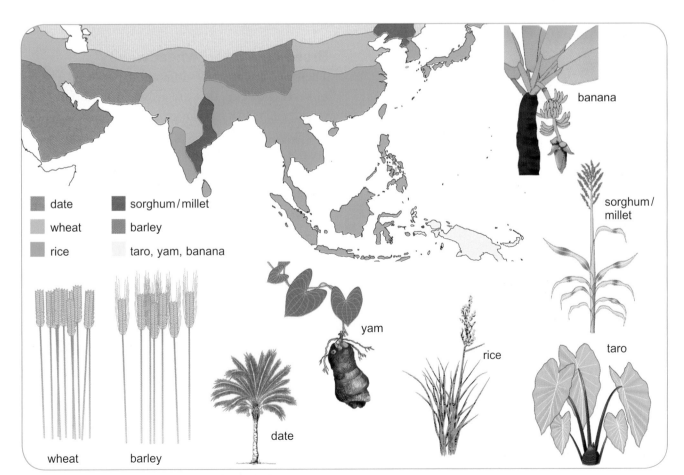

Figure 10.7 Staple foods in southern Asia.

date

wheat

rice

sorghum/millet

barley

taro, yam, banana

banana

sorghum/millet

yam

rice

taro

date

wheat

barley

Selective breeding

From the time that humans first farmed crops, thought to be around 10000 years ago, they have been selecting the 'best' individuals from which to breed. In a field of wheat, there may have been individual plants that had more seeds per ear, or larger seeds, or from which the seeds had less tendency to fall off the plant before they were ready for harvesting (Figure 10.8). Early farmers would have saved seeds from plants with such favourable characteristics, to sow the next year. Over time, the wheat crops that they grew would have come to have higher yields and better harvesting characteristics.

These early farmers knew nothing of genes and the laws of inheritance, yet the selection for particular characteristics over thousands of years has brought about great changes in the cultivated varieties of crop plants – not only wheat – that we grow today.

Although we now know much more about the genetic basis of variation in plants, we still use very similar techniques of **selective breeding** in order to produce new varieties. This is largely because most characteristics are not caused by a single gene, but by many different genes all making a small contribution towards a particular characteristic. Genetic modification has been used in some instances, to introduce a new gene into a crop plant, but selective breeding is by far the commonest method of developing varieties with desired characteristics.

The breeding of new plant varieties is now mostly done by specialist plant breeders, not by farmers. Selective breeding of animals is more likely to be done on a farm. We will look at three examples of selective wheat-breeding – to produce:
- a dwarf, high-yielding wheat variety
- rust-resistant wheat varieties
- a variety that is resistant to aphids.

We will then look at how selective breeding can produce herds of cattle with especially high body mass or milk yields.

Breeding a dwarf wheat variety

There are hundreds of different varieties of wheat, of several species, that are grown around the world, each with its own particular characteristics that make it suitable for growing in a particular area or for a specific purpose. The part of the wheat that we want is its grain, which is used to make flour. The rest of the plant is left behind after harvest, forming straw and stubble (Figure 10.9). The straw does have some uses – for example, as animal bedding – but it has only a low value and farmers often have to pay to get rid of it.

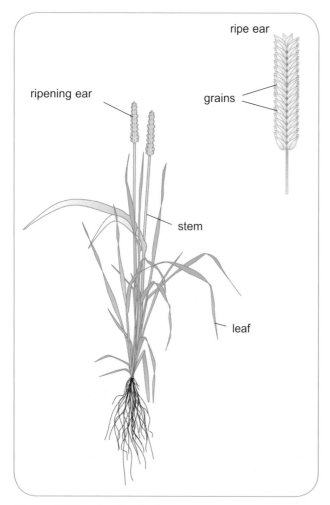

Figure 10.8 A wheat plant.

Figure 10.9 Harvesting a wheat crop. The harvester cuts the wheat stalks close to the ground, leaving behind stubble. In the harvester, the grain is separated from the straw.

In 2000, a breeding programme began to produce a new, dwarf variety of wheat that gives a higher yield than other dwarf varieties. The breeders chose to start with a very dwarf wheat, which did not have a particularly high yield, and another that had good yield. Figure 10.10 shows how the programme was carried out.

SAQ

4 a Using the information in Figure 10.10, state the number of generations of breeding that were needed before Perigee was ready to be marketed.

  b Farmers like to plant seed that grows into plants that are as identical as possible.

   i Suggest why this is advantageous for the farmer. [Hint]

   ii Explain how a wheat-breeding programme, such as the one that produced Perigee, can produce large quantities of genetically identical seed. [Answer]

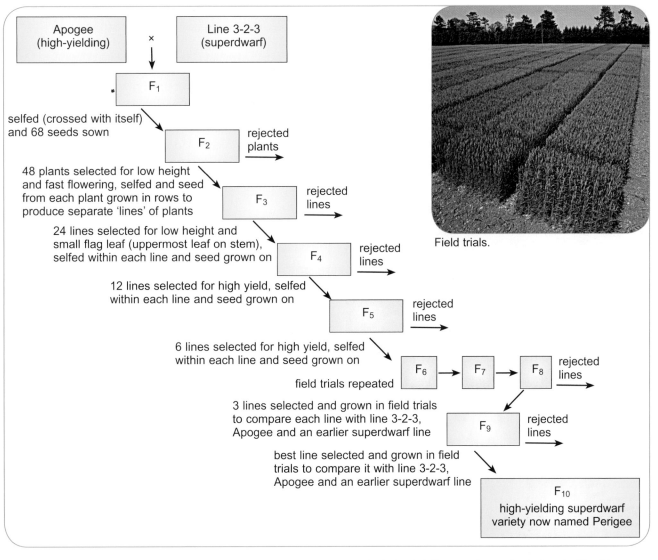

Field trials.

Figure 10.10 Selective breeding to produce Perigee, a dwarf, high-yielding variety of wheat. A 'line' is a group of plants of similar or identical genetic composition. A field trial involves growing plants in farmland to examine characteristics such as disease resistance, growth and yield of grain.

Breeding leaf-rust-resistant wheat varieties

Leaf rust is a disease of wheat caused by a fungus (Figure 10.11). It is a particular problem in warm, wet conditions. This makes it a real threat to wheat grown in many parts of Asia, where trying to avoid major epidemics of leaf rust is a constant concern.

Many of the cultivars (varieties) of wheat that are grown in Asia do have some resistance to leaf rust. If, however, two or more cultivars have the same resistance genes, then they could all quickly become susceptible if the rust fungus evolves to be able to evade their defences. So modern breeding programmes are working to try to prevent this situation before it arises.

The best strategy is to produce a cultivar with several different genes that help to confer resistance. Even if the rust fungus evolves a way of combating one of these genes, it is very unlikely to be able to overcome them all. Researchers have identified a number of rust-resistance genes in wheat, each of which has a small effect and which add up to produce excellent resistance overall (Figure 10.12).

It has been difficult to carry out selective breeding to produce varieties with many different rust-resistance genes. This is partly because it is not easy to find 'starter' varieties with more than one of the genes, so the breeders often have to work through many generations in order to produce a line of plants that has even five or six of them. Then they must also select for other characteristics, such as good yield. It was not until the 1990s that there was any good understanding of the genetics underlying rust resistance, so the choice of plants for breeding used to be based very much on trial and error. Now, it is possible to use DNA technology to detect particular genes in a plant, and so individual plants that have several of the rust-resistance genes can be identified more easily.

SAQ

5 Use the information in Figure 10.12 to describe how the number of resistance genes in a wheat plant affects its likelihood of being affected by rust.

Answer

Figure 10.11 a Rust fungus on wheat; **b** Light micrograph of the fungus on a wheat leaf (×240).

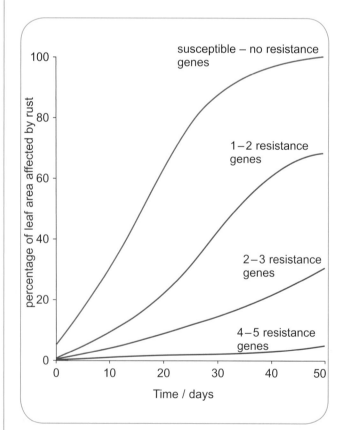

Figure 10.12 Additive effects of rust-resistance genes in wheat.

Breeding wheat resistant to Russian wheat aphid

Russian wheat aphid, *Diuraphis noxia*, is an insect that is a major pest of wheat plants in many countries. The aphids settle on the growing wheat plants and push their needle-like mouthparts into the plant's phloem tubes. The phloem sap flows through the mouthparts and into the aphid's digestive system. The wheat plants can lose a very large amount of fluid and sugars in this way, which greatly reduces their growth and the yield of grain. Moreover, the aphids often carry viruses that can infect the wheat plants, causing diseases that weaken the plants and reduce yields.

Pesticides can be sprayed to kill the aphids, but this is expensive. There is also a growing movement to reduce pesticide use, because of the potential harm that pesticides can do to other insects that may be beneficial, such as ladybirds. It is best all round (except for the aphids) if wheat varieties can be grown that have inbuilt resistance to these pests.

In Chapter 14, we will see how genetic engineering has introduced a gene coding for the production of a toxin into cotton plants, to provide them with resistance against cotton boll worms. There is no reason why GM wheat plants could not be produced in the same way, but it is an expensive process and there is still a lot of consumer resistance in Europe against consuming foods made from GM plants. Conventional selective breeding is still being used to produce new wheat cultivars that have resistance based on naturally occurring wheat genes.

Figure 10.13 shows the results of trials of three conventionally bred wheat varieties: Halt, TAM 107 and Arapahoe.

SAQ

6 a With reference to Figure 10.13a, explain which of the three varieties has the greatest resistance to Russian wheat aphid.

  b Are the results shown in Figure 10.13b consistent with those shown in Figure 10.13a? Explain your answer.

  c Russian wheat aphid is not a problem every year, although it is not possible to predict in which years this will be the case. Suggest reasons why not every wheat farmer will want to grow the most aphid-resistant variety of wheat in every year.

  > Hint

  > Answer

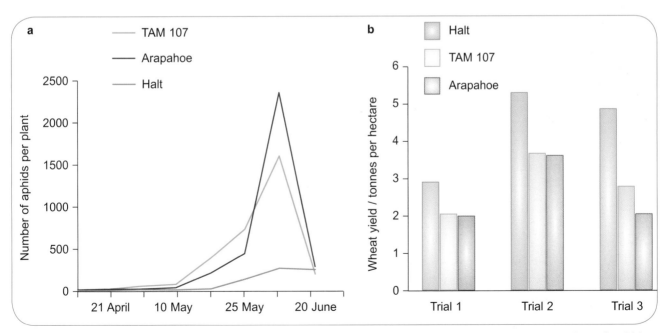

Figure 10.13 Results of trials of three wheat varieties for resistance to Russian wheat aphid: **a** number of aphids on each plant during a spring infestation; **b** yields following a spring infestation with Russian wheat aphids.

Breeding cattle for high productivity

There are many different cattle breeds in existence. Some are especially good for producing meat, and others for milk. Meat-producing breeds include Charolais (Figure 10.14), Hereford and Aberdeen Angus. Milk-producing breeds include Ayrshires, Friesians, Holsteins and Jerseys.

Figure 10.15 shows the effect of selective breeding for meat production in Charolais cattle. An intensive programme began in 1986. Bulls that had large bodies – a lot of muscle and therefore meat – were chosen to use as sires. Similarly, only the largest cows were used for breeding.

In cattle breeding, there is no longer a need to take bulls to cows. Semen is collected from chosen bulls, and then used for artificial insemination (AI). Farmers can look up the characteristics of particular bulls, and then order semen which comes from the one that farmers think will provide the best characteristics for their cattle herd. The semen can be frozen and kept for long periods of time, and transported over long distances. This means that one bull can be used for breeding with a very large number of cows.

Selective breeding for milk production is carried out in a similar way. Here, though, you obviously cannot choose a bull that produces high milk yields – instead, bulls are chosen whose female relatives have high milk yields, and who are known to produce female calves that grow up to have high milk yields. Figure 10.16 shows the effect of a ten-year selective breeding programme for high-volume milk production in Ayrshire cattle.

Care has to be taken with breeding programmes such as these, if the health and welfare of the animals is not to be compromised. For example, cattle that produce more milk also have a higher tendency to suffer from mastitis (inflammation of the udder) and lameness. Farmers may end up paying much more in veterinary fees to keep their cattle healthy. And, of course, the energy and materials that the cows use to make milk has to come from somewhere, so they will need to eat larger amounts of highly nutritious food.

Figure 10.14   A Charolais bull.

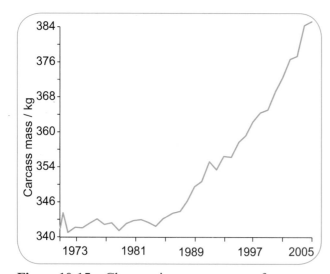

Figure 10.15   Changes in carcass mass of Charolais cattle involved in a selective breeding programme, between 1970 and 2005.

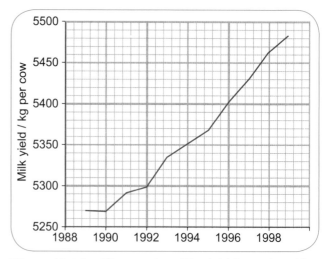

Figure 10.16   Changes in milk yield from Ayrshire cows involved in a selective breeding programme, between 1989 and 1999.

SAQ

7 Using the information in Figure 10.16, calculate the mean annual increase in milk yield per cow between 1989 and 1999.

[Answer]

Increasing food production

There are a lot of people in the world, and we all need to eat. As human populations grow, there is increasing pressure to get as much food as possible from farmed land. In many countries, farming has become increasingly **intensive** – there are large inputs into the system in order to get larger outputs. For example, fertilisers may be added to soils to increase crop yields, and pesticides sprayed onto crop plants to decrease losses to insects and other pests. Animals may be given food supplements or antibiotics to increase their growth rates, or the amount of body mass they put on from each kilogram of food that they eat.

In Britain, this trend really began just after World War II, in the 1950s. It had been difficult to supply the population with enough food during the war, because food could not be imported from overseas. The British government therefore encouraged farmers to produce more and more food. The quantity of fertiliser applied to arable land (land used for growing crops) soared, and so did the yields of crops.

Recently, there has been a backlash against this kind of intensive food production. Many people are prepared to pay more for 'organically' produced food. Organic production involves growing crops without the use of artificial fertilisers; 'natural' products such as manure are used instead (Figure 10.17). Only a limited range of pesticides is allowed. Animals are fed on organically produced feeds, and only certain medicinal products can be used.

Fertilisers

Fertilisers are added to the soil when it is deficient in one or more inorganic ions that the crop needs for its growth. The most widely used fertiliser is ammonium nitrate, which contains two ions that plants can absorb and use for making proteins: NH_4^+ and NO_3^-.

Fertilisers are expensive, and farmers only use them where they will give an increase in yield that more than outweighs the costs of buying them and applying them. Soil tests will show whether a field is lacking particular ions. Increasingly, farmers in industrialised countries use GPS systems to map the ion content of the soil in a field, allowing them to apply the fertiliser in the optimum quantities in different parts of the field (Figure 10.18). This precision can only be attained using manufactured fertilisers such as ammonium nitrate, because the farmer knows exactly the quantity of the ions that are contained in the fertiliser. If manure is used, it is only possible to have a general idea of how much should be applied to get the best results.

Figure 10.19 shows the results of an experiment into the effects of adding ammonium nitrate to the soil in a field used for growing wheat. The graph shows that adding fertiliser does increase yields, but only up to a point; after that, any extra fertiliser is effectively wasted. Other experiments have shown that, if very large quantities of fertiliser are added, they can actually *decrease* the yield of the crop, because the high concentration of dissolved ions in the soil decreases water potential below that in the root hairs of the plants, so water is lost from the plant.

Figure 10.17 Harvesting organically grown cotton.

Figure 10.18 Using an automated GPS system to apply fertiliser.

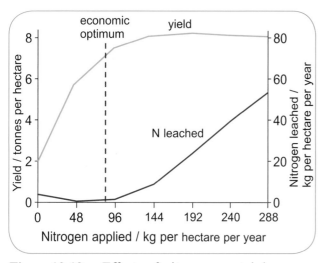

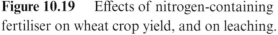

Figure 10.19 Effects of nitrogen-containing fertiliser on wheat crop yield, and on leaching.

Another problem that can arise if too much fertiliser is added – or if it is applied to the field at an inappropriate time – is that some of it may be leached from the soil and run into streams and rivers. Crops can make the best use of fertilisers if they are added while the crop is growing actively. It is very wasteful to apply fertiliser during the winter, or just before it is going to rain heavily. If the crop cannot absorb the ions before it rains, then there is a high chance that they will be washed out of the soil. Fertilisers running into streams and rivers are a major pollution problem; they cause considerable increases in the growth of algae, which shade out aquatic plants. As the plants die, bacteria feed on their remains, so the populations of bacteria increase. These respire aerobically, taking oxygen from the water and making it difficult for other organisms, such as fish, to live there.

SAQ

8 a Explain what is meant by 'economic optimum' in the graph in Figure 10.19.

   b Explain the shape of the curve for crop yield.

Hint

Answer

Pesticides

Pesticides, as their name suggests, kill pests. They include insecticides and fungicides.

In the past, some pesticides were highly damaging, largely because they were not biodegradable. An example is DDT, which does not break down inside an organism, and simply builds up in its body. Animals near the top of food chains could accumulate very large amounts of DDT in their tissues over their lifetimes, and this caused population crashes in several species of birds of prey in Britain and other parts of the world.

Insecticides like DDT are no longer used in Europe, the USA and several other parts of the world, but they are still the best way of fighting the serious problem of insect-borne diseases, especially malaria, in Africa.

Another difficulty with DDT is that it is a **broad-spectrum insecticide** – it kills all insects, not just the pests. For example, pollinating insects such as bees may be killed, and useful predators such as ladybirds. Several more specific insecticides have been developed, but these are more expensive.

Insecticides may have to be applied several times during the growing season, which again makes costs potentially very high. And there is always the problem of the development of resistance in the pest populations (page 159).

Yet another problem with pesticides is that traces of them may linger on the food that we buy and eat. There are strict regulations about allowable pesticide levels in food, but it is not possible to test every single batch of food that is on sale in a supermarket, and there are regular stories about these levels being exceeded. Evidence of harm done to people by pesticides is sketchy, but certainly most of us would prefer to eat food that does not contain them.

Organic growers are limited in the range of pesticides that they are allowed to use. Pest and disease management is a major problem in organic food production. For example, tomato plants are often infested with a fungus called *Septoria lycopersici* (Figure 10.20) and this has traditionally been controlled with fungicides containing copper. The use of these fungicides is

Figure 10.20 A tomato leaf infected with the fungus *Septoria lycopersici.*

now being questioned – copper may harm other beneficial organisms, and may even harm the plants themselves. Growers are looking for safer, more effective fungicides. Numerous alternatives have been tried. Table 10.3 shows the results of trials of two fungicides and two solutions made from compost on the yields of organically grown tomatoes. One of the fungicides contained copper, and the other contained bacteria called *Bacillus subtilis* which produce chemicals that kill fungi.

Fungicide	Total yield of tomatoes / kg ha^{-1}
copper-containing fungicide	5630
fungicide containing *Bacillus subtilis*	4020
compost solution type 1	4290
compost solution type 2	4290

Table 10.3 Effects of different anti-fungal treatments on tomato yield.

SAQ

9 a Look at Table 10.3, and compare the effects of the four anti-fungal treatments on the yield of the organically grown tomatoes.
   $\boxed{\text{Hint}}$

b Do you consider that products containing bacteria, such as the fungicide containing *Bacillus subtilis*, should be allowed to be used on crops certified as organically grown? Explain your opinion.
   $\boxed{\text{Answer}}$

Antibiotics

Antibiotics are chemicals that kill bacteria without harming the organism that is infected.

When animals are kept in intensive conditions, the chances that they will become infected with pathogenic bacteria increase. Research in the 1950s and later showed that regular 'treatment' of animals with antibiotics – even if the animals showed no symptoms of disease – could increase growth rates. The antibiotics kept down the overall numbers of bacteria, reducing the chance that diseases would occur. They help individual animals to make better use of their food, perhaps by destroying bacteria in their gut that might otherwise reduce the amount of nutrients absorbed. Such antibiotics have been widely used especially in the production of pigs and chickens.

However, the more the antibiotics are used, the more likely it is that resistance to them will evolve in populations of bacteria. This can reduce the usefulness of that antibiotic to treat bacterial infections in humans. Farmers are encouraged to limit the use of antibiotics to when they are needed – that is, to treat disease in animals.

SAQ

10 The table shows the results of a study into using antibiotics in feed on the growth rate of pigs. Two groups of pigs were used. One group was given antibiotics in its food, and the other was not. Both groups were kept in the same building.

Year	Average daily mass gain / kg	
	With antibiotics	**No antibiotics**
1	0.75	0.60
2	0.73	0.65
3	0.73	0.72
4	0.76	0.71

a Compare the results for the two groups of pigs in Year 1.
b Describe the trend over time in the results for the pigs that were not given antibiotics.
c Suggest reasons for the results you have described in **b**.
   $\boxed{\text{Hint}}$
   $\boxed{\text{Answer}}$

Microorganisms and food

Microorganisms can feed on the same foods as us. Food that is left unprotected can be colonised by bacteria and fungi, which spoil the food as they grow and feed on it. On the other hand, we can use microorganisms to make foods that we enjoy eating, such as yogurt and cheese.

Food spoilage

Bacteria and fungi feed by secreting enzymes onto the food on which they are growing. The enzymes hydrolyse substances within the food, converting them into molecules that the microorganisms can absorb and use for their growth. This changes the appearance, taste and smell of the food, and can make it dangerous to eat. Some microorganisms produce toxins as waste products, capable of making a person very ill if they eat even small amounts of them.

Preventing food spoilage by microorganisms is done by keeping the food in conditions that stop bacteria or fungi from growing. We have many different ways of doing this – some traditional and some only introduced recently.

Low temperatures

Metabolic reactions take place more slowly at low temperatures than at the usual temperatures found in a shop or a kitchen. By keeping food cool – in a fridge, for example, the temperature is about 4 °C – we considerably slow down the growth of microorganisms, allowing us to keep food safely for several days (Figure 10.21). Keeping food in a freezer, at a temperature of −10 °C or less, allows it to be kept for even longer. At this temperature, water in the cells of many microorganisms is frozen, and this prevents them growing. Food can be safely kept for many months in these conditions. However, many microorganisms are not killed in the freezer, and when the food is thawed they begin to grow again. This is why food that has been frozen and thawed should not be refrozen – the number of microorganisms will have increased, and could be enough to cause harm once the food is thawed again and eaten.

Figure 10.22 shows the effects that different temperatures have on microorganisms.

Figure 10.21 Fish is packed in ice on the boat while out at sea, to be kept cold until it is sold.

Some foods, such as fruit, can be **freeze-dried**. The food is frozen in a vacuum. This prevents the water from becoming ice – instead, because of the very low pressure around it, it turns into water vapour. This does less damage to the cells in the food, because no ice crystals are formed that could pierce and break the plasma membranes. The food keeps its texture much better than when conventional freezing is used.

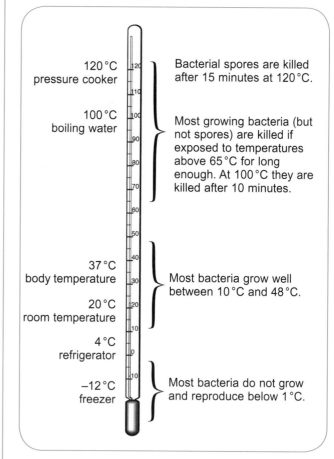

Figure 10.22 Effects of low and high temperatures on microorganisms.

Solutions with low water potential

We have seen in the section about osmosis in Chapter 2 that immersing a cell in a solution that has a lower water potential than its cytoplasm causes water to move out of the cell by osmosis, down a water potential gradient. This can destroy microorganisms, or at the very least prevent them from growing.

We make use of this when preserving food by **salting** (Figure 10.23). This is an ancient method of food preservation, traditionally used for fish, meat and some kinds of vegetables. Salt (usually sodium chloride) may be rubbed into the food, or the food may be submerged in a container full of either dry salt or a concentrated salt solution. This obviously greatly changes the flavour of the food, but many people enjoy the flavour of salted meats such as bacon, ham or pastrami.

Using concentrated sugar solutions has a similar effect. For example, jams and marmalades contain so much sugar that microorganisms are usually unable to grow in it.

Solutions with low pH

The enzymes and other proteins in microorganisms may lose their three-dimensional shape if they are placed in a highly acidic solution (see pH and enzyme activity in Chapter 9). Vinegar, a solution of ethanoic acid, is often used for food preservation. Pickles are foods preserved in vinegar, often with spices that not only taste good but also inhibit the growth of microorganisms.

Heat treatment

Many microorganisms are killed by high temperatures. However, some of them are able to produce highly resistant spores, which can survive temperatures considerably over 100 °C.

The temperatures in most kitchen ovens can be set to somewhere between 110 °C and 240 °C. Cooking food until it is piping hot will kill almost all of the microorganisms in it and make it safe to eat. Many cases of food poisoning occur when food has not been cooked or reheated to a high enough temperature.

Most of the milk that we buy has been heat-treated in some way. **Pasteurised** milk has been heated to a temperature of around 63 °C for around 30 minutes, and then rapidly cooled to 4 °C (Figure 10.24). This kills the potentially harmful bacteria in the milk, without spoiling the flavour. However, it does not kill *all* bacteria, so pasteurised milk can only be kept for a few days, even in a fridge, before it goes sour. For longer keeping, milk is **ultra heat treated** (UHT) – that is, heated to a temperature well above boiling point, at a high pressure. It is then sealed in airtight containers. UHT milk can be kept for a very long time, because it contains no active microorganisms.

Figure 10.23   Ham is made by salting pork.

Figure 10.24   A milk pasteurisation plant.

Irradiation

Ionising radiation can kill cells. The type that is generally used for food treatment is **gamma radiation**. This consists of short wavelength electromagnetic radiation, generated by radioisotopes such as cobalt-60. Gamma radiation can penetrate deeply, so a whole stack of packaged food can be irradiated at the same time.

The radiation kills most of the microorganisms in the food, but has very little effect on the food itself. You cannot tell if food has been irradiated just by looking at it (Figure 10.25)

Some people dislike the idea of eating irradiated food. Most people are very wary of anything to do with 'radiation', and fear that irradiated food might be 'radioactive'. These fears are unfounded. However, irradiation can cause some chemicals in the food to change into new substances, but investigations have shown absolutely no evidence that any of these could be harmful to health.

Figure 10.25   These two piles of strawberries were picked on the same day and kept under identical conditions. However, the ones on the left were irradiated with gamma rays, while those on the right were not.

SAQ

11 Explain the difference in the appearance of the two groups of strawberries in Figure 10.25.

(Answer)

Using microorganisms for food production

Humans have been using microorganisms for food production for thousands of years. For example, yogurt and similar milk products have traditionally been made in many countries in Asia and Europe (Figure 10.26). Making these milk products are ways of preserving milk (yogurt keeps much longer than fresh milk) as well as producing a food with a very different taste and texture. Cheese, also made from milk using microorganisms, keeps even longer.

More recently, a new type of food called **mycoprotein** has been developed. 'Myco' means 'fungus', and mycoprotein is made from a fungus called *Fusarium*. The main mycoprotein on sale in Europe and the USA is called Quorn™.

Figure 10.27 shows a fermenter used to make mycoprotein. The culture medium contains glucose, which is usually obtained from starch that has been hydrolysed by enzymes. This provides the growing fungus with a respiratory substrate for the release of energy, and also carbon that can be used to make new carbohydrate, protein and fat molecules for growth. Ammonium phosphate is added as a nitrogen source, so that the fungus can make proteins and nucleic acids, and small amounts of trace elements such as zinc and copper are also provided. Ammonia gas may be bubbled into the mixture.

Figure 10.26   Airag is made from the action of microorganisms on mare's milk. It has been made by Mongolian people for centuries, but is rather an acquired taste for others.

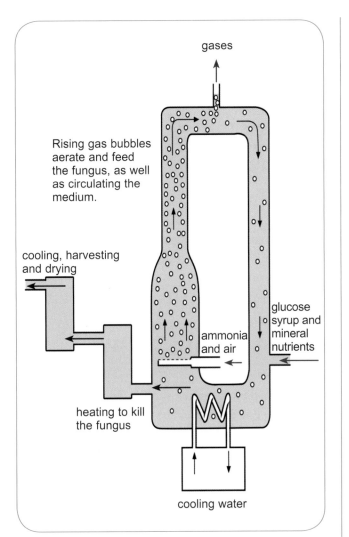

Rising gas bubbles aerate and feed the fungus, as well as circulating the medium.

gases

cooling, harvesting and drying

glucose syrup and mineral nutrients

ammonia and air

heating to kill the fungus

cooling water

Figure 10.27 A fermenter used to make mycoprotein.

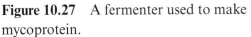

SAQ

12 Suggest why trace elements such as zinc and copper are needed by the fungus.

Hint

Answer

The temperature, pH and oxygen content of the fermenter are kept constant, providing optimum growing conditions. No stirrer is used, because the fungus is made of long, thread-like hyphae, and these are easily broken. The liquid culture containing the fungus is allowed to run off from the fermenter, and then centrifuged to separate the hyphae from the liquid.

The fungal hyphae contain a high concentration of RNA, which has a bitter taste. Enzymes are added to break this down. Mycoprotein makes an excellent food, rich in protein but low in fat.

Mycoprotein has not caught on in quite the way that manufacturers originally hoped that it would. It is fairly bland and tasteless, and really needs to be cooked imaginatively to make an interesting meal. It is sometimes used as a meat substitute by vegetarians.

So what *are* the advantages and disadvantages of using microorganisms to make food for human consumption? On the plus side, microorganisms are much cheaper and easier to work with than farm animals or even fields of crops. Microorganisms can be cultured in a relatively small area, anywhere in the world – they are not reliant on particular climatic conditions or soil type. The conditions in which they work can be kept constant, ensuring a product that always tastes just the same and has the same composition. They can be grown all year round, unaffected by weather or day-length. They can be grown on materials that might otherwise be wasted, such as wastes from food processing.

There are a few disadvantages. We have already seen the main one – mycoprotein is a much less interesting food than more conventional foods produced from crop plants or animals. For some types of food, specialist laboratory facilities may be needed, demanding investment that may not be possible in some developing countries. However, this is not normally the case, and historically people all over the world have found ways of making interesting, long-lived foods based on microorganisms using very simple processes that they can carry out in their homes.

Summary

Glossary

- Nutrition is taking in the substances that we need to provide energy and also the materials for building new cells. A balanced diet contains some of all the different nutrients, in suitable proportions, and the same amount of energy that is used by the body.

- Eating an unbalanced diet can lead to malnutrition. For example, if more energy is taken in than is used, the excess nutrients are stored as fat in adipose tissue. A person who is seriously overweight is said to be obese. Obesity increases the risk of developing heart disease, type II diabetes and arthritis.

- Almost all of the food that we eat ultimately comes from plants. Plants are producers, using energy from sunlight to make organic, energy-containing substances from inorganic ones.

- Selective breeding involves choosing individuals with desirable characteristics and breeding from them. The offspring with the best characteristics are chosen and bred together. This continues for several generations.

- Selective breeding has been used to produce crop plants (for example, wheat) with high yields, disease resistance and pest resistance, and animals (for example, cattle) with high body mass or milk yield.

- Chemicals, including fertilisers, pesticides and antibiotics, can be used to increase yields from crops and animals.

- Microorganisms can feed on food intended for humans, and spoil it. Exposing food to conditions that discourage microorganisms from growing can help to prevent food spoilage. This includes freezing, heating to high temperatures, using concentrated sugar or salt, pickling and irradiation.

- Microorganisms have been used for thousands of years to produce food. They are able to make use of foods that might otherwise go to waste, they grow easily and quickly, they can grow in almost any climate and any place, the foods that they produce often last longer than fresh foods and may have better taste, and a lot of food can be produced in a small space.

Questions

1 Much of the world's irrigated farmland has become too salty for growing crops.
Two varieties of tomato plant have been found that are tolerant of salty soil.
- Variety 1 can tolerate high concentrations of NaCl in its tissues, but has little ability to prevent the ions from entering the plant. The tomatoes produced are large, but not very tasty.
- Variety 2 cannot tolerate high concentrations of NaCl in its tissues, but is able to prevent excess ions from entering the plant. The tomatoes produced are small, but tasty.

Describe a programme for selectively breeding these two varieties to give tomato plants with high salt tolerance and large, tasty tomatoes. [8]

OCR Biology AS (2805/02) June 2005 [Total 8]

Answer

continued

2 In a 24 week study of a large sample of children with rickets in Nigeria, various treatments were carried out. The sample was divided into three groups. The groups were treated as follows:
- group 1 was given intramuscular injections of vitamin D and placebo glucose tablets
- group 2 was given calcium tablets and placebo injections of sterile water
- group 3 was given both vitamin D injections and calcium tablets.

An extra group of healthy children was included as a control (group 4).

A placebo is a treatment that is expected to have no effect, such as the injections of sterile water in group 2 or the glucose tablets group 1. Doctors took blood samples and measured the concentration of calcium ions before and after the treatment. They also took X-rays to look for signs of healing in the bones.

The results are shown in the table.

	Group			
	1	**2**	**3**	**4**
	Vitamin D injections + placebo (glucose) tablets	**Placebo (sterile water) injections + calcium tablets**	**Vitamin D injections + calcium tablets**	**Control group of healthy children**
average <u>dietary</u> calcium intake / $mg\,dm^{-1}$	200	200	200	greater than 450
mean calcium ion concentration in blood before treatment / $mg\,dm^{-3}$	77	77	77	90
mean calcium ion concentration in blood after treatment / $mg\,dm^{-3}$	83	90	90	90
% children showing some healing in X-rays after 24 weeks	83	86	93	–
% children showing complete healing in X-rays after 24 weeks	19	61	58	–

a The doctors concluded that the children in group 2 gained more benefit from their treatment than the children in group 1.
  Describe the evidence in the table that supports their conclusion. [3]
b Explain why the children in group 1 were given placebo tablets with their vitamin D injections. [2]
c Explain why group 4 was included in the study. [2]
OCR Biology AS (2802) January 2005 [Total 7]

Answer

Chapter 11

Health and disease

Background

e-Learning

Objectives

You know what you mean when you say that you are 'healthy' – but it is not easy to give this term a definition that everyone will agree with. The World Health Organization defines **health** as being 'a state of complete physical, mental and social well-being and not merely the absence of disease or infirmity'.

This definition includes the word **disease**, and this is another term that deserves some consideration. Many people use the word to mean an illness such as tuberculosis (TB) or perhaps cancer, but it can be used more widely than that. Disease is anything that impairs the normal functioning of the body. It certainly includes infectious diseases such as TB, and also problems that arise as we get older, such as coronary heart disease, or mental illnesses such as Alzheimer's disease, schizophrenia or clinical depression. There are also diseases that are inherited, such as cystic fibrosis.

Parasites and pathogens

Infectious diseases are ones that we can catch from someone else, such as a cold, TB, malaria and HIV/AIDS. These diseases are caused by **pathogens**. A pathogen can be defined as a microorganism that causes disease.

Pathogens are a kind of **parasite**. A parasite is an organism that lives in a very close relationship with another organism, called its host, and does it harm. The parasite gains from the relationship. So all pathogens are parasites, but not all parasites are pathogens. For example, you might have lice living in your hair, but they are not causing a disease so they are not pathogens.

A well-adapted parasite or pathogen does not kill its host. The parasite or pathogen is most likely to survive, and produce offspring that can move to a new host, if its host survives long enough for this to happen. Most of the infectious diseases that have been around for a long time, such as colds, measles and TB, either do not kill us – or do not kill us quickly.

Pathogens belong to one of four different groups of microorganisms – viruses, bacteria, fungi and protozoa. (Some may argue that viruses are not organisms at all.) Table 11.1 lists some examples of diseases caused by each of these groups.

Pathogen	Type of microorganism	Disease caused
human immunodeficiency virus (HIV)	virus	acquired immune deficiency syndrome (AIDS)
adenovirus	virus	colds
Mycobacterium	bacterium	tuberculosis (TB)
Tinea pedis	fungus	athlete's foot
Plasmodium	protozoan	malaria

Table 11.1   Causes of some infectious diseases.

Tuberculosis

Figure 11.1 shows the simplified structure of the bacterium *Mycobacterium tuberculosis*, which causes tuberculosis. These bacteria can enter the body if you breathe them in from the air around you. They will have come from someone else in whose body the bacteria are breeding. The most usual way for the bacterium to enter the body is when a person breathes in droplets of moisture that have been exhaled by an infected person.

Tuberculosis, usually known as TB, is not actually a very infectious disease – it is not very easy to catch it from someone. It seems that you need to be in close association with an infected person for some time before you run a high risk of getting TB. People who sleep in crowded conditions appear to be most at risk. This is partly why people living in substandard housing are most likely to get this disease. Malnutrition (especially if the diet is low in protein, minerals and vitamins), being infected with the human immunodeficiency virus (HIV) or having a weakened immune system also increases the risk.

TB can affect almost any organ of the body, but the most commonly affected part is the lungs. If the bacteria reach the alveoli of the lungs, macrophages (phagocytic white blood cells) engulf them. But, instead of being digested and destroyed, the bacteria remain undamaged inside the cells. They divide, releasing new bacteria which are in turn engulfed by other white blood cells. Slowly, more and more cells become infected with the bacterium.

Although it is estimated that around one-third of the world's population is infected with TB, it is only in about 10% to 15% of these people that the disease goes beyond this stage. In 85% to 90% of people, the immune system is able to contain the growth of the bacteria and the person has no symptoms of TB at all. But in others the bacteria continue to spread, causing severe tissue damage in the lungs and perhaps also in other parts of the body. As the disease progresses, the person loses weight, and suffers night sweats and a cough, eventually bringing up blood-stained mucus and pus. Untreated, a person in whom the disease has reached this stage is likely to die.

Up until the middle of the 19th century, TB was a common disease in Britain, where it was known as consumption. People from all walks of life suffered from it. Then improvements in sanitation and housing caused a decline in the number of people suffering from TB, and this decline continued steadily in all the industrialised countries of the world until about 1985. This was partly due to continued improvements in living conditions and also to the use of antibiotics to treat the disease and prevent infected people from passing it on.

Then, in the late 1980s, a dramatic change occurred. The number of people with TB began to increase, even in countries such as the USA and Britain. One of the main reasons for this has been the spread of HIV. The human immunodeficiency virus, which first appeared in the late 1970s, destroys one type of **lymphocyte** and so reduces

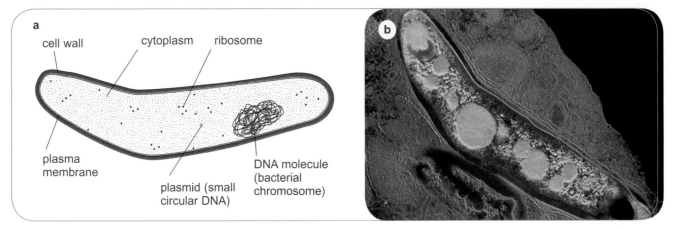

Figure 11.1   **a** *Mycobacterium tuberculosis*, the bacterium that causes TB.   **b** False-colour TEM of *Mycobacterium* inside a macrophage (× 11 700).

the body's ability to fight off bacteria and viruses. As the number of people with HIV has increased, so has the number of people with TB. Every year, three million people die from TB, worldwide. A disease that we thought we had beaten is getting out of control.

Most strains of TB can be treated successfully with antibiotics, but the drugs must be taken regularly over a long time in order to clear the bacteria completely from the body. A full six months of treatment must be followed to be sure that relapse will not occur. In Britain, quite a high proportion of people with TB live in difficult conditions with unstructured lifestyles, and need a lot of help and support to make sure that they take their drugs regularly. The World Health Organization advises that TB patients are asked to attend an outpatient clinic twice a week, where they take their drugs while someone watches them. This is called directly observed therapy, or DOTS.

Unfortunately, some strains of *M. tuberculosis* have now become resistant to some of the antibiotics that are used to kill them. Usually, therefore, two antibiotics are used together, as this increases the chances of destroying the bacteria.

SAQ

1 a Look at Figure 11.2. What is the overall aim of the WHO's 'Stop TB' strategy?
  b Outline how WHO hopes to achieve this aim.

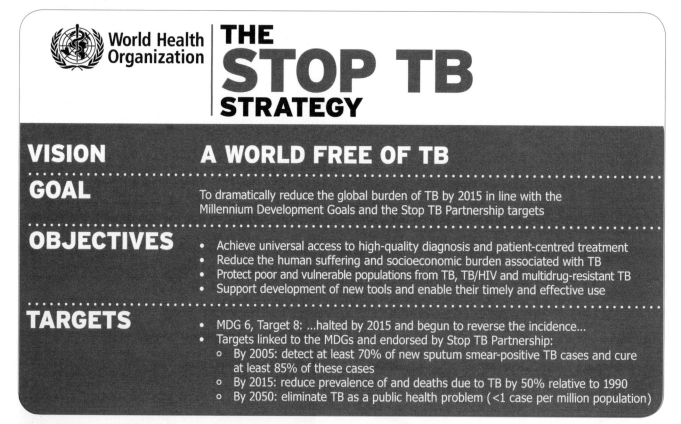

Figure 11.2 The World Health Organization's 'Stop TB' strategy.

HIV/AIDS

The devastating disease AIDS, acquired immunodeficiency syndrome, is caused by the human immunodeficiency virus, HIV. Figure 11.3 shows the structure of this virus. It is a **retrovirus**, containing RNA rather than DNA.

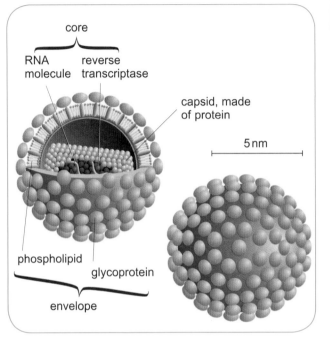

Figure 11.3 The structure of HIV.

Viruses are not cellular, and most are very much smaller than bacteria. HIV is basically a ball of protein and lipid around a core containing RNA (its genetic material) and the enzyme reverse transcriptase, which is required once the virus has entered a cell. The enzyme makes a 'DNA version' of the virus's RNA. The infected cell then follows the code on the DNA to make new viruses. The virus essentially hijacks the human cell's protein-making machinery.

Like all viruses, HIV can only reproduce when it is inside a host cell. HIV infects a type of blood cell called a **T lymphocyte** (Figure 11.4).

SAQ

2 Compare the structure of HIV with the structure of a bacterium.

> Hint

> Answer

HIV is passed from person to person when body fluids come into direct contact. The virus cannot survive outside the human body, except in blood (unlike the TB bacterium, which survives in exhaled droplets of moisture for some time). The main ways in which HIV is passed on are:

- during sexual intercourse – especially (but not only) if this involves damage to the linings of the vagina or anus, because the virus is most easily spread via blood
- sharing hypodermic needles – a needle used by someone with HIV may contain a small amount of fluid with the virus in it, which can enter the body of another person if they re-use the needle
- transfusions of blood from a person infected with HIV to another person
- from a mother to her unborn child – it is sometimes possible for the virus to cross the placenta, but it is more likely that the virus can be passed from the mother's blood to her baby's during the birth process.

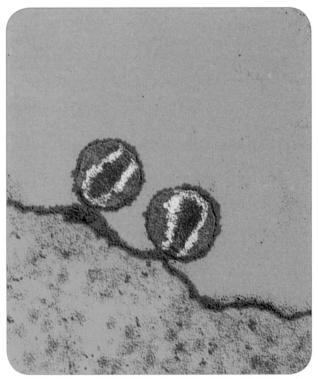

Figure 11.4 HIV 'docking' with a T lymphocyte (green); particular molecules on the plasma membrane of the lymphocyte act as receptors for molecules on the outside of the virus (× 280 000).

Most people who are infected with HIV eventually go on to develop AIDS. At first the virus lies low inside the T lymphocytes that it has infected. The cell makes copies of the virus's DNA and incorporates them into its own chromosomes. At this stage, the person has no symptoms, but if they take a blood test then antibodies (page 182) against the virus will be detected. The person is said to be HIV positive. Later, the virus may become active, producing many copies of itself inside the infected cells and then destroying them as it bursts out (Figure 11.5). More and more cells are infected and destroyed.

T lymphocytes are a very important group of cells because they help to protect us against infectious diseases, especially viral diseases. In a person infected by HIV, as T lymphocytes are destroyed, **opportunistic diseases** begin to occur. They include pneumonia and otherwise rare forms of cancer such as Kaposi's sarcoma (a type of skin cancer). The body becomes weaker, more and more infectious diseases take hold, and the person eventually dies. Globally, TB is the main cause of death for people with AIDS (Figure 11.6).

There are now some very successful treatments for HIV infection available, which can enable an HIV positive person to live a long and healthy life. However, these drugs are expensive and not freely available to people in many developing countries. The statistics for HIV infection are worrying. One of the worst affected countries is Botswana. This is a well-governed, stable, relatively well-off country in southern Africa, with a good record of education and health care. But here, in a population of about 1.6 million, it is estimated that almost 350 000 people are HIV positive, almost 25% of the population. Average life expectancy is only 39 years. Already, there are 60 000 children who have been orphaned as a result of AIDS.

SAQ

3 a Compare the distribution of HIV/AIDS and TB, shown in Figure 11.6.
  b Explain why a high level of HIV/AIDS in a country may be related to a high incidence of TB.

Answer

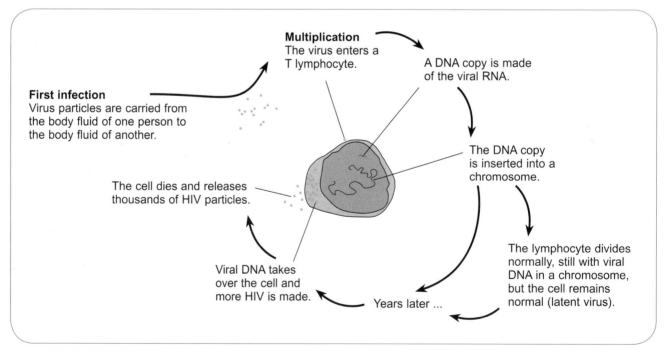

First infection
Virus particles are carried from the body fluid of one person to the body fluid of another.

Multiplication
The virus enters a T lymphocyte.

A DNA copy is made of the viral RNA.

The DNA copy is inserted into a chromosome.

The cell dies and releases thousands of HIV particles.

Viral DNA takes over the cell and more HIV is made.

Years later ...

The lymphocyte divides normally, still with viral DNA in a chromosome, but the cell remains normal (latent virus).

Figure 11.5   The life cycle of HIV.

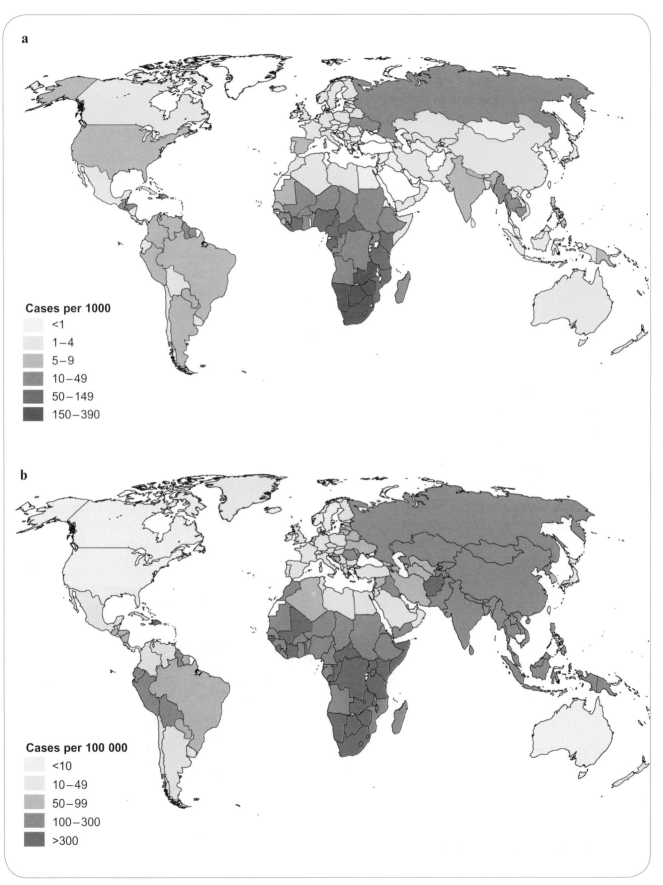

a

Cases per 1000
<1
1–4
5–9
10–49
50–149
150–390

b

Cases per 100 000
<10
10–49
50–99
100–300
>300

Figure 11.6 **a** Global distribution of HIV/AIDS (data from World Health Organization, 2003); **b** Global distribution of TB (data from World Health Organization, 2001).

Malaria

Malaria is a disease caused by a protozoan called *Plasmodium* (Figure 11.7). Malaria causes great suffering worldwide, especially in children (Figure 11.8). In 2007, it was estimated that a child died of malaria every 30 seconds. More than 500 million people become severely ill with malaria each year, and one million people die from it. Most of these deaths are in Africa, but malaria is also present in much of southern Asia and is spreading into areas where it has previously been absent, such as northern Australia. Approximately 40% of the world's population are at risk of malaria.

There are four species of *Plasmodium* that can cause malaria, although only two of these, *P. vivax* and *P. falciparum*, are common. They cause illness when they reproduce inside red blood cells, eventually bursting out of them and releasing chemicals that cause fever. The parasites then infect more red blood cells, multiply and burst out again. The symptoms of malaria therefore include repeated bouts of fever.

Figure 11.9 shows the life cycle of *Plasmodium* and how malaria is transmitted. This involves two hosts and several different stages. The second host is a female mosquito of the genus *Anopheles*. She sucks blood to obtain protein to make her eggs. When she bites, she takes up *Plasmodium* cells into her saliva. They reproduce in her salivary glands, so when she feeds again on someone else, she inadvertently injects them into that person's body.

The *Plasmodium* cells then invade the liver, where they multiply yet again. Millions of *Plasmodium* cells are released from the liver cells into the blood about eight days after infection. They invade red cells and the cycle begins again. Symptoms usually appear between 10 and 15 days after infection.

Malaria is a disease where prevention is a much better option than a cure. Several different drugs are used as **prophylactics** – they are taken *before* there is any chance of being infected by the disease, and prevent the disease developing even if a person is infected with *Plasmodium*. Until recently, the prophylactics that were most commonly prescribed were chloroquine and proguanil, but many strains of *Plasmodium* are now resistant to these drugs. Newer drugs, to which resistance has not yet widely evolved, include Lariam (mefloquine) and Malarone. If you are planning a trip to a country where malaria is present (Figure 11.10), you should check with your GP well before you go, so that you can be prescribed these drugs if you need them. Each year, a number of people develop malaria after returning home to Britain from an overseas holiday, and some of them die. The number of these deaths is increasing – 9 people died in 2002, and 16 in 2003. Many people simply do not think of malaria when they are going on holiday, and take no precautions to avoid infection.

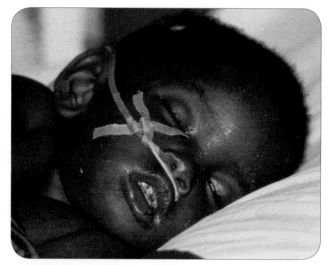

Figure 11.8 Each year, millions of children are infected with malaria. This young boy is in Tanzania, and is so ill he has to be fed through a tube.

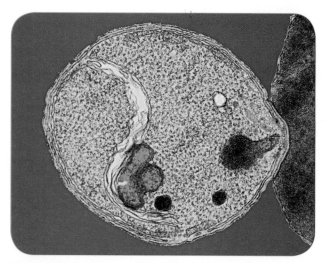

Figure 11.7 *Plasmodium* about to enter a red blood cell (× 45 000).

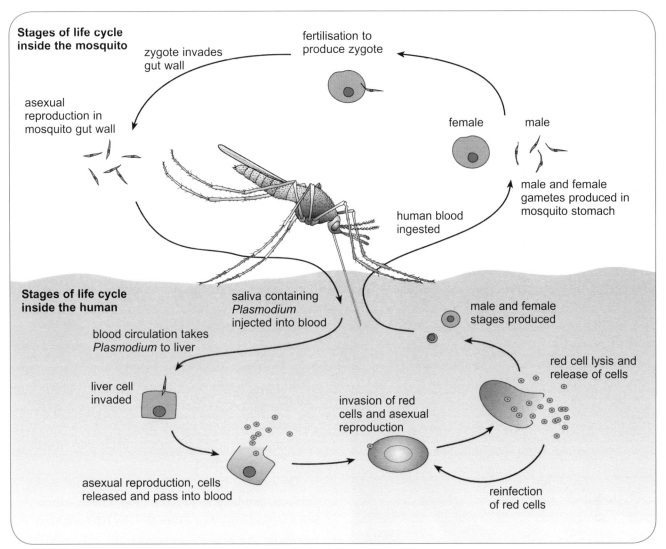

Figure 11.9   The life cycle of the malarial parasite, *Plasmodium*.

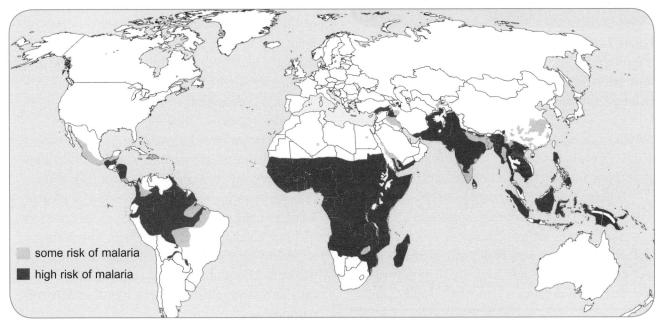

Figure 11.10   Countries where malaria was endemic in 2004 (World Health Organization).

Another way to reduce the chances of infection is to stop mosquitoes from biting (Figure 11.11). The mosquitoes that transmit malaria mostly feed in the evening and at night, so it is important to cover arms and legs at these times, and perhaps also to use insect repellent on skin and clothes.

Figure 11.11   Sleeping under a net, especially if it is impregnated with an insecticide, is a good protection against being bitten by the mosquitoes that transmit malaria.

SAQ

4 The mosquito *Anopheles* is a **vector** for malaria.
  a Using malaria as an example, explain the difference between a vector and a pathogen.
  b Find *two* more examples of vectors.
  c Suggest why targeting a vector, rather than a pathogen, may be a better way of reducing the incidence of an infectious disease.

  Answer

The immune response

We have numerous defences against invasion of our bodies by pathogens. The first line of defence is to stop them getting in at all. If they do gain access, then the **immune system** comes into action. The way in which white blood cells respond when pathogens enter the body is called the **immune response**.

Primary lines of defence

The best line of defence against pathogens is to prevent them from getting established in the body.

Skin is impermeable to most pathogens, although there are a few viruses, such as the ones that cause warts, that can penetrate unbroken skin. We have our own 'flora' of harmless bacteria that live on healthy skin, but most pathogenic bacteria cannot survive there, partly because lactic acid and fatty acid secreted from sweat glands and sebaceous glands provide a pH that is too low for them. However, the common bacterium *Staphylococcus aureus* can thrive even on undamaged skin, and it often infects hair follicles and sebaceous glands.

The normal bacterial flora living on our body surfaces can help to prevent infection by other microorganisms. For example, the bacteria that normally live in the vagina keep the pH low by secreting lactic acid. If a person takes antibiotics, these bacteria may be killed. Then the pH of the vagina rises, and this may allow other microorganisms, such as the fungus that causes thrush, *Candida*, to multiply to a much greater population density than usual.

If skin is damaged – for example, by cuts or extensive burns – then the way is open for bacteria to get into the underlying tissues. Blood clotting helps to seal wounds rapidly, until a more permanent repair is produced by mitosis of the cells surrounding the wound. A blood clot forms when soluble, globular fibrinogen is converted to the insoluble fibrous protein fibrin. This forms a mesh of strands across the wound in which platelets stick and red blood cells get trapped, thus preventing further loss of blood or entry of pathogens.

Moist body surfaces, such as the surface of the eyes and mouth, are bathed in fluids which have some bactericidal action. An enzyme called **lysozyme** is present in saliva and tears, and this enzyme can damage and destroy many bacteria. Semen contains a bactericide called spermine; milk contains a bactericidal enzyme called lactoperoxidase. The hydrochloric acid secreted into the stomach is very effective in destroying bacteria and other pathogens ingested in food.

Mucus helps to protect the digestive and respiratory tracts from infection. It acts as a barrier so that bacteria cannot make contact with the epithelial cells lining the walls of the tubes. Mucus is produced by goblet cells, which are part of the epithelium. A layer of cells containing goblet cells is sometimes known as a **mucous membrane** (but don't confuse this 'membrane' with a cell membrane). In the trachea and bronchi, the mucus is swept upwards to the back of the throat by cilia and then swallowed (Figure 11.12). Coughing and sneezing help to expel mucus containing microorganisms from the trachea and bronchi. If the mucus is swallowed, the acid and enzymes in the stomach destroy any bacteria trapped in it.

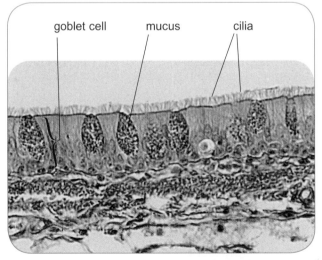

goblet cell   mucus   cilia

Figure 11.12 Light micrograph of the mucous membrane in the trachea. A mucous membrane is a layer of cells covering a surface inside the body, which secretes mucus.

Extension

Phagocytes

If pathogens do get through the body's outer defences, they may be destroyed by patrolling phagocytic white blood cells. The types of white blood cells known as **neutrophils** and **macrophages** are phagocytes. They engulf and digest foreign particles of almost any type or size (Figure 11.13). They crawl around within almost every part of the body – for example, over the surfaces of the alveoli in the lungs.

Neutrophils are found in the blood, where they make up about 60% of the white blood cells. They do not live very long, often dying after they have taken in and destroyed bacteria, and so new neutrophils are constantly being made in the bone marrow. They move around actively, and frequently leave the blood and patrol parts of the body where 'invaders' may be found.

Macrophages also leave the blood. (Indeed, when they are actually *in* the blood they are given a different name – monocytes.) They are present in especially large numbers in the liver, where they are known as Kupffer cells. They also line the passages through which lymph flows inside lymph nodes and are found on the inside of the alveolar walls. Unlike neutrophils, they are quite long-lived, tending to survive after taking in foreign particles. They break the particles up into their component molecules and place some of these molecules in their plasma membranes. Cells that do this are called **antigen-presenting cells**. By doing this, they display the molecules to other cells of the immune system, helping these cells to identify the invaders and be able to destroy them.

Lymphocytes

Lymphocytes are relatively small white blood cells. They are of two types, **B lymphocytes** and **T lymphocytes**. These two types look identical, and differ only in their functions. B lymphocytes are so-called because they develop in the bone marrow, while T lymphocytes need to spend time in the thymus gland during a person's childhood to become properly developed. This gland is found in the neck. It disappears by the time a person becomes a teenager.

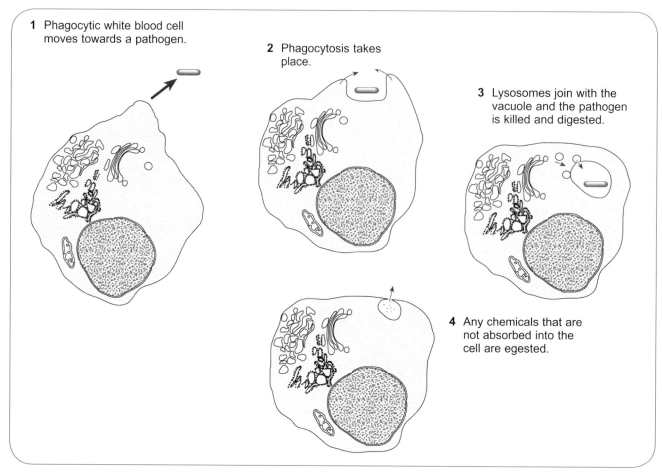

1 Phagocytic white blood cell moves towards a pathogen.

2 Phagocytosis takes place.

3 Lysosomes join with the vacuole and the pathogen is killed and digested.

4 Any chemicals that are not absorbed into the cell are egested.

Figure 11.13   Phagocytosis.

Lymphocytes are stimulated into action when they come into contact with molecules called **antigens**. Invading bacteria and viruses are recognised as foreign because they carry or produce antigens that are different from any of our own molecules. Antigens may be 'free' or they may be part of a bigger structure, such as the cell wall of a bacterium.

We have a huge number of different kinds of lymphocytes in our blood. Each one is capable of recognising and responding to one particular antigen.

As they mature, lymphocytes produce small quantities of particular glycoproteins called **antibodies** (page 182). We have perhaps a million different kinds of lymphocytes, each kind producing an antibody which is slightly different from other antibodies. At this stage, the antibodies are placed into the plasma membranes of the lymphocytes (Figure 11.14). Here, the antibodies act as receptors, able to bind with a particular antigen if this should appear in the body.

If bacteria enter the body, there is a good chance that some of the lymphocytes will have receptors than bind with antigens on the surface of the bacteria. If so, then a response is triggered. B lymphocytes and T lymphocytes respond in different ways.

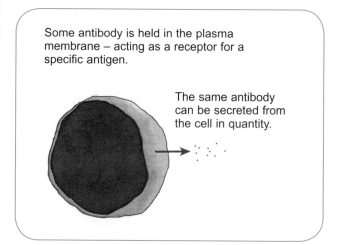

Some antibody is held in the plasma membrane – acting as a receptor for a specific antigen.

The same antibody can be secreted from the cell in quantity.

Figure 11.14   A lymphocyte can produce one specific type of antibody.

How B lymphocytes respond to antigens

Most B lymphocytes will spend all their lives without anything happening to them at all, because they never meet their particular antigen. But if a B lymphocyte does encounter an antigen which binds to the receptors in its plasma membrane, it is triggered into action. It could simply meet this antigen in the blood, or it could meet it as it is being displayed in the plasma membrane of an antigen-presenting cell (APC) such as a macrophage (Figure 11.15).

You can imagine the macrophages sitting in the lymph channels inside a lymph node, holding out the antigens they have discovered so that the lymphocytes will 'see' them as they pass by.

When it has encountered its specific antigen, the B lymphocyte responds by dividing repeatedly by mitosis. A large number of genetically identical cells is formed – a **clone** of the stimulated lymphocyte.

Some of these cells differentiate into **plasma cells**. These cells develop extra protein-making machinery – more endoplasmic reticulum, more ribosomes and more Golgi apparatus. They rapidly synthesise more and more molecules of their particular antibody and release them by exocytosis (Chapter 2). It has been estimated that a plasma cell can produce and release more than 2000 antibody molecules per second. Perhaps as a direct result of this tremendous rate of activity, plasma cells do not live long, mostly disappearing after only a few weeks.

The antibodies are secreted into the blood and so are carried to all parts of the body. They bind with the antigens on the invading bacteria, which results in the destruction of the bacteria – as we shall see on pages 178–179.

Other cells in the clone produced by the original B lymphocyte's division do not secrete antibodies. Instead, they remain as **memory cells**. These cells live for a long time, and remain circulating in the blood long after the invading bacteria have all been destroyed. They are capable of responding very quickly if the same type of bacterium enters the body again.

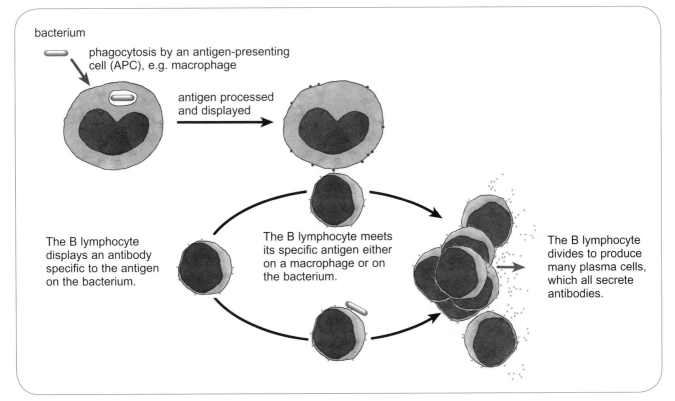

Figure 11.15   B lymphocyte response to antigen.

How T lymphocytes respond to antigens

T lymphocytes, like B lymphocytes, are activated if and when their particular antigen binds with the specific glycoproteins that are held in their plasma membranes. T lymphocytes, however, only respond to their antigen if they find it in the plasma membrane of another cell. This could be a macrophage that is displaying some of the molecules from a pathogen that it has taken up. Or it could be molecules on a body cell that has been invaded by a virus, and has placed virus particles in its plasma membrane as a 'help' signal (Figure 11.16).

There are several types of T lymphocytes, including **T helper cells** and **T killer cells**. A particular T helper cell with the complementary receptor binds to the antigen that it has found. It then divides to form a clone of itself. The cloned T helper cells then begin to secrete chemicals called **cytokines**. These chemicals stimulate other cells to fight against the invaders. For example, they may stimulate macrophages to carry out phagocytosis, or they may stimulate B lymphocytes specific to this antigen to divide rapidly and become plasma cells. They also help to stimulate appropriate T killer cells.

T killer cells actually destroy the cell to which they have become bound. A body cell displaying virus particles will be destroyed by T killer cells. This is the only way of destroying the viruses – it can't be done without destroying the cell in which they are multiplying. The T killer cells destroy the infected cell by secreting chemicals such as hydrogen peroxide. The T killer cells are our main defence against viral diseases.

We have seen that T lymphocytes, like B lymphocytes, divide to form clones when they meet their own particular antigen (Figure 11.17). While most of these cells act as helper cells or killer cells, some of them remain in the blood as memory cells. These, like the memory cells formed from B lymphocytes, help the body to respond more quickly and effectively if this same antigen ever invades again.

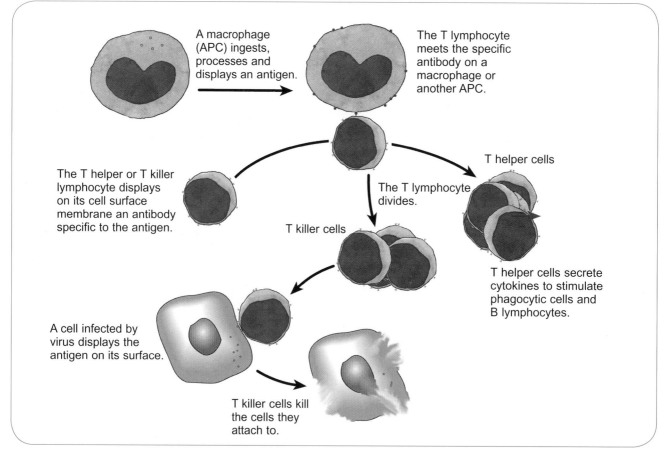

Figure 11.16 T lymphocyte response to antigen.

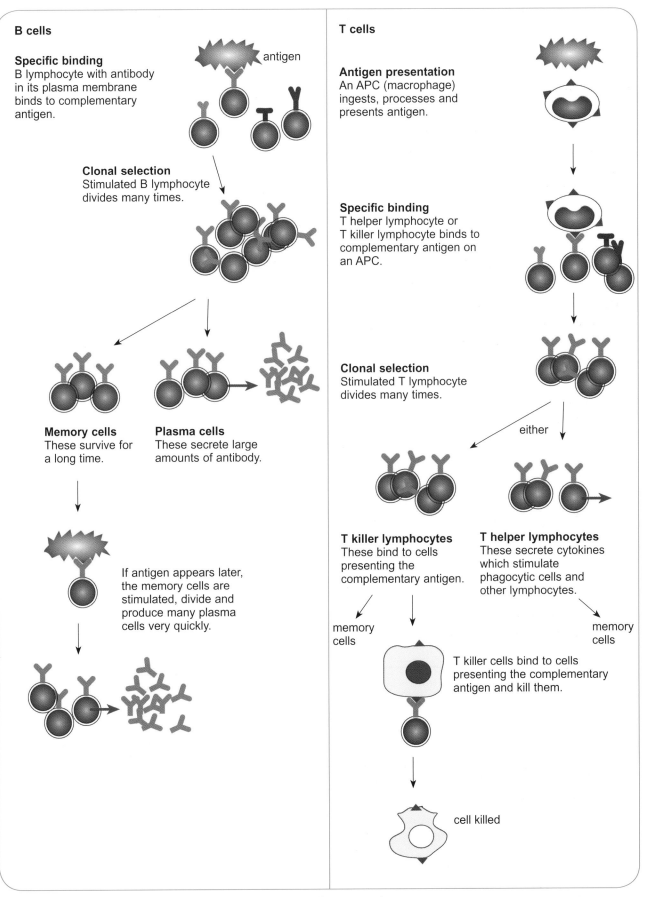

Figure 11.17 Summary of B lymphocyte and T lymphocyte actions.

How immunity develops

When a pathogen first enters the body, there will be only a few lymphocytes with receptors that fit into its antigens. It takes time for these lymphocytes to encounter and bind with these pathogens. It takes more time for them to divide to form clones, and for the B lymphocytes to secrete enough antibodies to destroy the pathogens, or for enough T lymphocytes to be produced to be able to destroy all the cells that are infected by them.

During this delay, the pathogens have the opportunity to divide repeatedly, forming large populations in the body tissues. The damage that they cause, and toxins that they may release, can make the person ill. It may be several days, or even weeks, before the lymphocytes get on top of the pathogen population and destroy it.

However, if the body survives this initial attack by the pathogen, memory cells will remain in the blood long after the pathogen has been destroyed. If the same pathogen invades again, these memory cells can mount a much faster and more effective response. More antibodies can be produced more quickly, usually destroying the pathogen before it has caused any illness.

The response to the first invasion of the pathogen is called the **primary response** (Figure 11.18). Subsequent invasions generate a **secondary response**. You can see that the secondary response happens more quickly, and produces many more antibodies. This is why we usually become **immune** to a disease if we have had it once.

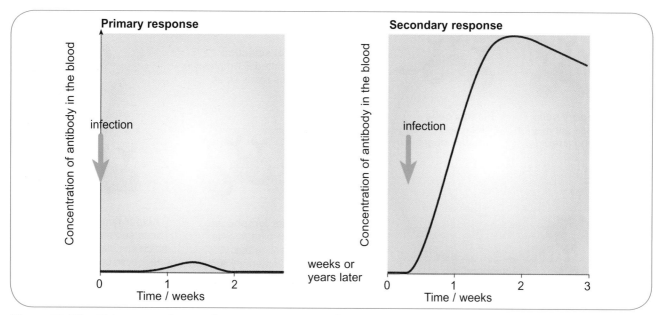

Figure 11.18   Primary and secondary responses to antigen.

SAQ

5 Match each word with its definition.
   antibody, antigen, pathogen, parasite,
   B lymphocyte, neutrophil, macrophage
   a a type of white blood cell that secretes
      antibodies
   b a phagocytic white blood cell with a
      multilobed nucleus and granular cytoplasm
   c a microorganism that causes disease
   d a glycoprotein secreted by some white blood
      cells, which binds to specific antigens
   e a phagocytic white blood cell that is relatively
      large, and which tends to be found in tissues

   such as the lungs, rather than in the blood
   f a molecule that is recognised by lymphocytes
      as being foreign to the body
   g an organism that lives in close association
      with a host, and does
      it harm.

6 With reference to the way in
   which they respond to antigens,
   suggest why T lymphocytes are more effective
   than B lymphocytes in dealing
   with infection by a virus.

Active and passive immunity

The kind of immunity described on the previous pages is a type of **active immunity**. The immune system has been stimulated to make a particular type of antibody, and can produce this same one more quickly and in larger quantity if it is exposed to the same pathogen again. The immunity has developed naturally, so it is a type of **natural immunity**.

Another way in which active immunity can develop is by **vaccination**. This involves injecting the antigen into the body (page 183–184). It may, for example, be in the form of viruses that have been made harmless, or as an inactivated toxin from a bacterium. The body responds in the same way as it would if invaded by the living pathogen, producing memory cells which will make the person immune to the disease if they should ever encounter it. This way of acquiring active immunity is not natural, so it is a form of **artificial immunity** (Figure 11.19).

A young baby's immune system takes time to develop. In the uterus, the fetus obtains antibodies from the mother's blood, across the placenta. After birth, the baby will continue to receive them in the mother's milk, if she decides to breastfeed. These ready-made antibodies help the baby to fight off pathogens. The baby has immunity to the same diseases as the mother. Because the baby's body has received ready-made antibodies, rather than making them itself, this is said to be **passive immunity**. It has happened naturally, so it is an example of natural immunity too.

Passive immunity can also be provided by injections. This is not a natural way of gaining immunity, so it is another example of artificial immunity. For example, if someone goes to the A and E department of a hospital with a cut that may have dirt in it, they may need to be protected against the bacterium that causes tetanus, *Clostridium tetani*. It is too late for a vaccination, because by the time the person's immune system responds, the bacterium could have multiplied and caused the fatal illness tetanus. Instead, the person will be given an injection of antitoxin. The antitoxin will bind to the toxin produced by the bacteria, rendering it harmless.

Passive immunity does not last as long as active immunity. No lymphocytes have been stimulated to make clones of themselves, so no memory cells have been formed. Passive immunity lasts only as long as the antibodies or antitoxins last. The body actually 'sees' them as being foreign, and they will be removed and destroyed quite quickly by cells in the liver and spleen.

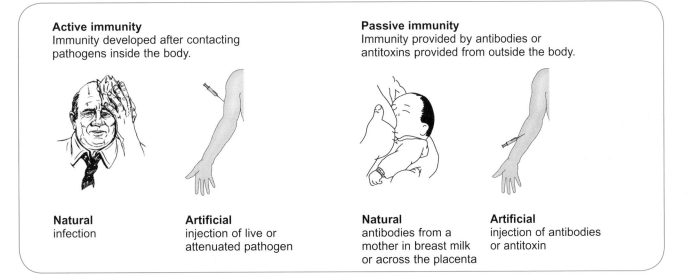

Active immunity
Immunity developed after contacting pathogens inside the body.

Natural
infection

Artificial
injection of live or attenuated pathogen

Passive immunity
Immunity provided by antibodies or antitoxins provided from outside the body.

Natural
antibodies from a mother in breast milk or across the placenta

Artificial
injection of antibodies or antitoxin

Figure 11.19   Active and passive immunity.

Antibodies

Antibodies are glycoproteins. Their molecules contain chains of amino acids, and also sugar units. Figure 11.20 shows the structure of an antibody molecule.

Antibodies are also known as **immunoglobulins**. There are several different kinds of them, given names such as IgG and IgA.

Each antibody contains a variable region that can bind specifically with a particular antigen. We have millions of different antibodies with different variable regions.

When an antibody molecule meets its specific antigen, it binds with it. The effect that this has depends on what the antigen is, and on what type of immunoglobulin has bound to it.

Some antibodies directly neutralise the antigen – for example, by binding with a toxin produced by a bacterium. Others may encourage phagocytes to destroy the pathogen, sometimes by making the pathogens clump together. Yet others may stop pathogens getting a foothold on body surfaces, by preventing them from attaching to cells or tissues (Figure 11.21 and Figure 11.22).

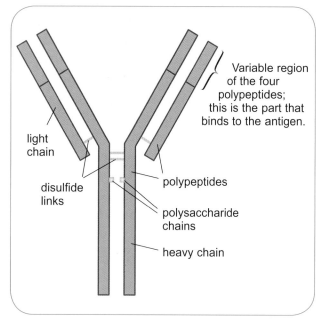

Figure 11.20   The structure of an antibody molecule.

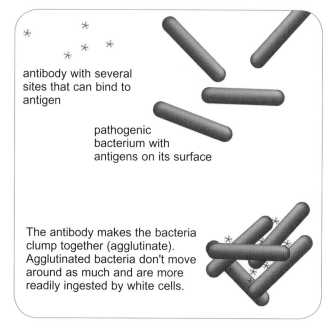

Figure 11.22   How antibodies agglutinate bacteria.

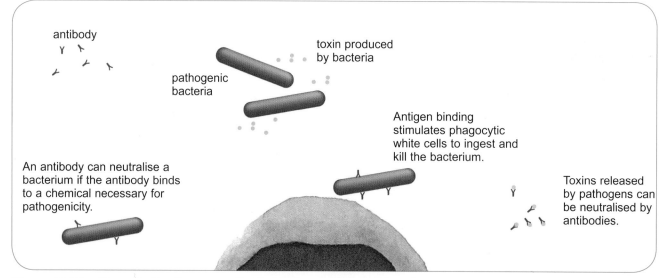

Figure 11.21   How antibodies neutralise bacteria and bacterial toxins.

Controlling infectious disease

Most of the infectious diseases that are common in Britain today are not especially dangerous to most people. Whereas infectious diseases were a major cause of death a century ago, nowadays we tend to worry more about heart disease and cancer. But we cannot afford to be complacent about infectious diseases. Bacteria are becoming resistant to the antibiotics that we have come to expect will protect us from them, and there is the constant threat of new infectious diseases emerging.

Vaccination

Vaccination is an excellent way of preventing a person from acquiring an infectious disease. The larger the proportion of people who are vaccinated in a population, the lower the chance that anyone – even those who have not been vaccinated – will get that disease. This is called **herd immunity**. For most diseases, at least 80–85% of the population need to be vaccinated to achieve herd immunity.

Vaccination involves giving a person a dose of a preparation that will cause the immune system to react as though an antigen from a pathogenic organism has entered the body. Most vaccinations are given by injection, but the polio vaccine is given by mouth. Many vaccines contain an **attenuated** (weakened) form of the bacterium or virus that causes the disease, while others contain a modified toxin produced by them.

When the vaccine enters the body, lymphocytes that recognise the antigen respond to it as if they had encountered live bacteria or viruses. They form clones of plasma cells, which secrete antibodies, and also memory cells. In most cases, a second 'booster' dose of the vaccine is given later on. This raises the antibody level much higher than the first dose, and helps to ensure that protection against the antigen lasts for some time (Figure 11.23).

SAQ

7 To answer this question, you will need to think back to your work on cells.

$\boxed{\text{Hint}}$

An experiment was carried out to follow what happens inside plasma cells as they make and secrete antibodies. Some cells were cultured in a solution containing amino acids which had been 'labelled' with a radioactive marker. The radioactivity in the Golgi body, endoplasmic reticulum and ribosomes was then measured over the next 40 minutes. The results are shown in the graph.

a In which order did the amino acids move through the three organelles? Use the results shown in the graph to justify your answer.

b Using your own knowledge, describe what happened to the amino acids in each organelle.

c Suggest why the peak values for the radioactivity in the ribosomes and the endoplasmic reticulum are the same, whereas the peak value for the Golgi body is lower. (There may be more than one possibility.)

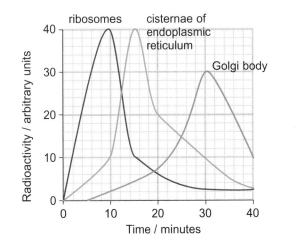

d Suggest how the amino acids would have been taken up into the cell at the beginning of the experiment.

e Describe how the antibody molecules would be secreted from the cell.

$\boxed{\text{Answer}}$

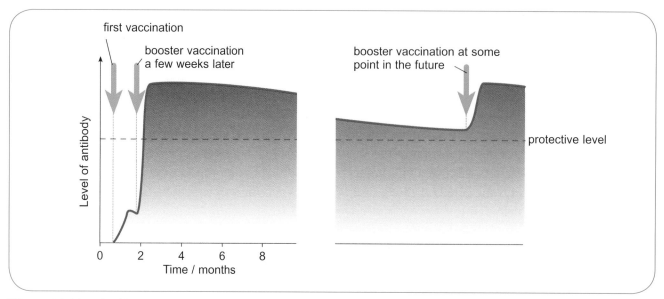

Figure 11.23 Antibody levels after vaccination.

The MMR controversy

In 1998, a small group of researchers published a paper in a well-respected medical journal. They had been looking to see if there was any link between autism and bowel diseases. They investigated 12 children who had both conditions. One of the researchers thought it might be possible that there was a link between the MMR vaccine and these conditions and, despite reservations from the other members of the research team, he mentioned in the published paper that there was a possibility of a link. He suggested that perhaps it would be a good idea for children to be given the three vaccinations separately, instead of all at once – even though there was absolutely no evidence to support the suggestion that this would be 'safer'.

His suggestions were picked up by the media and given huge publicity. People were already worried about this vaccine, as this same research group had suggested in 1993 that the MMR vaccine could cause Crohn's disease. This is a chronic inflammation of the alimentary canal. As a result, take-up of the vaccine had dropped.

But after the 1998 news, many more parents reacted by refusing to let their children have the MMR jab. Previously, more than 90% of babies had been having the vaccination, but in some parts of the country this now fell to less than 70%. Many further studies were undertaken by other researchers, but none found evidence to support the claims of a link between MMR and autism. But the press were having a field day with the story, and would not let it go.

Meanwhile, the number of children who had not had any vaccinations for measles, mumps and rubella was growing. Unsurprisingly, these diseases began to show up again. Although most children do recover from them with no problem, all three can have serious side effects and may be fatal. There is also the risk of a child with rubella coming into contact with a pregnant woman; rubella may deform or even kill her unborn child.

In 2004, ten of the thirteen scientists who contributed to the original research paper formally withdrew their support for any suggestion that there is a link between MMR and autism. Since then, there has been a lot of research that confirms there is no link. But even this has not put the argument to rest. Many people are so distrustful of the government's advice that they simply refuse to believe they are not putting their child at risk by allowing them to have the MMR jab.

There is no doubt that the UK vaccination programme (Table 11.2) provides most people with protection from diseases which could otherwise cause much suffering and even death.

Age	Vaccination given	How administered
2, 3 and 4 months	polio DTP-Hib (diphtheria, tetanus, pertussis, Hib) meningitis C	by mouth injection injection
13 months	MMR (measles, mumps and rubella)	injection
before starting school, 3 to 5 years	polio booster DTP booster MMR booster	by mouth injection injection
10 to 14 years	BCG (tuberculosis)	injection
13 to 18 years	tetanus	injection

Table 11.2 The United Kingdom vaccination programme.

Figure 11.24 shows the effect of the introduction of the MMR vaccine on the number of children under five years of age who were reported as having mumps or rubella. (MMR stands for measles, mumps and rubella.)

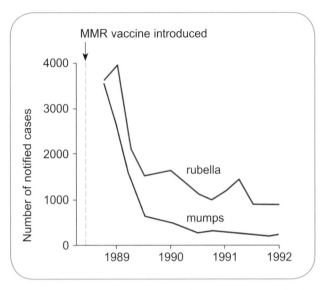

Figure 11.24 Notifications of mumps and rubella in children under five years old, in England and Wales between 1989 and 1992.

SAQ

8 In 2001, the percentage of children in London who had the MMR vaccine had fallen from over 90% to only 73%. In late December 2001 there was a measles outbreak in London. 90 confirmed cases of measles were reported over a period of about 10 weeks. The graph shows the number of suspected cases and the number of confirmed cases during this period.

a Suggest why a measles outbreak occurred in London during this time.

b Suggest reasons for the steep rise in suspected cases during weeks 2 to 6.

c Of these cases, 9% were in infants under 12 months, 46% in pre-school children, 22% in school children and 23% in young adults. Present these data in a suitable graph or diagram.

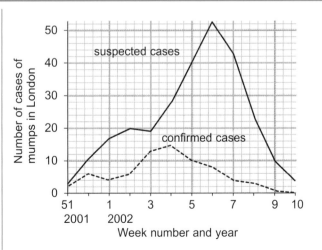

d Suggest why older people were apparently not affected by this measles outbreak.

The threat of new diseases

In 2003, a new and frightening disease emerged in south-east Asia. It was called SARS, short for severe acute respiratory syndrome. The disease is caused by a virus, which appeared to spread readily from person to person. What was so frightening about it was the high death rate among infected people; almost one in ten of them died.

The emergence of SARS was a wake-up call to the world. Here was a completely new virus which suddenly and without warning seemed to be sweeping across the world. With so many people now travelling over such large distances, it seemed to take no time for a disease that had erupted in China to spread to countries as far away as Canada and the United Kingdom. And as it was new, no-one had built up immunity to it.

Governments, charities and research organisations all over the world reacted quickly. The first 'official' death from SARS came on March 4th (there had been earlier ones that were not recorded or recognised at the time). By April 17th, the virus had been identified. Most countries, deeply worried by this completely new and potentially deadly disease, brought in measures to detect anyone suffering from it and keep them away from others. Information was shared between affected countries. The public were informed, so that they could be alert to the symptoms of the disease in themselves or others. Airlines screened passengers for signs of high fever.

We were lucky. This new disease was brought under control by the end of 2003.

The rapid spread of SARS illustrates just how important it is for us to be able to contain and control the spread of infectious diseases. We do not know exactly where SARS came from, although it seems probable that is was caused by a virus that 'jumped' from another animal – possibly one being sold for food at a market in China – to infect humans.

The World Health Organization estimates that at least 30 new diseases have emerged in the last 50 years. As well as SARS, there have been Ebola, HIV/AIDS, Lyme disease and West Nile fever. These are all caused by viruses. Many health experts think it is only a matter of time before we see the emergence of a new virus that is so dangerous and so easily spread that it could cause an epidemic even greater than that of HIV/AIDS.

It is possible, even probable, that this new disease will be a type of influenza. The flu virus is notorious for constantly changing slightly. If you have had flu in one year, you may not be immune from having it again the next year because the flu virus will be different – the lymphocytes that killed it last time won't have any effect this time. Flu is especially dangerous because it spreads easily and rapidly from person to person. In 1918–19, there was a pandemic (world-wide epidemic) of flu that killed around 20 million people – more than were killed in the First World War. The strain of flu responsible for this was called Spanish flu. There was another pandemic in 1957 (Asian flu) which killed an estimated 2 million people, and another in 1968, Hong Kong flu, which killed 1 million.

The UK government encourages elderly people to be vaccinated each year against the type of flu virus that is currently likely to cause infections. But it is difficult to keep up with the virus's constant changes, and a vaccination that works against one strain of flu will be useless against another. The drugs Tamiflu and Relenza can be used to reduce the severity of symptoms and length of infection with flu. However, there is now evidence that flu viruses are developing resistance against these drugs.

We are probably due for another flu pandemic. Scientists have their eye on a strain of the influenza virus called H5N1 (Figure 11.25). This virus mainly infects birds, so the disease is called avian flu, but the virus has jumped to humans on several

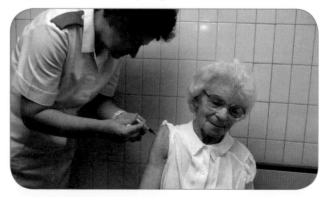

Figure 11.25 Flu vaccinations for elderly people can help to prevent deaths.

occasions. It is often deadly, with more than half of people infected with H5N1 dying from the disease. However, the virus is currently unable to spread from human to human, and only people who have close contact with infected birds run a risk of catching it. The worry is that the virus will mutate and create a slightly different form which is just as deadly, but which *can* spread between humans.

So what can we do? WHO is monitoring the situation closely, and encouraging governments where the disease has occurred to share their statistics and knowledge with other countries. If everyone works together, then we may be able to develop vaccines that could protect many people. WHO tries to get everyone working together for mutual benefit. They have published a document with a series of recommendations for governments to follow if the disease does break out. This includes keeping humans away from infected poultry to minimise the number of occasions on which the virus gets into humans in the first place; keeping records of who is infected and where; developing and stockpiling vaccinations; and sharing information and communicating with other countries. But WHO estimates that, even if these guidelines are followed, if there *was* a pandemic of H5N1 then between 2 million and 7 million people might die.

Sources of new drugs

If new diseases emerge, could we perhaps fight them with new drugs? The answer at the moment is probably 'no' – the new threats are mostly from viruses, and we have only a very few drugs that we can use against viral diseases.

We have seen, too, that many antibiotics are becoming less useful, as bacteria develop resistance to them. There is a constant search for new antibiotics. Many antibiotics come from microorganisms, such as fungi. It is thought that the fungi may produce them to prevent other microorganisms growing too close to them and competing for food. But antibiotics are being found in some surprising places. You may have read in Chapter 3 how sponges are providing a rich source of new molecules that may become new and

very useful drugs, perhaps including antibiotics. Finding drugs from completely new places is always exciting to researchers, because it is very unlikely that pathogenic bacteria will have been exposed to them before, and so resistance will not yet have built up.

At the moment, plants are our main source of medicinal drugs. Around 7000 drugs that are prescribed by doctors in the United Kingdom and other western countries are derived from plants. Approximately 3000 plant species are used as sources of these drugs, and of these plant species 70% grow in tropical rainforests. This is perhaps not altogether surprising, because the world's tropical rainforests are known to have by far the greatest plant biodiversity of any habitat in the world. This is one of many reasons why we need to conserve biodiversity in tropical rainforests.

Many plants have evolved chemical defences to stop themselves being eaten by animals such as insects or monkeys. Some of these chemicals are very toxic to humans, but even these may be used as drugs. For example, foxgloves contain a poison called digitalin. Taken in large quantities this is fatal, but extracts from foxgloves are widely used to treat abnormal heart rhythms (cardiac arrhythmias – in the section about electrocardiograms in Chapter 5).

The first drug to successfully treat malaria was discovered by a priest working in Peru. He heard about a kind of bark from a rainforest tree that the native people used to treat fever. Some of the bark was shipped back to Europe, and introduced to England in 1650. This was the main treatment for malaria until 1820, when two French chemists managed to separate the active ingredient, which they called quinine, from the bark. Quinine was a very effective antimalarial drug. It tasted bitter, but this became something in its favour, as it became fashionable to drink bitter-tasting 'tonic water', which contained quinine.

This is a classic example of how a new drug from a plant may be discovered. It often begins by finding out how native people use particular plants to treat illness. The study of the use of plants by native people has become so important that it now has a name of its own – ethnobotany.

Who benefits?

The development of new vaccines and new drugs costs huge amounts of money. It is usually done by large companies based in developed countries, as only they have the funding, expertise and facilities to produce and test the drugs. Developing just one new drug typically costs several hundred million pounds. Not surprisingly, the companies then sell these drugs in large volumes at quite high prices, in order to get back their investments, make a profit, and have funds available to continue research for the next new drugs.

However, there are problems here. The large drug companies may use materials that have come from developing countries. For example, to develop vaccines against the H5N1 virus, the company needs samples of the virus that have infected humans. The country where there are most human H5N1 infections is Indonesia. WHO wants Indonesia to let developed countries have these samples, so that vaccines can be developed. But after doing this for a while, Indonesia decided that it would no longer cooperate with richer countries by providing specimens taken from people with the disease, because these richer countries were planning to develop vaccines which would only be available to Indonesia at a considerable price. WHO has to try to work out ways in which all countries can share resources and get benefits from research that is done on them.

Similar issues arise when plants are used as the source of new drugs. Several large companies that produce and market drugs are interested in looking for new sources of plant-based drugs, and they fund researchers in the field and trials in laboratories. If a plant is found that has useful properties, then it might be developed into a drug that could potentially earn billions of pounds. There have been some arguments about the companies then making large profits – of which little or nothing goes back to the country in which the plant naturally grows.

For example, the San people in southern Africa have always used a plant called *Hoodia* as a way of staving off hunger and thirst in difficult periods when they may have had to go without food for several days while hunting or travelling. This usage was noticed by researchers from South Africa, and they investigated the plant to try to find the substance in it that had this anti-hunger effect. This active ingredient was isolated and patented by the Council for Scientific Investigation and Research (CSIR) in South Africa. The rights were then sold to the multinational drug company, Pfizer.

However, many people thought it was wrong that the San people would not benefit if this new drug is successful. After all, the plant grows on the land where they live, and it was information from them that alerted others to its potential as an anti-appetite drug. In 1992, the Convention on Biological Diversity gave countries the official ownership of their genetic resources. After much argument and discussion, it has now been decided that the San people will get royalties on every sale of the drug, if it passes clinical trials and can be successfully marketed.

San hunters in the Kalahari desert, in South Africa.

Smoking and health

In Britain in the 21st century, infectious diseases are not the major cause of death. Many more people die from heart diseases or diseases of the gas exchange system – and a high proportion of these deaths can be related to lifestyle, especially to smoking.

Tobacco smoke contains many different chemicals. These include:

- **tar** – a mixture of substances, some of which can cause cancer
- **nicotine** – the addictive substance in cigarette smoke; it affects the brain and other parts of the nervous system, and also the cardiovascular system
- **carbon monoxide** – a gas, produced by incomplete oxidation of some of the substances in tobacco, which reduces the oxygen-carrying capacity of the blood
- **particulates** – tiny particles, mostly of carbon, that cause irritation in the lungs and airways.

Each of these substances is potentially harmful to health. Compounds found in cigarette smoke are the direct cause of serious lung diseases, and increase the risk of developing CHD or suffering a stroke. Even breathing in someone else's cigarette smoke – passive smoking (Figure 11.26) – significantly increases the risk of developing these health problems.

Figure 11.26 Children may have little choice about passive smoking.

Lung diseases

Lung diseases are a major cause of illness and death. They include:

- **chronic obstructive pulmonary disease** (COPD) – this includes many related diseases, such as **emphysema**, that prevent the normal flow of air through the gas exchange system
- **lung cancer**, where cells in the lungs divide uncontrollably and form a tumour
- illnesses caused by **infectious organisms** (pathogens), such as bronchitis and tuberculosis.

Some lung diseases happen quickly and last for just a short time. They are called **acute illnesses**. An example is flu (influenza). Others, such as COPD, last over a long period of time, and the sufferer has to learn to live with them. These are called **chronic illnesses.**

Chronic obstructive pulmonary disease

COPD is an illness in which the airflow into and out of the lungs gradually and progressively becomes more and more obstructed. COPD happens to everyone to a certain extent as they get older, but it is hugely accelerated and worsened by smoking. It is thought that around 600 million people worldwide suffer from COPD, and that 300 million die from it each year. Somewhere between 80% and 90% of these cases are caused by smoking cigarettes.

Cigarette smoke contains a wide range of different chemicals, many of which stimulate **neutrophils** – a type of white blood cell (Figure 11.27) – to come to the scene. Neutrophils are an important part of the body's defence against infectious disease, but here they behave inappropriately and actually *cause* illness.

The neutrophils secrete an enzyme called **neutrophil elastase**. This enzyme is a protease and, as its name suggests, it breaks down elastin, which forms the elastic fibres in the tissues of the airways. Usually, there are inhibitors present that prevent this enzyme from doing very much harm. But, in a smoker, the balance between the concentrations of the protease enzymes and inhibitors tips too far in favour of the enzymes. The proteases gradually break down the elastin tissues in the lungs, causing irreversible damage.

One of the effects of this tissue damage is that the walls of many of the alveoli are broken down. Instead of millions of tiny alveoli, separated from blood capillaries by exceptionally thin walls, the lungs become filled with larger spaces, much more widely separated from the blood capillaries. What's more, many of these capillaries also disappear. The total surface area for gas exchange is therefore greatly reduced. This condition is called **emphysema** (Figure 11.27 and Figure 11.28). Not surprisingly, someone with emphysema has great difficulty in getting enough oxygen into their blood.

The progressive damage to the lungs causes them to lose their elasticity, while damage to the airways causes their walls to thicken. This happens because the attempts by the tissue to repair itself cause it to become fibrous. Both of these changes make it more difficult for air to move into and out of the lungs.

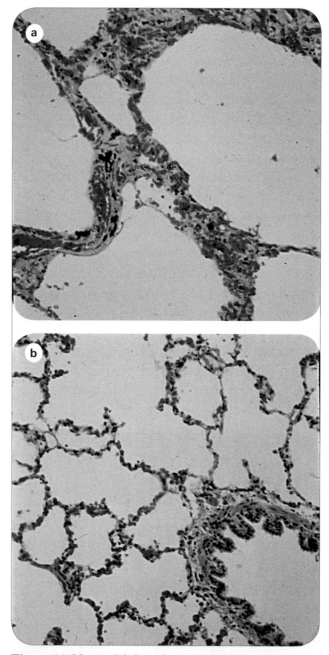

Figure 11.28 **a** Light micrograph of lung tissue from a person with chronic emphysema, showing large spaces where there should be many tiny alveoli; **b** light micrograph of normal lung tissue.

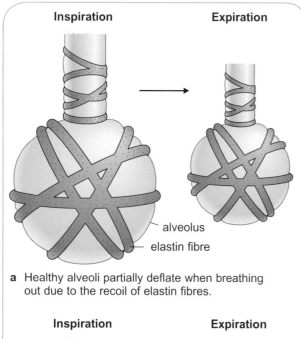

a Healthy alveoli partially deflate when breathing out due to the recoil of elastin fibres.

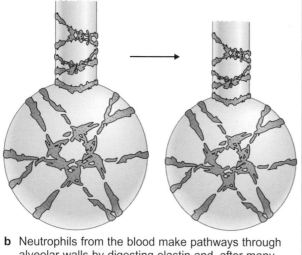

b Neutrophils from the blood make pathways through alveolar walls by digesting elastin and, after many years of this destruction, the alveoli do not deflate very much.

Figure 11.27 The development of emphysema.

The damage to the airways also involves the ciliated cells and the goblet (mucus-producing) cells, which normally help to keep the lungs clear of dust, bacteria and other foreign particles in the air that is breathed in. In smokers, the goblet cells often work even harder. More mucus is produced, but the cilia do not beat and so there is nothing to carry the mucus up and out of the bronchi and trachea. Instead, mucus accumulates in the airways, where it provides a breeding ground for bacteria. People with this condition therefore tend to suffer from bacterial infections of the bronchi, called **bronchitis**. They may have a chronic cough, as they attempt to clear the mucus from their lungs.

There is not really a great deal that can be done to help a person who has COPD. Once the tissues have been damaged, it is very difficult for them to recover. Usually, the best that can be done is to prevent the disease from getting any worse.

The first thing that anyone with COPD will be told to do is to stop smoking. This will almost immediately produce a reduction in the frequency and severity of infections, and may also reduce the cough. Ciliated cells and goblet cells can recover to a certain extent. But it is unlikely that large improvements will be made in the breathlessness that is caused by emphysema. Emphysema appears to be irreversible.

Many patients may be helped a little by drugs called beta agonists, which dilate the airways by causing the smooth muscle in their walls to relax (Chapter 4).

As the patient ages, and the symptoms get worse, they may need to breathe oxygen on a regular basis. This can be done at home, where the patient has an oxygen cylinder and breathing mask that they can use whenever they need to. In the advanced stages of the disease, even walking a few steps becomes impossible without getting out of breath.

Lung cancer

While COPD causes about 15% of smoking-related deaths, lung cancer causes almost double that number. Lung cancer causes around 35 000 deaths per year in England and Wales. Smokers are almost 20 times as likely to die from lung cancer as are non-smokers.

Cigarette smoke contains several chemicals which are **carcinogenic**. Carcinogens are substances that damage the control of cell division. Cells may begin to divide much more than they should, forming a lump of disorganised cells called a **tumour** (Figure 11.29). The tumour can be almost anywhere in the gas exchange system, but most frequently grows where the trachea branches into the two bronchi, or at other branching points.

As the tumour grows, it displaces other tissues. Eventually, this can lead to the blockage of the airways or other parts of the lungs. The person may find it difficult to get their breath, and may have a chronic cough, sometimes bringing up blood. They may experience pain or tightness in the chest. As the cancer progresses, they may lose weight.

Cancerous cells may break away from the primary (original) tumour and begin to form secondary tumours in other parts of the body. If this happens, survival rates are low.

Some of the carcinogenic substances enter the bloodstream in the lungs, and are carried all over the body. It is therefore not surprising that smoking significantly increases the risk of developing cancers in almost every part of the body.

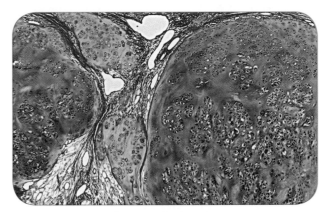

Figure 11.29 Micrograph showing a tumour (purple) in a human lung (×16).

Smoking and the cardiovascular system

Smoking increases the risk of developing CHD. Nearly everyone who develops CHD in their 30s or early 40s is a smoker. Smoking can cause high blood pressure. A smoker with high blood pressure has a 20 times greater risk of stroke than a non-smoker who does not have high blood pressure.

Nicotine

One of the culprits is the **nicotine** in cigarettes. Nicotine is a neurotoxin – a chemical that damages the nervous system. It is used as an insecticide. Nicotine is extremely addictive, and this is the reason why smokers find it so difficult to give up.

Nicotine molecules are relatively small, and they easily move out of the blood and into every part of the body, including the brain. Nicotine increases the levels of a transmitter substance called **dopamine** in the parts of the brain that are known as 'reward circuits'. Activation of these circuits gives feelings of pleasure, and this is why people enjoy smoking.

Nicotine also causes the release of adrenaline into the blood. Adrenaline increases the rate of heart beat, blood pressure and breathing rate.

Carbon monoxide

Carbon monoxide diffuses from the alveoli into the blood in the lung capillaries. Here it combines with haemoglobin, forming a bright red compound called **carboxyhaemoglobin**. It holds on tightly; haemoglobin has a very high affinity for carbon monoxide. With a proportion of the haemoglobin tied up in this way, there is less available for the transport of oxygen. Smoking therefore reduces the delivery of oxygen to the tissues, including the heart muscle. Smokers have less energy available to their muscles when they exercise.

Hypertension, CHD and stroke

We have seen that nicotine increases blood pressure, which can increase the risk of developing atherosclerosis and CHD (Chapter 10). It is not only the coronary arteries that are affected – atherosclerosis can develop in any arteries in the body. Smokers run a higher risk than non-smokers of atherosclerosis developing in blood vessels that supply the brain.

If a clot develops in one of these blood vessels, then part of the brain may be starved of an oxygen supply. Brain cells have a high metabolic rate and must have good supplies of oxygen and glucose for respiration. They begin to die if deprived of these for only a few minutes. The person suffers a **stroke**.

Although about 80% of strokes are caused by a blood clot, they may also be caused by a blood vessel bursting as a result of high blood pressure, flooding part of the brain with blood. This, too, kills brain cells.

The effects of a stroke depend on the parts of the brain in which nerve cells die. Damage to the right side of the brain affects the left side of the body, and vice versa. For example, a stroke in the right side of the cerebrum (the main part of the brain, which we use for thinking and which gives us our personality and emotions) is likely to affect movement on the left side of the body. As this side of the brain is concerned with spatial awareness, the person may have problems with judging distance and so have difficulty with walking and picking up objects. A stroke in the left side of the cerebrum is likely to affect language skills. Memory is often harmed no matter which side of the brain the stroke affects. Figure 11.30 shows a stroke patient receiving therapy to help re-learn some of the abilities lost.

Figure 11.30 This man lost his ability to speak clearly, because of a stroke. Therapy can help the brain to relearn, and to restore lost functions.

SAQ

9 The chart below is used to work out how likely a person is to have a heart attack or stroke.

a Use the chart to find the predicted risk for:
- a 56-year-old woman who smokes, has a blood pressure of 160/95 and whose total cholesterol : HDL-cholesterol ratio is 5
- a 45-year-old man who does not smoke, whose blood pressure reading is 160/95 and whose total cholesterol : HDL-cholesterol ratio is 8.

b What could each of these people do to reduce their risk of having a heart attack or stroke?

c Suggest how a risk calculator like this could be produced. [Hint]

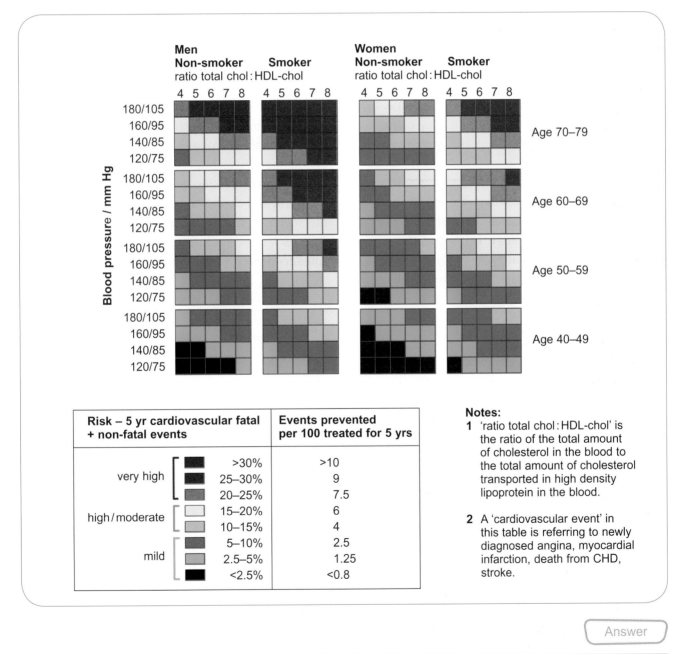

Risk – 5 yr cardiovascular fatal + non-fatal events		Events prevented per 100 treated for 5 yrs
very high	>30%	>10
	25–30%	9
	20–25%	7.5
high/moderate	15–20%	6
	10–15%	4
mild	5–10%	2.5
	2.5–5%	1.25
	<2.5%	<0.8

Notes:

1 'ratio total chol : HDL-chol' is the ratio of the total amount of cholesterol in the blood to the total amount of cholesterol transported in high density lipoprotein in the blood.

2 A 'cardiovascular event' in this table is referring to newly diagnosed angina, myocardial infarction, death from CHD, stroke.

[Answer]

Evidence for the effects of smoking on health

In the 1950s, 80% of adults in the UK smoked. Most people had no idea that it was bad for health. But deaths from lung cancer were increasing alarmingly, and no-one knew why. Interviews with 600 people with lung cancer revealed that almost all of them were smokers.

Figure 11.31 shows changes in smoking and lung cancer since 1911. This pattern could be explained if smoking causes lung cancer. The reason the link was not recognised sooner is that there is a time lag between smoking and developing lung cancer.

SAQ

10 Use Figure 11.31 to estimate the mean time-lag between smoking and developing lung cancer. Suggest why there is a time-lag.

> Answer

The study of disease in populations, and of the various factors that appear to affect who has the disease, is called **epidemiology**. It involves the collection and statistical analysis of large amounts of data. This forms the backbone of our evidence for the link between smoking and disease. It is difficult to obtain **experimental evidence** using people, but this kind of research can be done using cultures of human cells under controlled conditions in a laboratory, or on animals. In the 1960s, experiments were carried out on beagles, which were made to inhale cigarette smoke to find out if this increased their risk of developing lung cancer. It did. Today, animals are no longer used in this way.

Since the 1950s, huge quantities of research have been carried out on the effects of cigarette smoke on health. All of it supports the hypothesis that smoking increases the risk of developing not only lung cancer but also other types of cancer, COPD, coronary heart disease and stroke. We now understand how the carcinogens in cigarette smoke can affect the DNA in cells, so that the cells lose their normal control mechanisms and begin to divide uncontrollably. We understand how nicotine and carbon monoxide affect the physiology of the brain and cardiovascular system, and how this increases the risk of high blood pressure and atherosclerosis. We know that, on average, cigarette smokers die ten years younger than non-smokers.

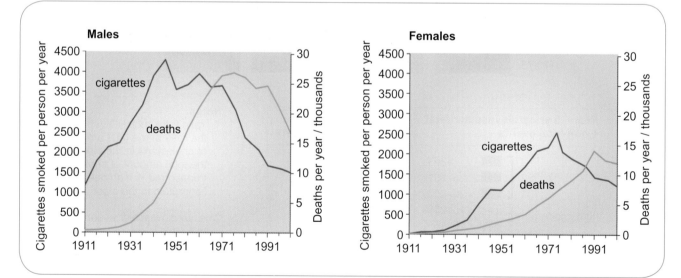

Figure 11.31   Lung cancer deaths and smoking rates from 1911.

Richard Doll

Richard Doll was born in London in 1912. He studied medicine, and worked for the Medical Research Council. He was asked to find out why cases of lung cancer were rising – they had increased fourfold between 1911 and 1950.

He set about the task by interviewing 600 people in London with lung cancer, trying to find a link between them. At first, he thought that tar used on roads could be the culprit – he knew that it contained many different carcinogens. But as the study continued, he became convinced that the link between the cancer sufferers was smoking. He was so sure of his findings that he immediately gave up smoking himself, and never smoked another cigarette. He extended his study to cover the whole country, and found even more convincing evidence that the rise in lung cancer was tightly linked to the rise in cigarette smoking.

Richard Doll's meticulous research provided the foundation for all the other investigations on the impact of smoking on health that followed.

He himself continued to research into the topic – and many others. He is credited with having saved millions of lives; his research has caused a massive reduction in smoking since the 1950s.

He died in 2006, aged 92.

Sir Richard Doll

SAQ

11 A study was carried out into the smoking habits and deaths of male doctors in Great Britain between 1951 and 1991. The men were classified as non-smokers, former smokers or current smokers. The numbers of men per 100 000 in each group who died during the 40-year period of cancer, cardiovascular disease or respiratory diseases were recorded. The results are shown in the table.

a Explain how the evidence in the table suggests that smoking causes lung cancer, CHD and COPD.   `Hint`

b Explain how smoking can cause cancer.

c Suggest a cause of death, other than CHD, that is classified under 'all cardiovascular disease'.   `Answer`

Cause of death	Annual mortality per 100 000 men		
	Non-smokers	**Former smokers**	**Current smokers**
lung cancer	14	58	209
all cancers	305	384	656
coronary heart disease	572	678	892
all cardiovascular disease	1037	1221	1643
chronic obstructive pulmonary disease	10	57	127
all respiratory disease	107	192	313

SAQ

12 A study was carried out into the effects of smokers, aged between 60 and 70 years, giving up smoking after having a heart attack. The graph shows the chance of survival for up to five years after the heart attack.

a What percentage of people who gave up smoking were still alive five years after their heart attack?

b Compare this with the results for people who continued smoking.

c Explain how giving up smoking could reduce the risk of death from a further heart attack.

Answer

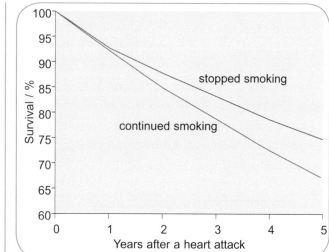

Summary

Glossary

- A pathogen is a microorganism that causes disease. Pathogens are a type of parasite. A parasite is an organism that lives in close association with a host and does it harm.

- Infectious diseases may be caused by viruses (e.g. AIDS), bacteria (e.g. TB), fungi (e.g. athlete's foot) or protozoa (e.g. malaria).

- TB is caused by *Mycobacterium tuberculosis*, which infects cells in the lungs. It is transmitted by breathing in droplets of moisture that have come from an infected person. TB has been successfully treated with antibiotics in the past, but it is now increasing worldwide and several antibiotic-resistant strains of the bacterium have appeared. People with HIV/AIDS often die from TB.

- AIDS is caused by HIV, the human immunodeficiency virus. It is transmitted through contact of body fluids. The numbers of people with HIV/AIDS is increasing worldwide. There is currently no cure, but drugs can enable an infected person to live a healthy life for many years.

- Malaria is caused by a protozoan called *Plasmodium*. It is transmitted in the saliva of female *Anopheles* mosquitoes when they bite first an infected person and then an uninfected one. Malaria is found only where these mosquitoes live, mostly in tropical and subtropical countries, but their range is currently increasing.

- Primary lines of defence prevent pathogens from entering the body. They include skin and mucous membranes.

- The way in which white cells (leucocytes) respond when a pathogen invades the body is called the immune response.

- Phagocytic cells – neutrophils and macrophages – destroy pathogens of any type by phagocytosis and digestion. Macrophages may act as antigen-presenting cells, placing molecules from the pathogens they have ingested in their plasma membranes, where other white cells may come into contact with them.

continued

- B and T lymphocytes only respond if the antigen to which they can make a specific response enters the body. If a B lymphocyte encounters its antigen, it forms a clone of plasma cells that secrete the antibody specific to that antigen, as well as memory cells. If a T lymphocyte encounters its antigen, it also forms a clone. T helper cells stimulate other cells to destroy the antigen, while T killer cells destroy the cell carrying the antigen. Activated T lymphocytes also produce memory cells.

- The first, primary, response of the body to a pathogen is often slow. Subsequent contact with the same pathogen produces a faster and more vigorous, response, the secondary response. This is often enough to prevent the disease occurring a second time, a condition known as immunity to that disease.

- Active immunity involves the body's production of its own B or T lymphocytes in response to an antigen. Passive immunity involves the body being given ready-made antibodies or antitoxins. Natural immunity includes the immunity that develops after having a disease, or from a mother's antibodies passing to her baby in the uterus or through breast milk. Artificial immunity develops through vaccination.

- New human diseases frequently appear. Most of them are caused by viruses. It is possible that a new disease could spread rapidly around the world and cause large numbers of deaths, so governments need to share information and work together to develop new vaccines and other means of preventing a new disease from spreading.

- Antibiotics and other medicinal drugs are often developed from other living organisms. For example, marine sponges may provide us with new antibiotics, while rainforest plants are a potential source of many new drugs.

- Smoking increases the risk of developing lung cancer, chronic obstructive pulmonary disease (COPD) and cardiovascular diseases.

- Bronchitis is inflammation of the airways, often caused by pathogens breeding in mucus that collects there. Tobacco smoke contains several different substances that irritate the ciliated cells and goblet cells lining the airways, increasing mucus production and stopping cilia from working.

- COPD prevents the normal flow of air through the lungs. It usually involves emphysema, in which the walls of the alveoli are broken down and lose their elasticity.

- Lung cancer is caused by carcinogens in tar, which damage genes that control cell division.

- Tobacco smoke contains nicotine, an addictive neurotoxin which increases blood pressure and the risk of developing cardiovascular diseases, including CHD and stroke.

- Carbon monoxide in tobacco smoke combines with haemoglobin, reducing the amount of oxygen that can be carried in the blood.

- Much of the evidence for the effects of smoking on health consists of epidemiological data. It is difficult to do controlled experiments that directly show that smoking *causes* a disease in humans.

Questions

1 The table shows the death rates from coronary heart disease (CHD) of men and women between the ages of 35 and 74 for some European countries. It also shows the prevalence of cigarette smoking among men and women of all ages in those countries. The prevalence of smoking is the percentage of men and women who smoke cigarettes every day.
(The data refer to the mid to late 1990s.)

	Deaths from CHD / deaths per 100 000		Prevalence of smoking / %	
Non-Mediterranean countries	**Men**	**Women**	**Men**	**Women**
Latvia	904	292	67	12
Russian Federation	639	230	67	27
Scotland	321	122	33	29
Finland	288	81	27	19
Czech Republic	318	115	43	31
Hungary	420	161	40	27
Mediterranean countries				
Greece	170	18	46	28
Italy	140	37	38	26
Spain	121	32	48	25
France	85	21	40	27

a Suggest <u>one</u> reason why health authorities are especially concerned about the death rates from CHD for people in the 35 to 74 age group. [1]

b Using <u>only</u> the information given in the table, explain whether or not the following hypotheses are supported by the data.
You should quote data from the table in support of your answers.
  i Mediterranean countries have lower death rates from CHD than non-Mediterranean countries.
  ii Men are more at risk of CHD than women.
  iii Death rates from CHD are highest in countries with the highest prevalence of smoking. [5]

OCR Biology AS (2802) January 2004 [Total 6]

Answer

2 Tuberculosis (TB) is one of the world's greatest killers. There is a pandemic of TB and this poses great threats to the world's population. It is a disease that is proving very difficult to eradicate.
  a Name the organism that causes tuberculosis (TB). [1]
  b Explain what is meant by the term <u>pandemic</u>. [1]
  c Discuss the problems that are involved in eradicating tuberculosis (TB) from the world. [9]

OCR Biology AS (2802) June 2003 [Total 11]

Answer

Chapter 12

Biodiversity

e-Learning

Objectives

No-one knows how many different species of living organisms there are on Earth. More than 1.5 million species of animals have been described and named to date. Around a quarter of a million flowering plant species and thousands of other plants (such as ferns and mosses) are known. Add to this the fungi, bacteria and other single-celled organisms, and we are looking at a very large number of species.

And these are only the ones that we know about. Some biologists think that there may be as many as 100 million species on Earth. One tree in a tropical rainforest can contain as many as 1200 species of beetles, and almost every time a biologist does a thorough count of beetles in a small area of rainforest they find many previously unknown species.

There is much interest in biodiversity. It is fundamental to sustainable life on Earth and we have at last recognised how much human activities affect it – generally in a negative way, because our increasing population and the demands that we put on the environment damage habitats and cause species extinction. But our influence is not always negative – for example, sunken ships can become new habitats for marine organisms, and worked-out quarries can form new lakes and wetlands that are valuable for wildlife.

An understanding of biodiversity can help us to understand, and hopefully limit, the damage that we do, and even to reverse it. Chapter 15 explores these issues, looking at how conservation measures can help to maintain biodiversity, and why this is important.

Measuring biodiversity

The more we understand about the living organisms around us, including how they live and where they live, the more we should be able to protect them and their environment. Ecologists attempt to find out what species are living in an area, how many of them there are and what they require from their habitats.

Some definitions

species – A species is a group of organisms with similar morphology and physiology. They are able to breed with each other to produce fertile offspring. They are usually unable to breed with other species. If this does happen, then the offspring are generally infertile.

habitat – A habitat is a place where an organism lives. Each species has its own requirements for a particular type of habitat.

population – A population is a group of organisms of the same species, living in the same place at the same time, and able to interbreed with each other.

community – A community is all the living organisms, of all species, living in the same place at the same time.

ecosystem – An ecosystem can be considered as a relatively self-contained system including all the living organisms and their environment, interacting with each other. An ecosystem is, as its name suggests, a system rather than a place. On a simple level, we can think of a pond as being an ecosystem, but the term really means the ways in which all the organisms in the pond interact with each other and also with the water in the pond, the mud at the bottom, the air above the water and the light that falls onto the pond.

Biodiversity is not an easy term to define. Most people have a rough idea of what it means, in terms of the number of different species in an area. But biodiversity means more than this – it includes the range of habitats, communities and species that are present in an area, and also the genetic variation that exists within each species. In 1992, 152 nations signed a Convention on Biological Diversity at which biodiversity was defined as: 'the variability among living organisms from all sources including ... terrestrial, marine and other aquatic ecosystems, and the ecological complexes of which they are part; this includes diversity within species, between species and of ecosystems.'

Sampling

To find out what species are present in a habitat, and the size of the population of each of them, the ideal method would be to find, identify and count every single organism that lives there. Obviously that is only rarely possible. Instead, we take samples from the area we are interested in, and use these to make an estimate of the total numbers in the area.

Sampling can be **random sampling** or **systematic sampling** (Figure 12.1). If an area looks reasonably uniform, or if it looks as though the species distribution is patchy, with no clear pattern, then it is best to sample the whole area randomly. This means that you use chance to determine your sampling points. It is important to do this because any element of choice that you give to yourself when deciding where to take your samples might mean that your overall sample becomes biased in some way, and therefore unrepresentative of the whole area. The usual way to ensure that a sample is random is to have a set of random numbers – for example, generated by a calculator – and use these as coordinates to determine the positions of the sampling points in relation to two axes.

Sometimes, however, you may have particular reasons for wanting to sample more systematically. For example, you may want to investigate how vegetation changes as a dry meadow grades into a wet, marshy area. In this case, you could lay out a string running in a straight line from the dry meadow to the marshy area. You then sample the organisms that are present along the line. This is called a **transect**.

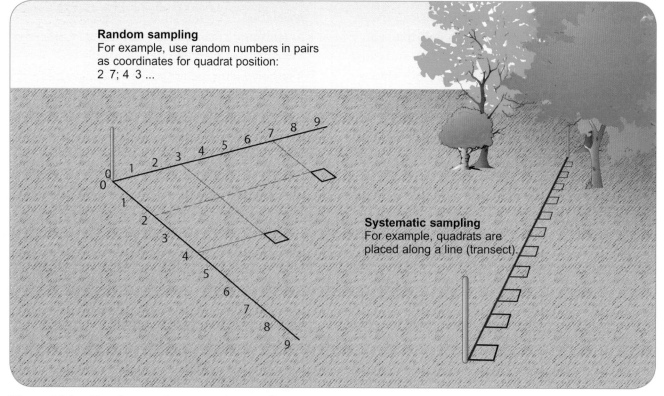

Random sampling
For example, use random numbers in pairs as coordinates for quadrat position:
2 7; 4 3 ...

Systematic sampling
For example, quadrats are placed along a line (transect).

Figure 12.1   Random and systematic sampling.

Random sampling methods

Using quadrats

Random sampling can be done using **quadrats**. A quadrat is a square frame that marks off an area of ground (or water) within which you can make a thorough survey of which species are present, and how many of each of them there are. You need to decide on a suitable size for the quadrats and how many you will use. There is a balance to be found between the ideal situation where you would completely cover the area with quadrats, and the more practical considerations of how much time you have at your disposal and the problems of scoring the organisms in the quadrats. Consideration should also be given to the possible damage to the environment that may be caused by the sampling procedure. Figure 12.2 shows how the choice of a suitable size of quadrat can be made.

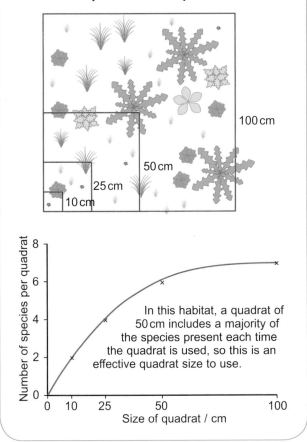

Frame quadrats – choice of size
Optimum size depends on the habitat. In meadowland it may have sides of 25 cm but to sample trees in woodland it may need to be many metres.

In this habitat, a quadrat of 50 cm includes a majority of the species present each time the quadrat is used, so this is an effective quadrat size to use.

Figure 12.2 Choosing quadrat size.

What you measure within the quadrat depends on what you want to know, and also on the types of organisms that are in it.

- You can simply record the different species that are present in the quadrat. This can be used to find the **species richness** or the **species frequency**. Species richness is the number of different species in the area you are studying. Species frequency is a measure of the chance of a particular species being found within any one quadrat. You simply record whether the species was present in each quadrat that you analyse. For example, if you placed your quadrat 50 times, and found daisy plants in 22 of these placings, then the species frequency for daisies is

$$\frac{22}{50} \times 100 = 44\%.$$

- You can count the numbers of each species present in the quadrat. This can be used to find the **species density**. This is a measure of how many individuals there are per square metre. You simply count the number of individuals of that species in each quadrat, and total all your results. This is then divided by the total area of all your quadrats (Worked example 1).

Worked example 1

Calculating species density

A survey gave the following results for a species of sea anemone on a rocky shore, using a quadrat with an area of $0.25\,m^2$.

Quadrat	1	2	3	4	5	6	7	8	9	10
Number of anemones	0	3	0	1	0	0	5	2	0	1

Ten quadrats were placed, so a total area of $10 \times 0.25\,m^2$, which equals $2.5\,m^2$, was sampled. The total number of sea anemones found in this area was 12. Therefore, the species density is

$$\frac{12}{2.5\,m^2} = 4.8\,per\,m^2.$$

● For many plants and animals, counting individuals in a quadrat is not an option. For example, how do you decide how many grass plants there are in a quadrat that you have placed on a lawn? In this case, you can estimate the **percentage cover** of the species within your quadrat (Figure 12.3). To help with this, you can use a 50 cm × 50 cm quadrat with wires running across it at 10 cm intervals in each direction, dividing the quadrat into 25 'mini quadrats'. You then decide approximately what percentage of the area inside the quadrat is occupied by each species. These percentages may not add up to 100%. For example, there might be bare ground in the quadrat, so the numbers will come to less than 100%. Or there may be plants overlying one another, in which case the numbers may add up to more than 100%.

An even more precise way of measuring percentage cover is to reduce your quadrat size to a point. Figure 12.4 shows how a **point quadrat** is used.

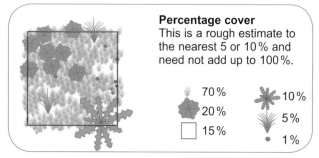

Percentage cover
This is a rough estimate to the nearest 5 or 10 % and need not add up to 100 %.

70 %
20 %
15 %
10 %
5 %
1 %

Figure 12.3 Estimating percentage cover.

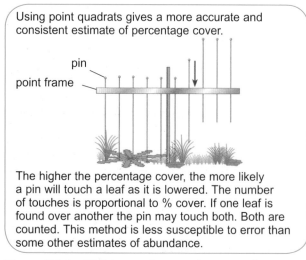

Using point quadrats gives a more accurate and consistent estimate of percentage cover.

pin
point frame

The higher the percentage cover, the more likely a pin will touch a leaf as it is lowered. The number of touches is proportional to % cover. If one leaf is found over another the pin may touch both. Both are counted. This method is less susceptible to error than some other estimates of abundance.

Figure 12.4 Using a point quadrat to estimate percentage cover.

1 A survey was made of dandelion plants growing on a lawn and in a cultivated vegetable patch. Ten 0.25 m² quadrats were placed randomly in each area, and the number of dandelion plants in each quadrat was counted. The results are shown in the table.

Quadrat	1	2	3	4	5	6	7	8	9	10
Number of dandelions on lawn	0	0	4	3	0	1	2	4	0	3
Number of dandelions in cultivated ground	0	0	0	2	5	0	0	1	0	0

Calculate the density of dandelions in each of the two areas. *Answer*

2 Five 0.25 m² quadrats were placed in a meadow. The percentage of each quadrat occupied by each species of plant was estimated to the nearest 5% and recorded in the following table.

Quadrat	1	2	3	4	5
Timothy grass	60	30	35	70	25
Yorkshire fog grass	25	70	30	15	40
plantain	0	5	0	5	0
meadow buttercup	0	0	15	0	10
dock	5	10	5	0	5
cowslip	0	0	0	5	0
white clover	15	0	25	25	10
bare ground	0	15	15	5	20

a Calculate the mean percentage cover for each species in this meadow.
b Explain why the percentage cover for all the species adds up to more than 100%.
c Suggest why the percentage cover was recorded to the nearest 5%.
d Could these results be used to obtain a valid estimate of the species density for each species? Explain your answer. *Answer*

Mobile animals

Quadrats are obviously no use for finding or counting mobile animals, so different methods have to be used for these.

Figure 12.5 shows some techniques that can be used to capture mobile organisms and estimate their population numbers. Small mammals, such as mice and voles, can be caught in a **Longworth trap**. Insects and other invertebrates, such as spiders, can be captured by **sweep netting**. Nets can also be used for capturing aquatic organisms. The techniques for this vary according to the size of the body of water, and whether it is still or moving.

A good method of estimating the population size of mobile organisms, if used with care, is the **mark, release, recapture** technique (Figure 12.6).

First, as many individuals as possible are caught. Each individual is marked, in a way that will not affect its future chance of survival (Figure 12.7). For example, a patch of fur can be clipped from a vole, or a small spot of waterproof paint put onto a water boatman. The marked individuals are counted, returned to their habitat and left to mix in with all the rest of the population. The reasoning behind this method assumes that this mixing is complete and random. Other assumptions are that the marked individuals are no more likely to die than unmarked ones, and that there will not be any births or immigrations between sampling, which would add extra unmarked individuals to the population.

A Longworth trap is used to catch small mammals. The traps are checked at least once a day and the captured animals marked and then released.

This trap is used for capturing night-flying moths. They are attracted to the light and fall into the box below.

Kick sampling involves one person disturbing the stream bed with their feet, so that organisms are swept down into a net held by another.

A sweep net captures insects in vegetation. Each type of vegetation requires a different standard method of sweeping the net.

Figure 12.5   Sampling populations and communities of mobile animals.

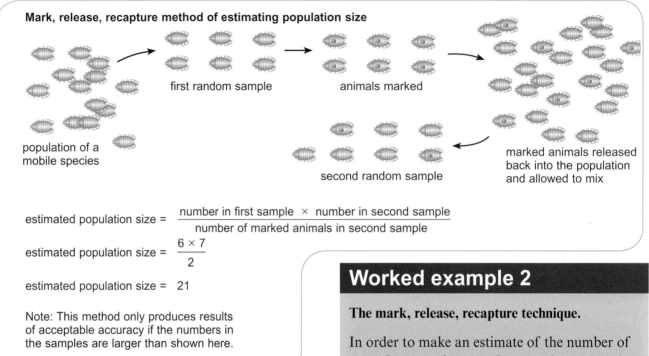

Mark, release, recapture method of estimating population size

first random sample

animals marked

population of a mobile species

second random sample

marked animals released back into the population and allowed to mix

estimated population size = $\dfrac{\text{number in first sample} \times \text{number in second sample}}{\text{number of marked animals in second sample}}$

estimated population size = $\dfrac{6 \times 7}{2}$

estimated population size = 21

Note: This method only produces results of acceptable accuracy if the numbers in the samples are larger than shown here.

Figure 12.6 The mark, release, recapture technique for estimating population size.

When enough time has elapsed for the mixing to take place, another large sample is captured. The number of marked individuals is counted, and also the number of unmarked individuals. The proportion of marked to unmarked can then be used to calculate the total number of individuals in the population (Worked example 2). For example, if you find that one-tenth of the second sample were marked, then you presume that you originally caught one-tenth of the population in your first sample. Your best estimate is therefore that the number in the population is ten times the number you caught and marked in your first sample.

Fig 12.7 Marking a woodlouse.

Worked example 2

The mark, release, recapture technique.

In order to make an estimate of the number of water boatmen in a pond, a sample was caught using a net. Each animal was marked with a very small spot of non-toxic waterproof paint and then released. The next day, a second large sample was caught.

Number caught and marked in first sample = 35

Number caught in second sample = 38

Number in the second sample that had been marked = 13

So estimated number in population

$= \dfrac{35 \times 38}{13} = 102$

SAQ

3 A sample of 39 woodlice was captured from beneath a piece of rotting wood. Each animal was marked and then released. A second sample of 35 was caught on the following day. Of these, 20 had been marked.
   a Use these results to estimate the number of woodlice in the population.
   b What assumptions must be made in order to make this estimate?

Answer

A lost world still to be discovered

Despite the huge and still growing population of humans on Earth, there are still some parts of which we know very little. The huge area of the sea floor has been only partly explored, and there must be many species of marine organisms that no-one has yet seen. There are even areas of land that have not been visited by humans, and new terrestrial species are regularly being discovered.

For example, in early 2006 a team of researchers from Australia and Indonesia spent a month searching and sampling an area of pristine rainforest in north-western New Guinea, in the Foja Mountains. They reported seeing absolutely no impact from humans. They themselves were dropped in by helicopter, because no roads or paths enter the region. The researchers found many new species of animals, such as the golden-mantled tree kangaroo. There were also many new plants, and they rediscovered some species were thought to have become extinct.

The team want to continue their research in the area. If they can find out more about it, then its value can be recognised and efforts made to conserve it and protect it from human interference in the future. But will the presence of the researchers themselves cause harm? Will their discoveries encourage other people to enter the previously untouched area of rainforest? Some people might argue that it would have been better to leave the forest alone, and that is certainly a suggestion worth considering. Others will consider that the benefit of knowing about the forest puts us in a stronger position to be able to protect it, and that this outweighs the potential risk of harm that we may inadvertently cause. Just being there will affect this previously undisturbed rainforest.

Species evenness

When we have data on the kinds of species in two habitats, and the approximate numbers of their populations, we can compare their **species evenness**. This is a measure of the relative abundance of each species in the area we have sampled. Species evenness is greatest when the population sizes of the different species are most similar.

For example, we might obtain these results for animals living on or near the surface of two ponds. The counts are from a 10 square metre area of each pond.

	Water boatmen	Water measurers	Pond skaters	Whirligig beetles	Water spiders
pond A	43	18	38	3	1
pond B	26	18	29	11	5

Pond B has a greater species evenness, because there is less variation between the population sizes of each species.

Simpson's Index of Diversity

When you have collected information about the numbers of species and their density in the area you are studying, you can use your results to calculate a value for the biodiversity in that area. One way of doing this is to use **Simpson's Index of Diversity**. The formula for this is:

$$D = 1 - \left(\Sigma \left(\frac{n}{N} \right)^2 \right)$$

where N is the total number of organisms of all species, and n is the total number of organisms of a particular species (Worked example 3).

Values of D range from 0 to 1. A Diversity Index value of 1 represents very low species richness. A value of 0 represents very high species richness – the value you get if there is only one species present, for example.

One big advantage of this method of calculating biodiversity is that you don't need to actually identify all, or even any, of the organisms present to species level. You can, for example, just decide to call the species of anemone that has lots of

Worked example 3

Simpson's Index of Diversity.

A sample was made of the animals living on two rocky shores. 10 quadrats were placed on each shore, and the number of animals of each species in each quadrat was counted. The results are shown in the table.

Species	Number of individuals, n	
	Shore A	Shore B
painted topshells	24	51
limpets	367	125
dogwhelks	192	63
snakelocks anemones	14	0
beadlet anemones	83	22
barnacles	112	391
mussels	207	116
periwinkles	108	93
total number of individuals, N	**1107**	**861**

To calculate Simpson's Index for shore A, we need to find $\frac{n}{N}$ for each of the eight species that were found, square each value and then add them up. We can do the same for shore B.

Species	Shore A		
	n	$\frac{n}{N}$	$\left(\frac{n}{N} \right)^2$
painted topshells	24	0.022	0.000
limpets	367	0.332	0.110
dogwhelks	192	0.173	0.030
snakelocks anemones	14	0.013	0.000
beadlet anemones	83	0.075	0.006
barnacles	112	0.101	0.010
mussels	207	0.187	0.035
periwinkles	108	0.098	0.010
total number of individuals, N	**1107**	$\Sigma \left(\frac{n}{N} \right)^2 = 0.201$	

For shore A, Simpson's Index of Diversity (D)
= 1 − 0.201 = **0.799**

SAQ

4 Calculate D for shore B.

Answer

short tentacles 'anemone A', and the species that has only a few very long tentacles 'anemone B'. So long as you can recognise that they are different species, you do not need to find their official names.

The higher the number we get for *D*, the greater the diversity. You can probably see that the diversity depends on the number of different species there are, and also the abundance of each of those species. A community with, say, 10 species but where one or two species are very dominant is less diverse than one with the same number of species but where several different species have a similar abundance.

SAQ

5 What is the species richness for each of shore A and for shore B?

Answer

The impact of sampling

Great care has to be taken that, when we are sampling a habitat, we do not damage the organisms that live there, or the habitat itself. We must try not to trample on plants in a field, or animals on a rocky shore – this could have a very big impact. If we catch mammals in traps, we need to ensure that we check the traps very regularly, so that no animal is caught for long enough to be harmed. If we take organisms from a pond or stream to count and identify them, we must replace them in their original habitat as quickly as possible. Before doing any trapping, you should look for specialist guidance on how to do this without harming the animals.

Nevertheless, sampling is bound to have some impact on the habitat. We have to weigh up this possible harm against the benefits to be gained from the knowledge we will have about what is living there. It is difficult to put forward a case for conserving a habitat if we do not know what lives in it. It is difficult to plan how to conserve an area if we do not have knowledge of the species that live in it, where they live and how many there are.

Summary Glossary

- Biodiversity can be defined as the variability among living organisms and habitats, including genetic diversity within species, between species and of ecosystems.

- We do not know how many species live on Earth, but it is likely that there are many millions of species, a vast number of which have not yet been discovered, described or named.

- To measure species diversity, estimate population numbers and investigate the distribution of species in a habitat, sampling methods are used. Random sampling involves taking samples at positions within the sampling area that are determined by chance. One way of this is to use random numbers as coordinates for the placing of quadrats.

- Sampling is necessary if we are to find out what species live in a habitat, how many of each type of organism are present and precisely where they are found. However, sampling always has some impact on the habitat and the organisms within it, and this must be minimised and taken into consideration when deciding on the sampling method and frequency to be used.

- Species richness is the number of different species in the area you are studying. Species frequency is a measure of the chance of a particular species being found within any one quadrat. Density is a measure of how many individuals there are per square metre.

- Simpson's Index of Diversity can be used to calculate a value for the biodiversity in an area.

  The formula is: $D = 1 - \left(\Sigma \left(\frac{n}{N} \right)^2 \right)$

Questions

1 A group of students used randomly placed $0.25\,m^2$ quadrats to analyse the distribution of plant species in an area of chalk grassland. The data they recorded on two particular species, yarrow, *Achillea millefolium*, and salad burnet, *Sanguisorba minor*, is shown in the table.

Quadrat	Number of individual plants per quadrat	
	Yarrow	**Salad burnet**
1	3	0
2	2	0
3	0	6
4	4	7
5	3	0
6	2	5
7	5	5
8	2	0
9	3	8
10	6	0
11	0	3
12	0	6
13	2	4
14	1	0
15	5	4
16	4	7
17	3	0
18	1	6
19	0	8
20	4	0

a Explain how the students would have determined the most suitable size of quadrat to use in this investigation. [3]

b State which of the two plants shows the highest species frequency. Explain your reasoning. [3]

c Calculate the mean number of salad burnet plants per square metre. Show your working. [3]

OCR Biology AS (2805/03) January 2002 [Total 9]

Answer

Chapter 13

Classification

Classification and taxonomy

With such a huge number of different kinds of organisms living on Earth, biologists have always wanted to arrange them into groups, a process called **classification**. We find it difficult to memorise or absorb information about thousands of different unrelated objects. By grouping them into different categories, it is much easier to understand them and to remember key features of them.

At first, the purpose of classification was to aid identification. This was the main reason behind Carolus Linnaeus's work on classification of living organisms in the 18th century. He built on previous attempts at classification, which had grouped plants and animals according to their visible features, putting those with similar appearance and structure into the same group.

However, whereas previous classifications had generally involved long descriptions of each kind of organism, Linnaeus introduced the neat and simple binomial system of naming them. Each type of organism was given two names – a **binomial**. This was in Latin, a language that would be understood by scientists all over the world. His idea was so good that it is still in use today – although Linnaeus would be amazed at the huge numbers of organisms that have now been discovered, described and named.

The way in which Linnaeus grouped organisms, which most biologists still use today, is called **taxonomy**. This involves placing organisms in a series of taxonomic units, or **taxa** (singular: taxon). In biological classification, these taxa form a **hierarchy**. Each kind of organism is assigned to its own **species**, and similar species are grouped into a **genus** (plural: genera). Similar genera are grouped into a **family**, families into an **order**, orders into a **class**, classes into a **phylum** (plural: phyla) and phyla into a **kingdom.**

Table 13.1 shows how a human and a daisy plant are classified.

Taxon	Human	Daisy
kingdom	animals	plants
phylum	chordates	angiosperms
class	mammals	dicotyledons
order	primates	Asterales
family	Hominidae	Asteraceae
genus	*Homo*	*Bellis*
species	*Homo sapiens*	*Bellis perennis*

Table 13.1 Taxonomic classification of a human and a daisy.

Notice that the names of the genus and species are written in italics. The name of the genus starts with a capital letter, and the name of the particular species within that genus starts with a small letter. The unique name for a species is its binomial – for example, *Homo sapiens* or *Bellis perennis*. This is a convention used in all scientific publications – though newspapers usually get it wrong. When you are writing by hand, you can underline the names to indicate that they should be in italics. Another convention is that the names start with a small letter if they are English words, and a capital letter if they are a Latin word – except for the species, which always has a small letter. Most taxa can be named using either English or Latin. For example, we can talk about the animal kingdom, or the kingdom Animalia.

SAQ

1 African elephants, *Loxodonta africana*, are mammals that belong to the order Proboscidea and the family Elephantidae. List the taxa to which an elephant belongs, as for the human and the daisy in Table 13.1.

Answer

The species concept

As we saw in the last chapter, we can define a species as a group of organisms that have similar morphology and physiology, and which can breed together to produce fertile offspring. Different species cannot normally interbreed, and if they do their offspring are generally not fertile.

This definition is all very well for organisms that are alive today, but it does not help us very much to decide whether two fossil ammonites belong to the same or different species, or whether two kinds of birds for which we only have skeletons or feathers in a museum were able to breed together.

Moreover, as in many instances in biology, by classifying organisms into species, we are sometimes trying to put things into neat and tidy groups that do not really exist. If one species can evolve into another, then we must expect to find some groups of organisms where it is difficult to decide if we are dealing with one species or two.

There are also difficulties where organisms do not normally reproduce sexually. For example, while everyone agrees that blackberry plants belong to the genus *Rubus*, there is less agreement about whether they all belong to the same species, *R. fruticosus,* or whether there are in fact several hundred different species (Figure 13.1). The difficulty here is that blackberries generally reproduce asexually. When, extremely rarely, they *do* reproduce sexually, there are slight variations in their offspring, each of which then goes on to produce many new plants genetically identical to itself (clones) by asexual reproduction.

Figure 13.1 There is disagreement about whether these two blackberry plants belong to the same or different species.

Phylogeny

Linnaeus classified organisms according to their observable features, so that they could easily be identified. Today, we do it rather differently. We place organisms into taxa according to what we think are their probable evolutionary relationships. The study of evolutionary relationships is called **phylogeny**.

It is not easy to determine the relationships between different species of living organisms. The clues that we have are mostly no more than circumstantial evidence. Species have changed over long periods of time, and biologists have to use whatever information they can in order to try to trace back their ancestries.

Similarities in structure are an obvious starting point. For example, any animal that has hair, in which the young develop attached to a placenta, and that suckles its young on milk, is classified in the class Mammalia. We deduce that all mammals have arisen from a common ancestor that lived millions of years ago. But, as ever in biology, things are not always straightforward. How, for example, should we classify the platypus, which has hair and suckles its young on milk, but which lays eggs? It seems that platypuses must be very closely related, in an evolutionary sense, to other mammals, and so they are placed in that class. Within the mammals, they belong to the order Monotremata, along with spiny anteaters (Figure 13.2), another mammal that lays eggs. We believe that the monotremes are a side branch of the mammalian family tree, which took its own individual line of evolution quite soon after the mammals first evolved.

Figure 13.2 A spiny anteater.

Sometimes, however, structural similarities or differences can be misleading. For example, there are several different mammals that have evolved to eat ants or termites. They include the spiny anteater, pangolin, giant anteater and aardvark (Figure 13.2 and Figure 13.3). They all have similar adaptations – strong front claws for grasping, small heads and long tongues for reaching into ants' nests, and no teeth. Yet they are not believed to be very closely related. Pangolins appear to be related to the carnivores, aardvarks – amazingly – show relationships with elephants, giant anteaters are related to sloths and – as we have seen – spiny anteaters branched off from the main mammalian family tree a long time ago; their nearest relatives are platypuses.

The observable similarities between these four species are the result of **convergent evolution**. They have evolved similar lifestyles, and therefore similar adaptations.

If we cannot always rely on observable structural features to decide how closely organisms are related to each other, then what else can we use? Today, the best information that we have is the DNA in an organism's cells. Different species have different base sequences in various regions of their DNA. The more similar the DNA, the more closely related the species. Modern phylogenetic taxonomists study similarities and differences between key regions of the DNA in different species. They can use these to build up possible family trees, suggesting how long ago different species evolved from common ancestors.

SAQ

2 Greenfinches, goldfinches and chaffinches all belong to the family Fringellidae. Their binomials are *Carduelis chloris*, *Carduelis carduelis* and *Fringella coelebs* respectively. What can you deduce from this information about the likely evolutionary relationships between these three species of birds?

greenfinch

goldfinch

chaffinch

Answer

Figure 13.3 a pangolin;   **b** giant anteater;
c aardvark.

Chapter 13: Classification

Are chimps a species of human?

Our closest relatives are the great apes – chimpanzees, gorillas and orang-utans. We share with them very similar body structures and physiology. We also share a lot of our DNA.

Traditional classification of humans and apes puts only humans in the genus *Homo*, so that we are the only species of *Homo* alive today – *Homo sapiens*. Fossil remains have been found of several human-like organisms that are now extinct, and some of these have also been placed in the genus *Homo*. They include *H. erectus*, *H. neanderthalensis* and the recently discovered, controversial species *H. floresiensis* – about which experts are still in dispute. The fossils of this species, found on an island in Indonesia, may represent a species of very small humans, but some scientists think they may just be small individuals of an already-known species.

The fossils of past humans are usually very fragmentary. Often, we only have just one or two bones to go on – for example, a jaw bone or part of the skull. With such a patchy fossil record, it is difficult to trace our evolutionary history in this way. There are constant revisions of classification and species names, as new fossils are found or new interpretations are made.

Studies of DNA can also help to sort out our relationships to other species. We have even managed to extract DNA from fossils. In 1997, DNA from some fossil neanderthals was sequenced. By looking at the number of differences in base sequences between modern human DNA and neanderthal DNA, researchers estimate that our most recent common ancestor lived about 500 000 years ago.

But what of our relationship to the modern great apes? They are all placed in different genera to us. Gorillas are in the genus *Gorilla*, chimps belong to *Pan* and orang-utans to *Pongo*.

Again, DNA studies give us some very interesting information. We have known for some time that we share almost 98% of our DNA with chimpanzees. This includes all of the DNA – much of which is non-coding. Non-coding DNA does not appear to be used for making proteins, and so it is assumed that it is easy for bases in it to change (mutate) without having any effect on the organism. But in 2003, Morris Goodman and other biologists working in Detroit, Michigan, made a careful analysis of the similarities and differences in the *coding* DNA of the great apes and humans. They reason that this is the DNA that really matters, and it is here that we should look for the degree of similarity between the genera *Homo, Pan, Pongo* and *Gorilla*.

Goodman found that we share more than 99% of our coding DNA with chimpanzees. He argues that the differences are so small that we should classify chimps in the same genus as humans. He suggests the name *Homo troglodytes* for the

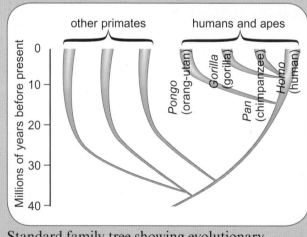

Standard family tree showing evolutionary relationships between humans and apes.

continued

212

common chimpanzee, and *Homo paniscus* for bonobo chimpanzees. In 2006, more DNA evidence was found that supports this view.

Goodman's suggested reclassification has met with considerable opposition. In particular, other researchers question the validity of his approach. Why should differences in coding DNA be more important than all the rest of the DNA in providing evidence of relationships between species? Is it reasonable to use a mathematical summary of the numbers of differences in base pairs to indicate how we should classify organisms? It is possible that just a very small change could have a large effect on the phenotype of a species – should we take into the account the *effects* of the base differences, and not just their numbers?

For example, in 2007, researchers discovered that humans have a variant of a gene involved with learning and memory which is not found in the great apes. The gene is almost the same in all the apes – the difference is that in humans there is a thymine nucleotide where in other apes there is an adenine. This has made the gene behave very differently, causing 45 more amino acids to be used to make the protein, called neurotopin, that the gene codes for. So just this one base change may be responsible for a big difference in the capacity for learning and memory in humans compared with the other apes.

To many people, especially non-biologists or creationists, it is impossible to think of any organism other than ourselves being classified as human. To others, it might be a way to save chimps from extinction. Goodman says: 'Moving chimps into the human genus might help us to realise our very great likeness, and therefore treasure more and treat humanely our closest relative.'

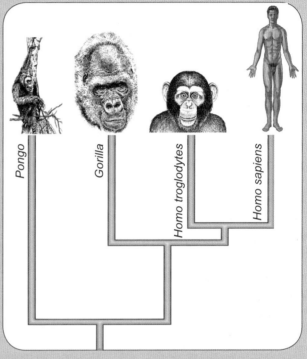

Goodman's suggested reclassification, which puts chimps and humans in the same genus.

Extension

SAQ

3 The table shows the percentage difference between the coding DNA of humans, chimpanzees, gorillas and orang-utans.
   a Which two animals appear to be most closely related?
   b Which two are most distantly related?
   c Explain why these data cannot provide us with firm guidelines about whether humans and chimpanzees should be placed in the same genus.

	% difference in coding DNA
humans and chimpanzees	0.87
humans and gorillas	1.04
humans and orang-utans	2.18
chimpanzees and gorillas	0.99
chimpanzees and orang-utans	2.14
gorillas and orang-utans	2.25

Answer

The five-kingdom classification

Traditionally, up until about a hundred years ago, all living organisms were divided into animals and plants. 'Plants' included anything that was not an animal – so not only green plants but also fungi and bacteria were included in this group. However, as microscopy allowed us to see more detail of cellular structure, and as investigations of physiology, biochemistry and molecular biology provided us with more detail of what organisms are made of and how they function, it became very clear that the 'plant' grouping contained several very distinct types of organisms.

In 1988, it was proposed by Margulis and Schwartz that all living organisms should be classified into five **kingdoms**. This classification is still used by some biologists today. The kingdoms are the Prokaryota (which used to be called Monera), Protoctista, Fungi, Plantae and Animalia. Their possible evolutionary relationships are shown in Figure 13.4.

Kingdom Prokaryota (Monera)

The Prokaryota include the bacteria and related organisms. Figure 13.5 shows the characteristic features of a prokaryotic cell.

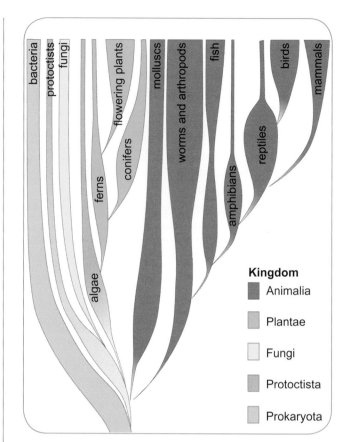

Figure 13.4 Possible evolutionary relationships of the five kingdoms.

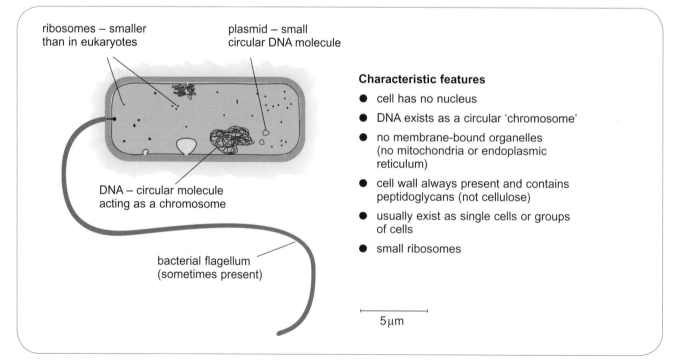

Characteristic features

- cell has no nucleus
- DNA exists as a circular 'chromosome'
- no membrane-bound organelles (no mitochondria or endoplasmic reticulum)
- cell wall always present and contains peptidoglycans (not cellulose)
- usually exist as single cells or groups of cells
- small ribosomes

Figure 13.5 Characteristic features of a prokaryotic cell.

Kingdom Protoctista

The Protoctista includes a very diverse range of organisms, which may actually be more closely related to organisms in other kingdoms than they are to each other. For example, there are strong arguments for classifying algae as plants. Any eukaryote that is not a fungus, plant or animal is classified as a protoctist. Some characteristic features of protoctists are shown in Figure 13.6.

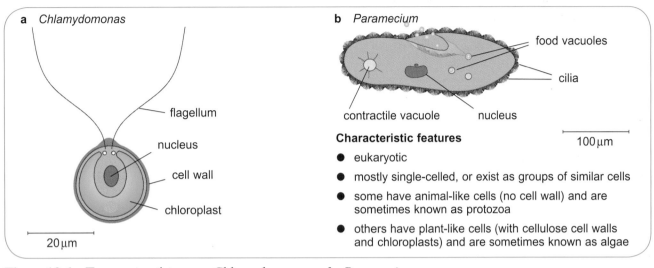

Figure 13.6 Two protoctists: **a** *Chlamydomonas;* **b** *Paramecium.*

Kingdom Fungi

Figure 13.7 shows characteristic features of fungi.

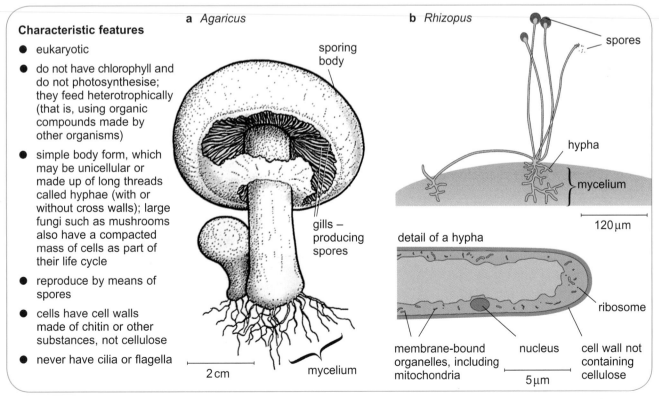

Figure 13.7 Two examples of fungi: **a** sporing body of a mushroom, *Agaricus campestris;* **b** *Rhizopus,* a mould that grows on substrates such as stale bread.

Kingdom Plantae

Figure 13.8 shows some characteristic features of plants.

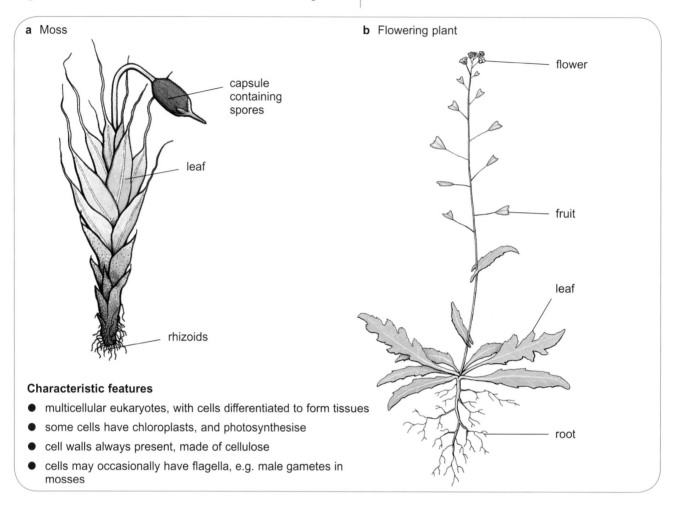

a Moss

capsule containing spores

leaf

rhizoids

b Flowering plant

flower

fruit

leaf

root

Characteristic features

- multicellular eukaryotes, with cells differentiated to form tissues
- some cells have chloroplasts, and photosynthesise
- cell walls always present, made of cellulose
- cells may occasionally have flagella, e.g. male gametes in mosses

Figure 13.8 Two examples of plants: **a** a moss, *Grimmia pulvinata*; **b** Shepherd's purse, *Capsella bursa-pastoris*.

Kingdom Animalia

Figure 13.9 shows some characteristic features of animals.

Characteristic features

- multicellular eukaryotes, with cells differentiated to form tissues
- do not have chloroplasts, and feed heterotrophically
- do not have cell walls
- cells sometimes have cilia or flagella

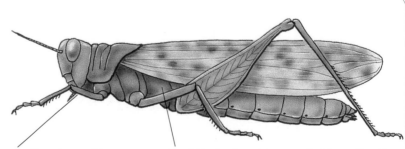

mouthparts used to feed heterotrophically

cells of the body not surrounded by cell walls (the outside of the insect is a non-cellular exoskeleton)

Figure 13.9 A locust – an example of an animal.

The three-domain classification

In 1990, a different set of major groups for the classification of organisms was proposed. It came about following a study of the genes coding for the RNA that makes up ribosomes in prokaryotes and eukaryotes. Although all prokaryotes look very similar under the microscope, they turn out to have some significant differences in their molecular structure and metabolic pathways. This indicates that the prokaryotes are made up of two distinct kinds of organisms, which have been named the Bacteria and Archaea (Figure 13.10). All the rest

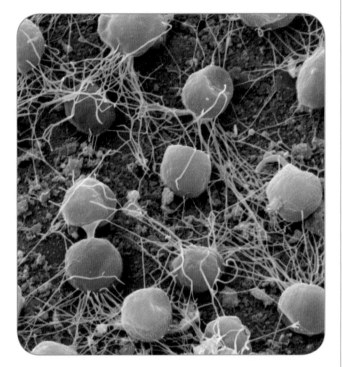

Figure 13.10 The archaean *Pyrococcus furiosus* lives near hot under-water vents. It can only survive in temperatures of 70 °C or more.

of life is placed in the Eukarya. These three groups are called **domains**. The three domains come right at the top of the hierarchy of taxa.

Since 1990, more evidence has been uncovered that supports this classification. Several metabolic pathways in the Bacteria are quite different from those in Archaea and Eukarya. Archaea and Bacteria have differences in the structure of their cell walls, cell membranes and flagella. And the methods by which DNA is used to provide instructions for making proteins in Bacteria are different from those used in Archaea and Eukarya.

Many Archaea live in extreme environments, such as hot springs, around deep volcanic vents (black smokers) in the oceans or in lakes where there is a very high concentration of salt. Some of them produce methane, cannot survive where there is oxygen and have many unusual enzymes.

In several ways, the Archaea appear to have more in common with the Eukarya than with the Bacteria. It is thought that Bacteria and Archaea separated from each other very early in the evolution of life. The Archaea and Eukarya probably diverged later (Figure 13.11).

Extension

SAQ

4 Discuss whether the five-kingdom and the three-domain classifications are completely different from one another, or if they could possibly be used together.

Answer

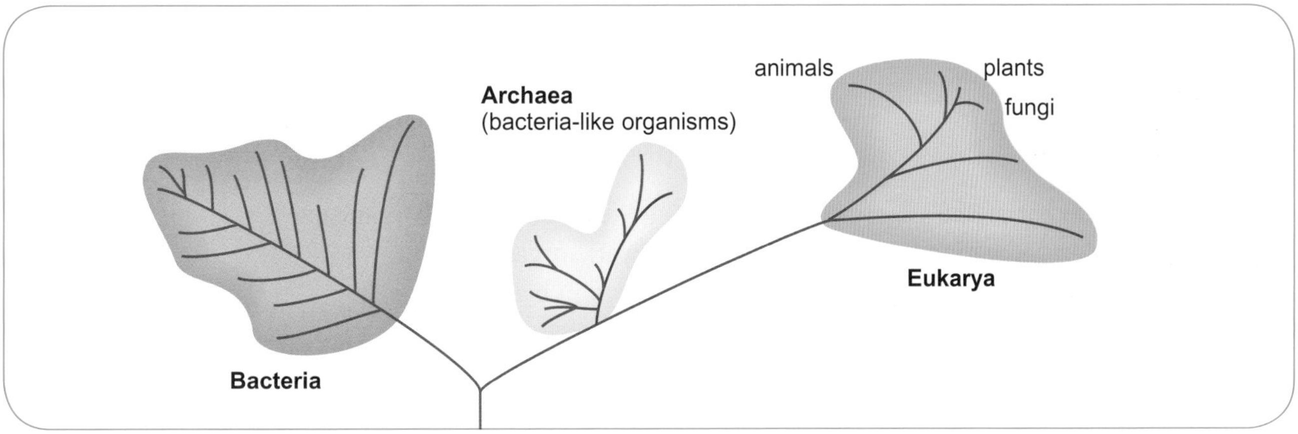

Figure 13.11 A possible phylogenetic tree supporting the grouping of organisms into three domains.

Summary

Glossary

- Classification means putting things into groups. Biologists use a taxonomic classification system, in which organisms are placed into groups called taxa, which have a hierarchical organisation.

- Biologists use natural classification, in which organisms are grouped into taxa according to how closely we believe they are related. Organisms that share physical and physiological characteristics, and that can interbreed to produce fertile offspring, are the most closely related, and they are placed in the same species. Closely related species are placed in the same genus, genera into families and then upwards into orders, classes, phyla and kingdoms.

- Classification helps us to study organisms, because we can deal with groups rather than with individuals.

- Each species has a unique binomial. Humans, for example, belong to the species *Homo sapiens*.

- Early classification systems were based on similarities in observable features. Today we can also use similarities and differences in metabolism and in DNA base sequences to work out relationships.

- One classification system places all organisms in five kingdoms – Prokaryota, Protoctista, Fungi, Plantae and Animalia. An alternative system is to divide them into three domains – the Bacteria, Archaea and Eukaryota.

Questions

1 In biological classification, there are seven principal taxonomic groups. For garlic, a flowering plant, they are listed below, but not in the correct sequence.

Number	Taxonomic group	Classification of garlic
1	order	Liliales
2	kingdom	Plantae
3	genus	*Allium*
4	phylum	Angiospermophyta
5	family	Liliaceae
6	species	*sativum*
7	subclass	Liliidae – Monocotyledons

a Using the numbers 1–7, list the taxonomic groups in the correct sequence starting with the highest group. [1]

Garlic is a member of the kingdom Plantae, which are all eukaryotic organisms.
b List the other <u>three</u> kingdoms that contain eukaryotic organisms. [3]
c State <u>three</u> features of the kingdom Plantae, other than being eukaryotic. [3]

OCR Biology AS (2804) June 2003 [Total 7]

Answer

Chapter 14

Evolution

Background

e-Learning

Objectives

Variation

In Chapter 13, we saw how organisms are classified into different species if they have differences in their structure and physiology, and if they are unable to interbreed successfully with one another. However, it is easy to see that individuals *within* a species also have differences. This is known as intraspecific **variation**.

Variation within a species has two causes – an organism's genes, and its environment.

Genetic variation

Some of the variations between individuals within a species are caused by differences in their genes – **genetic variation**. Different varieties of a gene for a particular characteristic are called **alleles**, and within a species not every individual will have the same combination of alleles.

In sexually reproducing organisms, alleles are shuffled each time a new organism is produced. You will remember that, in most plants and animals, there are two sets of chromosomes in the nucleus of each cell, one set from the male parent and one set from the female parent. Each nucleus therefore contains two copies of each gene. These copies may be the same, or they may be different.

When gametes are being formed, cell division by meiosis mixes up these sets of chromosomes, so that each sperm or egg that is made contains a different mixture of alleles. There is even more opportunity for variation when fertilisation occurs, because in principle any male gamete can fuse with any female gamete. This can give an almost infinite number of possible combinations of alleles among offspring produced by sexual reproduction.

While meiosis and fertilisation produce new *combinations* of alleles, it is also possible for completely new alleles to be produced occasionally. This happens when a mistake is made as DNA is being replicated. For example, a nucleotide may be missed out, or an extra one slipped in, or one nucleotide may be put in in place of another. This is called **mutation**.

Environmental variation

Some of the variation that you can see between individuals is not caused by their genes. For example, people with naturally fair skin may have very different skin colours, because one has been sunbathing and the other has not. Two people with combinations of alleles that would allow them to grow tall may be very different heights, because they ate different diets when they were young. Two plants with identical genes may have very different sizes and colours of leaves, because one is growing in shade, or in soil that is low in nitrate or magnesium ions, while the other is growing in the sun, or in soil that is rich in ions. Such differences are the result of **environmental variation**.

Differences like these arise during an individual's lifetime. Because they are not caused by differences in DNA, they cannot be passed on to offspring. Environmental variation cannot be inherited.

Discontinuous and continuous variation

Variation in some characteristics is very 'cut and dried'. For example, a person has one of four blood groups in the ABO system. There are no in-betweens – everyone is either A, B, AB or O. This kind of variation, where there are relatively few clearly defined groups to which an individual can belong, is called **discontinuous variation** (Figure 14.1).

SAQ

1 Suggest another example of discontinuous variation in humans.

Answer

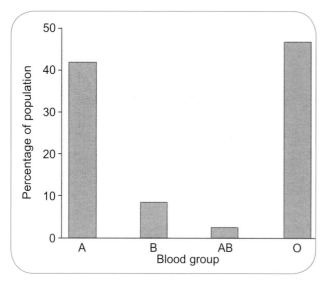

Figure 14.1 An example of discontinuous variation – ABO blood groups in the United Kingdom.

Discontinuous variation is almost always caused by genes, with little or no environmental influence. Usually, just one or two genes are involved, each of them having only a few alleles. Human ABO blood groups, for example, are controlled by a single gene with three alleles.

However, for most characteristics, variation is not so clear-cut. For example, human skin or eye colour is impossible to categorise into clearly defined colours. Leaf length in the Oxford ragwort can range between around 2 mm to 180 mm, with any length possible between these two extreme values. This kind of variation is called **continuous variation** (Figure 14.2).

A class is a chosen subdivision of a continuous variable.
The ragwort results are divided into length classes.
First the length of each leaf is measured and recorded in a table.
A leaf of 4.3 cm belongs to the class 4.00–5.99 cm.

Length class / cm	Number of leaves	Total
2.00–3.99	II	2
4.00–5.99	HHT HHT HHT II	17

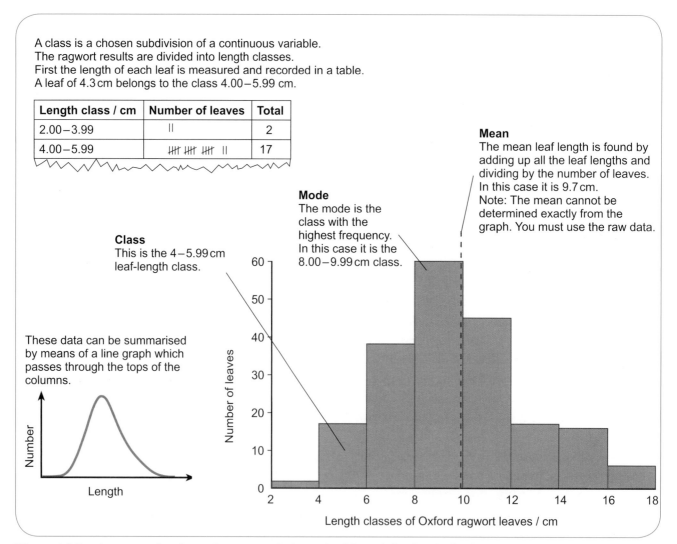

Class
This is the 4–5.99 cm leaf-length class.

Mode
The mode is the class with the highest frequency. In this case it is the 8.00–9.99 cm class.

Mean
The mean leaf length is found by adding up all the leaf lengths and dividing by the number of leaves. In this case it is 9.7 cm.
Note: The mean cannot be determined exactly from the graph. You must use the raw data.

These data can be summarised by means of a line graph which passes through the tops of the columns.

Figure 14.2 An example of continuous variation – leaf length in the Oxford ragwort, *Senecio squalida*. The classes into which the leaves have been divided in order to produce the graph are artificial – they have been decided by a person, for convenience.

Continuous variation may be caused by genes, or by the environment, or both (Figure 14.3). Continuous variation in human eye colour is caused entirely by genes. There are so many different genes, each with several different alleles, that there are hundreds of possible combinations producing all sorts of different colours that grade almost imperceptibly into one another. Variations in skin colour, on the other hand, are caused partly by genes (again there are many of these with many different alleles) and partly by the environment, in particular the degree of exposure to sunlight. Variations in leaf length on a single Oxford ragwort plant, however, must be caused entirely by the environment (for example, the degree of shading on the leaf) because all the cells in the plant were produced by mitosis from a single zygote and so contain exactly the same genes.

Figure 14.3 Most of the variation between humans is continuous variation, and is influenced by the environment as well as genes.

SAQ

2 For each of these examples of variation between sunflower plants, suggest whether they are caused by genes alone, environment alone, or interaction between genes and environment.
  a the height of the plant
  b the colour of the flower petals
  c the diameter of a mature flower
  d the percentage of seeds that develop after fertilisation.

Answer

Charles Darwin and the theory of natural selection

In 1856, a startling new theory was put forward by Charles Darwin and – quite independently – Alfred Russel Wallace. Darwin is by far the more famous of these two brilliant scientists, perhaps because his publications developed his theory more fully, and were widely read and discussed during the latter half of the 19th century. His book *On the Origin of Species* is still in the best-seller lists today.

Darwin was a thinker and experimenter. He made observations of the world around him, and then developed logical theories about how and why things happened. He worked on many different areas of biology, but he is best known for his theories about how living organisms may have evolved over time.

SAQ

3 The lengths of 50 petals of the flowers of a rush, *Luzula sylvatica*, were measured in millimetres. These were the results.

3.1	3.2	2.7	3.1	3.0	3.2	3.3
3.3	3.2	3.2	3.3	3.2	2.9	3.4
3.2	3.1	3.2	3.1	2.9	3.0	3.1
3.3	2.8	3.1	2.9	3.2	3.0	3.0
3.0	3.0	3.5	3.1	3.0	3.2	3.1
3.1	3.3	3.0	2.9	2.8	3.1	2.8
3.3	3.4	3.1	2.9	3.4	3.0	3.3
2.9						

a Calculate the mean petal length of this sample.
b Count up the number of petals of each length. Draw a histogram to display these results.
c What is the mode for these results?

Hint

d What is the median petal length?

Answer

Darwin proposed a mechanism called **natural selection** to explain how organisms might change over time. His theory grew out of four observations and three logical deductions from them.

Observations:

● All organisms over-reproduce – far more offspring are produced than are required to keep the population at a steady size.
● Population numbers tend to remain fairly constant over long periods of time.
● Organisms within a species vary.
● Some of these variations are inherited.

Deductions:

● There is competition for survival – the 'struggle for existence'.
● Individuals with characteristics that best adapt them for their environment are most likely to survive and reproduce.
● If these characteristics can be inherited, then the organisms will pass the characteristics on to their offspring.

Darwin argued that, if this happened over a long period of time, then the characteristics of a species could gradually change, as better-adapted individuals were more likely to survive and pass on their adaptations to their offspring. Gradually, the species would become better and better adapted to its environment.

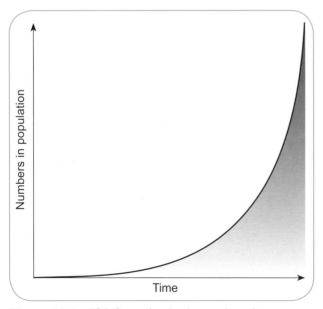

Figure 14.4 If left unchecked, numbers in a population can increase exponentially.

Overproduction

Almost all organisms have the reproductive potential to increase their populations. Rabbits, for example, produce several young in a litter, and each female may produce several litters each year. If all the young rabbits survived to adulthood and reproduced, then the rabbit population would increase rapidly. Figure 14.4 shows what could happen.

This sort of population growth actually did happen in Australia in the 19th century. In 1859, twelve pairs of rabbits from Britain were released on a ranch in Victoria, as a source of food. The rabbits found conditions to their liking. Rabbits feed on low-growing vegetation, especially grasses, of which there was an abundance. There were very few predators to feed on them, so the number of rabbits soared. Their numbers became so great that they seriously affected the availability of grazing for sheep (Figure 14.5).

Such population explosions are rare in normal circumstances. Although rabbit populations have the potential to increase at such a tremendous rate, they do not usually do so.

As a population of rabbits increases, various **environmental factors** come into play to keep down their numbers. These factors may be **biotic factors**

Figure 14.5 Attempts to control the rabbit population explosion in Australia in the mid-to-late 19th century included 'rabbit drives', in which huge numbers were rounded up and killed. Eventually, myxomatosis brought numbers down.

– that is, caused by other living organisms – such as predation, competition for food or infection by pathogens; or they may **abiotic factors** – that is, caused by non-living components of the environment, such as water supply or nutrient levels in the soil.

For example, the increasing number of rabbits eats an increasing amount of vegetation, until food is in short supply. The larger population may allow the populations of predators, such as foxes, stoats and weasels, to increase (Figure 14.6). Overcrowding may occur, increasing the ease with which diseases such as myxomatosis (Figure 14.7) can spread. Myxomatosis is caused by a virus that is transmitted by fleas. The closer together the rabbits live, the more easily fleas, and therefore viruses, will pass from one rabbit to another.

These environmental factors act to reduce the rate of growth of the rabbit population. Of all the rabbits born, many will die from lack of food, be killed by predators or die from myxomatosis. Only a small proportion of young will grow to adulthood and reproduce.

Figure 14.6   Stoats are predators of rabbits.

Figure 14.7   Myxomatosis is a deadly disease of rabbits, but some have developed resistance to it.

Natural selection

What determines which will be the few rabbits to survive, and which will die? It may be just luck. However, some rabbits will be born with a better chance of survival than others. Variation within a population of rabbits means that some will have features that give them an advantage in the 'struggle for existence'. The ones that are best adapted to their environment are most likely to survive and reproduce.

One feature that varies is coat colour. Most rabbits have alleles that give the normal agouti (brown) colour. A few, however, have darker coats. Such darker rabbits will stand out from the others and are more likely to be picked out by a fox. They are less likely to survive – at least, in their normal environment – than brown rabbits. The chances of a dark rabbit surviving long enough to reproduce and pass on its genes for coat colour to its offspring are less than the chances for a normal brown rabbit. Brown rabbits are better adapted to their environment.

Predation by foxes is an example of a **selection pressure**. Selection pressures increase the chances of some genetic variations being passed on to the next generation and decrease the chances for others. The effect of this is **natural selection**. Natural selection increases the frequency of certain characteristics within a population, at the expense of others. The characteristics that best adapt an organism to its environment are most likely to be passed on to the next generation.

SAQ

4 Skomer is a small island off the coast of Wales. Rabbits have been living on the island for many years. There are no predators on Skomer.
   a Rabbits on Skomer are not all brown. There are quite large numbers of rabbits of different colours, such as black or white. Suggest why this is so.
   b What might be important selection pressures acting on rabbits on Skomer?

Answer

Extension

Antibiotic resistance

The development of resistance to antibiotics and other medicinal drugs by bacteria is a good example of natural selection – and one that has great significance for us.

Antibiotics are chemicals produced by living organisms, which inhibit or kill bacteria but do not normally harm human tissue. Most antibiotics in general use are produced by fungi. The first antibiotic to be discovered was penicillin, which was first used during World War II to treat a wide range of infectious diseases caused by bacteria. Penicillin prevents cell wall formation in bacteria.

If someone takes penicillin to treat a bacterial infection, bacteria that are susceptible to penicillin will not be able to grow or reproduce (Figure 14.8). In most cases, this will be the entire population of bacteria. However, by chance, there may be among them one or more individuals that are resistant to penicillin. One example is found in the populations of the bacterium *Staphylococcus*, where some bacteria produce an enzyme, penicillinase, which inactivates penicillin.

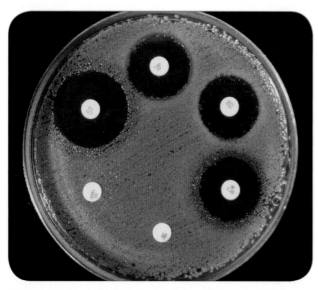

Figure 14.8 The green areas on the agar jelly in this Petri dish are colonies of the bacterium *Escherichia coli*. The white discs are pieces of card impregnated with different antibiotics. Where there is a clear area around a disc, the antibiotic has prevented the bacteria from growing. You can see that this strain of *E. coli* is resistant to the antibiotics on the discs at the bottom left and has been able to grow right up to the discs.

These individuals have a tremendous selective advantage. Bacteria that are not resistant are killed, while those with resistance can survive and reproduce. Bacteria reproduce very rapidly in ideal conditions, and even if there was initially only one resistant bacterium, it might produce ten billion descendants in 24 hours. A large population of penicillin-resistant *Staphylococcus* would result.

Such antibiotic-resistant strains of bacteria are constantly appearing. One of the most worrying is MRSA, which stands for methicillin-resistant *Staphylococcus aureus*. This bacterium, normally harmless, is capable of infecting people whose immune systems are not strong – perhaps because they have another illness. Many people who were already ill have picked up MRSA infections while in hospital and have died as a result. This bacterium has become resistant to almost all antibiotics, so infections are very difficult to treat. Figure 14.9 illustrates how the number of deaths from *Staphylococcus aureus* changed between 1993 and 2005, in England and Wales.

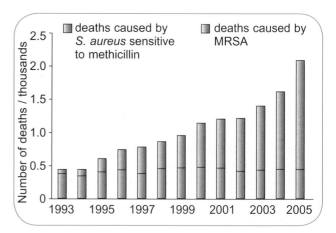

Figure 14.9 Deaths from *Staphylococcus aureus* between 1993 and 2005, in England and Wales.

SAQ

5 a Using Figure 14.9, describe the changes in the numbers of deaths from non-antibiotic-resistant *Staphylococcus aureus* and methicillin-resistant *S. aureus* between 1993 and 2005, in England and Wales.

    Hint

  b Suggest explanations for these changes.

    Hint

    Answer

By using antibiotics, we change the environment in which species of bacteria are living. We change the selection pressures. Individual bacteria that are lucky enough to have genes that make them better adapted to the new environment win the struggle for existence, and pass on their advantageous genes to their offspring. The more we use antibiotics, the greater the selection pressure we exert on bacteria to evolve resistance to them.

Alleles for antibiotic resistance often occur on **plasmids** (Chapter 1), small circles of DNA other than the main bacterial 'chromosome'. Plasmids are quite frequently transferred from one bacterium to another, even between different species. So it is possible for resistance to a particular antibiotic to arise in one species of bacterium and be passed to another.

(Extension)

Insecticide resistance

Just as natural selection has led to the development of populations of bacteria that are resistant to antibiotics, so it has led to the development of resistance to insecticides in some populations of insects.

There are many kinds of insects that we would like to see less of. Mosquitoes transmit malaria, a major cause of death, especially among children, in many tropical and subtropical parts of the world. Insects eat our stores of food, and damage crops. A wide range of insecticides has been developed to try to keep populations of insect pests to a reasonably low level.

Almost 20% of the insecticides that are used in the world are aimed at getting rid of insects that damage cotton plants. Cotton is a major crop in countries including USA, Australia, India, Pakistan and China (Figure 14.10 and Figure 14.11).

Figure 14.10 Cotton plants produce heads of seeds surrounded by silky fibres of cellulose, which in the wild would help the seeds to be dispersed by wind.

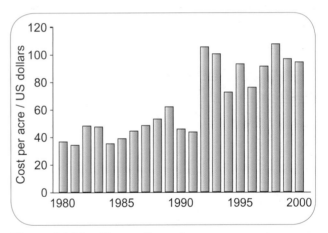

Figure 14.11 Costs of treating cotton against insect pests in the state of Mississippi, USA, between 1980 and 2000.

SAQ

6 a Using Figure 14.11, describe how the costs of controlling insect pests of cotton in Mississippi changed between 1980 and 2000.

  b One reason for these changes could be that the quantity of cotton that was grown changed over this time. Suggest at least two other possible explanations. (Answer)

The major pest of cotton is the cotton boll worm, *Helicoverpa armigera* (Figure 14.12 and Figure 14.13). This is a species of moth, and it is the caterpillars that cause all the damage. They feed not only on cotton, but also on crops of maize, groundnuts (peanuts) and sorghum. Resistance to several different insecticides has developed, and growers have sometimes fallen back on using highly toxic chemicals that not only kill boll worms but also other beneficial or harmless organisms.

Figure 14.12   The cotton boll worm, *Helicoverpa armigera*.

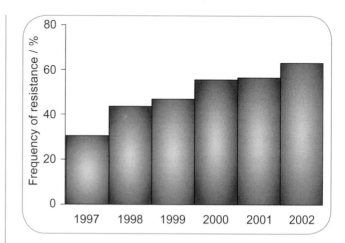

Figure 14.13   Changes in the frequency of resistance of cotton boll worms to a commonly used insecticide, in Australia.

SAQ

7 Explain how the increase in the percentage of boll worms showing resistance, illustrated in Figure 14.13, could have developed.

Answer

GM cotton to beat the boll worm

Today, there is a lot of pressure on growers to use fewer chemicals. But they still have to control cotton boll worms – if they did not then they could easily lose their entire crop. This did actually happen in Mississippi in 1999.

In an attempt to get around this problem – and to make large profits – the multinational company Monsanto has produced a genetically engineered variety of cotton plants. The cotton plants have had genes inserted into them that enable them to make a protein called Cry1Ac. The gene came from a bacterium called *Bacillus thuringiensis*, so the cotton plants are sometimes called Bt cotton. The protein is a toxin which kills insects that eat the cotton, by attaching to receptors on the plasma membranes of the cells lining the insects' guts and destroying the gut wall. This particular variety of the toxin only affects butterflies and moths (and their caterpillars), because only they have the receptors

to which the toxin can bind.

The cotton is marketed as INGARD®. Seeds are expensive – much more so than unmodified cotton – but growers should still gain good profits because they should not need to use insecticides, and should get high yields because less of the crop will be lost. The GM cotton could also be good for the environment, because it should only harm caterpillars that actually eat the cotton plants.

However, natural selection is still at work, and cotton boll worms are already becoming resistant to the toxin in the Bt cotton. Researchers in Australia investigated how resistance could arise. They took a large number of boll worms collected from different places, and fed them on crystals of the Cry1Ac protein and also spores from *Bacillus thuringiensis*. This gave the boll worms a much higher dose of the toxin than

continued

they would normally get if they ate the Bt cotton plants. After seven days, the researchers took the survivors and transferred them to a diet that did not contain the toxin, so that they could be sure to live long enough to produce the next generation. They repeated this procedure for 28 generations. The graph shows their results.

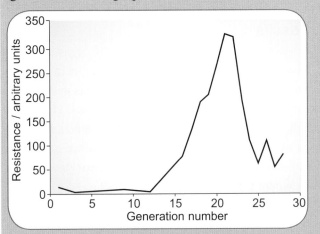

You can see that, to begin with, few of the boll worms were able to survive exposure to the toxin. But by the 12th generation, resistance was beginning to develop. The researchers found that this was caused by a lack of one of the binding sites on the plasma membranes of the boll worms' cells – the toxin could not bind to the cells, and so could not harm them. They think that one of the boll worms in the original population had a gene that caused it to lack this site (or perhaps a new mutation occurred), so this worm and its offspring survived and passed on the gene to their offspring. In each successive generation, more and more of the boll worms were resistant ones whose ancestor was the original resistant boll worm.

Interestingly, however, after generation 23 the level of resistance fell. The researchers think that perhaps there is a price that the boll worms have to pay for being resistant – perhaps lacking the receptor site disadvantages them in some way. However, these boll worms were still more resistant than the original colony, quite enough to cause problems in fields of Bt cotton.

So what can be done, if insect pests can even develop resistance to toxins in genetically modified cotton? At the moment, growers should use at least two different weapons against boll worms – two different insecticides, for example. It is much less likely that a boll worm will, by chance, have genes that make it resistant to both.

Speciation

If we take our definition of a species as a group of organisms that can interbreed to produce fertile offspring, then to produce a new species we need to produce a group that can no longer breed with the original species. The population has to become **reproductively isolated**.

The production of a new species is called **speciation**. It is a difficult event to study, because it seems that it often takes a long time to happen, and we cannot often watch the process all the way through. We can, though, look at populations that exist now, and use the patterns we can pick out to suggest what might have happened in the past.

One picture that emerges is that **geographical isolation** often plays a role in speciation (Figure 14.14). Two populations of the same species may become separated by a geographical barrier, such as a body of water or a mountain range. Because the environment in which each population lives is different, they will have different selection pressures acting on them, and so different adaptations will be selected for. Over time, this may cause heritable changes in the characteristics of one or both populations. Eventually, these changes might become so great that the two populations are no longer able to interbreed. They have become two different species. This is called **allopatric speciation**.

However, new species can sometimes evolve without being geographically separated. This is called **sympatric speciation**. For example, in North America and Canada there is a fly called *Rhagoletis pomonella*, whose maggots feed on various fruits such as apples and hawthorn berries. It looks as though the maggots used to feed on hawthorn berries, but that some of them began to feed on apples instead, soon after apples were

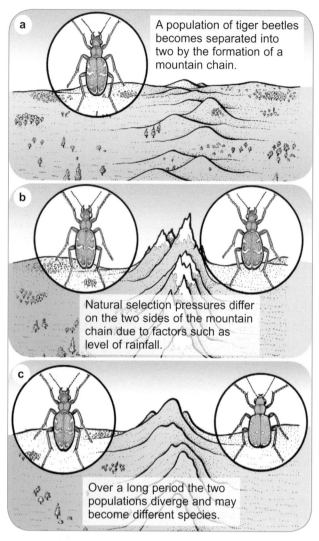

a A population of tiger beetles becomes separated into two by the formation of a mountain chain.

b Natural selection pressures differ on the two sides of the mountain chain due to factors such as level of rainfall.

c Over a long period the two populations diverge and may become different species.

Figure 14.14 Geographical isolation leading to speciation.

introduced into North America in the mid 19th century. Adult flies that grew up feeding on apples tend to lay their eggs on apples, and to mate with other flies that grew up on apples. The same is true for the ones that feed on hawthorn berries. Possibly these two populations will eventually become so distinct that they can no longer interbreed, and we can say that the apple fly and the hawthorn fly are two distinct species.

The inability of two populations to interbreed to produce fertile offspring is called **reproductive isolation**. There are many reasons for it, such as:
- they may have different courtship behaviour
- their sperms and eggs may be incompatible
- they may have different chromosome numbers, so cells of a hybrid cannot undergo meiosis, because not every chromosome will have a partner.

The evidence for evolution

Evolution by natural selection is a very convincing theory, and virtually all biologists support it. There is a huge range of evidence that it has happened, and is still happening now. We can only touch on a tiny part of it here, and will look briefly at how **fossils** and molecular evidence, including that from DNA, support the theory.

Fossils

Fossils are the preserved remains of organisms that lived and died long ago. Many fossils form from hard parts of organisms, such as bones and shells, that have gradually become mineralised. However, soft parts are sometimes also preserved as fossils, as well as other evidence of the existence and behaviour of animals such as dinosaur droppings or worm burrows.

Only a tiny proportion of organisms that die will be preserved as fossils, and we will only come across a very small proportion of fossils that have been formed. So fossils only give us a glimpse into what organisms were like long ago. Not surprisingly, there are large gaps in the fossil record.

Nevertheless, enough fossils of some kinds of organisms have been found to suggest how one form might have evolved into another over time. A prime example is horses (Figure 14.15). We have many different fossils, dating from 55 million years ago up to almost the present time. Fossils of different ages have different bone structures and arrangements. If the fossils are organised according to their ages, it can be seen how one structure could have changed to produce another, over time. There appears to be a sequence of changes, over time, culminating in the current species of horse, *Equus caballus*.

Fossil sequences such as this one provide us with circumstantial evidence that evolution of one species into another has happened, and also suggest *how* it may have happened. From the rocks in which they have been found, we can deduce the kind of environment in which each fossil species of horse lived. Early species, such as *Hyracotherium*, were small and had feet with several toes. They lived in wet, swampy conditions, where their size and foot structure would have allowed them to

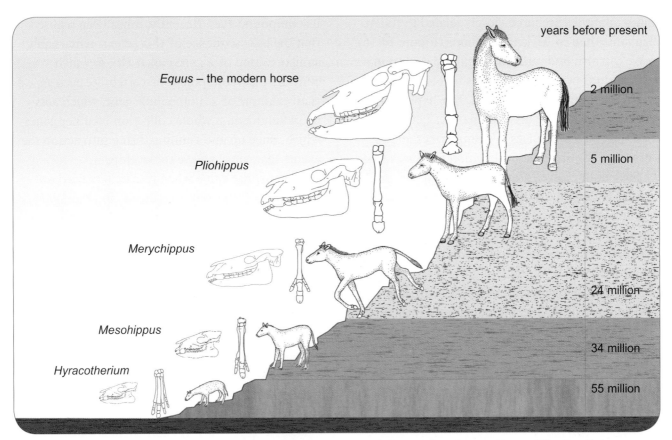

Equus – the modern horse

years before present

2 million

Pliohippus

5 million

Merychippus

24 million

Mesohippus

34 million

Hyracotherium

55 million

Figure 14.15 Some of the many species of fossil horses, and the modern horse *Equus*. The fossil sequence shows that, over time, horses have developed single-toed hooves, longer legs and longer faces with larger teeth adapted for grazing.

move around easily. Modern horses, with their single-toed feet forming hooves, would not have done well in that environment; they are adapted to run fast over firm ground. The changes that we see in the fossil horses can be explained by considering how natural selection might have favoured one characteristic over another, and how features that provided successful adaptations to the environment became more and more common in succeeding generations. As the environment changed, so did selection pressures, and this could have given rise to the succession of different species over time.

It is important to recognise that, even with horses where we have numerous fossils, we cannot ever say that *this* species evolved into *that* species. All that we can do is say that they appear to be related – that they probably share a common ancestor. There could well have been other species that existed, for which no fossils have ever been found. It is probable that the fossils we have do not include the common ancestor.

Molecular evidence

Structural similarities and differences between fossils of organisms that lived at different times can suggest to us how they might be related to each other. These features were caused by genes. By looking directly at the molecular structure of genes, rather than the features that they produce, we can find even more fundamental evidence for evolution.

Occasionally, ancient bones are found in such good condition that DNA can be extracted from them. For example, DNA has been found in the mitochondria of bones of woolly mammoths. The degree of similarity between the base sequences of the mammoth DNA and the base sequences of the DNA of modern elephants suggests that they had a common ancestor that lived about 6 million years ago. At that point, African elephants developed as a separate species. The DNA evidence suggests that mammoths and Asian elephants diverged around 440 000 years later. So we can say that mammoths are more closely related to Asian elephants than to African elephants (Figure 14.16).

We can also find out a lot about the evolutionary relationships between organisms that are alive today by comparing their DNA. In Chapter 13, we saw that there are great similarities between the DNA base sequences in chimpanzees and in ourselves. The simplest explanation for this is that we have both evolved from a common ancestor.

But DNA analysis can sometimes give us some very unexpected results. Many different kinds of animals have eyes, but they can be so different in structure that it has been assumed that eyes have evolved separately in different groups. For example, the structure of the compound eyes of insects seems to have little in common with the structure of the eyes of molluscs or vertebrates (Figure 14.17). The simplest explanation is that eyes of one type evolved in the ancestral line leading to insects, while eyes of a completely different type evolved separately in the line leading to vertebrates.

The fruit fly *Drosophila melanogaster* has a gene called *ey* that controls the development of its compound eyes. Recently, it has been realised that the base sequence of this gene is remarkably similar to that of a gene called *Pax-6*, which controls the development of vertebrate eyes. *Pax-6* is an example of a 'homeobox' gene, which acts by switching on a whole collection of other genes which, once up and running, bring into action the events that cause an eye to develop.

The surprise came when researchers tried out the effects of *Pax-6* from a mouse in *Drosophila* cells. They introduced the mouse *Pax-6* gene into cells that would develop into the wing of a larval *Drosophila*. To their amazement, they found that the wing grew an eye. And it was a *Drosophila* eye, not a mouse eye (Figure 14.18).

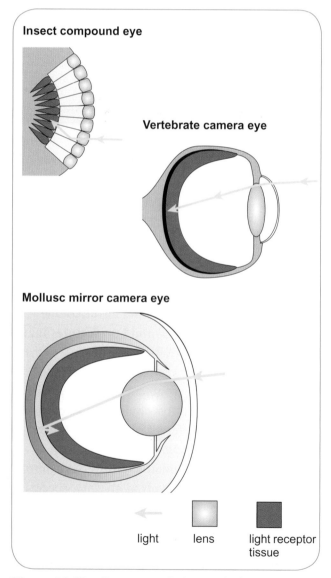

Figure 14.17 Structure of the eye in insects, vertebrates and molluscs.

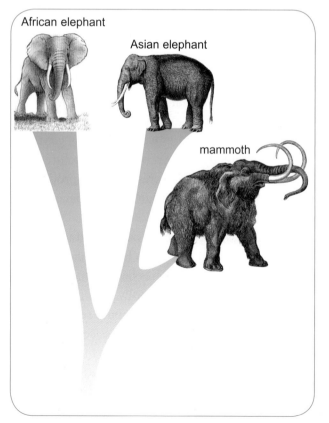

Figure 14.16 Probable evolutionary relationships of mammoths and modern elephants.

Figure 14.18 Coloured scanning electron micrograph of part of a fruit fly, *Drosophila melanogaster* (×80). At the right is the head, where one of its compound eyes is visible. The body of the fly is brown. You can see one of the fly's wings (grey) at the bottom left, and a red eye that has grown on it in response to instructions from a *Pax-6* gene from a mouse.

Since the original discovery, it has been found that *Pax-6* can also bring about the development of an eye in other organisms, such as squid (a kind of mollusc). It looks very much as though there *is* a common origin of eyes in all animals, despite their very different looks. The fact that such different organisms all have a similar sequence of DNA bases that controls the development of their eyes is very strong evidence for an evolutionary relationship between them. This is an ancient gene – it has been recycled and re-used in many different organisms, continuing to control the development of strikingly different structures.

Summary

Glossary

- There is variation between the individuals of a species. This may be caused by genes, by the environment, or both. In discontinuous variation, there are just a few distinct categories, and this type of variation is generally caused by genes. In continuous variation, there is a range with no clear-cut divisions between types, and this is often caused by interaction between genes and the environment. It may also be caused by genes alone, if there are several, each with several alleles.

- Charles Darwin put forward the theory of evolution by natural selection. He observed that most organisms produce more young than live to adulthood, and there is variation among them. He deduced that those that were best adapted to their environment would be more likely to survive long enough to reproduce, and that they would pass on the genes for their advantageous characteristics to their offspring. Over time, the features of a species could gradually change (evolve).

- New species arise when two groups that originally belonged to a single species become reproductively isolated. This can happen if, for example, they become separated by a geographical barrier. If the selection pressures in their two environments are different, then different features may be more favourable in each population. The two populations may eventually become so different from each other that they are no longer able to reproduce with each other.

- Evolution in action can be seen with the appearance of insects that are resistant to pesticides, and bacteria that are resistant to antibiotics. This poses problems for humans, as we have to find ways of reducing the risk that such resistance will develop. We also need to find new chemicals to which resistance has not yet developed.

- Fossil sequences suggest strongly that one species has given rise to another over time. Similarities in DNA suggest that animals which today look very different from one another share common origins.

Questions

1 a Explain the meaning of the term *species*. [3]

A recent study of populations of the house mouse, *Mus musculus*, on the island of Madeira, resulted in the following observations:

- there are six distinct populations
- the mice are associated with human settlements
- the populations are located in different valleys separated by steep mountains
- each population has a different diploid number of chromosomes.

As a result of these observations, it has been suggested that speciation is taking place. The diagram is a schematic representation of Madeira showing the distribution of the six populations.

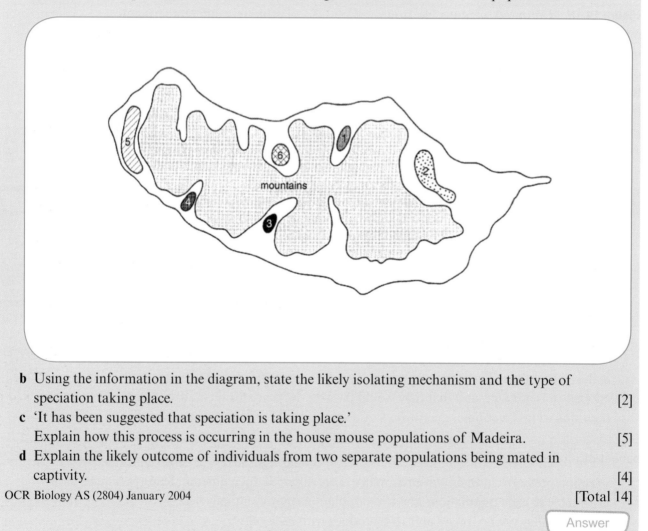

b Using the information in the diagram, state the likely isolating mechanism and the type of speciation taking place. [2]

c 'It has been suggested that speciation is taking place.'
Explain how this process is occurring in the house mouse populations of Madeira. [5]

d Explain the likely outcome of individuals from two separate populations being mated in captivity. [4]

OCR Biology AS (2804) January 2004 [Total 14]

Answer

Chapter 15

Humans, conservation and the future

Background

e-Learning

Objectives

From looking at fossils, it is apparent that there have been several occasions in the past when large numbers of species have quite suddenly become extinct. These occasions are known as **mass extinctions**. For example, one mass extinction happened around 65 million years ago. The fossil record suggests that about 16% of all the families of marine organisms, and 18% of families of terrestrial organisms – including the dinosaurs – became extinct at that time.

We are not certain what caused this mass extinction, but one theory is that a huge asteroid crashed into what is now the Yucatan peninsula, in Mexico. It would have caused massive climate change.

There appear to have been at least five mass extinctions during the history of life on Earth. We now seem to be at the beginning of another. This time, the cause is us.

Threats to biodiversity

In 2002, a summit meeting of the United Nations in Johannesburg, South Africa, made a commitment to 'achieve by 2010 a significant reduction of the current rate of biodiversity loss at the global, regional and national level as a contribution to poverty alleviation and to the benefit of all life on Earth'. This decision was made in the light of information suggesting that human activities are responsible for a huge loss of species in the recent past, and that this is getting worse. Some studies estimate that the current rate of extinctions is running at about 1000 times the 'natural' rate – the rate that would be expected if humans were not here. It is thought that we are currently experiencing the greatest mass extinction since that of the dinosaurs.

How humans cause extinction

What are we doing to cause such enormous loss of species? The fundamental problems are our rapidly increasing population, and the increasing impact that the average person has on the environment. There are about 6.5 billion of us, and the number continues to rise – although there are signs that the rate of increase is now slowing. We make increasing demands on the Earth (Figure 15.1). Our activities have caused wide-ranging pollution, altering the environments in which species live. We destroy habitats through deforestation, taking more land for building houses and roads, and through agriculture. We predate species for food or other resources, sometimes taking so many of them that we threaten them with extinction – for example, by overfishing (Figure 15.2). We introduce alien species into areas where they outcompete native species, or spread diseases which cause the alien species little harm but are fatal to the native ones (Figure 15.3).

Figure 15.1 Planet Earth is the only home for us and for the millions of other species.

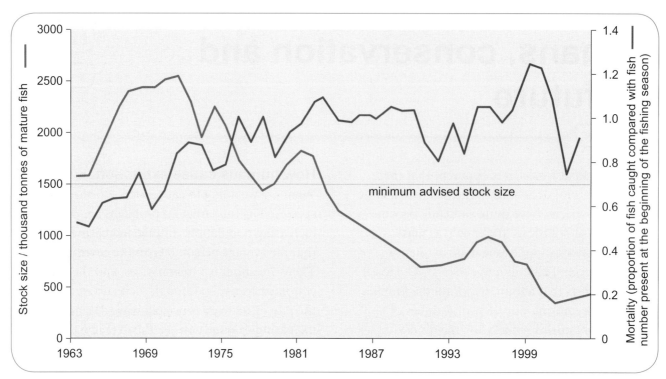

Figure 15.2 Stocks and fishing mortality in North Sea cod between 1963 and 2004. The population of North Sea cod has fallen greatly since the end of the 1960s, almost certainly as a direct result of overfishing. The horizontal line shows the minimum stock size that has been calculated will allow the cod population to be maintained at a viable level.

Figure 15.3 The native British white-clawed crayfish, **a** *Austropotamobius pallipes*, is being killed by a fungal infection carried by **b** the introduced American signal crayfish, *Pacifastacus leniusculus*. In some parts of Britain, the white-clawed crayfish has been completely wiped out, despite being a protected species.

Impact of climate change

There is no doubt that the mean global temperature on Earth is rising. This rise is almost certainly at least partly caused by the greenhouse gases emitted into the atmosphere as a result of human activities, especially carbon dioxide and methane. Climate change is already having a noticeable effect on species in Britain, as well as elsewhere in the world. We are experiencing warmer winters with fewer frosts, earlier springs and summers, and more 'extreme' weather events such as droughts and severe storms. Many species of animals and plants are now found further north than only a few years ago. Hornets, for example, previously only found in southern Britain, are now common in parts of the Midlands and even further north. Roesel's bush cricket, only found near the coast of south and southeast England until very recently, is spreading rapidly northwards, apparently as a direct result of the warmer climate (Figure 15.4a). There is concern that less welcome species, such as the mosquito that spreads malaria, may become resident in Britain.

While species such as these are benefiting from climate change, others may not be able to adapt to the changes. Species that are adapted to a cold climate may have to move northwards, as their habitats are increasingly colonised by warmer-climate species. Some of them will not be able to find new habitats to move into, and will become extinct (Figure 15.4b).

The importance of maintaining biodiversity

For many people, the main reason for trying to halt the damage that we are doing to biodiversity, by causing extinctions of species, is a simple moral or ethical one. We share our planet with a huge range of other organisms, and we have no right to make them extinct.

There are also aesthetic reasons. The enormous range of habitats and species on Earth is a delight to many of us – we get great pleasure from knowing that there is a rich and diverse world out there around us. Many people feel happier and more content when they have direct experience of 'wild' places inhabited by a wide variety of plants and animals – whether it is trekking in a tropical rainforest, walking on a remote part of Dartmoor, exploring rock pools on a beach or just meandering around a local park.

There are other, more practical, reasons to maintain biodiversity. We have seen that new drugs are being discovered and developed from plants and other organisms (Chapter 11). Around 7000 drugs that are prescribed by doctors in Britain are derived from plants. Almost 70% of these grow in tropical rainforests, and these are the places that are under the greatest threat. There must be thousands of species of plants and other organisms in these rainforests that we do not even know about, some of which could be sources of new medicinal drugs.

Figure 15.4 Some benefit, some lose: **a** Roesel's bush cricket is spreading rapidly northwards in Britain. **b** Moss campion is retreating to the tops of mountains in Scotland, and may soon be left with no suitable habitat at all.

235

Agriculture, too, can benefit from the maintenance of biodiversity. As we have seen, crop plants and farmed animals have been bred to possess a set of characteristics that enable farmers to produce the kinds of food that we want to eat, in large quantities and at relatively low cost. Many of these crop varieties and animal breeds have been selected to give high yields when farmed intensively, with high inputs of chemicals such as pesticides, fertilisers and high food value feedstuffs. In the future, we will almost certainly want to develop new crop varieties and animal breeds that do well in different conditions – perhaps farmed less intensively, or able to live in the different climate that is likely to develop in Britain as global warming progresses. Selective breeding has resulted in the loss of many alleles for currently 'unwanted' characteristics, so genetic diversity among crop plants and farmed animals is low. We may be able to use wild species to introduce new alleles, helping us to produce new varieties and breeds that are better suited to our new requirements.

For example, potatoes can be very badly affected by a fungus-like organism called *Phytophthora infestans*, which causes blight. This is already a problem in Britain, and may become even more so with climate change. Cultivated potato varieties were originally bred from wild species that grew in South America. Some of these wild species have excellent resistance to blight. Breeders are using these to introduce blight-resistance genes into commercially grown potato varieties, by selective breeding. If we had lost the wide variety of wild potato species, we would have lost these genes.

Conservation

Conservation attempts to maintain or increase biodiversity. It may be targeted at saving a particular species, or at conserving habitats such as an area of rainforest in Indonesia or a hillside rich in chalk downland vegetation in southern England.

The International Union for the Conservation of Nature and Natural Resources, IUCN, annually publishes a Red List of threatened species. The 2006 list contained 16 119 species (www.iucnredlist.org). Some of these have a very high profile – for example, tigers, giant pandas or orang-utans (Figure 15.6). Others are perhaps less photogenic – for example, the Kerry slug (Figure 15.7). Not surprisingly, the IUCN Red List has a very high proportion of vertebrates as opposed to invertebrates, and green plants as opposed to protoctists. There are no prokaryotes on the list. We have absolutely no idea how many of these are threatened.

Figure 15.6 Orang-utans live only in dense tropical rainforest in Borneo. Deforestation is threatening their survival.

Figure 15.7 Kerry slugs are found only in the south-west of Ireland.

SAQ

1 Suggest why the Red List contains more vertebrates than invertebrates. (You may be able to think of several reasons.)

Answer

Losing the Scottish flora

As the ice sheets slowly retreated from Britain at the end of the last Ice Age, many plants and animals that were adapted for life in these cold conditions disappeared. Some, however, hung on in the high ground in parts of Scotland. These mountainous areas support communities of plants that are found nowhere else in Britain. They are called arctic-alpine communities, and include plants such as the tufted saxifrage, *Saxifraga cespitosa* and lichens such as snow caloplaca, *Caloplaca nivalis*. As global warming takes place, it is estimated that the extent of the arctic-alpine environment in Scotland will decrease by at least 93%. While other species may survive by moving northwards or to higher altitudes as temperatures rise, there is nowhere left for the arctic-alpine species to go. We are likely to lose them entirely.

It is not only the arctic-alpine species that are threatened. There are many species that live at lower altitudes, but that are restricted to the extreme north of Scotland. They include twinflower, *Linnaea borealis* and the Scottish primrose, *Primula scotica*. These, too, are likely to have nowhere else in Britain to go as temperatures rise.

Scottish highlands in winter.

Scottish primrose, *Primula scotica*.

Twinflower, *Linnaea borealis*.

Northern Scotland, showing the distribution of the Scottish primrose, now restricted to the northern coast of the mainland and the Orkney Isles.

Tufted saxifrage, *Saxifraga cespitosa*.

Rescuing the oryx

We can get an idea of how an endangered species can be protected from extinction by looking at one example – the scimitar-horned oryx, *Oryx dammah* (Figure 15.8).

This oryx lives in semi-deserts in northern Africa. It has always been hunted for meat and its skin, but in the 1950s and 1960s hunting increased hugely as oil workers moved into the area and hunted the oryx using guns. During the 1960s and 1970s, it was recognised that if nothing was done, there would soon be no oryx left. So a few oryx were caught and transported to zoos in several places around the world.

A captive breeding programme then began. Each zoo tried to breed oryx and build up a herd. Care was taken not to breed closely related animals together, so that genetic diversity could be maintained. This often entailed animals from one zoo being moved to another. *In vitro* fertilisation (IVF) reduces the need for animals to be moved, because sperm can be collected from one male, then frozen and transported around the world to fertilise eggs from one or more females. (In some species, it has been possible to transplant embryos of the rare species into a female of another closely related one, who acts as a 'surrogate mother'.)

While the captive breeding programme was taking place, attempts were being made to provide a safe habitat for the oryx so that they could eventually be returned to the wild. Large reserves were set up in Tunisia, fenced off so that cattle could not get in. Local people were encouraged to be actively involved in this, and some of them were employed to look after the reserves.

By 1985, the first reserve was ready and ten oryx were released into it. They were kept in small pens for the first few months, to make sure they could acclimatise to these unfamiliar conditions. By 2000, the population had grown to more than 120.

This programme has been a great success. There are now other reserves, with more oryx in them. Many zoos have breeding herds. The scimitar-horned oryx appears to be safe, at least for the time being.

However, not every attempt to rescue an animal species in this way has been a success. Some

Figure 15.8 Marwell Zoological Park in Hampshire has helped to reintroduce the threatened *Oryx dammah* into its natural habitat in Tunisia.

animals simply refuse to breed in captivity. Often, it is not possible to create suitable habitats for them in the wild. Sometimes, even if a habitat exists, it is very difficult for the animals to adapt to living in it after being cared for in a zoo.

In situ or *ex situ*?

The oryx conservation programme illustrates how conservation of a species may need to involve programmes that are based in more than one area. The captive breeding programme has taken place ***ex situ*** – that is, not in the place where the oryx naturally lives. The creation and protection of a suitable habitat for the oryx has been done ***in situ*** – in the oryx's natural habitat.

In general, it is best if conservation can be concentrated *in situ*. The best way to conserve a threatened species is to protect it where it naturally lives. This could involve protecting its habitat, and preventing activities of people who live, work or take holidays there from further endangering the species. But this can be very difficult. Often, the threatened species lives where humans are themselves struggling for survival. There may be conflict between the needs of local human populations and the needs of the threatened species. The oryx programme has been successful because the people living in the area where the oryx has been reintroduced have been able to become involved in the project, making a living from working with the conservation programme rather than by keeping cattle on the land.

The African elephant, *Loxodonta africana*, looked to be in danger of extinction in the second half of the 20th century, and measures were put into place to conserve the elephants in their natural habitats. In many African countries, shooting elephants was banned, as was the sale of ivory from their tusks. The conservation measures were very successful, and in many areas elephant populations have grown considerably. There is no longer a danger of extinction.

However, the success of elephant conservation has not always been to the benefit of local people. Some of them have, indeed, benefited from employment in the ecotourism industry, which brings in tourists who want to see elephants in the wild. But many local people find themselves in direct conflict with elephants. Elephants damage their crops, food stores and water sources, and sometimes threaten human life (Figure 15.9). Conservation programmes must try to ensure that people who are already struggling to make a living are not themselves put under threat when protective measures are put into place for a threatened species. For example, people living in close proximity with elephants could be given help to fence their land to keep elephants out; selective culling of 'problem' elephants could take place; deep wells could be dug to ensure that there is always a good water supply for people.

It is not only people who may suffer in places where a particular species is conserved. For example, elephants can do huge damage to vegetation – they often push entire trees over in order to get at edible parts of the tree above their reach. A large elephant population can reduce the suitability of the habitat for other organisms – although it may also improve its suitability for others. Every time an *in situ* conservation programme takes place, it is important to assess the potential effects of that programme on other species and on people who live in that area.

Sometimes, the difficulties are so great that it looks unlikely that *in situ* conservation can be successful. This is especially likely when there is so little suitable habitat left that there is no chance of enough organisms being able to live there to maintain a viable population. In some instances, this is just a temporary situation: this was the case with the scimitar-horned oryx, where the population was so small, and the available safe habitat so limited, that there would have been no chance of saving the species just by working *in situ*. Here, the *ex situ* captive breeding programme bought time while suitable areas for the oryx to live in the wild were created. In some cases, sadly, it may be that we will never be able to protect enough suitable habitat for a species to survive in the wild. Some people think this may become the case with the tiger, where habitat loss and hunting by humans has reduced the area of land where tigers live to only 40% of what it was in 1995 (Figure 15.10). Tigers breed well in zoos, so there should be no danger of them becoming extinct, but it would be a great loss if, in the future, the only tigers in existence were those in captivity.

Figure 15.9 Elephants often come into conflict with humans.

Figure 15.10 Habitat loss and hunting may mean that it becomes impossible to conserve tigers *in situ*.

Zoos and botanic gardens

Zoos played a very important part in the rescue of the scimitar-horned oryx from extinction, through a captive breeding programme that has built up large, genetically diverse populations, from which some animals have been successfully returned to the wild. Another role of zoos is that they can bring the plight of endangered species to the attention of the public, which may help to raise awareness of the need for conservation. This may in turn lead to more public support for conservation projects and more funding for them.

Botanic gardens can play a similar role for endangered plants. Seeds or cuttings can be collected from species in the wild and then used to build up a population of plants from which, one day, some plants may be reintroduced to their natural habitats.

The Royal Botanic Gardens at Kew has been involved in several such projects, and also runs a hugely ambitious programme called the Millennium Seed Bank, which began in 2000. One of the Bank's ambitions is to collect and store seeds from at least 10% of the world's plant species, so that even if the species become extinct in the wild there will still be seeds from which they can be grown. If possible, seeds are collected from several different sites, so that they contain a good range of genetic variation.

Some seeds are easy to store, but others require very special conditions. It is also important to grow some of the seeds into plants every so often and then to collect new seeds from them, because most seeds do not survive for very many years. Some plants cannot be stored as seeds at all, and these have to be kept as adult plants.

SAQ

2 It has been suggested that seed banks put selection pressures on seeds that are different from the selection pressures the plants would experience in the wild.

   a How might these selection pressures differ?

   b How might this affect the chances of success when returning the plants to the wild?

   Answer

CITES

In 1973, 145 countries signed an agreement that controls the trade in endangered species and products from them, such as animal skins (Figure 15.11). More countries have joined since. This agreement is called the Convention on International Trade in Endangered Species of Wild Fauna and Flora, CITES for short.

CITES makes decisions about which species in the world are endangered and about how trade in these species should be limited. Species are assigned to one of three Appendices.

- Appendix I lists species that are considered to be the most endangered. These species are threatened with extinction, and CITES prohibits international trade in them or any products that come from them. Exemptions may be made in genuinely exceptional cases – for example, for research or for captive breeding programmes. This list includes animals such as the spiny anteater and plants such as *Nepenthes rajah*.

- Appendix II is a longer list than Appendix I, and it is made up of species that are not necessarily threatened with extinction now, but that may become so unless trade is closely controlled. Trade is only allowed in these species if an export permit is granted by the country from which the organism would be taken. It includes abundant species that look very similar to those in Appendix I, because this makes it less likely that an Appendix I species could be traded as an Appendix II species. So, for example, all *Nepenthes* species are listed in this Appendix (Figure 15.12).

- Appendix III includes species where there is regulated international trade. Again, permits are required to export or import these species, but these are more likely to be granted than for Appendix II species.

The species listed in the CITES appendices are constantly reviewed, and the list is growing. However, there is some concern that CITES listing does not always benefit a species. If trade in a species or its products becomes illegal, then the price that can be obtained for those products rises, and this can make it worthwhile for people to break the law. Particular problems arise when it is announced in advance that a species will go onto the list – in the months between the announcement and the introduction of the new law, trade in that species has often risen several-fold.

Biodiversity action plans

Figure 15.11 A policeman confiscating animal skins in Bolivia.

Figure 15.12 The Kinabalu pitcher plant, *Nepenthes kinabaluensis*, is protected by CITES.

In 1992, world leaders attended a conference in Rio de Janeiro, in Brazil, to consider the sustainable use of the world's resources. The conference was known as the Earth Summit, and out of it grew a Convention on Biological Diversity. This landmark agreement was signed by the leaders of 157 countries. Each country committed itself to develop national strategies to protect its biodiversity. Since then, many further meetings have been held, and more countries have signed up. In 2007, there were 190 countries involved.

In the UK, the Rio summit resulted in a strategy that was published in 1994 by the Department of the Environment, setting out an action plan to try to maintain biodiversity in the UK. The plan listed objectives for conserving species and their habitats. There are national targets and plans, and also local ones. Local Biodiversity Action Plans were drawn up for all parts of the UK. These plans are constantly being revised.

Initially, conservation efforts were focused on the protection of special areas, such as Sites of Special Scientific Interest (SSSIs). These are specially protected areas, usually chosen because they contain a wide variety of habitats, or an unusual community or a rare species. However, it is being increasingly realised that this is not enough, and that we need to look at *all* areas, not just specially designated nature reserves, and in towns and cities as well as in the countryside. For example, farmers can be given grants to maintain hedges on their land, or to create ponds or leave a wide, species-rich uncultivated margin around an arable field. Industries can be encouraged to create and maintain 'wild' areas in out-of-the-way corners of their sites. Gardens are now very important havens for wildlife. The addition of a small pond or an area of long grass – even a small one – can provide habitats for a wide variety of species that may be losing habitat elsewhere.

When any new development is planned – such as building a new housing estate, a new road or a new sewage treatment works, or making significant alterations to an existing one – then the company wishing to carry out the project has to submit an **environmental impact assessment**. This is intended to provide a full investigation into the likely effect of the development on local species. Usually, the developer will call in environmental consultants to survey the site, and the area around it that might be affected, to find out what is living there, including any species that are specially protected, such as great crested newts or bats. If the survey suggests that there may be harm done to the biodiversity or ecology of the area, then the developer will be expected to put measures into place to prevent this damage – for example, by making new ponds into which newts can be transferred if their original habitat is likely to be harmed (Figure 15.13).

This is all very expensive, and the cost has to be borne entirely by the developer. This can sometimes bring into question the true value of the assessment. It is in the developer's financial interest to employ a firm of consultants that does not cost too much, and that has a record of not finding too many potential problems that the development may cause.

Figure 15.13 Proposed work on a sewage treatment plant near Banbury required an environmental impact assessment, including a check on local populations of great crested newts. Here a garden pond is being investigated. Such ponds are important habitats for this species.

Extension

Summary

Glossary

- Human activity is a significant factor in causing species extinction and reducing biodiversity – for example, through damage to habitats and overpredation.

- Global climate change is changing the distribution of species, and may result in the extinction of some species that are adapted to cold environments.

- There are economic, ecological, ethical and aesthetic reasons for conserving species. For example, medicine and agriculture may benefit from the use of products or genes from 'wild' species.

- Conservation aims to maintain biodiversity. It may take place *in situ* and *ex situ*. *In situ* conservation is the ideal way to conserve species, as they remain in their natural habitat where they are part of the natural ecosystem. However, this is not always possible if there is great pressure on the habitat, or conflict with local human populations. *Ex situ* strategies, such as captive breeding, can frequently make a useful contribution to conservation projects.

- Zoos play an important role in conservation through captive breeding and release programmes, and by making people aware of the potential loss of animal species. Botanic gardens can play similar roles, and can help to store 'banks' of species in the form of seeds.

- International cooperation is essential for successful conservation. CITES regulates the movement of endangered species or products made from them between member countries. The Rio Convention on Biodiversity was the beginning of a worldwide effort by the signatory countries to maintain their own biodiversity. In the UK, this has resulted in Biodiversity Action Plans, and the use of environmental impact assessments.

Questions

1 a Asian elephants are now ten times as rare as African elephants in the wild. During the 1990s, their numbers halved to 20 000. It is estimated that if a similar rate of decline was to continue, they would face extinction in the wild within thirty years.
Suggest reasons for the decline in the numbers of Asian elephants in the wild. [3]

b Early in 2002, London Zoo's Asian elephants were transferred to Whipsnade Wildlife Park, in the hope that they might breed. At present, there is only one male and six females in this group of captive elephants. Only four or five Asian elephants are usually born in captivity each year.
Explain why captive breeding using only one male may be a disadvantage to this population. [3]

c State <u>three</u> reasons why animals often do <u>not</u> breed successfully when in captivity. [3]

Rare and endangered plant species can be maintained in botanic gardens and seed banks. Seeds are kept in seed banks at low temperature and in an atmosphere that contains very little oxygen.

d Explain why seeds are stored in seed banks under such conditions. [2]

e Explain the benefits of storing rare and endangered plant species in botanic gardens and seed banks. [5]

OCR Biology AS (2805/03) January 2004 [Total 16]

Answer

2 Preserving the diversity of life on Earth has come to be an accepted goal for many people. However, this goal can sometimes come into conflict with other goals, such as economic development.

In 1980, the International Union for the Conservation of Nature and Natural Resources (IUCN) proposed a statement to form the basis for conserving biodiversity. One of the points included in the statement is:

'All species have an inherent right to exist. The ecological processes that support the integrity of the biosphere and its diverse species and habitats are to be maintained.'

Within the UK, many initiatives have been set up to help maintain biodiversity. One is the Dartmoor Biodiversity Project, part of which is the Habitat Action Plan for moorland, which covers almost 50% of the National Park.

This Action Plan specifies many objectives, all of which aim to maintain the range of habitats on Dartmoor and ensure that all native plants and animals continue to breed successfully and maintain healthy populations.

a State what is meant by the term *biodiversity*. [2]

b Outline the <u>ecological</u>, <u>economic</u> and <u>ethical</u> reasons behind initiatives such as the Dartmoor Biodiversity Project and other similar projects around the world. [8]

OCR Biology AS (2805/03) June 2005 (modified) [Total 10]

Answer

Answers to SAQs

Chapter 1

1 $\text{magnification} = \dfrac{\text{size of image}}{\text{real size of object}}$

$= \dfrac{12}{5}$

$= \times 2.4$

2 maximum diameter of cell in micrograph

$= 30\,\text{mm}$

so magnification $= \dfrac{30 \times 1000}{50}$

$= \times 600$

3 length of scale bar $= 24.0\,\text{mm}$

so magnification $= \dfrac{24.0}{0.1}$

$= \times 240$

4 thickness of leaf on micrograph

$= 50.5\,\text{mm}$

$= 50.5 \times 1000\,\mu\text{m}$

magnification $= \times 240$

real thickness $= \dfrac{50.5 \times 1000}{240}$

$= 210\,\mu\text{m}$

6 They are TEMs, as they are not three-dimensional.

7 Ribosomes, details of mitochondria, centrioles, endoplasmic reticulum, nuclear pores, Golgi apparatus, lysosomes. (It is just possible to see Golgi apparatus and centrioles using a light microscope, but no detail of their structure.)

8 See the table at the bottom of this page.

Chapter 2

1 The outer surface of the membrane has chains of sugars – carbohydrate – that are part of the glycolipid and glycoprotein molecules.

2 Photosynthesis in the palisade cell uses carbon dioxide, maintaining a very low concentration inside the cell. The concentration of carbon dioxide in the air outside the leaf, and in the air spaces inside it, is higher than inside the cell, so carbon dioxide diffuses into the cell down its concentration gradient. The cell wall and plasma membrane of the cell are permeable to carbon dioxide.

5

Type of microscope	Best resolution that can be achieved	Best effective magnification that can be achieved
light microscope	200 nm	× 1400
transmission electron microscope	0.5 nm	× 300 000
scanning electron microscope	a little over 0.5 nm	× 300 000

8

Structure	Animal cell	Plant cell
plasma (cell surface) membrane	always present	always present
cell wall	not present	always present
nucleus, nuclear envelope, nucleolus	almost always present	almost always present
endoplasmic reticulum	both rough and smooth ER present	both rough and smooth ER present
Golgi apparatus	usually present	usually present
lysosomes	often present	sometimes present
chloroplasts	not present	present in many of the cells that are exposed to light
mitochondria	usually present	usually present
centrioles	usually present	not present
cilia and flagella	sometimes present	only very rarely present
cytoskeleton	always present	always present

3 Some pancreas cells secrete digestive enzymes, and they are moved out of the cell by exocytosis. Others secrete the hormones insulin and glucagon, which are moved out in the same way.

Chapter 3

1 a 12

b Of the 200 cells, 188 were in interphase, which suggests that $\frac{188}{200}$ of the time a cell is in interphase. So interphase probably makes up about 94% of this cell cycle. You can do similar calculations for each of the other stages. The cells seem to spend about 3% of the time in prophase, 1.5% in metaphase, 0.5% in anaphase and 1.0% in telophase.

2 a The ciliated epithelium in the bronchioles sweeps mucus (which has been produced by goblet cells – you may remember this from GCSE) upwards. The mucus traps small particles and organisms that were inhaled with air, so these are swept upwards away from the lungs to the throat, where the mucus can be swallowed.

b The cilia beat to move an egg along the oviduct towards the uterus.

Chapter 4

1 a See the table at the bottom of this page.

b The surface area : volume ratio (the last column of the table) decreases as the side length of the cube increases.

c The same is true for living organisms – even though they are not cubes. Large organisms tend to have a smaller surface area : volume ratio than smaller ones. This makes it difficult for substances to diffuse across the surface of a large organism fast enough to supply all of the contents of the body, or to get rid of waste products.

2 a 80 dm² for every 1 dm³ (80 : 1)

b 2.6 dm² for every 1 dm³ (2.6 : 1)

c 100 dm² for every 1 dm³ (100 : 1)

d The surface area : volume ratio for an earthworm is probably high enough for enough oxygen to be able to diffuse through its skin to supply its tissues, and carbon dioxide to be able to diffuse out. However, the surface area of a human's skin is much too low to be able to supply all of the person's volume. The lungs greatly increase this surface area, making the surface area : volume ratio even greater than that of an earthworm.

3 a The walls of the alveolus make up the surface inside the lungs. If parts of the walls disappear, the surface area is reduced. If the total volume of the lungs remains the same, this will cause a decrease in surface area : volume ratio.

b Emphysema causes a decrease in the surface area for gas exchange. There is less area across which oxygen can diffuse, and therefore less oxygen can move into the blood per unit time.

4 Cilia move, and this requires energy. Energy is provided by respiration. Aerobic respiration takes place inside mitochondria, where ATP is produced to fuel the movement of the cilia.
Goblet cells secrete mucus, which has molecules made of proteins and sugar units. Proteins are made on ribosomes on the rough endoplasmic reticulum and then transported to the Golgi apparatus. Here, the sugars are added to the proteins, and the resulting molecules are packaged into vesicles ready for export from the cell.

Length of one side of a cube / cm	Total surface area / cm²	Volume / cm³	Surface area divided by volume
1	6	1	6.0
2	24	8	3.0
3	54	27	2.0
4	96	64	1.5
5	150	125	1.2
6	216	216	1.0
7	294	343	0.9
8	384	512	0.8
9	486	729	0.7
10	600	1000	0.6

5 You will get a slightly different answer depending on whether you measure the breaths in or the breaths out. If measuring from bottom to top each time, and measuring to the nearest half square, the values are:

$3.5 + 4.0 + 4.0 + 4.0 = 15.5$ small squares.

So the mean value is

$$\frac{15.5}{5} = 3.1.$$

From the scale on the graph,
10 small squares = $1\,dm^3$.
So the mean value is $0.31\,dm^3$.

6 The bottom of the first breath was at time 0, and the bottom of the last complete breath was at 21 s. In that time, there were 4 complete breaths. So the breathing rate

is $\dfrac{60}{21} \times 4 = 11.4$ breaths per minute.

Ventilation rate is $11.4 \times 0.31 = 3.53\,dm^3$ per minute.

7 $3.4\,dm^3$

8 a Before: 10.0 breaths per minute. After: 17.1 breaths per minute.

b Before: $0.51\,dm^3$. After: $1.94\,dm^3$.

c Before: $0.3\,dm^3$ in approximately 24 s, so $0.75\,dm^3$ per minute. After: $1.4\,dm^3$ in approximately 14 s, so $6\,dm^3$ per minute.

d Before exercise, the person's muscle cells were at rest, so they would be respiring relatively slowly. The blood was able to supply them with all of the oxygen they needed, so their respiration would be aerobic. During exercise, they may have been respiring so quickly that the blood was unable to supply them with enough oxygen, so they also respired anaerobically. This produced lactic acid. After exercise had finished, the lactic acid needed to be broken down, and this process requires oxygen. The extra oxygen required was supplied by the faster, deeper breathing.

Chapter 5

1 a Size is important, but is not the only factor. Microscopic organisms such as *Paramecium* do not have transport systems, whereas all large organisms such as green plants, fish and mammals do. However, cnidarians do not have transport systems even though some of them are considerably larger than insects, which do.

b Surface area : volume ratio is important. Small organisms have large surface area : volume ratios, and generally do not have a transport system. Organisms with branching bodies, such as plants, can have large surface area : volume ratios even when they are large; they do have transport systems but, as you will see, these are not used for transporting gases, and they do not have pumps.

c Level of activity is important. Animals such as fish and mammals have a transport system containing a pump; plants, most of which are less active than most animals, do not have a pump. Insects have pumps in their transport system, even though they are smaller than the less active cnidarians, which do not have a pump.

2 a There are many small tracheoles, which together provide a large surface area.

b The chitin helps to prevent the tracheae from collapsing when air pressure inside them decreases – just as the rings of cartilage do around the trachea of humans.

c There is a risk that too much water vapour will diffuse out of the body through the spiracles. Closing the spiracles reduces this loss.

3 a A closed system; the blood is always inside vessels.

b Twice.

4 An insect has an open circulatory system, whereas a fish has a closed one. An insect's circulatory system is not used for transporting oxygen, whereas the circulatory system of a fish is.

5 a i 0.7–0.8 seconds

ii $\dfrac{60}{0.75} = 80$ beats per minute

For **b**, **c**, **d**, **e** and **f**, see graph on next page. The periods that are not atrial systole are atrial diastole.

6 a 1 beat = about 20 mm on the grid.
25 mm on the grid represents 1 second.
So 20 mm represents

$\dfrac{20}{25}$ seconds = 0.8 seconds.

If one beat lasts 0.8 second, then in 1 second there are

$\dfrac{1}{0.8}$ beats.

So in one minute there are

$\dfrac{1}{0.8} \times 60 = 75$ beats.

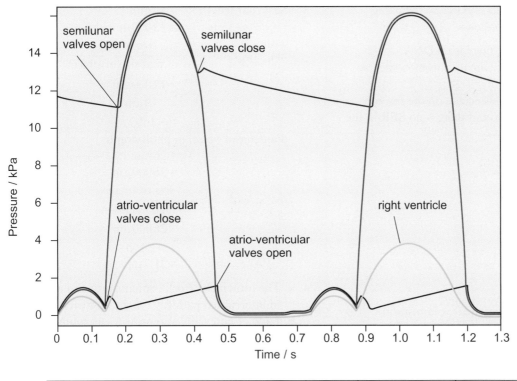

Stage	atrial systole	ventricular systole	ventricular diastole	atrial systole	ventricular systole	ventricular diastole

b i This is the time during which the ventricles are contracting.

ii On the grid, the distance between Q and T is about 7 mm.

This represents $\frac{7}{25} = 0.28$ seconds.

c i This is the time when the ventricles are relaxed and are filling with blood.

ii On the grid, the distance between T and Q is about 13 mm.

This represents $\frac{13}{25} = 0.52$ seconds.

A quicker way of working this out is to subtract your answer to **b ii** from 0.8 seconds.

7 Light passes through the cornea on its way to the retina. Blood vessels would absorb and scatter some of the light, reducing the clarity of the image.

8 a The arteries carry blood that has just come from the heart. When the ventricles contract, the blood surges into the arteries at high pressure, and the pressure falls when the ventricles relax.

b Blood pressure drops because the total cross-sectional area of the arterioles and capillaries is greater than that of the arteries. The same quantity of blood is therefore spread out into a larger volume, so its pressure is lower. Pressure also falls as plasma leaks out of the capillaries.

c The high blood pressure in the pulmonary artery is produced by the contraction of the right ventricle, and that in the aorta is produced by the contraction of the left ventricle. The muscle in the wall of the right ventricle is not as thick as in the left ventricle, so it does not produce as much force when it contracts.

9 a The larger the relative molecular mass of the substance, the lower the permeability of the capillary walls to it.

b Net diffusion for glucose would be into the muscle. Respiration within the muscle requires glucose, so that the concentration of glucose within the muscle cells is lower than in the blood plasma.

c Albumin in the blood plasma raises the solute concentration of the blood, thus helping to draw water back from the tissue fluid into capillaries. If albumin could diffuse out of capillaries into tissue fluid, more water would accumulate in the tissue fluid and not be returned to the circulation.

10 It has come from the cells making up the tissue, many of which secrete proteins.

11 a Protein synthesis – no; there is no DNA.
  b Cell division – no; there are no chromosomes, so mitosis cannot occur.
  c Lipid synthesis – no; this occurs on the smooth endoplasmic reticulum, and there is no SER in the cell.

12 a About 195 cm^3
  b 25 cm^3

13 a i 96.5%
    ii 1.25 cm^3
  b i 22.0%
    ii 0.29 cm^3

Chapter 6

1 Plants have a large surface area : volume ratio because of their branching shape. This allows gases to move quickly between the atmosphere and the cells by diffusion. Plants also have a relatively low metabolic rate, so they do not need such fast supplies of gases.

2 Root hairs and alveoli are both small, but present in large numbers, providing a very large surface area. They are both thin.

3 Scale bar length = 12 mm
  = 12 000 μm

$$\text{magnification} = \frac{\text{size of image}}{\text{real size of object}}$$

$$= \frac{12\,000\,\mu m}{10\,\mu m}$$

$$= \times 1200$$

diameter of vessel in photograph
  = 26 mm
  = 26 000 μm

$$\text{real size of object} = \frac{\text{size of image}}{\text{magnification}}$$

$$= \frac{26\,000\,\mu m}{1200}$$

$$= 21.7\,\mu m$$

4 a The total lack of cell contents provides an uninterrupted pathway for the flow of water.
  b Lack of end walls also provides an uninterrupted pathway for the flow of water.
  c The wider the diameter, the more water can be moved up through a xylem vessel per unit time. However, if the vessels are too wide, there is an increased tendency for the water column to break. The diameter of the xylem vessels is a compromise between these two requirements.
  d The lignified walls provide support, preventing the vessels from collapsing inwards. The lignin waterproofs the walls, keeping most of the water inside the vessel.
  e Pits in the walls of the vessels allow water to move into and out of them.

5 See table at the bottom of this page.

5

Feature	How it helps the plant to conserve water
Leaves can roll up	Less surface area is exposed to the air, and stomata can be hidden inside the rolled-up leaf, reducing the rate of diffusion of water vapour from the leaf.
Especially thick waterproof cuticle	Reduces the possibility of water vapour diffusing out of the cells on the surface of the leaf.
Hairs around stomata	The hairs trap a layer of relatively moist air next to the stomata, which reduces the concentration gradient for water vapour between the inside and outside of the leaf.
Sunken stomata	As with the hairs, a layer of moist air is trapped next to the stomata.
Stems, not leaves, used for photosynthesis (leaves may be reduced to spines)	The fewer the leaves, the less transpiration from them; stems have a relatively low surface area : volume ratio so less transpiration occurs.
Leaves in the form of needles	This shape has a smaller surface area : volume ratio than a broad, flat leaf and so diffusion of water vapour from it is reduced.
Swollen stems	These can store water, for use when supplies run short.

6 Sucrose, amino acids and plant growth substances are synthesised by the plant.

7 **a** Sink. **b** Sink. **c** Source. **d** Sink.

8

Feature	Xylem vessels	Phloem sieve tubes
cell contents	none	cytoplasm and organelles, but no nucleus
cell walls	contain lignin and cellulose	contain cellulose but not lignin
diameter	between 0.01 mm and 0.2 mm	can be smaller than xylem vessels
substances transported	water and mineral ions	substances made by the plant, especially sucrose and amino acids; also some mineral ions (but not nitrate)
method of transport	driven by the transpiration stream – a passive process	driven by active loading of sucrose – an active process

Chapter 7

1 Water moves up each xylem vessel as a tall column, by mass flow. Cohesion between the water molecules helps to hold the column together. If the column broke, then the pulling force exerted by transpiration in the leaves would not be transmitted to the whole of the column, and the water would not move up the plant in this way.

2 **a** 10
b $C_2NO_2H_5$

3 **a** $C_6H_{12}O_6$
b In α-glucose, the carbon shown on the right of the molecule (numbered 1) has an H above and a OH group below. In β-glucose, the OH group is above and the H below.

5 There are many places where this might happen, including the small intestine, where the enzyme lipase hydrolyses fats to fatty acids and glycerol.

6 **a** For example, $C_{45}H_{86}O_6$
b A glucose molecule has twice as many hydrogens as carbons, and the triglyceride also has very nearly twice as many hydrogens as carbons. But while the glucose molecule has the same number of carbon atoms as oxygen atoms, the triglyceride has more than seven times as many carbons as oxygens.

7 A monounsaturated fat contains one carbon–carbon double bond in one of its fatty acids. A polyunsaturated fat contains more than one carbon–carbon double bond.

4

	Amylose	Cellulose	Glycogen
Monosaccharide from which it is formed	α-glucose	β-glucose	α-glucose
Type(s) of glycosidic bond	α1–4	β1–4	α1–4, with α1–6 at branches
Overall shape of molecule	helix	straight chain	branched and slightly coiled
Hydrogen bonding within or between molecules	hydrogen bonds between sugar units in the chain	hydrogen bonds between sugar units in different chains	some hydrogen bonds between sugars units in the chain
Solubility in water	insoluble	insoluble	insoluble
Function	an energy store in plant cells	forms cell walls	an energy store in animal cells

Chapter 8

1 At the 5′ end, the covalent bond to the next nucleotide is with carbon number 5 on the deoxyribose. At the 3′ end, it is with carbon number 3.

2

	DNA	RNA
Sugar present	deoxyribose	ribose
Bases present	A, C, G, T	A, C, G, U
Number of strands	two	usually one
Where it is found	in the nucleus	both nucleus and cytoplasm
Function	stores the genetic code	copies the code from DNA and uses it to make proteins

Chapter 9

1 There is a risk of inaccuracy in a single measurement at 30 seconds. The shape of the curve is more likely to give an accurate value, because it is based on many readings taken over a period of time, rather than just one.

2

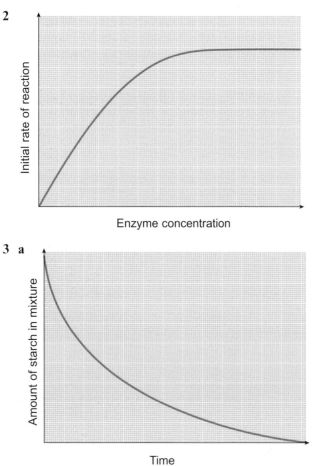

3 a

b Calculate the slope of the curve right at the beginning of the reaction.

4 Measure the volume of oxygen given off over time for several catalase–hydrogen peroxide reactions at different temperatures. In each case, all conditions other than temperature must remain constant. In particular, the same volume of hydrogen peroxide and of catalase solutions should be used each time. Plot total volume of oxygen against time for each reaction. Calculate the slope of the line at the beginning of the reaction in each case to give the initial reaction rate. Then plot initial reaction rate against time.

Chapter 10

1 a Carbohydrates, proteins, lipids and vitamins.
   b Carbohydrates, proteins and lipids.

2 a This means that everyone was alive at the start of the study.
   b Data were probably collected once a year, so the researchers did not know what happened in between. If one or more people died in a year, the graph goes down by a step.
   c There seems to be a clear difference between the results for people with an LDL : HDL ratio greater than 8 (red line) and those with an LDL : HDL ratio of less than or equal to 8 (blue line). Those with the higher ratio had a greater probability of survival.

3 **bread**: wheat ⟶ human
   yogurt: grass ⟶ cattle or goats or sheep (milk) ⟶ bacteria ⟶ human
   beef steak: grass ⟶ cattle ⟶ human
   eggs: wheat (or other grain) ⟶ hens ⟶ human

4 a Ten.

b i Genetically identical plants are more likely to grow to the same height and ripen at the same time. This makes harvesting easier. They are also more likely to produce grain of a consistent quality, which makes it easier for the farmer to sell it.

ii In each generation, a particular plant or line of plants was chosen and others discarded. This means that some alleles (varieties of genes) were lost in each generation. Finally, just one breeding line was used, which will have had just one particular set of alleles.

5 Over the 50 day period, all of the plants had an increasing area of leaf covered by rust. However, the plants with 4–5 resistance genes had only about 2% of leaf area affected after 50 days, while those that had no resistance genes had 100% of leaf area affected. In general, the greater the number of resistance genes, the less quickly the leaves became covered by rust and the smaller the area that was affected.

6 a Halt is the most resistant; the maximum number of aphids per plant was only just over 250, compared with 1600 on TAM 107 plants and 2300 on Arapahoe plants.

b Yes, the results are consistent. In all three trials, Halt gave the greatest yield following an infestation with aphids, which is what would be expected if it had fewer aphids feeding on it. TAM 107 gave slightly greater yields than Arapahoe, reflecting its slightly greater resistance shown in Figure 10.13a.

c There may be characteristics of other wheat varieties that farmers want – for example, resistance to a different pest, or characteristics of the grains that make them suitable for different buyers (for example, they may be especially suitable for making bread, or for making pasta). Farmers may be prepared to take a risk that aphids will not be a problem in a particular year and grow a non-resistant variety if it has these desirable features and could possibly be sold for a greater return than Halt.

7 Increase = 5483 − 5370 = 113 kg per cow.
So the mean annual increase is

$$\frac{113}{10} = 11.3 \text{ kg per cow.}$$

(You could work this out as a percentage increase too.)

8 a Up to this point, it is worth the farmer adding this quantity of fertiliser, as the increase in money he gets from the sale of the crop is greater than the extra costs of buying and applying the fertiliser. It is not worth adding any more fertiliser than this.

b The field in which the crop was being grown must have been lacking nitrogen-containing ions, such as ammonium ions or nitrate ions, in the soil. Adding nitrogen-containing fertiliser up to about $144 \text{ kg ha}^{-1} \text{ yr}^{-1}$ supplied extra nitrogen to the wheat plants, which the plants used for making proteins and therefore producing higher yields. Any extra fertiliser added had no effect, as the wheat plants now had as much as they required or could use. We can say that up to $144 \text{ kg ha}^{-1} \text{ yr}^{-1}$, availability of nitrogen-containing ions was a limiting factor, but beyond this value some other factor was limiting growth.

9 a The best anti-fungal treatment was the copper-containing fungicide, as this gave the greatest yield of tomatoes. The fungicide containing *B. subtilis* was the least effective, providing a yield that was 1610 kg ha^{-1} less. The copper-containing fungicide produced a 40% greater yield than the *B. subtilis* fungicide. The other two treatments gave identical results, between the yields from the two fungicides.

b This depends on two things – how organic production is defined, and your personal viewpoint. Organic production is normally defined as using only naturally occurring substances, rather than inorganic chemicals that have been produced artificially. So in that sense *B. subtilis* is a naturally occurring organism and could be used in organic growing. But you may have an opinion that it should not be used, and if you can support your view with reasons then that is a valid argument.

10 a In the first year, the pigs that were given antibiotics grew much faster than those with no antibiotics. There was a 0.15 kg difference in growth rate per day, which would add up to a very large difference in total body mass after one year. The percentage increase was

$$\frac{(0.75 - 0.60)}{0.60} \times 100 = 25\%$$

b The growth rate per day for the pigs that were not given antibiotics increased significantly during the first three years of the experiment, eventually settling down to a value that was similar to the growth rate for the pigs that were given antibiotics.

c It is likely that the use of antibiotics in some of the pigs reduced the overall numbers of bacteria in the building. This would have reduced the likelihood of the bacteria affecting the untreated pigs, so the untreated pigs benefited from the antibiotic treatment almost as much as the pigs that were treated.

11 The group on the right has been affected by microorganisms. The microorganisms (bacteria and fungi) have secreted enzymes which have hydrolysed substances in the strawberries, breaking down their structure and partially liquefying them. You can see fungal growth on some of the strawberries. The ones on the left have been irradiated; the gamma radiation killed the microorganisms that were already on the strawberries and, as yet, not enough microorganisms have re-colonised the strawberries to have any noticeable effect.

12 These trace elements may act as cofactors for enzymes.

Chapter 11

1 a They want to greatly reduce the global impact of TB by 2015.
  b They hope to ensure that everyone will have access to good diagnosis and treatment, so that suffering can be reduced. They want to protect poor and vulnerable people from TB. They want to support the development of new ways of treating TB.

2

Bacterium	HIV
cellular	not cellular
has a plasma membrane	has an envelope
has cytoplasm	no cytoplasm
much larger than a virus	much smaller than a bacterium
contains DNA	contains RNA
does not contain reverse transcriptase	contains reverse transcriptase
no capsid	has a capsid made of protein

3 a The distribution of these diseases is similar. Both are common in sub-Saharan Africa and in Eastern Europe, India and China.

b HIV/AIDS decreases the number of T lymphocytes, weakening the ability of the body to mount an effective immune response against HIV and other pathogens. This allows other infections, including TB, to take hold. About one-third of people are infected with *Mycobacterium tuberculosis*, which may progress to causing symptoms of TB when the immune system is weakened.

4 a A pathogen is a microorganism that causes a disease. A vector is an organism that transmits the pathogen from one person to another.
  b Examples include:
  rabies – bats, foxes, dogs
  plague – rat fleas
  Lyme disease – ticks
  c Vectors are outside the human body – if we know where they are and understand their life cycles, it is often easier to destroy or control them than it is to destroy pathogens inside the human body.

5 a B lymphocyte.
  b Neutrophil.
  c Pathogen.
  d Antibody.
  e Macrophage.
  f Antigen.
  g Parasite.

6 Viruses enter body cells, where they hijack the cell's machinery to reproduce themselves. If a cell is infected by a virus, it cuts up some of the virus molecules and puts them in its plasma membrane. T lymphocytes respond to antigens in the plasma membrane, so they recognise when a cell is infected by a virus. T helper lymphocytes then secrete cytokines, which alert other cells to respond. T killer lymphocytes bind to the cell that is infected by the virus and kill it.

  B lymphocytes, however, respond by secreting antibodies. These will not reach viruses that are safely inside a cell. Antibodies cannot cross plasma membranes to get into a cell.

7 a The results show that the radioactivity (and therefore the amino acids) was found first in the ribosomes, then in the endoplasmic reticulum, and then in the Golgi apparatus. As the radioactivity in ribosomes declines, it rises in the ER. As it declines in the ER, it rises in the Golgi apparatus.

b At the ribosomes, the labelled amino acids would have been used to make protein molecules. The ribosomes are attached to the membranes of the endoplasmic reticulum, and the proteins move into the cisternae of the endoplasmic reticulum as they are made. Pieces of the ER then break off to form small vesicles, containing the proteins. These vesicles travel to the Golgi apparatus, where they fuse with its membranes. In the Golgi, carbohydrates are added to the proteins to convert them to glycoproteins.

c This suggests that most of the proteins made on the ribosomes moved into the ER. However, not all of these proteins were transported to the Golgi apparatus. Some of them might have gone straight into the cytoplasm of the cell. Another possibility is that the radioactivity of the amino acids decreased over time.

d The amino acids might have been taken up by phagocytosis. In this case, the cell would have formed a vacuole containing amino acids and a droplet of the liquid surrounding them.

   They could have been taken up by active transport, through a protein channel in the plasma membrane.

e Small vesicles would pinch off from the Golgi apparatus, and travel to the cell surface membrane. They would then fuse with this membrane, emptying the contents of the vesicles outside the cell. This is an example of exocytosis.

8 a The low take-up of vaccine meant that quite large numbers of children had no immunity against measles.

b Once people knew that there was a measles epidemic, they were alert to the possibility that they or a child might get it. They may have thought that symptoms which they would normally not worry about could be measles.

c It is probably best to present this as a bar chart. The x-axis should be labelled 'group of people', with separate bars for each group. The y-axis should be labelled 'percentage of cases'. The bars should not touch.

d People who were children before the measles vaccine was introduced would probably have already been exposed to the live virus, so they had measles when they were young. Others would have been vaccinated against it when they were children.

9 a The woman: high/moderate risk, 10–15%. The man: mild risk, 5–10%.

b The woman should give up smoking, as this is by far the greatest factor contributing to her risk of having a heart attack or stroke. She should also try to reduce her total cholesterol:HDL-cholesterol ratio, perhaps by reducing the quantity of saturated fats in her diet, or by taking statins.

   The man needs to reduce his total cholesterol:HDL-cholesterol ratio. The fact that it is so high raises the possibility that he may be genetically liable to high cholesterol levels, in which case he will need to take statins or a prescribed medicine and not just try to get the level down by changing his diet.

c The risk calculators are built up by studying a large number of people over many years, recording various factors about their lifestyles (smoker or not, blood pressure readings, blood cholesterol levels) and all the cardiovascular events they have. These findings are then used to search for relationships between a particular lifestyle factor and the likelihood of suffering a cardiovascular event.

10 The peak for number of cigarettes smoked per year was around 1945, while the peak for deaths from lung cancer was around 1970–1975. The time-lag appears to be 25–30 years. There is a time-lag because the development of smoking-related lung cancer is slow. Typically, DNA damage takes time to occur, and several different genes may need to mutate before control of cell division is lost. It then takes time for the cancerous cells to form a tumour, and a person with lung cancer may live for several years.

11 a The annual mortality of smokers from lung cancer is about 15 times greater than that of non-smokers. Similarly, mortality from CHD is 1.5 times greater, and mortality from COPD is about 13 times greater. The strong links support the hypothesis that cigarette smoking causes these diseases. The evidence from former smokers also supports this idea – giving up smoking reduces the risk compared with smokers, but does not reduce it to the level of non-smokers.

b Carcinogens in tar damage DNA in cells in the gaseous exchange system (and also in other parts of the body). If genes that control cell division are damaged, this may allow the cell to divide uncontrollably, forming a tumour.

c Stroke.

12a 75%

b Only about 65% of continuing smokers were still alive, approximately 10% fewer than those who had given up.

c Nicotine in cigarette smoke increases blood pressure, and therefore the risk of developing atherosclerosis, which in turn can lead to coronary heart disease. Giving up smoking reduces the risk of all of these health problems.

Chapter 12

1 On the lawn:
total number of dandelions counted = 17

total area sampled is $\dfrac{10 \times 0.25}{2.5}\,\text{m}^2 = 2.5\,\text{m}^2$

so species density is $\dfrac{17}{2.5\,\text{m}^2} = 6.8\,\text{per}\,\text{m}^2$

On the cultivated vegetable patch:
total number of dandelions counted = 8

so species density is $\dfrac{8}{2.5\,\text{m}^2} = 3.2\,\text{per}\,\text{m}^2$

2 a Timothy grass 44, Yorkshire fog grass 36, plantain 2, meadow buttercup 5, dock 5, cowslip 1, clover 15.

b One plant may partly overlie another, so both would be included in the cover for that piece of ground.

c It is very difficult to estimate the percentage cover with any more precision than this.

d There may have been plants present that did not occupy enough area to be counted as covering at least 5% of a quadrat. For example, there could have been a cowslip plant in each quadrat, but only in quadrat 4 did this occupy at least 2.6 % of the area. (2.6% is the smallest number that could be rounded up to 5%.) These results can therefore not be used to estimate species frequency – they would give a considerable underestimate for small plants. Moreover, just five quadrats is a very small sample, and is unlikely to be truly representative of the whole area.

3 a estimated population size = $\dfrac{39 \times 35}{20} = 68$

b The marked woodlice were no more likely to be caught by predators, or die from other causes than the unmarked ones. The marked woodlice mixed freely, randomly and completely with the unmarked ones between the two samples being caught, and the number of births and amount of immigration between these times were not significant.

4

	Shore B		
Species	n	$\dfrac{n}{N}$	$\left(\dfrac{n}{N}\right)^2$
painted topshells	51	0.059	0.004
limpets	125	0.145	0.021
dogwhelks	63	0.073	0.005
snakelocks anemones	0	0.000	0.000
beadlet anemones	22	0.026	0.001
barnacles	391	0.454	0.206
mussels	116	0.135	0.018
periwinkles	93	0.108	0.012
total number of individuals, N	**861**	$\Sigma\left(\dfrac{n}{N}\right)^2 = 0.267$	

So D for shore B = $1 - 0.267 = 0.733$

5 Shore A: 8; shore B: 7.

Chapter 13

1 kingdom: Animalia (or animals)
phylum: Chordata (or chordates)
class: Mammalia (or mammals)
order: Proboscidea
family: Elephantidae
genus: Loxodonta
species: *Loxodonta africana*

2 Greenfinches and goldfinches both belong to the same genus, so they are considered to be more closely related to each other than they are to chaffinches. All three species belong to the same family, so they all had a common ancestor that gave rise to this family. We could show this possible relationship like this:

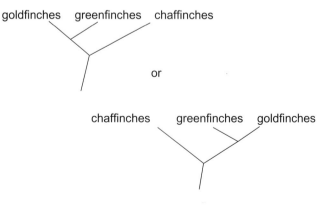

3 a Humans and chimpanzees.

b Gorillas and orang-utans.

c There is no clear definition of what a genus is and what criteria should be used for placing different species in the same genus. If we do use DNA sequences in this way, then there is no agreement about whether it is more valid to look at every part of the DNA in a species or whether we should concentrate on particular areas, such as just the regions that code for proteins (as was done here). We can also question whether sheer numbers of differences in DNA bases can justifiably be used to determine classification, or whether we should take into account their effects as well.

4 The three domains are the highest taxa. It is possible to have the domain Eukarya, with the kingdoms Protoctista, Fungi, Plantae and Animalia as subdivisions of it. However, we cannot keep the kingdom Prokaryota, as that is now split at a higher level.

Chapter 14

1 Sex is the clearest example. Tongue rolling and shape of earlobes are other possibilities.

2 a Both genes and environment.

b Probably genes only.

c Both genes and environment.

d Environment only. (It depends on how many ovules were fertilised.)

3 a 3.1 mm (Note that, even though your calculator will probably say 3.104 all the measurements were given only to the nearest 0.1 mm, so your value for the mean should given to the same degree of accuracy.)

b

Length / mm	2.7	2.8	2.9	3.0	3.1	3.2	3.3	3.4	3.5
Number	1	3	6	9	11	9	7	3	1

See histogram.

c The mode (the class with the highest frequency) is 3.1 mm.

d The median (the class at the midpoint of the range) is also 3.1 mm.

Histogram for question **3b**:

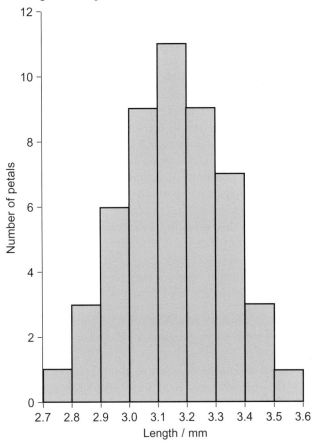

4 a There seems to be no selection pressure against unusual colours as there are no predators.

b Possible selection pressures include limited water and food supply, limited breeding space and disease (such as myxomatosis if this is present on the island).

5 a Deaths from *S. aureus* that are not specified as resistant have remained fairly constant, at between 350 and 500 per year over this time period. However, deaths from MRSA have increased from less than 100 in 1993 to around 1600 in 2005. This is an increase of over 16 times.

b The figures are for deaths, not for infections. It is likely that there have been many more infections than deaths, especially for non-resistant bacteria, which are easily treated with antibiotics. (The constant death rate from the non-resistant bacteria could possibly mask an increase in actual infections – but we cannot know this.) The figures suggest that there has been a steady increase in the number of people being infected with MRSA, and this could be because MRSA is becoming more common. The resistance arises as the result of selection – if antibiotics are used, then bacteria that have resistance to them are more likely to survive. They pass on their resistance genes to their offspring, producing a population of resistant bacteria. The numbers have increased because antibiotics continue to be used and so populations of resistant bacteria continue to breed more successfully than those that are not resistant.

6 a Costs remained relatively constant between 1980 and 1991, varying around a value of about $40 per acre. There was a sharp rise in 1992, when costs more than doubled, to about $100 per acre. Between 1992 and 2000, they varied around a value of about $85 per acre.

b There may have been more infestations with insect pests, so farmers had to spray more often. The pests may have become resistant to insecticides, so newer and more expensive ones may have been required.

7 Each time the insecticide is used, it provides a selection pressure. Boll worms that by chance are resistant are more likely to survive and breed. Their offspring are more likely to survive and breed than the offspring of non-resistant parents, and this continues over many generations. Over time, if the insecticide continues to be used, more and more of the boll worms in the population have the gene that confers resistance.

Chapter 15

1 One possibility is that people are much more aware of vertebrates than invertebrates, so we know more about them. They are larger and more visible than invertebrates. Many people find them more interesting than invertebrates. Moreover, vertebrates tend to be larger than invertebrates, and so may need larger areas of habitat. They are more likely to suffer from overhunting.

2 a Selection pressures in the natural habitat might include grazing, wide variations in rainfall or competition with other species. In the seed bank, none of these selection pressures will apply. Here, the greatest selection pressure will be the conditions in which the seeds are stored for long periods of time – seeds best able to survive storage will be the most successful.

b It is possible that plants grown from the saved seeds will not have the best set of characteristics for surviving the different selection pressures they will encounter in their natural habitat. This could reduce the chances of success when returning them to the wild.

Glossary

abiotic factor: an environmental factor caused by non-living components of the environment, e.g. water supply

acetylcholine: a transmitter substance; it is contained in vesicles in a presynaptic neurone, and diffuses across the cleft to the next neurone to set up an action potential (nerve impulse)

acrosome: a vesicle containing hydrolytic enzymes, in the head of a sperm

activation energy: the initial energy that must be given to a substrate in order for it to change into a product

active immunity: the ability to produce antibodies to destroy a pathogen

active loading: the movement of sucrose into sieve tubes, using active transport, carried out by proteins in the plasma membranes of companion cells

active site: the part of an enzyme molecule to which the substrate binds

active transport: the movement of molecules or ions through transport proteins across a cell membrane, against their concentration gradient, involving the use of energy from ATP

acute illness: a disease that lasts for only a short time

adenine: one of the four nitrogenous bases found in DNA and RNA

adhesion: a force that attracts water molecules to a surface, by hydrogen bonding

adipose tissue: a tissue made up of cells containing large lipid droplets

adrenaline: a hormone secreted by the adrenal glands in times of stress or excitement

aerobic respiration: a series of metabolic reactions that releases energy from glucose or other substrates, using oxygen

allele: one of two or more varieties of a gene

allopatric speciation: the production of new species from populations that are geographically separated from one another

alveoli: tiny blind-ending sacs in the lungs, where gas exchange takes place between air and the blood

amino acid: a molecule containing carbon, hydrogen, oxygen and nitrogen (and sometimes sulfur); it has a hydroxyl group and an amino group and one of 20 R groups attached to a central carbon atom

amino group: $-NH_2$; this group readily ionises to form $-NH_3^+$, so it is basic

amylose: a polysaccharide made of many α-glucose molecules linked together

anaphase: the stage in cell division when chromatids (or chromosomes in meiosis I) are pulled apart and travel to opposite ends of the dividing cell

angina: a pain felt in the chest and left arm, caused by poor blood flow in the coronary arteries

antibiotic: a substance that kills bacteria but does not harm animal cells

antibody: a small protein secreted by B lymphocytes in response to a particular antigen

antigen: a molecule or cell that is recognised as foreign by the immune system

antigen-presenting cell: a cell that takes in a pathogen, or molecules from it, and holds them in its plasma membrane where they may be encountered by a lymphocyte

anti-parallel: running in opposite directions; the two polynucleotide strands in a DNA molecule are anti-parallel

aorta: the large artery that carries blood out of the left ventricle of the heart

apoplast pathway: a route taken by water as it moves across a plant tissue by passing through the cell walls and the spaces between the cells

arteriole: a small artery, which carries blood between an artery and capillaries

artery: a thick-walled vessel with a relatively narrow lumen which carries blood away from the heart

artificial immunity: immunity acquired through vaccination, for example being given weakened pathogens, or antibodies

asexual: reproduction that does not involve gametes or fertilisation

assimilates: substances synthesised by a plant during or following photosynthesis

atheromatous plaque: a deposit of cholesterol in the wall of an artery

atherosclerosis: the hardening and stiffening of artery walls, often caused by deposits of plaque

ATP: adenosine triphosphate, the universal energy currency of cells

ATPase: an enzyme that catalyses the production or breakdown of ATP

atrial systole: the part of the cardiac cycle in which the muscles in the walls of the atria contract

atrio-ventricular node: the AVN; an area of tissue in the septum between the atria, which delays the electrical impulse from the atria briefly, before it passes to the Purkyne tissue

atrio-ventricular valve: one of the valves between the atria and the ventricles, which prevents blood flowing back up into the atria from the ventricles

atrium: one of the two upper chambers of the heart, which receive blood from the veins and pass it on to the ventricles

attenuated: when pathogens have been treated so that they are not able to cause disease

autotroph: an organism that does not require organic nutrients; plants are autotrophs

AVN: the atrio-ventricular node

B lymphocyte: a white blood cell that secretes antibodies to a specific antigen

balanced diet: a diet that includes some of all the required nutrients in suitable proportions, and the correct amount of energy

basement membrane: a layer of extracellular material that holds the base of an epithelial tissue in place

bicuspid valve: the atrio-ventricular valve on the left side of the heart; also called the mitral valve

bilayer: a structure made up of two layers of molecules, e.g. the phospholipid bilayer in a cell membrane

binomial: the two-word Latin name given to a species

biodiversity: the variety of habitats, communities and species in an area, and the genetic diversity within populations

biological catalyst: an enzyme; a protein that acts as a catalyst in living organisms

biotic factor: an environmental factor caused by other living organisms

blastocyst: the tiny ball of cells formed by a zygote as its cells repeatedly divide

blood capillary: the smallest type of blood vessel, with walls a single cell thick

Bohr effect: the decrease in the affinity of haemoglobin for oxygen in the presence of carbon dioxide

bone marrow: a cavity in the middle of some bones in which red and white blood cells are produced

breathing: muscular movements that cause air to move into and out of the lungs

breathing rate: the mean number of breaths per minute

broad-spectrum insecticide: a substance that kills a wide range of insects, not only the pests

bronchiole: a small tube branching from a bronchus and leading to the alveoli

bronchitis: inflammation of the bronchi, often caused by bacterial infection

bronchus: one of two tubes which branch from the trachea and carry air into the lungs

callose: a complex carbohydrate produced by plants to seal wounds in phloem tissue

cambium: a cylinder of cells in plant stems and roots, whose cells are able to divide and produce new cells so that the stem or root grows wider

capillary: the smallest type of blood vessel, which has walls a single cell thick

capillary bed: an area where there are many capillaries, spreading out within a tissue

carbaminohaemoglobin: a compound formed when carbon dioxide combines with haemoglobin

carbon dioxide: a gas found in very low concentrations, less than 0.04 %, in air, used by plants in photosynthesis and released by all organisms in respiration

carbon monoxide: CO; a substance produced by incomplete combustion, which binds with haemoglobin and reduces its ability to carry oxygen

carbonic anhydrase: an enzyme found, for example, in red blood cells, which catalyses the reaction of carbon dioxide with water to form carbonic acid

carboxyhaemoglobin: a compound formed when carbon monoxide combines with haemoglobin

carboxyl group: $-COOH$; this group readily ionises to form $-COO^-$ and H^+, so it is acidic

carcinogenic: causing cancer

cardiac arrest: a heart attack, when the heart muscle stops contracting

cardiac cycle: the series of events that take place in the heart during one heart beat

cartilage: a strong but flexible tissue, found for example covering the ends of bones at joints, and in the form of C-shaped supporting rings in the trachea

Casparian strip: a band of suberin in the walls of cells making up the endodermis of plant roots, preventing water from passing between the cells

cell cycle: the sequence of events that takes place from one cell division until the next; it is made up of interphase, mitosis and cytokinesis

cell signalling: communication between one cell and another by means of chemicals

cell surface membrane: the plasma membrane, made up of a phospholipid bilayer in which protein molecules float

cell wall: a structure that is present outside the plasma membrane in plant cells, fungal cells and bacterial cells; in plants, it is made of criss-crossing layers of cellulose fibres

cellulose: a polysaccharide made of many β-glucose molecules linked together

centrioles: a pair of organelles found in animal cells, which build the microtubules to form the spindle during cell division

centromere: the place where two chromatids are held together, and where the microtubules of the spindle attach during cell division

channel protein: a protein that forms a pathway through a membrane, through which molecules that would not be able to move through the phospholipid bilayer can pass

chloroplast: an organelle found only in plant cells, where photosynthesis takes place; it is surrounded by an envelope of two membranes, and contains chlorophyll; photosynthesis takes place here

cholesterol: a lipid (or a lipid-like substance) that helps to maintain the fluidity of cell membranes

chromatid: one of two identical parts of a chromosome, held together by a centromere, formed during interphase by the replication of the DNA molecule

chromatin: the DNA in a nucleus when the chromosomes have not condensed

chromosome: a structure made of DNA and histones, found in the nucleus of a eukaryotic cell; the term bacterial chromosome is now commonly used for the circular strand of DNA present in a prokaryotic cell

chronic illness: an illness that lasts a long time

chronic obstructive pulmonary disease (COPD): a long-term illness caused by damage to the lungs and airways

ciliated cell: a cell that has cilia on its surface, which are able to move in unison and cause movement

ciliated epithelium: a layer of cells covering a surface in an animal, in which some of the cells have cilia

cisterna: a space enclosed by the membranes of the endoplasmic reticulum

class: a group of similar orders

classification: putting things into groups

clone: a group of genetically identical cells

closed circulatory system: a circulatory system in which the blood is always within blood vessels

coenzyme: a non-protein substance that is required for an enzyme to catalyse a reaction

coenzyme A: a coenzyme required for many metabolic reactions to take place, including respiration

cofactor: a non-protein substance, often an inorganic ion, that is required for an enzyme to catalyse a reaction

cohesion: the attractive force that holds water molecules together by hydrogen bonding

collagen: a fibrous protein found in skin, bones and tendons

community: all the organisms of all the different species living in the same place at the same time

companion cells: cells that are closely associated with sieve elements; they have a nucleus and many organelles and provide energy to enable translocation to take place

competitive inhibition: inhibition in which an enzyme inhibitor has a similar shape to the substrate molecule, and competes with it for the enzyme's active site

complementary base pairing: the pattern of pairing between the nitrogenous bases in a polynucleotide; in DNA, A pairs with T and C with G

concentration gradient: a difference in concentration of a substance between one area and another

condensation reaction: a reaction in which two molecules are linked together, involving the formation of water

condenser lens: the lens on a microscope that focuses rays of light from the light source onto the specimen

continuous variation: variation in which there is a continuous range of values between two extremes

contraction time: the time interval between phases Q and T in an electrocardiogram

convergent evolution: the development of similar structures in organisms that are not closely related, as a result of adaptation for similar lifestyles

coronary artery: one of the arteries that branches off from the aorta and supplies oxygenated blood to the heart muscle

coronary heart disease (CHD): a disorder affecting the blood vessels (coronary arteries) that supply the muscle in the heart walls with blood

coronary thrombosis: a blood clot in a coronary artery

cortex: the area of a stem or root between the surface layers and the centre; it is made up of parenchyma tissue

covalent bond: a bond formed by two atoms sharing a pair of electrons

crenated: the shape that red blood cells become when they have lost a lot of water by osmosis

cyclic AMP: a 'second messenger' substance, which is affected when particular molecules bind to receptors in a plasma membrane and which, in turn, affects another molecule within the cell

cytosine: one of the four nitrogenous bases found in DNA and RNA

cytoskeleton: a network of microtubules and microfibres that provides support in eukaryotic cells

denatured: when a protein molecule, for example an enzyme, has lost its molecular shape, so that its function can no longer be carried out

deoxyribonucleic acid (DNA): the genetic material contained in chromosomes; a polynucleotide in which the five-carbon sugar is deoxyribose

deoxyribose: a five-carbon sugar found in DNA

diaphragm: a dome-shaped sheet of tissue which separates the thorax from the abdomen; contraction of its muscles pulls it flatter, which increases the volume inside the thorax and helps to draw air into the lungs

differentiation: the development of a cell to become specialised for a particular function

diffusion: the net movement, as a result of random motion of its molecules or ions, of a substance from an area of high concentration to an area of low concentration

diffusion gradient: a difference in concentration of a substance between one place and another; if the substance has particles that are free to move, their net movement will be down the diffusion gradient

diploid cell: a cell that possesses two complete sets of chromosomes

disaccharide: a sugar whose molecules are made of two sugar units

discontinuous variation: variation in which each organism belongs to one of a few clearly defined groups

disease: a condition that impairs the normal function of the body

dissociate: to break apart; for example, carbonic acid dissociates to form hydrogen ions and hydrogencarbonate ions

dissociation curve: a graph showing the percentage saturation of a blood pigment, for example haemoglobin, at different concentrations of oxygen

dissolving: the separation and dispersal of molecules or ions of a substance in between the molecules of a solvent

disulfide bond: a covalent bond formed between the sulfur atoms of two cysteine molecules

domain: one of three major groups into which all living organisms are classified; an alternative classification to the five-kingdom system

dopamine: a neurotransmitter found in the brain

double circulatory system: a circulatory system in which there are two circuits, the systemic circulation and the pulmonary circulation; the blood returns to the heart after being oxygenated and before flowing to other parts of the body

ecosystem: the interactions between all the organisms, and their environment, in a particular area

elastic fibres: microscopic fibres containing the protein elastin, that are able to stretch and recoil back to their original length

electrocardiogram (ECG): a recording of the heart's electrical activity

emphysema: a disorder caused by the breakdown of the alveolar walls, making it difficult to obtain sufficient oxygen in the blood

endocytosis: the movement of bulk liquids or solids into a cell, by the indentation of the plasma membrane to form vesicles containing the substance; it is an active process requiring ATP

endodermis: the outer layer of the stele in a plant root

endoplasmic reticulum: often abbreviated to ER; a network of membranes within a eukaryotic cell, where various metabolic reactions take place

endothelium: a tissue lining the inner surface of an organ, for example the inside of a blood vessel

envelope: two membranes surrounding an organelle; nuclei, mitochondria and chloroplasts have envelopes

environmental factor: a feature of the environment that has an effect on an organism

environmental impact assessment: a study of possible environmental effects that must be carried out before a new development is approved

environmental variation: differences between organisms caused by their environment

enzyme: a protein that works as a catalyst

enzyme–substrate complex: the temporary association between an enzyme and its substrate during an enzyme-catalysed reaction

epidemiology: the study of patterns of disease in populations, in order to work out the causes of the disease

epithelial tissue: a layer of cells lining a surface in an animal

equator: the mid-line of a cell, where the chromosomes are lined up during metaphase of mitosis or meiosis

erythrocyte: a red blood cell

ester bond: a bond linking a fatty acid to a glycerol molecule in a lipid

eukaryotic: a cell containing a nucleus and other membrane-bound organelles

ex situ: away from the place where an organism normally lives

exocytosis: the movement of bulk liquids or solids out of a cell, by the fusion of the vesicles containing the substance with the plasma membrane; it is an active process requiring ATP

experimental evidence: data obtained from planned, controlled experiments

expiratory reserve volume: the maximum volume of air, over and above the tidal volume, that can be breathed out with one breath

extracellular: outside a cell

eyepiece lens: the part of a microscope through which you look; it contains a lens that focuses light onto your eye

facilitated diffusion: the diffusion of a substance through protein channels in a cell membrane; the proteins provide hydrophilic areas that allow the molecules or ions to pass through a membrane that would otherwise be less permeable to them; it is an active process requiring ATP

family: a group of similar genera

fatty acid: a molecule containing a hydrocarbon chain, with a carboxyl group at one end

fibre: a grouping of fibrils of a substance, for example in collagen or cellulose; fibres are generally large enough to be seen with a light microscope, whereas fibrils are of an order of magnitude smaller

fibril: a grouping of several molecules held side-by-side by bonds between them, for example in collagen or cellulose

fibrous protein: a protein with a linear three-dimensional shape; fibrous proteins have structural roles and are insoluble in water

filling time: the stage in the cardiac cycle during which the heart is filling with blood

flaccid: a plant cell is said to be flaccid if it has lost a lot of water, and its volume has shrunk so much that the cell no longer pushes outwards on the cell wall

fluid mosaic model: the universally accepted model of membrane structure, in which proteins float in a phospholipid bilayer

fossil: the remains of a long-dead organism, preserved in stone

freeze-dried: (food) frozen in a vacuum, so that most of the water in it is lost as water vapour

gamma radiation: short wavelength electromagnetic radiation that destroys living cells

gene: a sequence of DNA nucleotides that codes for a polypeptide

genetic variation: differences between organisms caused by their genes

genetically different: containing a different collection of alleles of genes

genus: a group of similar species; plural genera

geographical isolation: the separation of two populations of a species by a geographical barrier, for example a stretch of water

globular protein: a protein with a roughly spherical three-dimensional shape; many are metabolically active and soluble in water

glucose: a hexose sugar; the form in which carbohydrate is transported in the blood of mammals

glycogen: a polysaccharide made of many alpha glucose molecules linked together; it is the storage polysaccharide in animals and fungi

glycogen phosphorylase: an enzyme that catalyses the breakdown of glycogen to form glucose, especially in liver cells and muscle cells

glycolipid: a molecule made of a lipid to which sugars are attached

glycoprotein: a molecule made of a protein to which sugars are attached

glycosidic bond: the bond that links sugar molecules together in a disaccharide or polysaccharide

goblet cell: an epithelial cell that secretes mucus

Golgi apparatus: a stack of curved membranes inside a cell, in which protein molecules are packaged and modified, for example by adding sugars to them to produce glycoproteins

G-protein: a protein that is linked to a receptor in a plasma membrane, and that brings about a reaction when a signal molecule links with the receptor

grana: (singular: granum) membranes inside a chloroplast, containing chlorophyll

guanine: one of the four nitrogenous bases found in DNA and RNA

habitat: a place where an organism lives

haem: a group of atoms with an Fe^{2+} ion at the centre, found in several proteins including haemoglobin and cytochrome

haemocoel: a space within the body of an animal, for example an insect, in which blood is contained

haemoglobin: the red pigment found in red blood cells; it transports oxygen and carbon dioxide between lungs and body cells

haemoglobinic acid: the compound formed when hydrogen ions combine with haemoglobin

haploid cell: a cell that possesses only one set of chromosomes

HDL: high-density lipoprotein

health: a state of complete physical, mental and social well-being

herd immunity: immunity possessed by a large proportion of individuals in a population, lowering the chances of even those individuals that are not immune from getting an infectious disease

heterotroph: an organism that requires organic nutrients; all animals and fungi are heterotrophs

hexose: a sugar with six carbon atoms, $C_6H_{12}O_6$

hierarchy: a series of groups in which each group is made up of several smaller ones

histones: protein molecules that are associated with DNA in chromosomes

homologous chromosomes: a pair of chromosomes in a diploid cell that have the same structure as each other, with the same genes (but not necessarily the same alleles of those genes) at the same loci; they that pair together to form a bivalent during the first division of meiosis

humidity: the quantity of water vapour held in the air

hydrogen bond: an attractive force between a slight negative charge on one atom, for example oxygen, and a slight positive charge on another, for example hydrogen

hydrolase: an enzyme that catalyses a hydrolysis reaction

hydrolysis: a reaction in which two molecules are separated from each other, involving the combination of water

hydrophilic: attracted to water; hydrophilic substances have small electric charges that are attracted to the small electric charges (dipoles) on water molecule

hydrophobic interaction: a weak bond formed between two groups of atoms that are repelled by water

hydrophobic: repelled by water; hydrophobic substances do not have electric charges, and are not attracted to water molecules

hypertension: high blood pressure

immune: able to destroy a pathogen before it can harm the body

immune response: the way in which lymphocytes respond to infection by pathogens

immune system: the organs and cells in the body that help to destroy pathogens

immunoglobulin: an antibody; a small protein molecule that is able to bind with a specific antigen

in situ: in the place where an organism normally lives

induced fit: the change of shape of an enzyme when it binds with its substrate, caused by contact with the substrate

inhibitor: a substance that reduces the rate of an enzyme-catalysed reaction

initial rate of reaction: the rate at which substrate is converted to product right at the beginning of a reaction

inorganic ions: charged particles of elements or their compounds, such as potassium, K^+ and nitrate, NO_3^-

inspiratory reserve volume: the maximum volume of air, over and above the tidal volume, that can be breathed in with one breath

insulin: a small peptide hormone secreted by the cells in the islets of Langerhans in the pancreas; it reduces blood glucose levels

intensive farming: producing as much as possible on a small area of land, using high inputs such as fertilisers or high-energy animal feeds

intercostal muscle: one of the muscles between the ribs, which contract and relax to raise and lower the ribcage during breathing

interphase: the longest stage in the cell cycle; this is when the replication of DNA takes place

intracellular: within cells

involuntary: an action that takes place with no conscious thought

ionic bond: a strong bond formed by attraction between a positively charged ion and a negatively charged ion

irreversible inhibition: inhibition of an enzyme that is permanent, and that is not affected by the addition of more substrate

karyotype: the chromosomes of an individual; usually, photographs are taken of the cell during mitosis when the chromosomes are visible, and the pictures of each chromosome are then arranged in their pairs, from largest to smallest

kingdom: one of the five major groups into which organisms are classified

latent heat: the amount of heat energy absorbed by a substance, without raising its temperature, as it changes from one state (e.g. liquid) to another (e.g. gas)

LDL: low-density lipoprotein

leucocyte: a white blood cell

light microscope: a microscope that uses light rays

lignin: a strong, waterproof substance found in the walls of xylem elements

lipids: fats, oils and waxes

lipoprotein: a tiny ball of lipid and protein; the form in which cholesterol and other lipids are transported in the blood

Longworth trap: a metal trap used for catching small rodents

lung cancer: a disorder caused by the uncontrollable division of cells in the lungs, producing tumours

lymph: the fluid inside lymphatic vessels; it is formed from tissue fluid

lymphatic: a blind-ending vessel containing valves which transports tissue fluid back to the blood stream; also called lymph vessel

lymphocyte: a white blood cell that responds to a specific antigen in the body

lysosomes: small vesicles containing hydrolytic enzymes, surrounded by a membrane

lysozyme: an enzyme found in body fluids such as tears, that destroys bacteria

macrophage: a type of leucocyte; it is a large cell and it destroys bacteria and other foreign material by phagocytosis; also known as a monocyte when in the blood

magnification: the number of times greater that an image is than the actual object;

$$\text{magnification} = \frac{\text{image size}}{\text{object size}}$$

malnutrition: the effects of an unbalanced diet

maltase: an enzyme that catalyses the hydrolysis of maltose to glucose

maltose: a disaccharide made of two α-glucose molecules joined together

mark, release, recapture: a method of estimating population size of mobile animals by marking a sample, releasing them and then catching a second sample

mass extinction: the loss of many different species in a relatively short period of time

mass flow: the movement of a bulk liquid, like water flowing in a river

meiosis: a type of cell division in which a diploid cell divides twice to form four haploid, genetically different cells

memory cell: a cell derived from a B lymphocyte or T lymphocyte following contact with an antigen; it is able to divide rapidly if the same antigen is encountered later

meristem: a region in a plant where cells are actively dividing

metabolic poison: a substance that prevents a metabolic reaction from taking place, for example a heavy metal that inhibits enzymes

metabolic reactions: the chemical reactions that take place in living organisms

metaphase: the stage of cell division just after the disappearance of the nuclear envelope during which chromosome centromeres are aligned to the equator

microfilaments: long, thin filaments of protein that help to make up the cytoskeleton in a eukaryotic cell

micrometre (μm): one thousandth of a millimetre; 1×10^{-6} metres

microtubules: long, thin tubes of protein that help to make up the cytoskeleton in a eukaryotic cell

mitochondria: organelles found in most eukaryotic cells, in which aerobic respiration takes place; they are surrounded by an envelope, of which the inner membrane is folded to form cristae

mitosis: the division of a nucleus such that the two daughter cells acquire exactly the same number and type of chromosomes as the parent cell

mitral valve: the bicuspid valve; the atrio-ventricular valve on the left side of the heart

monosaccharide: a sugar whose molecules are made of a single sugar unit

mucous membrane: a tissue containing goblet cells and often ciliated cells

mucus: a substance made from glycoproteins; it coats the inside of the digestive system and protects it from attack by acids and enzymes; it coats airways and traps particles in the air being inhaled into the lungs

multicellular: made of many cells

mutation: a random change in the sequence of nucleotides in DNA, or in the structure and number of chromosomes

mycoprotein: food made from the culture of fungi in a fermenter

myocardial infarction: death of muscle cells in the heart wall

myogenic: a property of cardiac muscle; its contraction is initiated within the muscle itself, not by impulses from a nerve

nanometre (nm): one millionth of a millimetre; 1×10^{-9} metres

natural immunity: immunity acquired naturally, for example following an infection or through breast-feeding

natural selection: the way in which individuals with particular characteristics have a greater chance of survival than individuals without those characteristics; they are therefore more likely to reproduce and pass on genes for those characteristics to their offspring

neutrophil: a leucocyte (white blood cell) which destroys pathogens by phagocytosis

neutrophil elastase: an enzyme, produced by neutrophils, which breaks down elastin

nicotine: the addictive substance in cigarette smoke

non-competitive inhibition: inhibition in which an enzyme inhibitor does not resemble the substrate, and binds with the enzyme molecule at a place other than its active site

nuclear envelope: two membranes that surround the nucleus and separate it from the cytoplasm; it contains pores through which messenger RNA can pass

nucleotide: a molecule consisting of a five-carbon sugar, a phosphate group and a nitrogenous base

nucleus: a large organelle found in eukaryotic cells; it is surrounded by an envelope and contains the chromosomes

obesity: being seriously overweight; having a body mass index of more than 30

objective lens: the lens that collects light rays after they have passed through the specimen, and focuses them onto the eyepiece lens

oedema: the build-up of tissue fluid in the tissues, caused by poor drainage through the lymphatics

open circulatory system: a circulatory system in which the blood is not contained within vessels for at least part of its journey around the body

opportunistic disease: a disease that occurs because the body's immune system is not functioning properly, allowing infections by pathogens

optimum temperature: the temperature at which a reaction occurs most rapidly

order: a group of similar families

organ: a structure within a multicellular organism that is made up of different types of tissues working together to perform a particular function, e.g. the stomach in a human or a leaf in a plant

organelle: a functionally and structurally distinct part of a cell, for example a ribosome or mitochondrion

organic nutrients: substances containing carbon, hydrogen and oxygen, required by all living cells; they include amino acids, sugars and lipids

osmosis: the net movement of water molecules from a region of high water potential to a region of low water potential, through a partially permeable membrane, as a result of their random motion

oxygen: a gas that makes up about 16 % of air, produced by plants in photosynthesis and used by organisms in aerobic respiration

oxyhaemoglobin: the compound formed when oxygen combines with haemoglobin

pacemaker: the SAN; its inbuilt rhythm of contraction sets the pace for all the muscle of the heart

palisade cell: one of the cells in a leaf found just below the upper epidermis; these cells contain many chloroplasts and are the main site of photosynthesis

parasite: an organism that lives closely with another, its host, and does it harm

partial pressure: a measure of the concentration of a gas

partially permeable: allowing some types of molecule or ion to pass through, but not others

particulates: tiny carbon particles, found for example in cigarette smoke and exhaust fumes from diesel engines, that accumulate in lungs and cause irritation

passive immunity: possessing antibodies that were produced in another organism's body

passive transport: the movement of a substance using only its own energy of motion; no ATP is involved, and the substance moves down its concentration gradient

pasteurised milk: milk that has been heated to around 63 °C for 30 minutes, killing most microorganisms in it

pathogen: an organism that causes disease

peptide bond: the −CO−N− linkage between two amino acids

peptidoglycans: molecules made of chains of amino acids and sugars; they are found in bacterial cell walls

percentage cover: the percentage of the ground covered by a particular species

phloem sap: the contents of sieve tubes, mostly sucrose and water

phloem tissue: tissue containing sieve tubes and other cells; it transports substances such as sucrose throughout the plant

phylogeny: the study of evolutionary relationships

phylum: a group of similar classes; plural phyla

pit: part of a xylem element wall in which there is no lignin

plasma: the liquid part of blood

plasma cell: a cell derived from a B lymphocyte, which secretes antibodies

plasma membrane: the cell surface membrane, made up of a phospholipid bilayer in which protein molecules float

plasma proteins: proteins that are dissolved in blood plasma; they include albumin and fibrinogen

plasmid: a small, single-stranded molecule of DNA found in bacteria

plasmodesmata: direct connections between the cytoplasm of one plant and cell and an adjacent cell, made up of plasma membrane and endoplasmic reticulum directly linking the two cells

plasmolysed: when a cell has lost so much water that the plasma membrane has torn away from the cell wall

pleural fluid: the viscous fluid between the two pleural membranes that surround the lungs

pleural membrane: one of two membranes that surround the lungs, making them airtight

point quadrat: a quadrat so small that it consists of the end of a rod; the plants touched by the rod are recorded as present in the quadrat

poles: the areas at each end of a dividing cell towards which the chromatids are pulled during anaphase of mitosis

polynucleotide: a substance made of many nucleotides linked together in a chain; RNA and DNA are polynucleotides

polypeptide: a chain of amino acids

polysaccharide: a substance whose molecules are made of many sugar units linked together in a long chain

population: a group of organisms of the same species, living in the same place at the same time and able to breed with one another

potassium ions: K^+; small, positively charged ions that a cell keeps at a higher concentration inside than outside

potometer: an instrument used to measure the rate of uptake of water by a cut stem

pressure potential: the pressure exerted by a cell pushing outwards on the cell wall

primary response: the response of the immune system when an antigen is encountered for the first time

primary structure: the sequence of amino acids linked together in a polypeptide or protein

product: a new substance that is made by a chemical reaction

prokaryotic: a cell that does not contain a nucleus or any other membrane-bound organelles; bacteria are prokaryotes

prophase: the stage of cell division during which the chromosomes first appear

prophylactic: a drug taken to prevent a disease occurring

protein: a substance whose molecules are made of chains of amino acids

pulmonary artery: the artery that carries deoxygenated blood from the right ventricle of the heart to the lungs

pulmonary circulation: the part of the circulatory system that carries blood from the heart to the lungs and back

pulmonary vein: the vein that carries oxygenated blood from the lungs to the left atrium of the heart

purine base: a nitrogenous base whose molecules contain two carbon–nitrogen rings; adenine and guanine are purines

Purkyne tissue: cells that conduct an electrical impulse very rapidly down through the septum of the heart

pyrimidine base: a nitrogenous base whose molecules contain one carbon–nitrogen ring; thymine, cytosine and uracil are pyrimidines

quadrat: a square area within which a survey of organisms is made

quaternary structure: the overall shape of a protein molecule that is made up of two or more intertwined polypeptides

R group: one of the twenty or so possible groups of atoms that are attached to the central C atom in an amino acid

random sampling: investigating small parts of a habitat that have been chosen by chance, for example by using random numbers as coordinates

reproductively isolated: unable to breed with other members of the species

resolution: the ability to distinguish between two objects very close together; the higher the resolution of an image, the greater the detail that can be seen

retrovirus: a virus that contains RNA, for example HIV

reversible inhibition: inhibition of an enzyme that lasts for only a short time, or that can be reduced by the addition of more substrate

rib: one of the bones that forms a protective cage around the thorax

ribonucleic acid (RNA): a polynucleotide made of nucleotides containing ribose

ribose: a five-carbon sugar found in RNA

ribosomes: very small organelles found in both prokaryotic and eukaryotic cells, where protein synthesis takes place

root hair cell: a root epidermal cell that has a long, thin extension which grows between soil particles and provides a large surface area for the uptake of water and mineral ions

root hairs: extension of cells in the epidermis of plant roots, which absorb water and mineral ions from soil

rough endoplasmic reticulum: endoplasmic reticulum that has ribosomes attached to it, where protein synthesis takes place

salting: adding salt to food to preserve it

sampling: investigating a small part of the whole

SAN: the sino-atrial node, the pacemaker; its inbuilt rhythm of contraction sets the pace for all the muscle of the heart

saturated fat: a fat in which there are no double bonds between carbon atoms

scanning electron microscope: a microscope that forms three-dimensional images of surfaces, using electron beams**secretion**: the production and release of a useful substance; for example, salivary glands secrete saliva

secondary response: the response of the immune system when an antigen is encountered again

secondary structure: a regular, repeating pattern of shape in a polypeptide chain, for example an α-helix or β-fold

selection pressure: an environmental factor that decreases or increases the chance of survival of organisms with particular variations

selective breeding: choosing parents that are most likely to give rise to offspring with desired characteristics, generally carried out over several generations

semi-conservative replication: the way in which new DNA molecules are formed; each new molecule contains one old strand and one new one

septum: the wall of tissue that separates the left and right sides of the heart

sieve element: a cell found in phloem tissue, with non-thickened cellulose walls, through which sap containing sucrose is transported. The cells have very little cytoplasm, no nucleus and end walls perforated to form sieve plates.

sieve plate: the end wall of a sieve element, which has many holes through which water and solutes can pass

Simpson's Index of Diversity: a measure of the biodiversity in an area

single circulatory system: a circulatory system in which the blood flows on from the lungs or gills to the rest of the body, without first returning to the heart

sink: in plants, an area where sucrose is used

sino-atrial node: the SAN, the pacemaker; its inbuilt rhythm of contraction sets the pace for all the muscle of the heart

smooth endoplasmic reticulum: endoplasmic reticulum that does not have ribosomes associated with it; it carries out various metabolic reactions, such as the synthesis of steroids

smooth muscle: the type of muscle found in the walls of blood vessels and the alimentary canal; it contracts and relaxes slowly and steadily and rarely tires; it is not under conscious control

sodium ions: Na^+; small, positively charged ions that a cell keeps at a lower concentration inside than outside

sodium–potassium pump: protein molecules in a plasma membrane that use ATP to move sodium ions out of a cell and potassium into it, against their concentration gradient

source: in plants, an area where sucrose is produced

speciation: the production of a new species

species: a group of organisms with similar morphology and physiology, which are able to breed together to produce fertile offspring

species density: the numbers of a species per unit area

species evenness: a measure of the relative abundance of all the different species in a habitat; the less difference between their population sizes, the greater the species evenness

species frequency: the percentage of quadrats containing a particular species

species richness: the number of different species per unit area

specific: if an enzyme is specific it is able to bind with only a particular substrate

specific heat capacity: the amount of energy required to raise the temperature of 1 kg of a substance by 1 °C

spermatozoa: male gametes

spindle: a structure made up of microtubules that is formed during cell division and manoeuvres the chromosomes into position

spirometer: an instrument that can be used to measure the volume of air moved in and out during breathing

spongy mesophyll: a tissue in plant leaves, made up of cells containing chloroplasts, with large air spaces between the cells

squamous epithelium: an epithelium made up of thin cells interlocked closely together to produce a very smooth surface

stain: a substance that is taken up by various parts of cells, so that they can be distinguished by their colours

starch: a polysaccharide containing a mixture of amylose and amylopectin, both of which are made of many α-glucose molecules linked together; it is the storage polysaccharide in plants

statins: drugs that reduce the synthesis of cholesterol by the liver

stele: the central area of a root, containing xylem and phloem tissues

stem cell: a cell that has not differentiated, and is able to divide to form specialised types of cells

steroid: a lipid-like substance with molecules based on cholesterol; testosterone and oestrogen are steroids

stomata: small holes in the epidermis of a leaf, mostly in the lower epidermis, bounded by two guard cells

stroke: damage to the brain caused by a burst or blocked blood vessel

stroma: the 'background' material in a chloroplast, where the light-independent reactions of photosynthesis take place

structural protein: a protein with a structural role, such as collagen or keratin; many structural proteins, but by no means all, are fibrous proteins

subclavian vein: a large vein that carries blood back from the arms to the heart, into which lymph flows from the lymphatics

suberin: a waterproof substance that makes up the walls of cells in the endodermis; also in the walls of cork cells

substrate: the substance that is altered by an enzyme during an enzyme-catalysed reaction

sugar: a carbohydrate made up of one or two sugar units; sugars are soluble and they taste sweet

surface tension: an effect produced by the attractive forces between water molecules that pull downwards on the molecules at the surface, resulting in the surface molecules packing more tightly together

surfactant: a substance secreted by some of the cells lining the alveoli, which acts like detergent and reduces surface tension, stopping the alveoli from sticking shut

sweep netting: collecting insects and other organisms by sweeping a net through vegetation

sympatric speciation: the production of a new species from populations that are living in the same place

symplast pathway: a route taken by water as it moves across a plant tissue by passing through the cells

system: a group of organs that work together to carry out a function

systematic sampling: taking samples at places selected for a reason, for example along a transect

systemic circulation: the part of the circulatory system that carries blood from the heart to all parts of the body other than the lungs

T helper cell: a T lymphocyte that secretes cytokines, stimulating other white cells to destroy a pathogen

T killer cell: a T lymphocyte that attaches to a cell containing an antigen and destroys the cell

T lymphocyte: a white blood cell that binds to a cell containing a specific antigen and either destroys the cell or stimulates other cells to do so

tar: a mixture of chemicals in cigarette smoke, several of which are carcinogenic

taxa: the hierarchical groups used in classification – for example kingdom, phylum, genus, species; singular taxon

taxonomy: grouping organisms into a hierarchy of taxa

telophase: the stage in cell division where chromosomes have arrived at opposite ends of the dividing cell; they decondense and become surrounded by nuclear membranes

tertiary structure: the overall three-dimensional shape of a protein molecule

thorax: the chest; the part of the body below the neck and above the diaphragm

thylakoids: stacks of grana inside a chloroplast, where the light-dependent reactions of photosynthesis take place

thymine: one of the four nitrogenous bases found in DNA

tidal volume: the volume of air breathed in or out during a single breath

tissue: a layer or group of cells of similar type, which together perform a particular function

tissue fluid: the fluid which fills spaces between the cells within body tissues; it is formed from blood plasma

tonoplast: the membrane that surrounds a vacuole in a plant cell

totipotent: a stem cell is said to be totipotent if it is able to divide to form any of the different types of specialised cell in the body

trachea: the windpipe

tracheae: tubes of the gas exchange system in insects

transect: a line along which samples are taken, for example by placing quadrats

translocation: transport of organic substances made by the plant, such as sucrose, in phloem tissue

transmission electron microscope: a microscope that forms images of thin specimens, using electron beams

transpiration: the loss of water vapour from a leaf

transpiration stream: the continuous movement of water from soil to air through a plant, brought about by the loss of water vapour from the leaves

transporter protein: a protein molecule in a plasma membrane that uses ATP to move ions or molecules across the membrane against their concentration gradient

tricuspid valve: the atrio-ventricular valve on the right side of the heart

triglyceride: a lipid whose molecules are made from three fatty acids linked to a glycerol molecule

tubulin: a globular protein that makes up microtubules

tumour: a lump of cells; if these are able to spread around the body and cause tumours elsewhere, the tumour is said to be malignant; if not, then it is said to be benign

tunica externa: the outer layer of the wall of an artery or vein

tunica media: the central layer of the wall of an artery or vein

turgid: a turgid plant cell contains plenty of water, so that its volume is high and it pushes outwards on its cell wall

ultra heat treatment: a treatment for milk or fruit juice in which the substance is heated, under pressure, to a temperature above 100 °C, killing all microorganisms in it

ultrastructure: detailed structure, including very small things; electron microscopes reveal the ultrastructure of cells

unicellular: made of only one cell

unsaturated fat: a fat in which there is at least one double bond between carbon atoms

uracil: one of the four nitrogenous bases found in RNA

variation: differences between individuals within a species

vector: an organism that transmits a pathogen

vein: a thin-walled blood vessel with a relatively large lumen, containing valves, which carries blood towards the heart

ventilation rate: the volume of air moved into and out of the lungs per minute

ventricle: one of the two lower chambers of the heart, which receives blood from the atria and pumps it out into the arteries

ventricular diastole: the stage of the cardiac cycle in which the muscles in the walls of the ventricles relax

ventricular systole: the stage of the cardiac cycle in which the muscles in the walls of the ventricles contract

venule: a small vein, which carries blood between capillaries and a vein

vesicle: a tiny 'space' inside a cell, surrounded by a single membrane and containing substances such as enzymes

vital capacity: the maximum volume of air that can be breathed out after breathing in as deeply as possible

water potential: the tendency of a solution to lose water; water moves from a solution with high water potential to a solution with low water potential. Water potential is decreased by the addition of solute, and increased by the application of pressure. Symbol is ψ.

water potential gradient: a difference in water potential between one place and another; water moves down a water potential gradient

xerophyte: a plant that is adapted to live in conditions where water is in short supply or difficult to obtain

xylem element: a long, narrow, empty, dead cell with no end walls and with lignified side walls, through which water travels

xylem vessel: a dead, empty vessel with lignified walls and no end walls, through which water is transported in a plant

zygote: a diploid cell produced by the fusion of two gametes

Index